Inside the

Apple //e

Gary B. Little

Brady Communications Company, Inc.

A Prentice-Hall Publishing Company

Bowie, MD 20715

Inside the Apple //e

Library of Congress Cataloging in Publication Data

Little, Gary B., 1954–
Inside the Apple IIe.

Title appears on t.p. as: Inside the Apple //e.
Includes bibliographies and index.
1. Apple IIe (Computer) I. Title.
QA76.8A6623L38 1984 001.64 84–12461

ISBN 0-89303-551-3

Prentice-Hall International, Inc., London
Prentice-Hall Canada, Inc., Scarborough, Ontario
Prentice-Hall of Australia, Pty., Ltd., Sydney
Prentice-Hall of India Private Limited, New Delhi
Prentice-Hall of Japan, Inc., Tokyo
Prentice-Hall of Southeast Asia Pte. Ltd., Singapore
Whitehall Books, Limited, Petone, New Zealand
Editora Prentice-Hall Do Brasil LTDA., Rio de Janeiro

Printed in the United States of America

85 86 87 88 89 90 91 92 93 94 95 2 3 4 5 6 7 8 9 10

Publishing Director: David Culverwell
Acquisitions Editor: Chris Williams
Production Editor/Text Designer: Michael J. Rogers
Art Director: Don Sellers
Assistant Art Director: Bernard Vervin
Cover Design: George Dodson
Manufacturing Director: John A. Komsa

Copy Editor: Keith R. Tidman
Photo of protoboard and DIP jumper cable: Tony Szary
Typesetting: Electronic Publishing Services, Baltimore, MD
Printing: Fairfield Graphics, Fairfield, PA
Typefaces: Eurostile (display), Aster (text), and Universal Monotype #3 H-P (computer programs)

To my grandfather,
Richard V. Robinson (1899–1978)

Limits of Liability and Disclaimer of Warranty

Trademarks of Material Mentioned in This Text

Note to Authors

Do you have a manuscript or software program related to personal computers? Do you have an idea for developing such a project? If so, we would like to hear from you. The Brady Company produces a complete range of books and applications software for the personal computer market. We invite you to write to David Culverwell, Publishing Director, Brady Communications Company, Inc., Bowie, MD 20715.

CONTENTS

PREFACE

I can sense what you're saying right now: "Oh, no, not another book on the Apple!" Well, yes, it is, but don't put it down just yet. It's not simply another book on how to write programs in Applesoft BASIC or on how to use your favorite spreadsheet program. Rather, it's a detailed study of how the Apple //e works (from a software point of view) and how you can control it with your own programs.

You will first be introduced to the 65Ø2 microprocessor that controls the //e and to some important 65Ø2 programming concepts. You will then be conducted on an internal tour of the //e's operating systems (the system monitor, DOS 3.3, and ProDOS) and of its primary language, Applesoft BASIC. Along the way several programming examples (written in Applesoft and 65Ø2 assembly language) will be presented to illustrate important principles and features.

Once this background information has been presented, you will be shown how the //e reads information from the keyboard, displays information on the video screen, and how you can write and install your own input/output subroutines. In addition, all of the //e's video display modes, including 8Ø-column text and double-width graphics, will be explained.

The last few chapters of the book will show you how to manage the //e's internal and expansion memory spaces, how to use the speaker and cassette port, and how the //e's peripheral expansion slots are used.

I am sure this book will be of great interest to all readers who want to know what makes the //e tick. It is geared to the more advanced reader: You will be assumed to have a working knowledge of Applesoft and at least some familiarity with 65Ø2 assembly language. If you are a computer novice, then the references that are included at the end of each chapter should be consulted for further information on programming techniques. No matter what your level of expertise, however, you should find this book an excellent source of programming tips and ideas.

I would like to thank two people in particular for reviewing portions of the manuscript before publication: Archie Reid and Vern Little. Archie set me straight on how to generate music on the //e's speaker and how to digitize voice through the cassette port. Vern is an electrical engineer and he prevented me from putting my foot in my mouth when talking about anything other than software. Thanks are also due to Vern for helping to convince me to shell out $1,800 for a 16K Apple II in 1978 when I should have been saving money to finance my stay at law school; it turns out to have been the most important purchase I have ever made.

Brady Communications also arranged for several independent technical reviewers to review the manuscript and I thank them for all their invaluable assistance, particularly Val Golding and Cecil Fretwell.

Gary B. Little
Vancouver, British Columbia
September 1984

About the Author

Gary B. Little has been programming Apple computers for fun and profit since 1978. He is a founding member of Apple's British Columbia Computer Society and of SAGE (Serious Apple Group, Eh!). He is currently a director of the Pacific Coast Computer Fair Association, the Software Industry Development Association, and Vancouver PC Users Group. When he isn't tinkering with computers, he practices law in a downtown Vancouver, British Columbia law firm. Gary lives in Vancouver with his wife Pamela and their two little ones, Sam and Roo.

1

Introduction to Apple and the Apple //e

The Apple //e represents Apple Computer, Inc.'s latest full-size model in its highly popular Apple II family of computers and was first announced in January 1983. The earlier members of this family are the original Apple II (1977) and the Apple II Plus (1979); the newest member is the portable Apple //c (1984).

In this book we will be taking an advanced "inside" look at the Apple //e itself. Bear in mind, however, that much of what will be said will also apply to its two predecessors and to the Apple //c because Apple has made a substantial effort to maintain a high degree of compatibility with other members of the Apple II family. The discussion will be limited to the //e's built-in language and operating system (Applesoft and the system monitor) and to the two disk operating systems used with them, DOS 3.3 and ProDOS.

Apple Computer, Inc. is an interesting and exciting company. It not only produces innovative products, it also ensures that important technical information concerning these products is divulged to whoever needs it. This goes against every rule that the computer industry was following back in 1977 when Apple first made its presence felt. This "open-system" policy fuels software development, and this is one of the main reasons Apple has been so successful—after all, who wants to buy a computer for which no software is available?

A CONDENSED HISTORY OF APPLE COMPUTER, INC.

The history of Apple Computer, Inc. is a fascinating one and represents a real rags-to-riches (or is that "garage-to-multinational-corporation"?) story. Let's take a look at what Apple has been up to since it was first formed in 1976 and how the Apple II slowly evolved into the Apple //e.

1976

In the beginning, Apple was made up of just two individuals: Stephen Wozniak ("Woz") and Steven Jobs. Woz provided the hardware and software expertise and almost single-handedly designed the company's first two computers, the Apple I and the Apple II (Rod Holt helped; he designed the Apple II's power supply). A patent application was subsequently filed with respect to the Apple II on April 11, 1977, and U.S. patent #4,136,359 was eventually issued in early 1979. Jobs was largely responsible for marketing and raising financing, and it was he who came up with the "Apple" name (Jobs was apparently thinking of a job that he had recently had in an Oregon orchard). In the early going, both partners were still working for other computer companies in California's Silicon Valley, Jobs with Atari and Woz with Hewlett-Packard. Fortunately for Apple, Hewlett-Packard was not interested in Woz's design for a personal computer and gave him a release so that he could deal with it as he saw fit.

The Apple I was designed to be sold to and used by hobbyists; only about 175 were sold. The Apple II, however, was designed with a much larger market in mind (although Woz claims he simply wanted to build a computer with which he could play Atari's "Breakout" game). That market quickly materialized as a result of the startling combination (for 1977) of excellent hardware, attractive packaging, and superb documentation. The Apple //e, which was released six years later, still resembles the original Apple II and it still operates in much the same way.

Woz decided to use the MOS Technology 65Ø2 microprocessor to control the Apple II. This decision was dictated not by the 65Ø2's reliability, powerful instruction set, or any other design characteristic, but rather by its price. Whereas other microprocessors were selling for hundreds of dollars in 1976 and were difficult to find, the 65Ø2 was readily available and it cost only about $2Ø.

Wozniak wrote all the software for the original Apple II that was stored in its read-only memory (ROM). This included a version of the BASIC programming language called Integer BASIC (which can't handle decimal numbers but is great for games), a system monitor for debugging and for handling fundamental input/output operations, a set of mathematical subroutines, a mini-assembler for entering programs in assembly language, and "Sweet 16," a software-simulated 16-bit microprocessor (Woz was way ahead of his time).

To raise a little money for their fledgling venture, Wozniak sold his Hewlett-Packard pocket calculator and Jobs sold his Volkswagen bus. Overhead expenses were cut to the bare minimum by setting up operation in the garage of Jobs' parents. As 1977 rolled around, however, it became clear that more money, a lot more money, was going to be needed.

1977

Since Jobs was the partner responsible for marketing the Apple II, it was he who began searching for venture capital. That search eventually led him to Mike Markkula, a former marketing manager at Intel, an integrated-circuit designing company. Markkula, Jobs, and Wozniak quickly struck a deal whereby Markkula agreed to put $25Ø,ØØØ into Apple in exchange for an equal partnership interest. He then proceeded to use his expertise to line up bank financing and additional capital funding. Apple was then finally ready for the mass market!

The Apple II was formally announced for sale at the 1st West Coast Computer Faire in early 1977 and it was an instant success. The main reasons for its early success were that it was easily expandable (more memory could easily be added to it and eight slots were available for peripheral devices when they became available), it had a full-size keyboard, and it had *color* graphics. Oh, yes, it also looked great!

Not that there weren't any problems, however. For example, lower-case characters could not be produced by the keyboard and the video display was only forty columns wide. These shortcomings officially persisted until the introduction of the Apple //e, although several other sources of upper- and lower-case keyboards and 8Ø-column boards did pop up in the interim.

One software problem had to be remedied quickly. Integer BASIC did not support decimal (floating-point) numbers or functions, and so business and scientific use of the Apple II was necessarily limited. Apple began to take steps to remedy this in the summer of 1977 when it negotiated the purchase of about 1Ø,ØØØ lines of program source code for a floating-point version of BASIC from Microsoft Corporation. This code was written in 65Ø2 assembly language and so could be readily adapted to run on the Apple II.

By this time Apple had a few employees, one of which was a young programmer by the name of Randy Wigginton. Wigginton reworked the Microsoft source code and came out with a preliminary version of a floating-point BASIC that would run on the Apple II. This version was called "Applesoft - Extended Precision Floating Point BASIC Language" and was released in October 1977. Further work was required to polish Applesoft into a final product and this was done during the winter of 1977.

1978

The final version of Applesoft, Applesoft][, was finally released in May 1978 and this same version is still in use today on the Apple //e. It was first available on cassette tape only, but was later provided in ROM on a card that could be plugged into a slot on the Apple II; it eventually replaced Integer BASIC on the motherboard when the Apple II Plus was released in 1979.

Probably the most important new product released in 1978 was the Disk II disk drive and controller card which are still used on the Apple //e today. The disk drive revolutionized the software business because for the first time it was feasible to develop sophisticated programs that could be easily loaded and that could quickly and reliably access large data bases. Until the disk drive was released, all programs had to be saved to and loaded from cassette tape, which was invariably an exercise in frustration. Many a cottage software business started up after the disk drive became available.

The Disk II was controlled by a program called the Disk Operating System (DOS), first written by Bob Shepardson and later substantially modified by Randy Wigginton. DOS has undergone several revisions throughout the years and the current version is DOS 3.3. This version is still being shipped with the Apple //e (together with a brand-new DOS called ProDOS).

1979

Sales really ballooned for Apple in 1979. It was able to increase sales by a total of forty million dollars (!) over the previous year, to a total of forty-eight million dollars. By this time, the Apple II was selling not only because it was an excellent hardware package but also because an ever-increasing supply of software was available that could be run on it. One important piece of software, VisiCalc, the very first financial spreadsheet program, is reputed to have been directly responsible for stimulating the purchase of tens of thousands of Apple II computers.

The Apple II underwent a minor operation in 1979 and came out of it with a new name, Apple II Plus. The Apple II Plus is essentially the same as an Apple II, except that its ROM chips contain Applesoft][rather than Integer BASIC and its system monitor has been changed to support more powerful screen-editing commands and to allow the Apple II to automatically run a program from diskette whenever the power is turned on. At the same time, a couple of handy debugging commands (step and trace) were taken out of the system monitor, but they were not missed by many users. The modifications to the system monitor were written by John Arkley.

Apple announced its Pascal Operating System in 1979 as well. Because Pascal requires a huge amount of memory in which to operate, Apple also released a new peripheral card, called a language card, at the same time. The language card effectively added another 16K of memory to the Apple II, which could "replace" the Applesoft ROMs when Pascal was being used. The language card was plugged into slot #0 of the Apple II but in the //e it is simulated in the memory chips on the motherboard. These different implementations, however, are transparent to the user.

1980-1982

Apple's sales continued to explode in the early eighties: $117 million in 198Ø, $334.8 million in 1981, and $583.1 million in 1982! Most of these sales were generated by the Apple II Plus which eventually set a record for monthly sales in December 1982.

The infamous Apple /// was released in 1980. For several reasons, notably its early unreliability and high price, it never established a significant market presence even though a modified version (known as the Apple /// Plus) was still being produced in 1984. It comes with an Apple II emulation mode that allows it to run most, but not all, of the software that runs on the Apple II.

In the winter of 198Ø-81, Apple made a public offering of stock, which was quickly snapped up. The proceeds were largely directed into intensive (and expensive) research and development projects. We'll see in a moment what those projects led to.

If imitation is the sincerest form of flattery, then Apple must surely be crimson red. Since about 198Ø, tens of thousands of unofficial Apple II "clones" (euphemistically called "compatibles") have been manufactured, mostly by Taiwanese concerns. To achieve absolute compatibility with the Apple II, most of these clones contain ROMs that are direct copies of the Applesoft and system monitor ROMs. Not surprisingly, Apple considers this to be highly improper and has successfully instituted legal proceedings in the United States and many other countries against several manufacturers in order to protect its copyrights and patent rights. The importation of Apple II clones to the United States has also been reduced because Apple has registered its copyrights with U.S. Customs. The Customs authorities have the power to confiscate shipments of products that violate Apple's copyrights.

1983

At Apple's Annual General Meeting on January 19, 1983, two major announcements were made. First, the Lisa computer was announced, a computer that was immediately recognized as a technological and innovative triumph because of its ease of use and excellent operating system. Its retail price, however, was initially too high for it to sell in the quantities that Apple would have liked. Subsequent price reductions, coupled with increasing availability of software, has helped to remedy this problem.

The more important announcement as far as we are concerned was the introduction of the successor to the Apple II Plus, the Apple //e. The Apple //e was carefully designed to maintain as high a degree of compatibility with the Apple II Plus as possible so that the thousands of software packages developed for the Apple II Plus would not have to be rewritten. Several new features were added to the //e, however, that make it a significantly different computer: built-in support for an 8Ø-column display, an upper- and lowercase keyboard, self-testing subroutines, and enhanced editing capabilities.

In addition, Apple significantly simplified the construction of the //e by reducing the number of integrated circuits on the motherboard from 1Ø9 on the Apple II Plus to only 31! It did this by designing two special integrated circuits, called the IOU (input/output unit) and MMU (memory management unit), to replace many of the discrete components used on the II Plus.

The manager of the team that designed the Apple //e was Peter Quinn. The hardware was designed by Walt Broedner and most of the modifications to the old system monitor were made by Rick Auricchio and Bryan Stearns.

There was also a major change at the managerial level at Apple in 1983. On April 8, Apple announced that Mike Markkula had resigned as President and that John Sculley had been named to succeed him. Sculley was formerly president of Pepsi-Cola and it is reported that his salary is in excess of one million dollars per year.

1984

At its January 24, 1984, Annual General Meeting Apple announced the Macintosh computer ("Mac"), a scaled-down version of Lisa. Mac undoubtedly represents another mass-market best seller for Apple because it is easy to use and it is priced affordably. Within a month of its release, at least two Mac-specific magazines and several books had been published. This is reminiscent of what happened in 1979 when sales of the Apple II began to skyrocket.

On the //e front there was one major announcement at the Annual General Meeting: the release of a successor to DOS 3.3 called ProDOS. This disk operating system is significantly different from, but upwardly compatible with, DOS 3.3. Most Applesoft programs, when transferred to ProDOS-formatted diskettes, will run without modification. Programs and other files can be transferred between DOS 3.3 and ProDOS by using a utility program supplied with ProDOS. The main advantages of ProDOS are that it is faster, it is easier for programmers to use, it supports a directory structure that is more convenient for use with larger-capacity diskettes or hard disks, and it creates files that can be read by the Apple ///.

On April 24, 1984, Apple announced a scaled-down, portable version of the Apple //e called the Apple //c and made it known to the world that it will be supporting the Apple II concept for a long time to come. This was apparent from the theme of the event at which the Apple //c was announced: "The Apple II forever." As expected, the Apple //c will run almost all software written for the //e.

UNDER THE HOOD OF THE APPLE //e

Although this book is primarily concerned with software, let's begin by taking a quick look at the hardware that makes up the Apple //e. You can't see much with its lid on, except the keyboard at the front and the video, cassette, and game paddle connectors at the back. So, turn off the power and take the lid off.

The biggest component under the hood is the power supply on the left side. The main circuit board (called the "motherboard") contains only 31 integrated circuit packages; these include the 65Ø2 microprocessor (see Chapter 2), the IOU and MMU, eight random-access memory (RAM) chips, three read-only memory (ROM) chips (which contain Applesoft, the system monitor, and the keyboard decoder), and miscellaneous support chips.

Lined up at the back of the motherboard are seven 5Ø-pin connectors called slots. These slots are numbered consecutively from 1 through 7, with slot 1 being the leftmost slot. Peripheral cards can be installed in these slots to allow the //e to control a variety of input/output (I/O) devices. In fact, you undoubtedly have a peripheral card already installed that is connected by a ribbon cable to a disk drive. There is an eighth slot, called the auxiliary connector, that is located at the left center of the motherboard (or directly in front of slot 3 if you are using a United Kingdom Apple //e). This 6Ø-pin connector is designed for use by an optional 8Ø-column text card available from Apple (and, now, from others). This card permits the use of a video display mode in which 8Ø characters may be displayed on one screen line instead of the standard 4Ø. An extended 8Ø-column text card is also available that contains 64K of memory and that can be used to generate special double-width graphics that were unavailable on the Apple II and Apple II Plus. The peripheral-card expansion slots will be discussed in Chapter 11.

On the right near the back you will see the 16-pin game I/O connector to which joysticks, push buttons, and other game-playing paraphernalia can be attached. We'll see some examples of how to attach these, and other, devices in Chapter 1Ø.

The last item of interest is the //e's built-in speaker. As we will see in Chapter 9, the speaker can be used to produce both harsh sound and beautiful music. It is mounted to the bottom plate of the //e and is connected to the motherboard through a twisted pair of wires.

So much for the //e's hardware!

LEARNING THE FUNDAMENTALS

The purpose of this section is to introduce you to some of the fundamental concepts and terminology that will be used in this book. You should realize, however, that this book has not been written for computer novices and that more general books should be consulted if more background information is required.

Numbering Systems

We are all familiar with the decimal numbering system that makes use of ten fundamental digits. This system, however, is not sacred and we could, if we preferred, use other systems that use fewer or more digits.

When dealing with computers, it is often convenient to use the binary numbering system and the hexadecimal numbering system. The binary numbering system uses only two digits, Ø and 1. The hexadecimal system uses the following sixteen digits:

Ø,1,2,3,4,5,6,7,8,9,A,B,C,D,E,F .

which represent decimal numbers Ø through 15, respectively.

The //e's 65Ø2 microprocessor performs all its internal operations using binary numbers because it has available to it thousands of logic cells that can easily be turned either "on" or "off" to represent the binary digits "1" or "Ø", respectively. Binary numbers, however, are usually not used when writing a program because they are difficult to read and are prone to transcription errors. Decimal-number equivalents of binary numbers are often used instead, but the pattern of binary ones and zeros to which they refer are often not immediately obvious (quick now, what is the binary representation of 225?). The hexadecimal numbering system, however, is an ideal alternative because each hexadecimal digit defines exactly one of the sixteen four-digit patterns of binary ones and zeros, making conversion between binary and hexadecimal very easy.

In this book, hexadecimal numbers will be preceded by "$" to distinguish them from decimal numbers. They will be used when referring to data values or to memory addresses.

Bit Numbering and "Significance"

As you undoubtedly know, the basic unit of storage in the Apple //e, and most other microcomputers, is the byte. As far as the 65Ø2 microprocessor is concerned, each byte is made up of eight bits, each of which can be either on or off (a computer likes things that can exist in only one of two states). This means that binary numbers from ØØØØØØØØ to 11111111 (Ø to 255 decimal) can be stored in a byte.

Each bit in a byte is associated with a certain binary weight equal to the number that the byte would represent if that bit were on and all the other bits were off. These binary weights are as shown in Figure 1-1.

(Notice that the bits within the byte are numbered from Ø to 7 and not from 1 to 8.) To determine the decimal representation of the bit pattern, it is simply necessary to add up the binary weights of all bits in the byte that are on. Since bit 7 contributes most, it is called the most-significant bit or "high-order" bit. Conversely, bit Ø is referred to as the least-significant bit or "low-order" bit.

7	6	5	4	3	2	1	Ø	←bit numbers
128	64	32	16	8	4	2	1	←binary weights

Figure 1-1. Binary weights of each bit in a byte.

Bit 7 of a byte is also called the "sign bit" because it is often used to indicate whether the number stored in the byte is positive or negative (if it is 1, then the number is considered to be negative). The 65Ø2 microprocessor that controls the //e uses a special internal status register which, among other things, holds a flag that represents the sign of any number being dealt with (see Chapter 2). Special 65Ø2 instructions are available that can change the flow of a program depending on the state of this sign flag (they are called "BPL," branch on plus, and "BMI," branch on minus). We are going to see in later chapters that the //e uses bit 7 of several special memory locations to hold information relating to the state of the system. When these status locations are examined in an assembly-language program, BPL can be used to transfer control if the status is off (bit 7 is Ø) and BMI can be used to transfer control if the status is on (bit 7 is 1). The same thing can be done from an Applesoft program by using the PEEK command to read the number stored at the status location. If bit 7 is on, then the value read will be greater than or equal to 128 (since the binary weight of bit 7 is 128).

We will also come across situations in this book where more than one byte is required to store a number (i.e., the number is larger than 255). In these cases, the byte that contains information on the highest-weighted bits for the number is called the most-significant byte or high-order byte, and the byte that contains information on the lowest-weighted bits is called the least-significant byte or low-order byte.

Pointers and Vectors

As we will see in Chapter 2, the 65Ø2 microprocessor is capable of controlling a memory space that is mapped to the addresses from $ØØØØ . . . $FFFF. Since one byte can hold exactly two hexadecimal digits, any address in the 65Ø2's memory space can be stored in two bytes.

A pointer or "vector" is a pair of memory locations that contains the address of another location to which the pointer is said to be pointing. The least-significant byte of the pair is always stored in the first memory location and the other byte in the next higher location. To determine the address stored in a pointer, you can use the following Applesoft formula:

```
ADDR = PEEK(X)+256*PEEK(X+1)
```

where X represents the first memory location that the pointer occupies. The second byte in the pair is multiplied by 256 since it represents the number of 256-byte units that make up the address.

The 6502 microprocessor makes extensive use of pointers to access data arrays and to handle interrupts (see Chapter 2). Applesoft also maintains a great many pointers for keeping track of its many data areas (see Chapter 4).

Control Characters

Control characters are special characters that are entered from the keyboard by using the CONTROL key. Although they do not represent visible symbols, they often cause the //e to perform special functions. Such characters will be denoted in this book by <CTRL-X>, where X refers to any alphabetic character (A. . .Z) or one of the following six special symbols: & [\] ^ _. The CONTROL key acts just like another SHIFT key in that it and one other key must be pressed at the same time in order to enter a control character from the keyboard. The procedure involves first pressing the CONTROL key and then, while still holding it down, pressing the other key ("X" in the above example).

6502 Assembly Language

Many of the programs presented in this book are written in a programming language that can be used to generate a series of bytes (which represent microprocessor instructions and data) that can be interpreted and directly executed by the //e's 6502 microprocessor. This programming language is called "6502 assembly language."

There are two steps involved in developing an assembly-language program. First, a source code for the program must be entered that defines the program in a human-readable form using symbolic labels for addresses and data, special three-character mnemonics for the permitted 6502 instructions, and special symbols to indicate the addressing modes used by the instructions (see Chapter 3 for a detailed discussion of 6502 instructions and addressing modes).

A typical line of source code looks something like this:

```
LABEL    LDA ($28),Y        ;This is a comment
```

and is made up of four distinct fields. The first field is the label field and it holds the symbolic name (if any) for the current location within the program. The next field is the instruction field and it holds the three-character mnemonic for the 65Ø2 instruction ("LDA" in the example). It is immediately followed by the operand field, which holds the addressing mode used by the instruction, that is, information relating to the method the instruction is to use to access the data or memory location on which it is to act ("($28),Y" in the example). The last field is the comment field and is used for documenting the program. Each field is separated from the other by at least one blank space; in addition, most assemblers require comments to be preceded by a semicolon.

The second step is to interpret or "assemble" the program source code using a 65Ø2 assembler. This is done in order to produce a file that contains the bytes defined by the program in a format that the 65Ø2 can directly execute (the "object code" or "machine language").

The assembly-language programs presented in this book were all entered and assembled using the BIG MAC Macro Assembler published by A.P.P.L.E. (21246 68th Ave. S., Kent, WA 98Ø32). If you want to modify and reassemble the programs presented in this book and you are not using BIG MAC, then you will likely have to make several changes to the program source codes to account for any differences in syntax and command structure. Differences usually arise in the area of "pseudo-instructions"; these are assembler-specific commands that appear in the 65Ø2 instruction field of a line of source code, but that represent commands to the assembler rather than 65Ø2 instructions. They can be used to place data bytes at specific locations within the program (DFB, DS, and ASC), to define symbolic labels (EQU), to indicate the starting address of the program (ORG), and for several other purposes.

Here are descriptions of some of BIG MAC's more commonly used pseudo-opcodes:

DFB—Define a byte of data
DS—Define a data space
ASC—Define an ASCII string
EQU—Equate a symbolic label to a number or a memory location
ORG—Specify origin (starting address) of object code

Some of the more popular assemblers available for the //e are listed in the references at the end of Chapter 2.

Running Assembly-Language Programs

To run an assembly-language program, two steps must take place. The first step is obvious: the program must be loaded into memory. This can be done by storing the bytes that make up the programs into the appropriate area of memory by using Applesoft POKE statements or by using the system monitor STORE command (see Chapter 3). The easier method, however, is to load it from the binary file on diskette in which it is contained (a "B" is displayed to the left of a binary file's name when a diskette is CATALOGued) by using the DOS BLOAD command. The BLOAD command must be entered while you are in Applesoft and is of the form

```
BLOAD FILENAME,Aaddr
```

where "FILENAME" represents the name of the binary program and "addr" represents the memory location at which it is to be loaded, in hexadecimal (if preceded by "$") or decimal notation. The ",Aaddr" suffix can be omitted if you wish; if it is, then the file will be loaded into memory at the same position it was in when the BSAVE command was used to save it to diskette.

The second step is to actually run the program. This can be done by using the Applesoft CALL command, which is of the form

```
CALL start
```

where "start" represents the decimal starting address of the program. For example, to run a program that begins at location $3ØØ (768 decimal), you would enter the command CALL 768. The alternate way of starting the program is to use the system monitor's GO command (see Chapter 3). This can be done by entering the system monitor from Applesoft using a CALL -151 command and then, for a program beginning at location $3ØØ, entering the command "3ØØG".

Some of the programs in this book will not operate properly if they are loaded and called in this way (they will be specifically noted). Instead, the DOS BRUN command must be used to load and execute them directly from diskette. This command can be entered as follows:

```
BRUN FILENAME
```

where "FILENAME" represents the name of the binary program.

When the BRUN command is used, the program will be loaded into memory at the location from which it was saved to diskette using the DOS BSAVE command. To save a copy of a binary program that you have already entered into memory to a diskette, enter the command

```
BSAVE FILENAME,Aaddr,Lnum
```

where "addr" represents the starting address of the program and "num" represents the number of bytes in the program.

WHAT WON'T BE COVERED

There are a few topics that will not be discussed at length in this book. Integer BASIC, the BASIC that was built into the first few thousand Apple IIs, will not be discussed because it is rarely used anymore and is fast becoming obsolete. In fact, the new ProDOS operating system does not allow Integer BASIC programs to be run at all.

The only language that will be discussed at length will be Applesoft. For more information on Apple Pascal or Apple Logo, you will have to go elsewhere.

Although Apple produces a wide range of interface cards (super serial card, parallel printer card, etc.) and peripheral devices (printers, modems, graphics tablets, etc.), these will not be discussed. The general techniques used to interface these devices to the //e, however, will be discussed in Chapter 11.

USING THE OPTIONAL DISKETTE

This book can be purchased either with or without a program diskette, or the diskette can be purchased separately. The diskette contains all the programs that are presented as examples in the following chapters and will allow you to quickly load a program into memory, or modify a program, without having to endure the pleasure of typing it in from scratch.

As an added bonus, several useful programs are included on the diskette that are not described in the main body of this book. Instructions on how to operate these programs can be found in Appendix V.

The diskette has been initialized in the Apple DOS 3.3 format rather than the ProDOS format. If the programs are to be transferred to a ProDOS-formatted diskette, then the CONVERT program on the Apple ProDOS system diskette must be used. One of the programs presented in this book, READ.BLOCK, can be run only in a ProDOS environment.

The files on the diskette are either Applesoft programs (marked by "A" in the catalog), text files (marked by "T"), or binary programs (marked by "B").

The text files on the diskette are the source-code listings for the binary programs and are in the format expected by the BIG MAC assembler (use the "R" command from BIG MAC to load them). Most other assemblers are also able to read text files. Keep in mind that the source-code formats used by different assemblers do vary and it may be necessary to modify a source code file to take into account any such differences before the file can be properly assembled.

The Applesoft programs and binary programs can usually be run by using the standard RUN and BRUN commands, respectively. Some of the binary programs, however, are designed to be called from an Applesoft program only and should simply be loaded into memory using the BLOAD command. Such exceptions will be noted in the discussions that relate to these programs in this book.

FURTHER READING FOR CHAPTER 1

Historical background . . .

"Photograph of Apple I," *Apple Orchard*, April 1983, front cover. The original Apple product.

A.L. Taylor III, "Striking it Rich," *Time*, February 15, 1982, pp. 42-47. Apple makes the front cover of Time!

P. Lopiccola, "Core of a New Apple," *Popular Computing*, March 1983, pp. 114-117. How the Apple II Plus was transformed into the Apple //e.

Standard reference work . . .

Reference Manual for //e Only, Apple Computer, Inc., 1982. Includes detailed information on the hardware and software that make up the Apple //e.

2

The 65Ø2 Microprocessor

The "brains" of every microcomputer are represented by a complex integrated circuit called a microprocessor that controls the operation of the system as a whole. The microprocessor used in the //e is called a 65Ø2.

The 65Ø2 is an example of what is usually called an "8-bit" microprocessor. These types of microprocessors can handle data only one byte at a time and they typically use 16 address lines. Since each of these lines can be on or off, the 65Ø2 is capable of addressing 65,536 (2^16) memory locations at any given time. (Since one "K" of memory is equal to 1,Ø24 bytes, this represents a "64K" memory space). This is in contrast to the newer wave of 16-bit microprocessors that can manipulate two bytes of data at once and have typical address spaces of one megabyte or more.

While the 65Ø2 is operating, it is continuously interpreting a stream of bytes in order to determine what it should do next. The bytes in this stream are controlled by the computer program that is being executed. This program contains instructions that enable the 65Ø2 to perform data transfers, input/output operations, logical operations, simple arithmetic, and other fundamental control operations.

In this chapter, we will take a brief look at the 65Ø2 instruction set and internal registers and describe how the 65Ø2 has been implemented on the //e. Note, however, that the purpose of this chapter is not to teach you 65Ø2 assembly-language programming, but rather to review some of the more important principles relating to the 65Ø2 microprocessor. Consult the references at the end of the chapter for a list of books that are available to teach you the art of programming the 65Ø2.

IMPORTANT 65Ø2 CONCEPTS

The 65Ø2 forms only one part of a microcomputer system such as the //e. The other important parts are the system memory (RAM and ROM) and the system input/output (I/O) devices. It is the 65Ø2, however, that is in charge of controlling both the accessing of memory and the passing of data to and from the I/O devices.

The 65Ø2 is told how and when to perform its chores by a series of instructions that it is constantly interpreting. These instructions will be discussed in the next section. In brief, they cause the 65Ø2 to perform a variety of data-manipulation tasks using a set of six internal registers that will be discussed below in the section entitled "65Ø2 Registers."

Zero Page and the Stack

This is a convenient time to introduce you to two rather important areas of memory that are used in special ways by the 65Ø2 microprocessor: zero page and the stack.

Each 256 bytes of memory that starts at an address that is an integer multiple of $1ØØ (256), i.e., $ØØØØ, $Ø1ØØ, $Ø2ØØ, . . ., $FFØØ is called a "page" of memory. For example, the area of memory from $BFØØ through $BFFF is referred to as page $BF. Zero page, the page of memory from $ØØØØ . . . $ØØFF, is treated in a special way by the 65Ø2. Generally speaking, whenever the address on which a 65Ø2 instruction acts is contained in zero page, the highest two hexadecimal digits of the address do not have to be specified (since they are always zero by definition). This not only reduces the size of the program, it also allows the program to be executed more quickly. No wonder, then, that zero page is prime real estate as far as the 65Ø2 is concerned.

Page one of memory ($1ØØ . . . $1FF) holds the 65Ø2 stack. The stack is used as a temporary data area by the 65Ø2 and several instructions can be used to implicitly read data from it or store data to it. These instructions are executed very quickly because they automatically calculate where to store the data or where to read it from by examining a special internal 65Ø2 "stack pointer" register. This register always points to the next free position available in the stack. When a byte is stored on the stack, it is stored at the position within page one given by the stack pointer and then the stack pointer is decremented by one. When a byte is removed from the stack, it is taken from the position within page one given by the stack pointer plus one and then the stack pointer is incremented by one.

We will be discussing the stack pointer, and other registers, in greater detail below.

65Ø2 INSTRUCTION SET

There are 56 general types of instructions that the 65Ø2 is capable of executing; they are listed in Table 2-1. (An enhanced version of the 65Ø2, called the 65CØ2, supports all of these instructions and a few more—the 65CØ2 is used in the Apple //c.) Each instruction is actually a binary number that can be interpreted by the 65Ø2 but is usually represented by a three-character mnemonic name that is easier to remember. These mnemonics are used whenever an assembly-language program is being developed. The assembler that is used takes care of translating them into the corresponding binary numbers (the "machine language") that the 65Ø2 can execute directly.

Table 2-1. 65Ø2 instruction set mnemonics in alphabetical order.

Mnemonic	Description
ADC	Add to accumulator
AND	"And" with accumulator
ASL	Arithmetic bit-shift left
BCC	Branch on carry clear
BCS	Branch on carry set
BEQ	Branch on result zero
BIT	Test bits
BMI	Branch on result minus
BNE	Branch on result not zero
BPL	Branch on result plus
BRK	Software interrupt
BVC	Branch on overflow clear
BVS	Branch on overflow set
CLC	Clear carry flag
CLD	Clear decimal mode flag
CLI	Clear interrupt disable flag
CLV	Clear overflow flag
CMP	Compare with accumulator
CPX	Compare with X register
CPY	Compare with Y register
DEC	Decrement memory by one
DEX	Decrement X register by one
DEY	Decrement Y register by one
EOR	"Exclusive-or" with accumulator
INC	Increment memory by one
INX	Increment X register by one
INY	Increment Y register by one
JMP	Jump to new location
JSR	Jump + save return address
LDA	Load accumulator
LDX	Load X register
LDY	Load Y register
LSR	Logical bit-shift right
NOP	No operation
ORA	"Or" with accumulator
PHA	Push accumulator on stack
PHP	Push status on stack

(continued)

Table 2-1. 65Ø2 instruction set mnemonics in alphabetical order (continued).

PLA	Pull accumulator from stack	**STA**	Store accumulator
PLP	Pull status from stack	**STX**	Store X register
ROL	Rotate left through carry	**STY**	Store Y register
ROR	Rotate right through carry	**TAX**	Transfer accumulator to X
RTI	Return from interrupt	**TAY**	Transfer accumulator to Y
RTS	Return from subroutine	**TSX**	Transfer stack pointer to X
SBC	Subtract from accumulator	**TXA**	Transfer X to accumulator
SEC	Set carry flag	**TXS**	Transfer X to stack pointer
SED	Set decimal mode flag	**TYA**	Transfer Y to accumulator
SEI	Set interrupt disable flag		

The 65Ø2 instructions can be used to perform a wide variety of functions. For example, they can be used to pass data between two registers or between registers and memory, to perform simple arithmetic, to increment and decrement index registers and memory locations, to pass data between registers and the stack, to perform logical functions, and so on. Figure 2-1 illustrates, in a general way, how each of the 65Ø2's instructions affect memory and the 65Ø2 registers.

As you might expect, it takes a finite period of time for any particular instruction to be executed by the 65Ø2. The time required to execute one instruction, however, is not necessarily the same as the time required to execute another. In fact, the time it takes to execute one general type of instruction will even vary depending on how the instruction is told to access the data on which it is to operate (i.e., its "addressing mode").

Table 2-2 sets out the times required to execute each instruction in units of 65Ø2 *machine cycles* for each valid addressing mode (addressing modes will be discussed in detail later in this chapter). The length of a 65Ø2 machine cycle is fixed by the frequency of the clock signal fed into the 65Ø2 microprocessor. On the //e, this clock signal is 1.Ø23 megahertz, which means that every machine cycle takes Ø.9775 (1/1.Ø23) microsecond to perform.

It is often convenient to know exactly how long it will take to execute a particular instruction when precise timing loops must

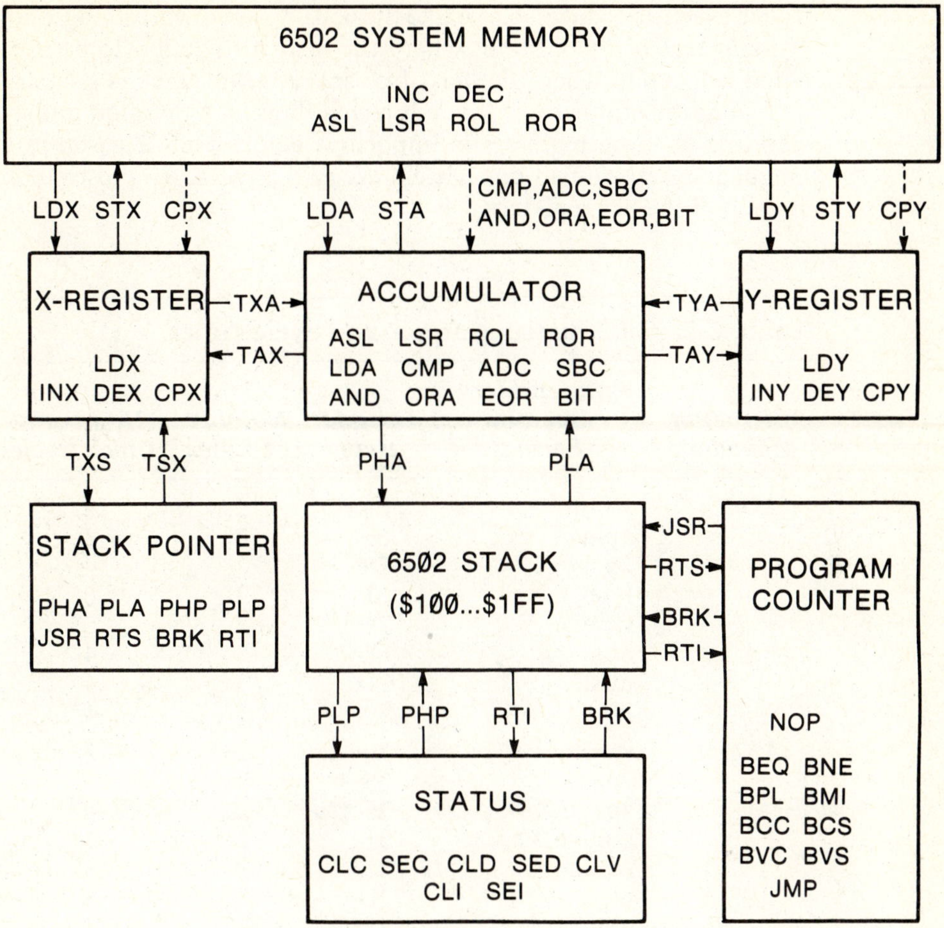

NOTE: Solid arrows indicate a transfer of data.
Dashed arrows indicate a transfer of information.

Figure 2-1. Usage chart of 65Ø2 instructions.

be generated in software. We will see an example of this in Chapter 9, where a program is presented that can generate musical notes of specific frequencies.

65Ø2 REGISTERS

While the 65Ø2 is executing a program, it makes use of the six internal registers that are shown in Figure 2-2. These registers are used to manipulate data in the manner dictated by the program that is executing and also to make the 65Ø2 aware of various aspects of the status of the system: where the next instruction to be executed is located, where the next free space in the stack is located, and what the status of its seven internal flags is. A detailed understanding of these registers is important before a 65Ø2 assembly-language program can be written. We will now take a closer look at each of the six registers.

Table 2-2. 65Ø2 instruction set and cycle times.

Instruction Mnemonic	*Assembler Operand Format*	*Opcode Byte*	*Number of Bytes*	*Number of Clock Cycles*
ADC	#num	69	2	2
	zpage	65	2	3
	zpage,X	75	2	4
	(zpage,X)	61	2	6
	(zpage),Y	71	2	5*
	abs	6D	3	4
	abs,X	7D	3	4*
	abs,Y	79	3	4*
AND	#num	29	2	2
	zpage	25	2	3
	zpage,X	35	2	4
	(zpage,X)	21	2	6
	(zpage),Y	31	2	5*
	abs	2D	3	4
	abs,X	3D	3	4*
	abs,Y	39	3	4*
ASL	[accumulator]	ØA	1	2
	zpage	Ø6	2	5
	zpage,X	16	2	6
	abs	ØE	3	6
	abs,X	1E	3	7
BCC	disp	9Ø	2	2**
BCS	disp	BØ	2	2**
BEQ	disp	FØ	2	2**
BIT	zpage	24	2	3
	abs	2C	3	4
BMI	disp	3Ø	2	2**
BNE	disp	DØ	2	2**
BPL	disp	1Ø	2	2**

Table 2-2. 6502 instruction set and cycle times (continued).

Instruction Mnemonic	*Assembler Operand Format*	*Opcode Byte*	*Number of Bytes*	*Number of Clock Cycles*
BRK	[implied]	00	1	7
BVC	disp	50	2	2**
BVS	disp	70	2	2**
CLC	[implied]	18	1	2
CLD	[implied]	D8	1	2
CLI	[implied]	58	1	2
CLV	[implied]	B8	1	2
CMP	#num	C9	2	2
	zpage	C5	2	3
	zpage,X	D5	2	4
	(zpage,X)	C1	2	6
	(zpage),Y	D1	2	5*
	abs	CD	3	4
	abs,X	DD	3	4*
	abs,Y	D9	3	4*
CPX	#num	E0	2	2
	zpage	E4	2	3
	abs	EC	3	4
CPY	#num	C0	2	2
	zpage	C4	2	3
	abs	CC	3	4
DEC	zpage	C6	2	5
	zpage,X	D6	2	6
	abs	CE	3	6
	abs,X	DE	3	7
DEX	[implied]	CA	1	2
DEY	[implied]	88	1	2
EOR	#num	49	2	2
	zpage	45	2	3
	zpage,X	55	2	4
	(zpage,X)	41	2	6
	(zpage),Y	51	2	5*
	abs	4D	3	4
	abs,X	5D	3	4*
	abs,Y	59	3	4*

(continued)

Table 2-2. 65Ø2 instruction set and cycle times (continued).

Instruction Mnemonic	*Assembler Operand Format*	*Opcode Byte*	*Number of Bytes*	*Number of Clock Cycles*
INC	zpage	E6	2	5
	zpage,X		2	6
	abs	EE	3	6
	abs,X	FE	3	7
INX	[implied]	E8	1	2
INY	[implied]	C8	1	2
JMP	abs	4C	3	3
	(abs)	6C	3	5
JSR	abs	2Ø	3	6
LDA	#num	A9	2	2
	zpage	A5	2	3
	zpage,X	B5	2	4
	(zpage,X)	A1	2	6
	(zpage),Y	B1	2	5*
	abs	AD	3	4
	abs,X	BD	3	4*
	abs,Y	B9	3	4*
LDX	#num	A2	2	2
	zpage	A6	2	3
	zpage,Y	B6	2	4
	abs	AE	3	4
	abs,Y	BE	3	4*
LDY	#num	AØ	2	2
	zpage	A4	2	3
	zpage,X	B4	2	4
	abs	AC	3	4
	abs,X	BC	3	4*
LSR	[accumulator]	4A	1	2
	zpage	46	2	5
	zpage,X	56	2	6
	abs	4E	3	6
	abs,X	5E	3	7
NOP	[implied]	EA	1	2
ORA	#num	Ø9	2	2
	zpage	Ø5	2	3
	zpage,X	15	2	4
	(zpage,X)	Ø1	2	6
	(zpage),Y	11	2	5*
	abs	ØD	3	4

Table 2-2. 65Ø2 instruction set and cycle times (continued).

Instruction Mnemonic	*Assembler Operand Format*	*Opcode Byte*	*Number of Bytes*	*Number of Clock Cycles*
	abs,X	1D	3	4*
	abs,Y	19	3	4*
PHA	[implied]	48	1	3
PHP	[implied]	Ø8	1	3
PLA	[implied]	68	1	4
PLP	[implied]	28	1	4
ROL	[accumulator]	2A	1	2
	zpage	26	2	5
	zpage,X	36	2	6
	abs	2E	3	6
	abs,X	3E	3	7
ROR	[accumulator]	6A	1	2
	zpage	66	2	5
	zpage,X	76	2	6
	abs	6E	3	6
	abs,X	7E	3	7
RTI	[implied]	4Ø	1	6
RTS	[implied]	6Ø	1	6
SBC	#num	E9	2	2
	zpage	E5	2	3
	zpage,X	F5	2	4
	(zpage,X)	E1	2	6
	(zpage),Y	F1	2	5*
	abs	ED	3	4
	abs,X	FD	3	4*
	abs,Y	F9	3	4*
SEC	[implied]	38	1	2
SED	[implied]	F8	1	2
SEI	[implied]	78	1	2
STA	zpage	85	2	3
	zpage,X	95	2	4
	(zpage,X)	81	2	6
	(zpage),Y	91	2	5*
	abs	8D	3	4
	abs,X	9D	3	4*
	abs,Y	99	3	4*

(continued)

Table 2-2. 65Ø2 instruction set and cycle times (continued).

Instruction Mnemonic	*Assembler Operand Format*	*Opcode Byte*	*Number of Bytes*	*Number of Clock Cycles*
STX	zpage	86	2	3
	zpage,Y	96	2	4
	abs	8E	3	4
STY	zpage	84	2	3
	zpage,X	94	2	4
	abs	8C	3	4
TAX	[implied]	AA	1	2
TAY	[implied]	A8	1	2
TSX	[implied]	BA	1	2
TXA	[implied]	8A	1	2
TXS	[implied]	9A	1	2
TYA	[implied]	98	1	2

*Add one clock cycle if a page boundary is crossed.
**Add one clock cycle if a branch occurs to a location in the same page; add two clock cycles if a branch occurs to a location in a different page.
See Table 2-3 for a description of the assembler operand formats.

The Accumulator—A

The 65Ø2 supports two simple arithmetic instructions: ADC (add with carry) and SBC (subtract with carry). Both of them require that the first of the two operands in the addition or subtraction be contained in the accumulator register, A. After the arithmetic has been performed, the result is stored in A, and this is how it gets its name—it "accumulates" the results of arithmetic operations that are performed. The accumulator is an 8-bit register and so can hold numbers from Ø to 255 only.

The accumulator is unique in that it is the only one of the 65Ø2's registers that can be used to perform the logical instructions, namely, EOR (logical "exclusive-or"), ORA (logical "or"), and AND (logical "and"), or any of the bit-shifting instructions, namely, ASL (arithmetic shift left), LSR (logical shift right), ROL (rotate left), and ROR (rotate right). (You should note, however, that the bit-shifting instructions can also operate directly on memory locations.)

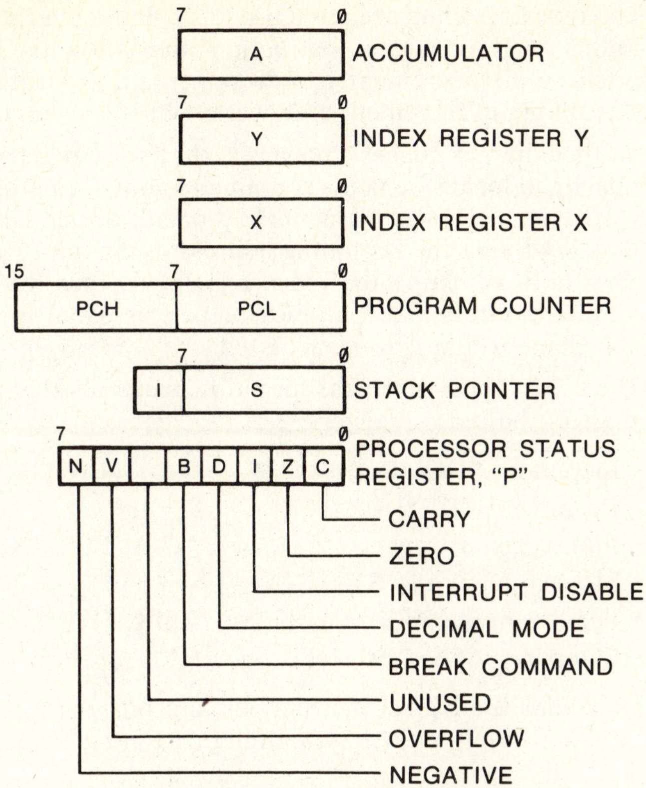

Figure 2-2. The 65Ø2 registers.

Here are the 65Ø2 instructions that directly use and affect the accumulator:

- Arithmetic : ADC, SBC
- Logical : AND, ORA, EOR
- Bit-shifting : ASL, LSR, ROL, ROR
- Compare : CMP
- Store in memory : STA
- Load from memory or with data : LDA
- Store on stack : PHA
- Load from stack : PLA
- Inter-register transfer : TAX, TAY, TXA, TYA

The Index Registers—X and Y

Like the accumulator, the X and Y index registers are eight bits in size and can contain numbers from Ø to 255.

The index registers are often used as counters because the 65Ø2 contains special one-byte instructions that allow the index registers to be easily incremented or decremented. No such instructions are available to increment and decrement the accumulator.

As their names suggest, however, the index registers are used primarily to locate elements contained in data structures in memory, such as a series of elements in a one-dimensional array. This is done by fixing the beginning address of the data structure and then simply adjusting the index register so that the sum of the beginning address and the index register is equal to the address of the element that is to be accessed.

The 65Ø2 supports several special instructions that directly use and affect the index registers:

- Increment : INX, INY
- Decrement : DEX, DEY
- Inter-register transfer : TAX, TAY, TXA, TYA, TXS, TSX
- Store in memory : STX, STY
- Load from memory or with data : LDX, LDY
- Compare : CPX, CPY

Note that the logical instructions and bit-shifting instructions that can be used with the accumulator cannot be used with the index registers.

The Processor Status Register—P

The 8-bit processor status register holds the states of seven one-bit flags or "status" bits that are referenced by the 65Ø2 when it is executing many of its instructions. (One bit in the processor status register, bit 5, is not used by the 65Ø2.) Each of these flags has a specific meaning and can markedly affect how instructions are executed. For example, the 65Ø2 supports a series of "branch on condition" instructions (BCC, BCS, BPL, BMI, BEQ, BNE, BVC, BVS), each of which can be used to examine the status of a particular flag and to cause the program to "jump" to a new location if the condition is met or to continue on with the next instruction in memory if it is not.

Although almost all instructions will cause flags in the processor status register to be adjusted after they have been executed, the following instructions *explicitly* affect them:

- Clear and set the carry flag : CLC, SEC
- Clear and set the decimal flag : CLD, SED

- Clear and set the interrupt flag : CLI, SEI
- Clear the overflow flag : CLV

Let's take a look at each of these seven flags right now.

Carry Flag (C)

The 65Ø2 uses the carry flag in three quite different ways. First, the carry flag represents the "ninth" bit in any unsigned addition (ADC) or subtraction (SBC) operation that is performed. ("Unsigned" means that all eight bits of a byte are used to represent the magnitude of a number.) It can be examined after the addition or subtraction in order to determine whether the result is outside the range of numbers that can be stored in the 8-bit accumulator. This allows for easy manipulation of numbers that use more than one byte.

The 65Ø2 can perform arithmetic in one of two modes: binary and decimal. The mode used depends on the setting of the status register's decimal mode flag (see below).

In binary mode, each byte is considered to represent a simple unsigned binary number from Ø . . . 255. When arithmetic operations are performed, the standard rules for adding or subtracting two binary numbers are followed.

In decimal mode, however, each half of the byte is considered to represent a single decimal digit from Ø to 9; this means that only those decimal numbers from Ø . . . 99 can be represented. When arithmetic operations are performed on such numbers, the result is always stored in the same decimal format.

In either mode, before any arithmetic is performed, the carry flag must be cleared with a CLC instruction, in the case of addition, or set with a SEC instruction, in the case of subtraction. (If multibyte arithmetic is being performed, then the carry is adjusted only at the beginning of the sequence of additions or subtractions.) If the state of the carry flag changes after an addition operation, then the true answer is 256 (if in binary mode) or 1ØØ (if in decimal mode) more than the number in the accumulator. If the carry flag changes after a subtraction, then the true answer is 256 (if in binary mode) or 1ØØ (if in decimal mode) less than the number in the accumulator.

The second use of the carry flag is as a ninth bit that participates whenever the ASL, LSR, ROL, and ROR bit-shifting instructions are executed.

Third, the carry flag is used as a general-purpose flag that is acted on by the BCC (branch if C-flag is Ø) and BCS (branch if C-flag is 1) instructions. As with all of the 65Ø2's "branch on condition" instructions, BCC and BCS allow control of the program flow to be manipulated by simply changing the state of a flag in the processor status register (in this case, the carry flag).

Zero Flag (Z)

This flag is used to indicate whether the last data movement or arithmetic operation involved a zero result. If it did, then the Z-flag will be set (1); otherwise it will be cleared (Ø).

There are two branch instructions that examine the status of the Z-flag to determine whether the branch should be performed: BEQ (branch if Z-flag is 1) and BNE (branch if Z-flag is Ø).

Interrupt Disable Flag (I)

This flag is used to control how the 65Ø2 will react when the electrical signal on its IRQ (interrupt request) pin is brought near Ø volts. Such an interrupt can be generated by certain peripheral cards whenever they are ready to send information to, or receive information from, the //e. If the I-flag is set using the SEI instruction, then all IRQ signals that may be generated will be ignored. If, however, the I-flag is cleared using the CLI instruction, then the 65Ø2 will respond to IRQ signals when they occur by beginning a special interrupt sequence that is described in detail below in the section entitled "65Ø2 INTERRUPTS."

Decimal Mode Flag (D)

This flag is used to control how the 65Ø2 is to perform addition and subtraction operations. If standard binary arithmetic is to be performed using the ADC and SBC instructions, then this flag must be cleared to Ø using the CLD instruction. As we saw when discussing the accumulator, in binary mode bytes are treated as unsigned binary numbers from Ø to 255.

If, however, the D-flag is set to 1 using the SED instruction, all arithmetic will be performed under the assumption that all numbers are stored in a special decimal format. In this format, one byte is used to store exactly two decimal digits from Ø to 9. The first digit is stored in the high-order four bits and the other in the low-order four bits and the maximum number that can be stored is 99. When arithmetic operations are performed, the results will also be stored in this format.

Break Flag (B)

This flag is adjusted internally by the 65Ø2 whenever an IRQ (interrupt request) interrupt is recognized by the 65Ø2 or a BRK (break) instruction is executed. See the section below entitled "65Ø2 INTERRUPTS" for more information on these types of interrupts. When an IRQ interrupt is recognized, then the B-flag is cleared to Ø; if a BRK instruction is executed, then it is set to 1.

Whenever an IRQ or a BRK interrupt is generated, the 65Ø2 begins to execute the same program (its address is held at locations $FFFE and $FFFF). It is often convenient, however, to determine what the source of the interrupt was so that a different action can be taken for each source. This is most easily done by having the interrupt-servicing program examine the state of the B-flag.

Overflow Flag (V)

The overflow flag is used primarily when performing arithmetic operations on signed numbers. Signed numbers are those that use bit 7 of a byte to hold the sign of the number (1 for negative, Ø for positive). Bits Ø . . . 6 are used to store the magnitude of the number in a special "two's complement" format that will be described in Chapter 4. If the result of an addition or subtraction of two signed numbers is outside the range of numbers that can be stored in this format (−128 . . . +127), then the V-flag will be set to 1; if the number is in range, however, the V-flag will be cleared to Ø.

The V-flag can be explicitly cleared by using the CLV instruction. Surprisingly, there is no corresponding instruction to explicitly set the V-flag.

The state of the V-flag can also be affected by using the BIT instruction. If you "BIT" any memory location, then a copy of bit 6 of the byte stored there will be placed in the V-flag.

Two branch instructions make use of the V-flag: BVS (branch if V-flag is 1) and BVC (branch if V-flag is Ø).

Negative Flag (N)

The negative flag is used to indicate the sign of the last value that was directly transferred into the A, X, or Y register or that was put there by an instruction that performed an arithmetic operation (DEX, DEY, INX, INY, ADC, SBC, and so on). The 65Ø2 considers any byte that contains a one in bit 7 to be negative.

Two branch instructions make use of the N-flag: BPL (branch on plus, i.e., N-flag is Ø) and BMI (branch on negative, i.e., N-flag is 1).

A BIT instruction can also be used to directly affect the state of the N-flag. When you "BIT" any memory address, a copy of bit 7 of the byte stored there will be placed in the N-flag. If bit 7 is used to hold the status of some condition, then you can use BPL to branch if the status is off (Ø) or BMI to branch if it is on (1). We will see in later chapters that the //e uses bit 7 of several locations to represent the status of different hardware switches that can be controlled by software.

The Stack Pointer—S

As we saw earlier in this chapter, the 65Ø2 uses the 256-byte area from $1ØØ to $1FF as a hardware stack. This is a "last-in, first-out" data area: the most recent information stored on the stack is always removed first. Information is usually placed on the stack by the "push" instructions, PHA and PHP, and removed from the stack by the "pull" instructions, PLA and PLP. (Information does not actually disappear after a pull, but it will be overwritten as soon as more information is pushed on to the stack.)

The JSR (jump-to-subroutine) instruction also causes information to be placed on the stack. When the JSR instruction is executed, the address of the next instruction in memory after the JSR, minus one, is pushed on the stack (high-order byte first). When the corresponding RTS (return-from-subroutine) instruction is executed, this address is removed and the program resumes at that address (plus 1).

The stack pointer register, S, is used to keep track of where in the 256-byte stack area the bytes are to be pushed to or pulled from; it always points to the next free space available in the stack area. When the system is first initialized, S is set equal to $FF. Then, whenever a byte is pushed on the stack, it is stored at location $1ØØ+S and then the stack pointer is *decremented* by one. Because S is decremented, the stack grows downward in memory. When bytes are pulled from the stack, they are taken from the top of the stack (location $1ØØ+S+1). The stack pointer is automatically incremented each time a byte is removed from the stack in this way.

Interrupt conditions and interrupt-related instructions also affect the stack pointer (see the section below entitled "65Ø2 INTERRUPTS" for a detailed discussion of interrupts). When an interrupt from a peripheral device is recognized (or one is generated by a BRK (break) instruction), a two-byte address and a copy of the processor status register is placed on the stack and the stack pointer is decremented by three. When the corresponding RTI (return-from-interrupt) instruction is executed, the stack pointer will be incremented by three, thus effectively "removing" these bytes from the stack.

Here are the 65Ø2 instructions that directly affect the stack pointer register:

- Inter-register transfer : TXS, TSX
- Push data on stack : JSR, PHA, PHP, BRK
- Pull data from stack : PLA, PLP, RTS, RTI

The Program Counter—PC

The program counter (sometimes called the instruction pointer) is the only 16-bit register that the 65Ø2 supports and is used to hold the address of the next instruction to be executed. This address will normally be that of the next instruction in the program, but not necessarily. There are several instructions that can be used to manipulate the flow of the program and to pass control to other parts of the program by adjusting the program counter accordingly. These are the JMP (jump) instruction, which acts like an Applesoft GOTO, the JSR (jump-to-subroutine) and RTS (return-from-subroutine) instructions, which act like an Applesoft GOSUB/RETURN combination, and the branch-on-condition instructions (BCC, BCS, BEQ, BNE, BPL, BMI, BVC, BVS). The program counter is also affected by any hardware or software interrupt (BRK) and by the RTI (return-from-interrupt) instruction.

65Ø2 ADDRESSING MODES

A complete 65Ø2 instruction is either one, two, or three bytes long. The first byte always represents the operation code ("op-code") for the instruction itself and the remaining bytes (if any) represent the operand; if an operand is specified, it is either an address (one byte or two bytes) or immediate data (one byte). If the operand represents a two-byte address, then the first byte is always the lower two digits of the four-digit hexadecimal address (the allowable addresses are in the range $ØØØØ to $FFFF).

An address that is specified after an opcode is not necessarily the address from which the instruction will read data or to which it will store data. In many instances, the 65Ø2 uses this address to calculate another address (called the "effective address") on which it does operate. Exactly how this calculation is to be performed depends on which of several *addressing modes* that can be used by that instruction has been selected. The 65Ø2 determines which addressing mode has been selected by examining the value of the opcode itself—each general type of instruction can have several opcode values associated with it, one for each valid addressing mode. The value of the opcode also dictates whether the operand is to be interpreted as immediate data instead of an address.

We will now outline the various addressing modes that the 65Ø2 supports. Before beginning, you should note that not all instructions are permitted to use each addressing mode. The ones that are supported by each instruction are indicated by entries in Table 2-2. The names of each of the addressing modes that the 65Ø2 uses, and the operand formats used to represent these modes in an assembly-language program, are summarized in Table 2-3 Note that these operand formats are those used by the BIG MAC assembler that was used to develop the examples presented in this book; other assemblers may require that slightly different formats be used.

Immediate

Immediate addressing is used whenever you want an instruction to act on a specific 8-bit number rather than on a byte stored somewhere in memory. This 8-bit number is stored in the byte immediately following the opcode itself and forms the operand for the instruction.

The immediate addressing mode is most useful for initializing a register to a constant value and for providing specific data on which an instruction is to operate. To select this addressing mode when using an assembler, the "#" symbol must be placed in front of the number in the instruction's operand:

`LDA #49`—load the accumulator with 49 (decimal)
`LDX #$43`—load X with $43 (hexadecimal)

It is often necessary to deal with the high-order or low-order byte of a two-byte address as an immediate quantity. To do this, you must use an assembler operand of the form "#<ADDRESS" (for

Table 2-3. 65Ø2 addressing modes and assembler operand formats.

Addressing Mode	*Assembler Operand Format*	*Example of Instruction*
Immediate	#num	LDA #$45
	#<abs	LDA #<$FD1B
	#>abs	LDA #>$FD1B
Absolute	abs	LDX $FE44
	zpage	LDA $24
Accumulator	[Not applicable]	ASL
Implied	[Not applicable]	CLC
Indexed indirect	(zpage, X)	LDA ($EØ, X)
Indirect indexed	(zpage), Y	STA ($28), Y
Absolute indexed	abs, X	LDA $2ØØØ, X
	abs, Y	STA $Ø4ØØ, Y
	zpage, X	LDA $28, X
	zpage, Y	STX $22, Y
Relative*	disp	BNE $BEAF
Indirect	(abs)	JMP ($Ø3EE)

Note: "num" = 1-byte number
"abs" = 2-byte address
"<abs" = low-order byte of a 2-byte address (or constant)
">abs" = high-order byte of a 2-byte address (or constant)
"zpage" = 1-byte zero page address
"disp" = 1-byte signed displacement

*Relative addressing: An absolute address is usually specified in the operand when the program is written; the assembler converts the operand to a one-byte displacement to this address when the program is assembled.

the low-order byte) and "#>ADDRESS" (for the high-order byte), where "ADDRESS" is the address being dealt with. Note, however, that the form of this type of operand applies to the BIG MAC assembler only; most other assemblers require that a different method be used to specify which half of an address is to be dealt with. One assembler, the Apple 65Ø2 Editor/Assembler, uses the same general method, but it reverses the meaning: "#>" is used to specify the low-order byte and "#<" is used to specify the high-order byte!

Absolute

The absolute addressing mode is used whenever the operand itself contains the absolute address in memory on which the opcode is to operate. The two bytes required to store this address are stored low-byte first.

Here are some examples of how to use the absolute addressing mode:

LDA $FE43—load the accumulator with the number stored at $FE43
STY $1238—store the Y register at location $1238

Some instructions support an important variant of the absolute addressing mode, called zero page absolute, if the address specified is in the 65Ø2 zero page (the first 256 bytes of memory). In this mode, the opcode is followed by a one-byte address only because the high-order byte is implicitly zero. Most assemblers will recognize when a zero page location is being specified and will automatically select this addressing mode for you by changing the value of the opcode byte used by the instruction when the program is assembled.

Accumulator

Accumulator addressing is the mode used by all those opcodes that act on the accumulator alone and that require no address or immediate data on which to operate. These are the bit-shifting opcodes LSR, ASL, ROL, and ROR. There are no operand bytes for these instructions. Note, however, that some assemblers other than BIG MAC (notably, the Apple 65Ø2 Editor/Assembler) require that the letter "A" be entered in the operand field before the program source code can be properly assembled.

Implied

The 65Ø2 supports many opcodes that do not act on immediate data or on memory locations, but rather on internal registers and status flags only. These opcodes require no operands because their actions are implicitly defined by the opcode itself and so the addressing mode used is called implied.

Here are some examples of opcodes that use the implied addressing mode: PHA, PLA, PHP, PLP, CLD, CLI, BRK, DEX, INX, NOP, RTS, TAX.

Indexed Indirect

When the indexed indirect addressing mode is used, the operand is only one byte long and represents a location in zero page. The effective address on which the instruction acts is calculated by first adding the contents of the X register to the zero page location specified in the operand to obtain a resultant address. The effective address is represented by the two bytes that are stored at the resultant address and the very next address (low-order byte first).

You can select this addressing mode when using an assembler by using an instruction of the form

```
STA ($E0,X)
```

where the parentheses indicate that the effective address is not $EØ+X but rather the address stored at that location.

Indirect Indexed

Indirect indexed is a powerful addressing mode that is often used to access a block of memory that may not always begin at the same location in memory or that is longer than 256 bytes in length. The operand is one byte long and represents a zero page location; this zero page location, and the one immediately following it, contain the address (low-byte first) of the beginning of a data block in memory. These locations are said to "point to" this data block.

When this addressing mode is used, the effective address on which the instruction is to operate is calculated by first taking the address of this data block from the zero page locations and then adding to it the contents of the Y register.

Here is an example of how you would select the indirect indexed addressing mode when using an assembler:

```
LDA ($26),Y
```

The parentheses around $26 mean "contents of"; it is the address stored at $26 (and $27) that will be used to calculate the effective address, and not $26 itself. If the Y-register contains $FE and the address $4ØØ is stored at $26/$27, then the accumulator will be loaded with the contents of memory location $4FE ($4FE = $400 + $FE).

Absolute Indexed

The operand for the absolute indexed addressing mode is two bytes long and contains the absolute address of a memory location called a "base address." The effective address on which the instruction is to operate is calculated by taking this base address and adding to it the contents of the X register (if X indexing is selected) or of the Y register (if Y indexing is selected).

Here are some examples of the use of this addressing mode:

LDA $400,X—load the accumulator with the contents of the location specified by $4ØØ+X.

STA $A032,Y—store the accumulator at the location specified by $AØ32+Y

There is a special version of this addressing mode, called zero page absolute indexed, that can be used by some instructions when the base address is in page zero. In this case, the operand is only one byte long and represents this zero page address. Most assemblers will automatically select this addressing mode for you if the operand is, indeed, in page zero.

Relative

The 65Ø2 supports a series of branch instructions that examine the 65Ø2 status register to determine whether a change in the flow of the program should be made or not: BEQ, BNE, BPL, BMI, BCC, BCS, BVC, and BVS. The first byte represents, as usual, the opcode for the instruction. The second byte represents the number that must be added to the address of the next instruction in memory in order to calculate the destination address of the branch. Because this byte represents a displacement from an instruction's location rather than an absolute location, this addressing mode is called "relative."

There are restrictions on how far you can branch using relative addressing. In particular, you can only specify a relative address that is at most 127 bytes higher in memory or 128 bytes lower in memory (as measured from the address of the next higher instruction). Values from $ØØ . . . $7F represent the positive branches (Ø . . . 127), and values from $8Ø . . . $FF represent the negative branches (−128, −127, . . . ,−1). Note that the values for negative branches are stored in a special "two's complement" format; see Chapter 4 for a detailed description of this format.

If you must transfer control to a destination location that is outside this range, you will have to use a JMP instruction instead.

Indirect

This addressing mode is used by only one instruction, JMP. A two-byte operand is used and these two bytes define a location in memory that contains the low half of the address that is to be jumped to; the high half is stored in the next memory location.

If you are using an assembler, then you would select this addressing mode by entering an instruction that looks like this:

```
JMP ($1234)
```

The parentheses around the operand indicate that it is not $1234 that is being jumped to but rather the address stored at $1234 (and $1235).

The indirect addressing mode is useful in situations where the ultimate destination of the jump instruction may be changed, perhaps by another program. Even if this other program places a new address at the operand address, the main program itself need not be changed. On the other hand, if the absolute addressing mode were used instead, then it would be necessary to modify the program and this may be difficult to do. The //c uses the indirect addressing mode whenever it has to jump to its character input or output subroutines. Whenever new input or output devices are activated, all that need be done is to change the address stored at the address specified in the operand—the main program will remain the same (see the discussion of the //e's input and output links in Chapters 6 and 7).

You should note that there is a serious hardware bug in the 65Ø2 chip itself that affects the use of the indirect addressing mode. It turns out that if the address specified in the operand begins at the end of a page (that is, at $xxFF), then the effective address will not be the one found at $xxFF and $xxFF + 1 as expected but rather at $xxFF and $xxØØ. This bug has been eliminated in the 65CØ2 microprocessor that controls the Apple //c.

65Ø2 INPUT/OUTPUT HANDLING

Unlike those of some microprocessors, the 65Ø2 instruction set does not include any instructions that are specifically designed to perform input/output (I/O) operations. Instead, all I/O operations are performed by using standard instructions to read data from or write data to addresses within the 65Ø2's standard 64K address space to which I/O devices are "connected." These addresses do not usually represent real RAM or ROM memory locations (memory that holds video display information is one exception) but, nevertheless, are accessed in exactly the same way as if they did.

This method of handling I/O is called "memory-mapped I/O" because the I/O devices form a logical part of the 65Ø2's 64K memory space itself and so no special instructions are required to make use of them. The //e contains several addresses that are used to control various aspects of its hardware environment. As we will see at the end of this chapter, except for those addresses that relate to the video display, these addresses are all contained in locations $CØØØ ... $CØFF. Note that some of these I/O locations can be accessed in order to switch between one of two hardware states, for example, text or graphics display, primary or alternate character set, and 4Ø-column or 8Ø-column display. Thus, they are called "soft switch" I/O memory locations.

65Ø2 INTERRUPTS

There are three input pins on the 65Ø2 integrated circuit that are called RESET, IRQ (interrupt request), and NMI (non-maskable interrupt). When the electrical signals at each of these three pins is high (near +5 volts) the 65Ø2 goes about performing its normal functions. If, however, one of these pins is suddenly brought low (near Ø volts), one of three special *interrupt* sequences may begin, depending on which pin has been affected. An interrupt sequence can also be generated in software by using the BRK instruction.

One especially useful type of hardware interrupt, IRQ, is commonly generated by devices found on peripheral cards that are plugged into one of the //e's seven expansion slots (see Chapter 11). These interrupts indicate to the 65Ø2 microprocessor that an event has taken place that should be dealt with before continuing to run the main program. For example, a clock card may generate an interrupt once per second to allow the new time to be displayed on the video screen.

Each type of 65Ø2 interrupt has associated with it a two-byte vector that holds the address of the interrupt-handling subroutine that will be called when the interrupt occurs. These vectors are all stored in the high end of of the 65Ø2 memory space from $FFFA to $FFFF. The specific vector locations for each type of interrupt and the addresses of the interrupt-handling routines to which they point are shown in Table 2-4. Note that all of the vector addresses (except the one for NMI) change when ProDOS is being used. Most of ProDOS resides in a special "bank-switched RAM" area that occupies the addresses from $DØØØ ... $FFFF that are normally occupied by the Applesoft and the system monitor ROMs (see Chapter 8). Thus, the interrupt vectors within this RAM area (from $FFFA to $FFFF) can be changed as desired and they will take effect whenever bank-switched RAM is active. ProDOS takes advantage of the power to change the interrupt vectors by storing in

Table 2-4. 65Ø2-Apple //e interrupt locations.

Interrupt Type	*Interrupt Vector Location*	*Address of Interrupt Handler*	*Location of User Vector*
NMI	$FFFA/$FFFB	$Ø3FB	n/a
RESET	$FFFC/$FFFD	$FA62 or $FFCB	$Ø3F2*
IRQ	$FFFE/$FFFF	$FA4Ø or $FF9B	$Ø3FE
BRK	$FFFE/$FFFF	$FA4Ø or $FF9B	$Ø3FØ

($FF9B: when the ProDOS bank-switched RAM area is active only)

*Control is passed to the Reset user vector only if the number stored at $3F4 (the powered-up byte) is equal to the logical exclusive-OR of the number stored at $3F3 and the constant $A5.

them the addresses of routines that handle interrupts more safely and efficiently than the normal subroutines that are pointed to by the ROM interrupt vectors. We will see examples of this later in this section.

The interrupt-handling routines on the //e ultimately pass control to other addresses that are specified in user-definable vector locations. These user vector locations are also shown in Table 2-4. Note that a user-defined interrupt subroutine that is used to handle interrupts generated by an IRQ or NMI signal, or a BRK command, must end by executing an RTI (return-from-interrupt) instruction and that when it ends the 65Ø2's A, X, and Y registers must contain the same values as when the subroutine was first called.

Interrupts are often generated by I/O devices whenever they have information available to be read (input devices) or whenever they are ready to receive information (output devices). Because the 65Ø2 can be interrupted by the device, it is not necessary for the program to continuously monitor (poll) the I/O devices to determine when one is ready to be used. This means that the program is able to execute much more efficiently.

The four basic types of interrupts supported by the 65Ø2 will now be discussed in detail.

Reset Interrupt

The reset interrupt is used to cause the system to stop executing the current program and to begin a sequence of instructions that start at the address stored in the reset vector at $FFFC/$FFFD (low-order byte first). On the //e, the reset vector points to a subroutine beginning at $FA62 (the ProDOS reset vector actually points to another subroutine that ultimately calls $FA62). This subroutine takes care of initializing the //e to a known state and will pass control to a user-definable subroutine whose address is stored at $3F2 and $3F3 (low byte first) if the logical exclusive-OR of the value stored at $3F3 and the constant $A5 is the same as the value stored at $3F4 (which is called the powered-up byte). If it isn't, then the disk drive will start up just as it does when the //e is first turned on.

The reset interrupt is automatically generated whenever the power to the 65Ø2 is first turned on. As we will see in Chapter 6, it can also be generated by pressing the CONTROL and RESET keys on the //e's keyboard at the same time. Specific examples of "trapping" the reset interrupt by adjusting the user vector at $3F2/$3F3 and the powered-up byte at $3F4 will also be given in Chapter 6.

A reset interrupt is normally used only in panic situations where the program that is running must be stopped immediately.

Non-Maskable Interrupt (NMI)

If an NMI interrupt is generated, the 65Ø2 always responds by first completing the current instruction being executed. The following sequence of events then takes place:

1. The current program counter is stored on the stack (this will be the address of the next instruction in the program to be executed after the interrupt has been dealt with).
2. The processor status register is stored on the stack.
3. The I-flag in the processor status register is set to 1 (this disables subsequent IRQ operations; see below).

After these operations have been performed, the program counter is loaded with the address that is stored in the NMI vector at $FFFA/$FFFB (low-order byte first), and then the interrupt-handling program that begins at that address is executed. The address stored in the NMI vector on the //e is $3FB. Thus, to properly trap an NMI signal, a three-byte JMP (jump) instruction must be placed at this address that passes control to the main body of the interrupt-handling subroutine.

To end an interrupt-handling program, an RTI (return-from-interrupt) instruction must be executed. This will cause the old program counter and flags to be restored (by pulling them from the stack), thus allowing the main program to start up again where it last left off.

As you might expect from its name, there is no way that you can prevent an active NMI signal from being dealt with by the 65Ø2, that is, it cannot be "masked." This can cause serious difficulties in situations where time-critical operations such as timing loops and disk accesses are being performed, so devices do not generally use the NMI signal except for the most important reasons (for example, an anticipated power loss).

Interrupt Request (IRQ)

The maskable equivalent to the NMI signal is the IRQ signal. When an IRQ signal is generated, the 65Ø2 will take action on it only if the I-flag in the processor status register is Ø (this can be achieved using the CLI instruction). If the I-flag is set to 1 (using the SEI instruction), then the IRQ signal will be ignored and no further IRQ interrupts will be dealt with until one occurs after the I-flag is cleared to Ø using a CLI instruction.

If the I-flag is Ø and an active IRQ signal is generated, then the 65Ø2 will handle the interrupt by performing virtually the same operations that take place when an NMI signal is generated. In fact, the only differences are that the break flag in the processor status register is cleared to Ø before it is placed on the stack and that the address of the interrupt-handling routine is loaded from the IRQ vector at $FFFE/$FFFF (low-order byte first). The address stored at the IRQ vector on the //e is usually $FA4Ø (unless ProDOS is active; see below).

The subroutine beginning at $FA4Ø first stores the contents of the accumulator at location $45 and then determines whether the cause of the interrupt was an IRQ signal or a BRK instruction (BRK is discussed in the next section). If it was caused by an IRQ signal, then control will pass to the address stored at user vector locations $3FE and $3FF. Thus, to properly handle an IRQ interrupt, an interrupt-handling subroutine must be placed in memory and its starting address must be stored at $3FE/$3FF. Alternately, if ProDOS is being used, you can install your interrupt-handling routine by using a special ProDOS interrupt function. See Apple's *ProDOS Technical Reference Manual* for more information on this feature of ProDOS.)

The major shortcoming in the standard IRQ subroutine beginning at $FA4Ø is that it destroys the contents of location $45. This location is used by DOS 3.3 as a temporary storage location and if an interrupt occurs just before $45 is to be read, the results can be disastrous.

If ProDOS is being used, however, then the $45 problem no longer exists. When ProDOS is performing any instructions that may use $45, the IRQ vector (in bank-switched RAM) points to $FF9B, which is the location of a subroutine that first saves the contents of $45 in a safe place in memory and then stores the accumulator in $45 as usual. It then modifies the stack so that when the user-installed interrupt-handling subroutine ends, control will return to another ProDOS subroutine that will restore the original value of $45 before finally returning control to the main program. Lastly, it passes control to location $FA42, which is just past the "STA $45" instruction at the beginning of the standard IRQ subroutine that begins at $FA4Ø.

The BRK Instruction

One of the 65Ø2's instructions allows you to simulate the effect of an IRQ signal in software. This is the one-byte BRK (break) instruction represented by a "ØØ" byte. BRK is primarily used when debugging a program because when a program encounters it, control will be directed to a user-definable subroutine that can display information relating to the state of the program at that particular point. For example, the contents of important memory locations and of the 65Ø2 registers can be displayed. If the state is not as expected, then you can start bug-hunting.

Whenever the 65Ø2 encounters a BRK instruction, the B-flag in the processor status register is set to 1 and then an interrupt sequence much like the one generated by an IRQ signal is started (the main difference is that the address stored on the stack is the address of the BRK instruction plus two). Since the interrupt-handling routine used is the same one as that used for IRQ interrupts, that routine should properly check the status of the B-flag to determine how the interrupt was caused. In fact, this is what is done on the //e. Once the //e determines that the interrupt was caused by a BRK, control is passed to the address stored at the user vector locations $3FØ and $3F1 (low-order byte first). This vector usually contains $FA59, the address of the subroutine that displays the current contents of all the registers, but can be changed to point to any other interrupt-handling routine that you care to use.

THE 65Ø2 MEMORY SPACE ON THE //e

In this section, we are going to take a look at the layout of the memory space that is available to the 65Ø2 as implemented on the //e. This memory space can be thought of as being composed of three parts: RAM, ROM, and input/output memory addresses. The //e's RAM memory map is shown in Figure 2-3. Its ROM and I/O memory map is shown in Figure 2-4.

In the following sections, we will encounter several situations where the same logical memory address is used by more than one actual physical memory location. The //e uses a set of special "soft

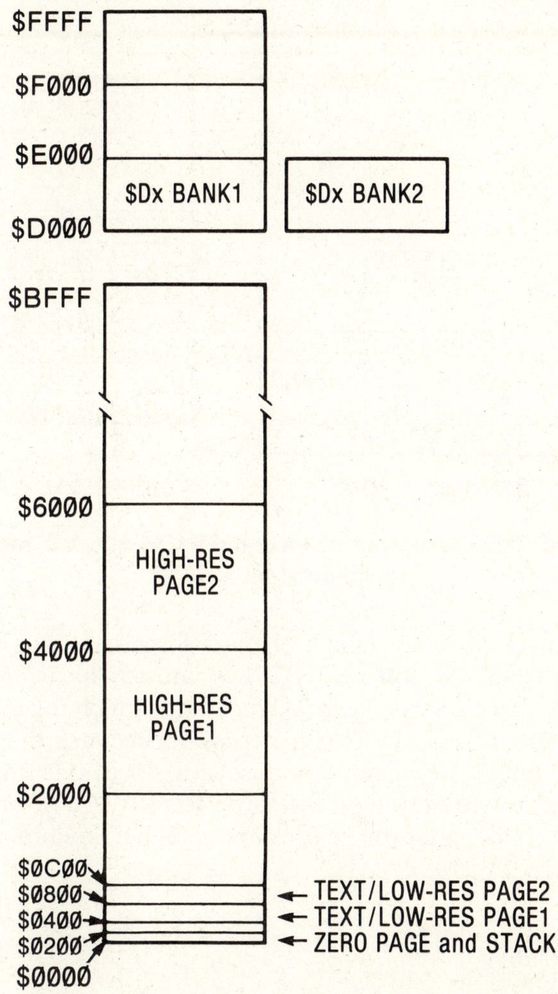

Figure 2-3. Memory map of internal RAM.

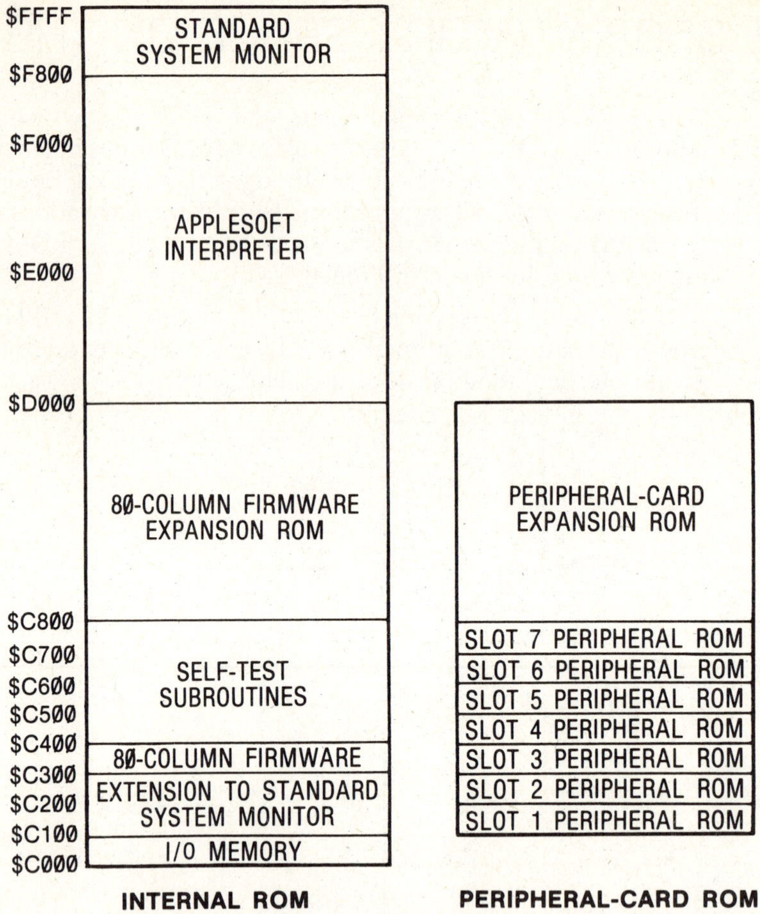

Figure 2-4. Memory map of internal ROM and I/O memory and peripheral-card ROM.

switches" to select which of these locations is to be active at any given time. (A "soft switch" is a memory location that, when accessed from a software program, causes a change in the //e's hardware environment.) This is necessary because the 65Ø2 would become hopelessly confused if several locations sharing the same address were active at the same time. We will be looking at the soft switches that the //e uses to manage its memory space in Chapter 8.

RAM Memory

The area of RAM memory that is most often used on the //e extends from locations $ØØØØ to $BFFF and is contained in eight memory chips built in to the system motherboard. As indicated in Figure 2-3, some regions within this range are dedicated for special uses. Here is a summary of the usage of the internal (or "main") RAM memory locations:

- **$ØØØØ-$ØØFF.** This is the 65Ø2 zero page and it is used extensively by all parts of the //e's operating system, including the system monitor (see Chapter 3), the Applesoft interpreter (see Chapter 4), and the disk operating system (see Chapter 5). Those locations available for use by your own programs are set out in Table 2-5.
- **$Ø1ØØ-$Ø1FF.** This is the 65Ø2 stack area and is also used for temporary data storage by the Applesoft interpreter (see Chapter 4).
- **$Ø2ØØ-$Ø2FF.** This area of memory is normally used as an input buffer whenever character information is entered from the keyboard or from diskette (see Chapter 6).
- **$Ø3ØØ-$Ø3CF.** This area of memory is not used by any of the built-in programs in the //e and so is available for use by your own programs. It is an ideal location for storing small assembly-language programs that are called from Applesoft and most of the examples presented in this book are to be loaded here.
- **$Ø3DØ-$Ø3FF.** This area of memory is used by the disk operating system, Applesoft, and the system monitor for the purpose of storing position-independent vectors to important subroutines that can be located anywhere in memory (such as interrupt-handling subroutines). See Appendix IV for a complete description of how this area is used.
- **$Ø4ØØ-$Ø7FF.** This is page1 of video memory that is used for displaying both the primary text screen and the primary low-resolution graphics screen (see Chapter 7). It is also used for displaying one-half of the text screen when in 80-column mode.
- **$Ø8ØØ-$ØBFF.** This is page2 of video memory that is used for displaying both the secondary text screen and the secondary low-resolution graphics screen (see Chapter 7). Since page2 is rarely used, this area of memory is normally used for program storage; in fact, the default starting position for an Applesoft program is $8Ø1.
- **$ØCØØ-$1FFF.** This area of memory is free for use.
- **$2ØØØ-$3FFF.** This is page1 of video memory that is used for displaying the primary high-resolution graphics screen (see Chapter 7).
- **$4ØØØ-$5FFF.** This is page2 of video memory that is used for displaying the secondary high-resolution graphics screen (see Chapter 7).

- **$6000-$BFFF.** This area of memory is normally free for use. However, the upper part of it (above $9600) will be used if a disk operating system is installed (see Chapter 5).

The motherboard also contains an additional 16K of RAM memory that is located from $D000 to $FFFF (the 4K block from $D000 to $DFFF is duplicated). The ProDOS disk operating system occupies most of this area but if DOS 3.3 is being used, this area is free for use by a program. This 16K area is called bank-switched RAM and will be discussed in detail in Chapter 8.

If you have a standard 80-column text card installed in the auxiliary slot of the //e, another 1K of RAM memory suddenly becomes available to the 6502. This memory extends from $400 to $7FF and is used to support the //e's special 80-column text display mode and double-width low-resolution graphics mode (see Chapter 7).

If an extended 80-column text card is in the auxiliary slot, then a total of 64K of auxiliary RAM memory is added to the //e. This memory occupies the same address spaces as the 64K of built-in RAM memory and so can be thought of as a "twin" memory space. There are slight differences, however, in how some of the areas within this memory are interpreted. For example, the two memory areas corresponding to the page2 video areas in main memory are not reserved for those purposes in auxiliary memory. Furthermore, the two areas corresponding to page1 video areas are not used for video display purposes unless 80-column text mode is active or unless a double-width graphics mode is active. These differences will be discussed in greater detail in Chapter 7.

Input/Output (I/O) Memory

The //e's I/O memory space corresponds to those addresses from $C000 to $C0FF. Although these addresses may be read from or written to in exactly the same way as normal RAM or ROM memory locations, there is no memory stored at these locations. Instead, whenever these locations are accessed, a physical change in the system can be effected (e.g., the graphics display can be turned on, the character set can be changed, or the disk drive motor can be turned on), the status of an I/O device can be read, or data can be transferred to or from the I/O device. This method of handling I/O operations is called memory-mapped I/O.

For example, consider the //e's keyboard. The keyboard has been wired into the system in such a way that it can be be controlled by using the locations $C000 and $C010 (see Chapter 6). To determine whether a key has been entered, address $C000 is examined; if bit 7 at this "location" (the keyboard strobe bit) is 1, then a key has indeed been entered. Address $CØ1Ø is accessed to clear the keyboard strobe bit. Even though an address is referred to in order to read and clear the keyboard, there is no memory chip on the //e that corresponds to this address.

All of the //e's I/O memory locations will be discussed in later chapters. A summary of the meaning of each of these locations is contained in Appendix III.

ROM Memory

As you can see from Figure 2-4, ROM memory on the //e extends from locations $C1ØØ to $FFFF. However, part of this memory space (from $C1ØØ to $CFFF) is duplicated: one area represents built-in internal ROM, and the other represents memory contained on devices connected to the //e's seven peripheral slots. Here is a summary of ROM memory usage:

- **$C1ØØ-$C7FF.** This is the peripheral-card ROM space. One page of ROM is reserved for use at each slot: $C1ØØ . . . $C1FF for slot 1, $C2ØØ . . . $C2FF for slot 2, and so on (see Chapter 11).
- **$C8ØØ-$CFFF.** This is the peripheral-card expansion ROM space. Each peripheral card can contain a block of memory that uses these addresses (see Chapter 11).
- **$C1ØØ-$CFFF.** This is the internal 8Ø-column firmware ROM that contains extensions to the system monitor, subroutines to support the 80-column text display, and self-test subroutines.
- **$DØØØ-$F7FF.** This is the Applesoft ROM space (see Chapter 4).
- **$F8ØØ-$FFFF.** This is the standard system monitor ROM space (see Chapter 3).

Table 2-5. 65Ø2 zero page locations not used by the System Monitor, Applesoft, DOS 3.3, or ProDOS

Available Locations:

```
$06 $07 $08 $09
$19 $1A $1B $1C $1D $1E
$CE $CF
    $D7
$E3
$EB $EC $ED $EE $EF
    $FA $FB $FC $FD $FE $FF
```

The permanent programs contained within these ROM areas are often called "firmware" to distinguish them from "software" that is loaded into RAM memory from a diskette.

Note that the addresses used by the Applesoft and system monitor ROMs ($DØØØ . . . $FFFF) are the same as the ones used by the //e's bank-switched RAM space.

FURTHER READING FOR CHAPTER 2

On 65Ø2 assembly-language programming . . .

MCS65ØØ Microcomputer Family Programming Manual, MOS Technology, Inc., 1976. This book comes straight from the manufacturer.

R. Zaks, *Programming the 65Ø2,* Sybex, 1978.

L.A. Leventhal, *65Ø2 Assembly Language Programming,* Osborne/McGraw Hill, 1979.

M.L. De Jong, *Programming & Interfacing the 65Ø2, With Experiments,* Howard W. Sams & Co., Inc., 198Ø.

D. Inman and K. Inman, *Apple Machine Language,* Reston Publishing Company, Inc., 1981.

R. Wagner, *Assembly Lines: The Book,* Softalk Books, 1982.

R.C. Haskell, *Apple II 65Ø2 Assembly Language Tutor,* Prentice-Hall Inc., 1983.

On enhancements to the 65Ø2 microprocessor . . .

S. Hendrix, "The CMOS 65Ø2," *Byte,* December 1983, pp. 443-452. This article reviews some of the limitations of the 65Ø2 and introduces the new 65CØ2 microprocessor.

On machine cycle time . . .

S. Wozniak, "Impossible Dream: Computing e to 116,ØØØ Places With a Personal Computer," *Byte,* June 1981, pp. 392-4Ø7. This article has interesting comments on the 65Ø2's effective machine cycle time on the Apple II.

On interrupts . . .

G.M. White, "Using Interrupts on the Apple II System," *Byte,* May 1981, pp. 28Ø-294. A good analysis of how interrupts are handled on the Apple II (in software and hardware).

D. Fischer and M.P. Caffrey, "Go On and Interrupt Your Apple," *Softalk,* March 1982, p. 47

D. Fischer and M.P. Caffrey, "Go On and Interrupt Your Apple," *Softalk,* April 1982, p. 65

R.L. Emerson, "Interrupts and Apples," *Call -A.P.P.L.E.*, February 1983, p. 35.

On memory usage by the 65Ø2/Apple II . . .

W.F. Luebbert, *What's Where in the Apple*, Micro Ink, Inc., 1982. This book contains a comprehensive memory map for the Apple II.

Assemblers (software) . . .

The following assemblers operate in DOS 3.3:

G. Bredon, *BIG MAC Macro Assembler*, A.P.P.L.E., 1981.

Apple 65Ø2 Assembler/Editor, Apple Computer, Inc., 198Ø.

B. Sander-Cederlof, *S-C Macro Assembler*, S-C Software Corporation, 1983.

R. Hyde, *LISA*, Sierra On-Line Inc., 1981.

G. Bredon, *Merlin*, Roger Wagner Publishing, Inc., 1982.

The following assemblers operate in ProDOS:

G. Bredon, *Merlin Pro*, Roger Wagner Publishing, Inc., 1984.

ProDOS Assembler Tools, Apple Computer, Inc., 1983.

3

The System Monitor

The system monitor is a machine-language program that resides in the //e's ROM area and whose "cold-start" entry point to a special command interpreter is located at $FF59. It is called a "monitor" because it supports several commands that allow you to quickly and easily view and modify the contents of memory locations, programs loaded into memory, or 65Ø2 registers. In addition, commands are available that can be used to run programs, to assist in the debugging of programs, and to perform general housekeeping functions (such as data movement or data comparison).

The subroutines that make up the system monitor take up two large parts of the //e's internal ROM area. The first part resides from $F8ØØ to $FFFF and the second part from $C1ØØ to $CFFF. Generally speaking, the first part is comparable to the standard system monitor ROM that resided at the same locations in the earlier Apple II and Apple II Plus computers; the code is not identical, but virtually all of the starting addresses for its commonly used subroutines are the same as on older models. The internal ROM area from $C1ØØ to $CFFF is found on the //e only and provides the additional space needed for the longer subroutines required to support the //e's 8Ø-column video display mode and also to hold its special self-test subroutines (see Chapter 5). The areas used to support these two new functions are as follows:

`$C100-$C3FF`)—Contains extensions to standard system
`$C800-$CFFF`) monitor subroutines and special subroutines that are used when an 8Ø-column text card has been installed.

`$C400-$C4FF`—Self-test subroutines

The subroutines contained within the system monitor perform most of the fundamental input/output (I/O) tasks needed to support programs running on the //e. Such tasks include reading a character from the keyboard, displaying a character on the video display, displaying graphics on the video display, and reading the game paddle input. Other subroutines required to support the monitor commands themselves are also found here, of course. In addition, there are numerous utility subroutines used by the code performing these tasks and commands. In the last section of this chapter, we will identify some of the more useful subroutines that can be accessed from Applesoft by using the CALL command or from assembly language by using the JSR (jump-to-subroutine) or JMP (jump) instructions.

The usefulness of the system monitor is greatly enhanced by the fact that, being in ROM, its subroutines and command interpreter are always easily accessible. There are three main entry points to the system monitor command interpreter—OLDRST ($FF59), MON ($FF65), and MONZ ($FF69)—and control can be passed to them from Applesoft direct mode by entering the commands "CALL −167", "CALL −155", and "CALL −151", respectively. (Note that Applesoft considers a "negative" decimal address to be equivalent to the standard positive address minus 65536; for example, $FF69 can be represented as 65385 or 65385 − 65536 = −151.) After this has been done, the system monitor prompt symbol (the asterisk—"*") will appear and you can begin to enter any of the commands that the system monitor supports (or, if DOS is active, any valid DOS commands).

The //e reacts slightly differently to each of the above three CALLs to its standard entry points. The cold-start entry point, OLDRST (−167), will initialize "normal" video mode (white characters on a black background), select the full-screen text video mode, and then enable the standard keyboard input and video screen output subroutines. It also deactivates the //e's disk operating system (DOS) so that it must be reactivated before returning to Applesoft (see the discussion below of the BASIC and CONTINUE BASIC commands). After this has been done, control passes to the primary warm-start entry point, MON (−155), where the 65Ø2's decimal mode flag is cleared (to force binary arithmetic) and the speaker is beeped. Control then passes to the secondary warm-start entry point, MONZ (−151), which takes care of setting up the "*" prompt symbol and interpreting commands that are entered from the keyboard. MONZ is the entry point that is most commonly used to enter the system monitor command interpreter.

THE SYSTEM MONITOR COMMANDS

The commands that the system monitor supports are summarized in Table 3-1. Before we take a detailed look at these commands, let's review the general command entry rules that must be followed.

First of all, the system monitor "thinks" in hexadecimal. This means that it displays all addresses or data in a standard hexadecimal format and that all information must be provided to it in this format as well. Decimal numbers cannot be used.

Addresses (from $ØØØØ. . .$FFFF) must normally be specified as four hexadecimal digits but leading zeros may be omitted if you wish. If an address is entered that is longer than four digits, only the last four digits specified are used. Similarly, byte values (from $ØØ. . .$FF) must normally be specified as two hexadecimal digits but, again, a leading zero may be omitted. If more than two digits are specified for a byte value, only the last two are used.

The DISPLAY Command : Displaying the Contents of Memory

After you have entered the system monitor, you can quickly read and display what is stored in any particular memory location by simply entering the hexadecimal address of the location and pressing <RETURN>. For example, to display the number that has been stored at $FDØC, you would enter

```
FD0C
```

(followed by <RETURN>, of course) and the system monitor will respond with

```
FD0C- A4
```

where A4 is the hexadecimal value of the byte stored at $FDØC. You can also just press <RETURN> by itself to display the contents of the locations immediately after the last one acted on, up to the edge of the next 8-byte boundary (i.e., locations ending in "7" or "F").

The contents of an entire range of memory can be displayed at once by typing in the first address, a period ("."), and then the last address. For example, to examine the 17 bytes of the system monitor ROM area from $F8Ø1 to $F811, you would enter

```
F801.F811
```

and you would see the following values displayed (this is called a "hex dump"):

```
F801- 08 20 47 F8 28 A9 0F
F808- 90 02 69 E0 85 2E B1 26
F810- 45 30
```

After the first line, where only those bytes up to the edge of the next 8-byte boundary are displayed, eight bytes will be displayed per line until the very last line where the last few remaining bytes are displayed. The two-digit values after the dash in each line represent the bytes stored at the address displayed immediately before the dash and in succeeding memory locations.

Table 3-1. Summary of system monitor commands.

Command Name	*Syntax*	*Description*
DISPLAY	addr1.addr2	Displays the contents of memory from "addr1" to "addr2".
STORE	addr1:b1 b2 . . .	Stores the values of bytes "b1", "b2", . . . into memory locations beginning at "addr1".
MOVE	addr3<addr1.addr2M	Moves the block of memory from "addr1" to "addr2" to the block beginning at "addr3".
VERIFY	addr3<addr1.addr2V	Compares the block of memory from "addr1" to "addr2" to the block beginning at "addr3" and displays any differences.
EXAMINE	<CTRL-E>	Displays the current values stored in the 6502 registers.
GO	addr1G	Runs the program beginning at "addr1".
LIST	addr1L	Disassembles 20 lines of a machine language program beginning at "addr1".
NORMAL	N	Set normal video.
INVERSE	I	Set inverse video.
ADD	b1 + b2	Adds the bytes "b1" and "b2" and displays the result.
SUBTRACT	b1 − b2	Subtracts byte "b2" from byte "b1" and displays the result.
BASIC	<CTRL-B>	Causes the system to enter Applesoft (cold).
CONTINUE BASIC	<CTRL-C>	Causes the system to enter Applesoft (warm).

Table 3-1. Summary of system monitor commands (continued).

Command Name	*Syntax*	*Description*
USER	<CTRL-Y>	Causes the system to jump to location $3F8.
READ	addr1.addr2R	Reads data from cassette tape into memory from "addr1" to "addr2".
WRITE	addr1.addr2W	Writes data from "addr1" to "addr2" to cassette tape.
KEYBOARD	slot <CTRL-K>	Causes the device in "slot" to become source of input.
PRINTER	slot <CTRL-P>	Causes the device in "slot" to become the current output device.

"b1", "b2" represent byte values (in hexadecimal)

"addr1", "addr2", "addr3" represent addresses of memory locations (in hexadecimal)

"slot" represents a peripheral expansion slot number (1 . . . 7)

The STORE Command : Changing the Contents of Memory

It is often handy to be able to quickly enter data into memory locations. You may want to do this in order to provide data to a program, or even to enter the program itself. The system monitor makes this easy by providing you with a convenient command to do this.

To change the contents of memory, you must first type in the address of the first location to be changed, followed by the STORE command (a colon), and then the values of the bytes to be stored in that location and succeeding locations, separated by spaces. For example, to place the values $3E, $22, $24, $ØØ, and $29 into addresses $3ØØ through $3Ø4, you would enter the command

```
300:3E 22 24 0 29
```

(The number of bytes that can be stored after the colon is limited by the fact that only 255 characters can be entered on one line. This allows about 83 data bytes to be specified.)

To continue entering values at this point, you can simply type a colon followed by more data bytes separated by spaces. The address at which the first byte will be stored will automatically be assumed to be the one after the last one that was accessed. Thus, if you entered the command

```
:44 33
```

immediately after entering the above command, address $305 would contain $44 and address $3Ø6 would contain $33.

All of the machine language programs that will be presented in this book can be entered using this technique. To understand how to do this, first refer to Table 3-2, which sets out the assembler source listing of a sample program after the assembly process has been completed. This program doesn't do anything really useful, it just prints out all digits from Ø to 9 on the video screen and then stops. What we are really interested in is seeing how to interpret this listing and how it can be used to allow you to enter the program into memory.

First remember that the assembler-listing format used in this book is that used by the BIG MAC assembler only and that if you are using any other assembler the format may be different. Fortunately, however, formats from one assembler to another are generally quite similar.

The assembler-listing format is made up of six general fields. The first field is the address and data field and can be found at the far left of the listing. Each line in this field contains an address used by the program followed by the data byte stored at that address and, in certain cases depending on the type of instruction, at the following one or two addresses as well. This information is all you need to be able to enter the program from the monitor because it is in exactly the same format used by the STORE command. To enter the program, all you must do is enter the following STORE commands:

```
300:A2 0
302:8A
303:9 B0
305:20 ED FD
308:E8
309:E0 A
30B:D0 F5
30D:60
```

Since the program is so short, you could also enter the whole program using just one long STORE command:

```
300:A2 0 8A 9 B0 20 ED FD E8 E0 A D0 F5 60
```

The rest of the fields in the listing simply relate to the source

Table 3-2. An example of a 65Ø2 assembly-language program.

```
Page #01

: A S M
                 1    ******************
                 2    * SAMPLE PROGRAM *
                 3    ******************
                 4
                 5    COUT     EQU $FDED      ;Character output subroutine
                 6
                 7             ORG $300
                 8
0300: A2 00      9             LDX #0
0302: 8A        10    DIGITOUT TXA            ;Put digit in A
0303: 09 B0     11             ORA #$B0       ;Convert to ASCII digit
0305: 20 ED FD  12             JSR COUT
0308: E8        13             INX            ;Go to next digit
0309: E0 0A     14             CPX #10        ;Done?
030B: D0 F5     15             BNE DIGITOUT   ;No, so loop
030D: 60        16             RTS
                17
```

Address and data field	Line number field	Label field	Instruction field	Operand field	Comment field

code that gave rise to the machine language bytes that make up the program. These are, in order, the line number field, the label field, the instruction field, the operand field, and the comment field.

A faster way to enter a machine language program is, of course, to load it directly from diskette using the DOS 3.3 or ProDOS BLOAD command. This is done by entering the command

```
BLOAD FILENAME,Aaddr
```

where "FILENAME" represents the name of the binary file to be loaded and "addr" represents the decimal starting address at which it is to be loaded, or, if the address is preceded by "$", the hexadecimal starting address. The ",Aaddr" suffix is optional; if the suffix is omitted, the program will be loaded at the position it was in when it was originally saved to diskette using the BSAVE command.

The MOVE Command : Copying the Contents of Memory

It is sometimes necessary to copy the contents of one block of memory to another part of memory. Two common situations where such a move would be performed are when an assembly-language program is being relocated or when a data block is being duplicated because it may be overwritten by subsequent operations and you don't want to lose it.

You could perform the move by examining the contents of all the memory locations in question and then entering these values at the new locations using the DISPLAY and STORE commands, but there is an easier way: you can use the MOVE command. The syntax of this command is as follows:

```
{destination}<{sourceS}.{sourceE}M
```

where {destination} represents the address to which the block of memory is to be moved (the destination address), {sourceS} represents the starting address of the block to be moved (the source starting address), and {sourceE} represents the ending address of the block to be moved (the source ending address). For example, to move the program that you just entered in the previous section, which resides from $3ØØ through $3ØD, to locations $1ØØØ through $1ØØD, you would enter the command

```
1000<300.30DM
```

To see that the move has, in fact, been performed, enter the following two commands:

```
300.30D
1000.100D
```

and compare the two hex dumps. They will be identical apart from the address indicators.

When moving a block of memory, you must ensure that the destination address is not within the range of addresses defined by the source block. If it is, then the block will not be properly moved because the area of the source block from the destination location to the end of the block will be overwritten before it is actually moved. This occurs because the byte stored at the lowest-addressed location in the source block is moved first, followed by the rest of the bytes in increasing order of address until the end of the block is reached. For example, if the move command

```
301<300.30DM
```

is entered, the block of memory from $3Ø1 to $3ØE will *not* contain an image of $3ØØ to $3ØD before the move but rather will be filled with the value of the byte stored at $3ØØ. You can see why by visualizing the steps that are followed to perform the move: first, the byte at $3ØØ is moved into $3Ø1, then the byte at $3Ø1 (which has just been overwritten) is moved into $3Ø2, and so on. This type of move is handy for quickly storing the same values at locations throughout an area of memory, but not much else.

One important note on using the MOVE command to relocate machine language programs: many programs will not operate properly at their new locations unless they are modified first. Any program that uses JMP (jump) or JSR (jump-to-subroutine) instructions to transfer control to areas that are within the block being moved, or that read from or write to addresses within that block, fall within this "unrelocatable" category. This problem arises because such instructions refer to *absolute* memory locations, locations that will not be meaningful after the program has been moved. The easiest way to make a program operate at a new location is to reassemble it at the new location and then enter the new data bytes that the assembler generates. This can be done by changing the operand of the ORG (for "origin") statement in the assembler source listing (see line 7 of the sample program in Table 3-2) to reflect the new starting address of the program. You could also patch the program manually to fix up all such absolute references in the program by replacing them with the new absolute addresses (low-order byte first), but this is time consuming and prone to error.

The VERIFY Command : Comparing Ranges of Memory

Another useful chore that can be performed by the system monitor is the comparison of the contents of two blocks of memory. Comparisons are commonly made for the purposes of determining the locations at which two similar programs (usually related revisions) differ from one another.

You could perform the comparison manually by repeatedly using the DISPLAY command but this would be tedious at best, especially for long data blocks. The process can be automated, however, by using the VERIFY command. The syntax for this command is as follows:

```
{block2}<{blockS}.{blockE}V
```

where {block2} represents the starting address of the block of memory to which comparisons will be made, {blockS} represents the starting location of the main block, and {blockE} represents the ending location of the main block. When the command begins to execute, each byte in the main block will be compared with its corresponding byte in the other block. If there are any differences, then they will be printed out in the following format:

```
{address}-34 (EA)
```

where {address} is the address of the byte in the main block that is different, the first (unbracketed) data byte represents the value of that byte in the main block and the second number represents the value of that byte in the other block.

The EXAMINE Command : Examining the 65Ø2's Registers

The system monitor reserves several locations in zero page for temporary storage of the 65Ø2's internal registers, A, X, Y, P, and S. All of these registers (except for the stack pointer, S) are loaded with the values stored at these locations whenever the monitor's GO command is entered (see below). This allows you to properly initialize the 65Ø2 registers before executing any assembly-language program.

The saved contents of the 65Ø2's internal registers can be examined at any time by using the EXAMINE command by entering the following control character:

```
<CTRL-E>
```

(Recall that this notation means "press the CONTROL key and, while it is being held down, press the E key.") When the EXAMINE command is entered, the currently saved values of each of the five 65Ø2 registers will be displayed in the following format:

```
A=02 X=CC Y=D8 P=00 S=B7
```

In this list, A represents the accumulator, X and Y represent the X and Y index registers, P represents the processor status register, and S represents the stack pointer. The two-digit hexadecimal number after each "equal" sign indicates the current value of the corresponding register.

Immediately after the <CTRL-E> command has been entered and the contents of the registers have been displayed, you can set any of the register locations to any value that you want by entering a colon followed by the new values for the contents of the registers, separated by spaces. The new values must be entered in the order in which the registers are displayed. If you want to change some, but not all, of the registers, then you will have to enter the current values for those of the other registers that are displayed before the last one that you wish to change.

For example, if you want to set the X register to $33 and leave the other registers unchanged, you would enter the command

```
:02 33
```

where Ø2 represents the current value of the accumulator.

The <CTRL-E> command is primarily used as a debugging tool when developing an assembly-language program. Program subroutines that require certain registers to be initialized in certain ways before they will perform properly can easily be tested by setting up the registers after entering <CTRL-E> and then executing the subroutine.

The GO Command : Running a Program

You can run any machine-language program that is contained in memory by using the monitor's GO command. To do this, you must type in the starting address of the program followed by "G" and then press <RETURN>. Before control is passed to the program, the 65Ø2's A, X, Y, and P registers are loaded with the values last set by the EXAMINE command (see above). When the program stops running, you will usually return to the system monitor command interpreter and see the "*" prompt symbol once again.

For example, if you want to run a program that starts at location

$3ØØ, then you would enter the command

```
300G
```

When the program stops running, the monitor's prompt symbol will reappear.

The LIST Command : Disassembling Assembly-Language Programs

The LIST command can be used to translate bytes in any area of memory into the assembly-language mnemonics they represent and to display the listing on the screen. This command essentially reverses the process performed by an assembler and so the function it performs is called "disassembly."

A disassembled listing of memory is much more comprehensible and informative to a programmer than a simple hex dump that only displays raw numbers. It is especially useful as an aid in debugging assembly-language programs that have been loaded into memory. The syntax associated with the LIST command is as follows:

```
{address}L
```

where {address} represents the address at which you want to begin the listing. A total of twenty disassembled lines will be displayed for each "L" specified after the address.

Let's examine an area of the //e's system monitor ROM to observe the format in which the LIST command generates its output. As we will see later, the basic character input routine used by the monitor begins at location $FDØC and is called RDKEY. To disassemble the RDKEY subroutine, enter the command

```
FDOCL
```

and you will see the following 2Ø-line display:

```
*FDOCL

FD0C-     A4 24          LDY    $24
FD0E-     B1 28          LDA    ($28),Y
FD10-     48             PHA
FD11-     29 3F          AND    #$3F
FD13-     09 40          ORA    #$40
FD15-     91 28          STA    ($28),Y
FD17-     68             PLA
FD18-     6C 38 00       JMP    ($0038)
FD1B-     A0 06          LDY    #$06
FD1D-     4C B4 FB       JMP    $FBB4
```

he NORMAL and INVERSE Commands : hanging Video Display Modes

Monitor operations that affect the video display can be performed either in normal video (white characters on a black background) or in inverse video (black characters on a white background). To select the inverse video format, enter the command

```
I <RETURN>
```

To select the normal video format, enter the command

```
N <RETURN>
```

You will probably not have to use these commands very often.

e ADD and SUBTRACT Commands : Simple ithmetic

You can perform simple one-byte hexadecimal arithmetic while in the system monitor by taking advantage of its ADD and SUBTRACT commands. To add two numbers together, you would enter the command

```
{number1}+{number2}
```

where {number1} and {number2} represent the two one-byte hexadecimal numbers to be added. The result of the addition will be shown on the next video display line.

The subtraction command is similar. To subtract one number, say {number2}, from another, say {number1}, you would enter the command

```
{number1}-{number2}
```

and the result will be calculated and displayed.

The result that either the ADD or SUBTRACT command displays is a one-byte number only. This means that any overflow or underflow in the arithmetic calculation is ignored.

e BASIC and CONTINUE BASIC Commands : tering Applesoft

The system monitor supports two commands that can be used to transfer control from the monitor to Applesoft direct mode (as indicated by the "]" prompt symbol). These are the <CTRL-B> and <CTRL-C> commands. There are also subroutines that can

```
FD20-      EA                NOP
FD21-      20  0C  FD        JSR     $FI
FD24-      A0  07            LDY     #$(
FD26-      4C  B4  FB        JMP     $FI
FD29-      8D  06  C0        STA     $C(
FD2C-      28                PLP
FD2D-      60                RTS
FD2E-      60                RTS
FD2F-      20  21  FD        JSR     $F
FD32-      20  A5  FB        JSR     $F
```

Each line in this listing represents a startir chine language bytes representing the 65Ø2 ins its operand, the three-letter mnemonic for the formatted operand. Note that operands that h resent an address and that those that have a " immediate hexadecimal data. In addition, th branch instruction (BEQ, BNE, BPL, and so address of the "branched-to" location rather dress of that location. The 65Ø2 uses relative it is the absolute address that is usually more it allows a programmer to more easily follow gram.

Note that you can continue to disassembl beginning at the address immediately after t byte by entering the "L" command without "L"'s can also be entered to disassemble m at once; for example, "LLLL" allows you t consecutive lines.

When you are disassembling an area of m times see a "???" indicator in the opcode fiel 65Ø2 mnemonic. The system monitor's dis uses this triad of question marks whenever the contents of memory into a valid 65Ø2 i happen if you are attempting to disassemb that contains program data or ASCII text ra or if you begin disassembling in the "mid (remember that 65Ø2 instructions can be u If you suspect that you have started in the m try disassembling from a location that is on from the original starting location.

In many cases, a data area will erroneou series of valid instructions by the disasse zeroed out data area would appear as a seri This is because the machine language by data areas are usually obvious, however, they appear to define is clearly meaningle be called to enter Applesoft that begin at $ØØØØ (with or without DOS) and $Ø3DØ (only when DOS is being used).

The BASIC command, <CTRL-B>, is used to re-enter Applesoft in such a way as to cause it to be reinitialized. This is called a "cold start" and will cause any Applesoft program which may be residing in memory to be destroyed.

The CONTINUE BASIC command, <CTRL-C>, is used to re-enter Applesoft in such a way that the existing Applesoft program and the values of its variables are not affected at all. This is called a "warm start." An alternate way to warm-start Applesoft is to call a subroutine that begins at $ØØØØ by entering the command "ØG".

The effect on the disk operating system, be it DOS 3.3 or ProDOS, must also be considered when moving to Applesoft from the monitor. If you are using DOS 3.3 and the monitor was entered with either a CALL −151 or CALL −155 command (the warm-start entry points), then DOS 3.3 will still be active upon the return to Applesoft using <CTRL-B> or <CTRL-C>. If you are using ProDOS, the <CTRL-C> command works fine, but the <CTRL-B> command will cause a NO BUFFERS AVAILABLE error message to be displayed whenever a ProDOS I/O command is attempted. This renders ProDOS useless and so you should never use <CTRL-B> to return to ProDOS.

If the monitor was entered via its cold-start entry point with a CALL −167 command, both DOS 3.3 and ProDOS will be deactivated after a <CTRL-B> and <CTRL-C> command is entered to cause a return to Applesoft. In this situation, DOS 3.3 can be reactivated by entering a CALL 1ØØ2 command and the program and its variables will not be affected. Similarly, ProDOS can be reactivated by entering a CALL 976 command, but this causes the values of any active program variables to be cleared. Note, however, that even after the CALL 976 is entered, ProDOS will still be rendered unusable if it was entered with a <CTRL-B> command for the reasons given in the previous paragraph.

Applesoft can always be entered with the DOS active by using a "3DØG" command ($3DØ is the address of a subroutine that performs a warm-start of DOS 3.3 or ProDOS), but this method is not recommended because of zero page memory conflicts between DOS 3.3 or ProDOS and the system monitor. A further problem arises if ProDOS is being used: a 3DØG re-entry will clear any active program variables.

In summary, to ensure that you never deactivate DOS (either DOS 3.3 or ProDOS) or clear the values of any active Applesoft program variables, you should always enter the monitor at one of its two warm-start entry points (−151 or −155) and always return to BASIC using the <CTRL-C> command.

The USER Command : User-Defined Commands

The system monitor is flexible enough to allow you to define the actions to be taken whenever its special USER command, <CTRL-Y>, is entered. The <CTRL-Y> command causes the monitor to perform an unconditional jump to location $3F8. By placing a 65Ø2 JMP instruction there (which behaves like an Applesoft GOTO), followed by the two-byte address (low byte first) of the start of the subroutine that you want to execute, you can easily make the <CTRL-Y> command execute any program you wish.

Let's take a look at a simple example of how to take advantage of the USER command. The first thing you have to decide is what you want to happen when <CTRL-Y> is pressed—that's easy. Then you must write the program to perform what it is you want to do—not so easy. We can, however, make use of subroutines that already exist in the //e's ROM areas to perform many useful chores. For example, there is a subroutine beginning at $FC58 that can be called to clear the video screen and a subroutine beginning at $FDØC to read a key from the keyboard. To set things up so that when the USER command is entered, the system pauses until a key is pressed and then clears the screen, a "JMP $Ø3ØØ" instruction must be set up at $3F8 and then "JSR $FDØC" and "JMP $FC58" instructions must be stored beginning at $3ØØ. This can be done by using two STORE commands as follows:

```
3F8:4C 00 03
```

("4C" is the opcode for the JMP instruction and "ØØ Ø3" is the address of the user-defined subroutine—low-order byte first) and

```
300:20 0C FD 4C 58 FC
```

where "2Ø ØC FD" are the data bytes for "JSR $FDØC" ($2Ø is the opcode for the JSR instruction) and "4C 58 FC" are the data bytes for "JMP $FC58". Now when you enter <CTRL-Y> the //e will wait until you press a key and then the screen will be cleared!

Note that you cannot simply place the entire subroutine at $3F8, because only locations $3F8 to $3FA are reserved for use by the USER command. Locations after that are reserved for other purposes and must not be overwritten.

Parameters can be passed to the USER command by storing them in memory just before the monitor executes the USER command. This can be done by using the STORE command. If the parameters to be passed represent addresses, there is a much more convenient way to pass up to three of them. For example, if the USER command is entered as follows:

```
addr1<addr2.addr3<CTRL-Y>
```

then "addr1" will be stored at monitor locations A4L ($42) and A4H ($43), "addr2" will be stored at A1L ($3C) and A1H ($3D), and "addr3" will be stored at A2L ($3E) and A2H ($3F). Each of these addresses is stored with its lower two digits in the first of the two memory locations specified for each parameter. Two addresses can be passed (in A1L/A1H and A2L/A2H) by removing the "addr1<" part in the above command line and one address can be passed (in A1L/A1H) by removing the "addr1<addr2." part.

The READ and WRITE Commands : Cassette Tape I/O Commands

The system monitor also supports two commands that can be used to save a block of data on cassette tape or to read a block of data from cassette tape.

The WRITE command is used to to save a block of bytes to tape and is used by entering the following command:

```
{address1}.{address2}W
```

where {address1} represents the starting address of the block and {address2} represents the ending address of the block. Just before you press <RETURN> to enter this command, the tape recorder must be properly connected to the //e and placed in record mode.

The READ command is used to retrieve a block of bytes from tape and is used by entering the following command:

```
{address1}.{address2}R
```

where {address1} and {address2} represent the starting and ending addresses of the block of data to be read in. Of course, just after you press <RETURN> you must begin playing the tape by pressing the PLAY button on the recorder.

You should note that if the block size specified in the READ command is not the same size as the block you are attempting to read from the tape, then an error message will be displayed. To avoid this type of error, you should always write down the starting and ending locations of a block of memory whenever it is saved to tape.

The KEYBOARD and PRINTER Commands : Redirecting Input and Output

The system monitor provides two simple commands that allow you to easily redirect the source of character input and output to a program that resides on any one of the //e's seven expansion slots. These are the KEYBOARD, <CTRL-K>, and PRINTER, <CTRL-P>, commands, respectively. They perform exactly the same functions as Applesoft's IN# and PR# commands.

The syntax associated with both of these commands is similar:

```
{slot number}<CTRL-K>
```

for the KEYBOARD command and

```
{slot number}<CTRL-P>
```

for the PRINTER command, where {slot number} is a digit from 1 to 7 representing the peripheral expansion slot to which you wish to pass control. You can also specify a slot number of Ø; if you do this when entering the KEYBOARD command, the keyboard will become the source of character information. If you do this when entering the PRINTER command, the video screen will become the current output device.

The KEYBOARD command is usually used to "connect" alternate input devices such as an external keyboard or a modem to the //e by vectoring all requests for input to them. The PRINTER command is usually used to activate a printer so that you can obtain a hardcopy printout of your activities while in the monitor. To turn on a printer that is connected to an interface card in slot 1, you would enter the command

```
1<CTRL-P>
```

After this is done, all outputted characters will be sent to the printer instead of the video screen.

Another common use for the PRINTER command is to "boot" the disk drive. If your disk drive is connected to a disk interface card in slot 6, then the command to be entered is

```
6<CTRL-P>
```

Note that whenever the KEYBOARD or PRINTER command is entered, the monitor jumps to location $CsØØ (where "s" is the slot number specified), which is the first address of a program located in a ROM area dedicated to the particular slot in question (see Chapter 11). Thus, it is the program in the ROM that dictates exactly how the I/O is to be redirected and it is conceivable that I/O may not be redirected at all.

I/O is redirected on the //e by changing the addresses stored in two vectors in zero page, the input link and the output link. The use of these links will be discussed in detail in Chapters 6 and 7.

Note that because of the way DOS 3.3 and ProDOS operate, the KEYBOARD and PRINTER commands may not work properly in a DOS environment. This is because DOS is forever storing the addresses of its input and output subroutines in the I/O links; as soon as this is done, the new input or output device is disconnected. Methods of avoiding these problems will also be discussed in Chapters 6 and 7.

MULTIPLE COMMANDS ON ONE LINE

All of the examples that we have given so far have contained only one monitor command per line. The monitor is not fussy about this, however, and you can actually put as many commands on one line as that line can hold (a line must be less than 256 characters long).

There are a few syntactical rules to follow, however. First of all, each command on the line must be separated from the next one by a space unless both adjacent commands are one of the letter commands (L, G, W, R, M, V, I, N), in which case they can be jammed together.

Second, any command that immediately follows the data bytes after the STORE command must be a letter command without a preceding address. A convenient command to use for this purpose is the NORMAL command ("N") since it is really a "do-nothing" letter command.

Let's look at a few examples of multiple command entry to see how it works.

1. **3ØØLLL** will disassemble 6Ø lines of a program at once.
2. **3ØØ:4C 3A FF N 3ØØG** will enter a short program beginning at $3ØØ to beep the speaker and then execute it (note the "N" after the data bytes of the STORE command).
3. **3ØØ.32Ø 8ØØ.83Ø** will display two separate blocks of memory, one after the other.
4. **3F8:4C ØØ Ø3 N 3ØØ:4C 58 FC N <CTRL-Y>** will set up the USER command jump address, enter the program to be

jumped to, and then execute the USER command (which causes the screen to clear).

SYSTEM MONITOR SUBROUTINES

As we have already seen, the system monitor is made up of several useful subroutines. Most of these subroutines can easily be accessed from Applesoft or assembly-language programs.

Direct access from Applesoft is achieved by using the Applesoft CALL command. Note, however, that only those monitor subroutines that require no initialization of the 65Ø2 registers can be CALLed in this way because there are no Applesoft commands available to you to set up these registers directly.

One way to access subroutines that require register initialization would be to CALL a RAM-based program that would set up these registers explicitly and then call the requested subroutine. An alternate method makes use of the monitor's GO command and the fact that GO initializes the 65Ø2's registers to the values stored in zero page by the EXAMINE command before control is passed to the subroutine whose address is stored at $3A and $3B (low-order byte first). The values of the registers A, X, Y, and P are stored at locations $45, $46, $47, and $48, respectively. To execute the subroutine, you must first use the Applesoft POKE command to store the address of the subroutine to be executed at $3A/$3B and to store the appropriate register values at locations $45-$48. The final step is to execute the GO command by entering it at the point where it sets up the registers before passing control to the address at $3A/$3B. This is location $FEB9 (652Ø9).

For example, you can set up a simple decimal-to-hexadecimal conversion program from Applesoft by calling a monitor subroutine called PRINTYX ($F94Ø). This subroutine prints out the Y and X registers as four hexadecimal digits (the two most-significant digits are held in Y). To get the converter to work, all you have to do is take your decimal number, divide it by 256, and put the quotient in Y (this represents the decimal value of the two high-order digits) and the remainder in X (this represents the decimal value of the two low-order digits). Here is an example of such a program:

```
100 DEF FN MD(Z) = Z - 256 * INT(Z / 256)
110 INPUT "ENTER A NUMBER: ";N
120 ADDR = 63808 : REM ADDRESS OF "PRINTYX" ($F940)
130 POKE 70,FN MD(N):REM SET UP "X"
140 POKE 71,INT (N/256):REM SET UP "Y"
```

```
150 POKE 58,FN MD(ADDR) : REM SET UP ADDR LOW
160 POKE 59,INT (ADDR/256) : REM SET UP ADDR HIGH
170 CALL 65209 : REM CALL "GO" AT $FEB9
```

Line 100 in this program defines a "modulo 256" function that can be used to calculate the decimal value of the lower two digits of a hexadecimal number (0 . . . 255).

These complications do not really arise when calling monitor subroutines from an assembly-language program because the 6502 has explicit commands for initializing registers (LDA, LDX, LDY, and so on). Once the registers have been properly set up, you can execute the subroutine by using a JSR instruction (like an Applesoft GOSUB) or a JMP instruction (like an Applesoft GOTO).

Some of the more useful subroutines available in the system monitor are set out in Table 3-3. These subroutines are presented in increasing order of address and the symbolic name for each address (as published by Apple in "Reference Manual Addendum: Monitor ROM Listings") is shown immediately after the address.

Table 3-3 by no means represents a complete list of the monitor's subroutines. To examine all the subroutines for yourself, you should consult Apple's published source listing of the monitor ROM in "Reference Manual Addendum: Monitor ROM Listings."

Table 3-3. Apple //e system monitor subroutines.

Address Hex	*Address* (Dec)	*Symbolic Name*	*Description*
$F940	(63808)	PRINTYX	Prints out the number held in X (low) and Y (high) as four hexadecimal digits.
$FB1E	(64286)	PREAD	Reads the current value of the game paddle input. On entry, X=game paddle number (0 . . . 3). On exit, Y=game paddle value (0 . . . 255) and A is destroyed.
$FBC1	(64449)	BASCALC	Calculates the address of the first location used by the current video line. On entry, A=video line number (0 . . . 23). On exit, the address is stored in BASL ($28) and BASH ($29), low byte first, and A is destroyed.
$FC22	(64546)	VTAB	Moves the cursor to the video display line indicated by CV ($25).

Table 3-3. Apple //e system monitor subroutines (continued).

Address *Hex*	*(Dec)*	*Symbolic Name*	*Description*
			On entry, CV must contain the line number required (Ø . . . 23). On exit, the base address for the line is set up in BASL ($28) and BASH ($29) and A is destroyed.
$FC42	(64578)	CLREOP	Clears the screen display from the current cursor position to the end of the screen without changing the position of the cursor. On exit, A and Y are destroyed.
$FC58	(646ØØ)	HOME	Clears the screen display and positions the cursor at the left of the first line on the screen. On exit, A and Y are destroyed.
$FC62	(6461Ø)	CR	Moves the cursor to the first position of the next video display line (and scrolls if required). On exit, A and Y are destroyed.
$FC9C	(64668)	CLREOL	Clears the screen display from the current cursor position to the end of the line without changing the cursor position. On exit, A and Y are destroyed.
$FCA8	(6468Ø)	WAIT	Causes a delay of Ø.5*(26+27*A+5*A*A) microseconds. On exit, A is destroyed.
$FDØC	(6478Ø)	RDKEY	Receives a character of information from the currently active input device (the address for the input subroutine for this device is held in KSWL ($38) and KSWH ($39)). On exit, A contains the inputted character and Y is destroyed; other registers may be destroyed, depending on the input subroutine for the input device.
$FD1B	(64795)	KEYIN	Receives a character of information from the keyboard. On exit, A contains the inputted character and Y is destroyed.

Table 3-3. Apple //e system monitor subroutines (continued).

Address Hex	(Dec)	Symbolic Name	Description
$FD35	(64821)	RDCHAR	Receives a character of information from the currently active input device and handles any valid escape sequences. On exit, A contains the inputted character and Y is destroyed; other registers may be destroyed, depending on the input subroutine for the input device.
$FD6A	(64874)	GETLN	Receives a line of information (terminated by RETURN) from the currently active input device and places it into the input buffer at $200 . . . $2FF. On entry, the prompt symbol to be used must be stored in PROMPT ($33). On exit, the line is stored in the input buffer beginning at $200, X contains the number of characters in the line, and A and Y are destroyed.
$FDDA	(64986)	PRBYTE	Displays a byte as two hexadecimal digits. On entry, A contains the byte to be displayed. On exit, A is destroyed.
$FDED	(65005)	COUT	Sends a character of information to the currently active output device (the address for the output subroutine for this device is held in CSWL ($36) and CSWH ($37)). On entry, A contains the byte to be sent. On exit, registers may be destroyed, depending on the output subroutine for the output device.
$FDF0	(65008)	COUT1	Displays a character of information on the video display screen at the current cursor position. The display mode is set by logically ANDing the byte with INVFLG ($32). On entry, A contains the byte to be displayed (with its high bit

Table 3-3. Apple //e system monitor subroutines (continued).

Address Hex	*(Dec)*	*Symbolic Name*	*Description*
			set to one). On exit, all registers are preserved.
$FF69	(65385)	MONZ	Enters the //e's system monitor. On exit, all registers are destroyed.

FURTHER READING FOR CHAPTER 3

On system monitor subroutines . . .

Reference Manual Addendum: Monitor ROM Listings, Apple Computer, Inc., 1982. All the source code for the system monitor except from $C4Ø1 . . . $C7FF (self-test subroutines).

W.E. Dougherty, *The Apple II Monitors Peeled*, Apple Computer, Inc., 1981. A detailed look at the system monitors for the Apple II and Apple II Plus.

4

Applesoft BASIC

Applesoft BASIC is a high-level programming language interpreter that occupies 10K of the //e's ROM space from location \$DØØØ through location \$F7FF. (BASIC is an acronym for Beginner's All-Purpose Symbolic Instruction Code.) It is yet another version of the "basic" BASIC developed by Microsoft Corporation of Bellevue, Washington, and so is structurally similar to Microsoft-developed BASICs running on many other personal computers, including those manufactured by Tandy, Commodore, and IBM.

What exactly is the Applesoft programming language, anyway? Well, it's really just another 65Ø2 assembly-language program, but one that has a special goal: to allow you to easily write your own programs using straightforward, English-like commands. These commands can be used in such a way as to allow you to manipulate various types of data and to perform input/output functions. In addition, Applesoft comes with a built-in editing environment that facilitates creation of its programs.

Applesoft is actually a language *interpreter* and a program is simply a set of data that the Applesoft code in ROM is continuously analyzing (interpreting) to determine what commands are to be executed and in what order. Other types of BASICs, called "compilers," are also available. Compilers are simply preprocessors that convert your program source code into directly executable machine language that can then be run just like any other machine language program. Since directly executable code is generated, no interpretation is necessary when the code is actually executed (except, of course, by the microprocessor) and so the program will run much faster than its interpreted counterpart. Although Applesoft compilers have been written for the //e, none have been officially released by Apple itself.

The purpose of this chapter is *not* to teach you how to program in the Applesoft language. In fact, you will be presumed to be familiar with Applesoft already. What we are going to do is take a close look at the internals of Applesoft to see how the interpreter performs its various duties. This will include a look at how an Applesoft program and its variables are stored and arranged in memory and how the program is actually executed by the Applesoft interpreter. We will also take a look at how Applesoft can be linked to machine-language subroutines to improve program speed and efficiency.

The study of the internal structure of Applesoft is difficult and frustrating because no official source listing for its code has been made available by Apple. Such a study is not totally futile, however, because it is possible to disassemble the contents of the Applesoft ROM (using the monitor's "L" command) to view the language in a convenient assembler-language form that can sometimes be made intelligible (if you're lucky). In addition, at least two "unofficial" source listings of Applesoft have been published (see the references at the end of this chapter).

Knowledge of the internal structure of Applesoft is important for three main reasons. First, by analyzing the work of the professional programmers who wrote the language you might develop better personal programming practices. Second, you can generally write much more elegant and efficient assembly-language routines to be used in conjunction with Applesoft programs if the routines use the standard routines found in Applesoft because this spares you from having to redevelop the same code from scratch. Third, it is possible to write much more efficient Applesoft programs if you understand how they are being executed.

APPLESOFT MEMORY MAP

The Applesoft interpreter makes use of most of the RAM space located from $ØØØØ to $95FF on the //e for program and variable storage and for work areas. The area of RAM memory above this, from $96ØØ to $BFFF, is reserved for use by DOS 3.3 or ProDOS.

Much of the 65Ø2 zero page ($ØØØØ. . .$ØØFF) is used by Applesoft to hold short subroutines, temporary data areas, and several two-byte pointers that contain the addresses of important data areas used by the program. For example, there are pointers that indicate the starting and ending addresses of the program itself, of the space reserved for simple variables and array variables, and of the space reserved for string data. We'll be looking at these pointers in greater detail later on in this section.

(To review, a pointer is a pair of bytes that are positioned in adjacent memory locations and that contain the base address of an area in memory to which they are said to be pointing. The lower half of this address is stored in the byte that is lower in memory. To calculate the absolute address of the area being pointed to, take the number held in the first location and add it to 256 times the number in the second location.)

Page one of memory ($100. . .$1FF) is implicitly used by Applesoft since the 6502 microprocessor uses this page as its stack. In addition, Applesoft uses the stack area for temporary storage of information when it executes instructions such as FOR/NEXT, GOSUB/RETURN, and ONERR GOTO that need space to hold transfer-of-control information and when it converts binary numbers into decimal numbers.

Applesoft uses page two of memory ($200. . .$2FF) as its character input buffer. For example, whenever an Applesoft program executes the INPUT command to read a line from the keyboard, it initially stores the response in this buffer and then processes it and moves it up into a space reserved for string data near the end of the RAM space reserved for use by Applesoft.

The lower part of page three of memory from $300. . .$3CF is not used by Applesoft and so is a good place to store short assembly-language programs or other data. However, the entire upper part of this page, from $3D0. . .$3FF, is reserved for use by the disk operating system (DOS 3.3 or ProDOS), the system monitor (to handle the USER command and the 6502 RESET, IRQ, NMI, and BRK interrupts), and by Applesoft. Applesoft reserves the three bytes beginning with $3F5 for use with its & (ampersand) command. Thus, the upper part of memory should not be overwritten unless it is for the specific purpose of modifying the information stored there. Appendix IV contains a complete memory map of the area in page three from $3D0. . .$3FF.

Pages four through seven ($400. . .$7FF) are used for the //e's primary text display screen. (A secondary text display screen can also be enabled that uses pages eight through eleven ($800. . .$BFF), but it is rarely used.) See Chapter 7 for more information on how the //e interprets these pages.

The rest of the RAM space, from $800 up to $95FF, is usually available for storage of the Applesoft program itself and of any variables that it may use. Figure 4-1 shows a generalized Applesoft memory map that indicates the relative positions of the program and its variable spaces. The pointers to these areas are all held in zero page and are summarized in Table 4-1.

The Applesoft program itself is usually stored beginning at location $801, which is the default value of TXTTAB ($67), the start-

Table 4-1. Applesoft pointer locations.

Pointer Hex	*Location (Dec)*	*Symbolic Name*	*Description*
$67 $68	(1Ø3) (1Ø4)	TXTTAB (low) (high)	Start of Applesoft program (normally $8Ø1).
$69 $6A	(1Ø5) (1Ø6)	VARTAB (low) (high)	Start of simple variable space. This space usually begins right after the end of the program. However, it can be set higher by using the Applesoft LOMEM: command.
$6B $6C	(1Ø7) (1Ø8)	ARYTAB (low) (high)	Start of array space. This space begins right after the end of simple variable space.
$6D $6E	(1Ø9) (11Ø)	STREND (low) (high)	End of variable space.
$6F $7Ø	(111) (112)	FRETOP (low) (high)	Start of string space. Applesoft strings are stored from here to just before the address pointed to by MEMSIZ ($73).
$73 $74	(115) (116)	MEMSIZ (low) (high)	End of string space plus 1 and last location available to Applesoft plus 1. Applesoft strings are stored from FRETOP ($6F) to this location. This location is usually $96ØØ (when using DOS) but can be set lower by using the Applesoft HIMEM: command.
$AF $BØ	(175) (176)	PRGEND (low) (high)	End of Applesoft program plus 1 or 2. The end of an Applesoft program is signified by three consecutive "Ø" bytes. The first "Ø" is the end-of-line marker for the last line in the program and the next two "Ø"'s are the "address" of the next line.

and the beginning of the string data will become smaller and smaller as more variables are defined and as more strings are defined. When all of the free space has been used up, an OUT OF MEMORY error message will be generated.

In the next few sections, we will discuss the data spaces used by Applesoft in greater detail.

TOKENIZATION OF APPLESOFT PROGRAMS

An Applesoft program is simply the data the Applesoft interpreter acts on in order to determine exactly what instructions it is to execute and in what order. This data is put into memory with a LOAD or RUN command or is simply typed in from the keyboard.

You might think that an Applesoft program is stored in memory in exactly the same format in which it is displayed when it is listed. To save valuable memory space (an Applesoft program and its variables cannot use up more than about 36,ØØØ bytes when DOS is being used), and to speed up program execution, however, each line of an Applesoft program is analyzed and compressed before it is actually inserted into the proper area of memory. This process is called "tokenization" because it involves, among other things, substituting one-byte tokens for Applesoft keywords. For example, if you enter the line

```
100 HGR2
```

it is not stored as nine bytes in memory as it would be if you used a standard line editor to create the source file (eight bytes of text plus one byte for the carriage return that follows the line). Rather, it is stored as six bytes: two for the line number, one for the token for the HGR2 keyword, and three for overhead information (these overhead bytes will be described below).

It is the tokenized program that is analyzed by the Applesoft interpreter and not the original source listing. By the way, listing a program is the same as "detokenizing" it because the LIST command essentially converts tokens back into their full keywords.

Let's take a detailed look at what happens when you add a new line to an Applesoft program while in direct mode (that is, when the program is not running and the "]" prompt symbol is being displayed).

When you type in a line of characters (each line can be up to 239 characters in length) and then press the RETURN key to enter it, Applesoft scans the input line and checks to see whether it begins with a valid line number. If it doesn't, then Applesoft thinks that this is a direct command and attempts to execute it right away; if it does begin with a line number, then Applesoft interprets it as a deferred command (that is, one that is to be executed only when the program is executed) and will tokenize it and store it in the proper position in memory.

The line is placed in memory in such a way that the ascending numeric sequence of the line numbers in the program is maintained. The lowest-numbered line is stored lowest in memory at the location pointed to by the beginning-of-program pointer, TXTTAB ($67), and the higher-numbered lines are stored sequentially upward in memory.

The bytes that make up a tokenized line are arranged in memory as follows:

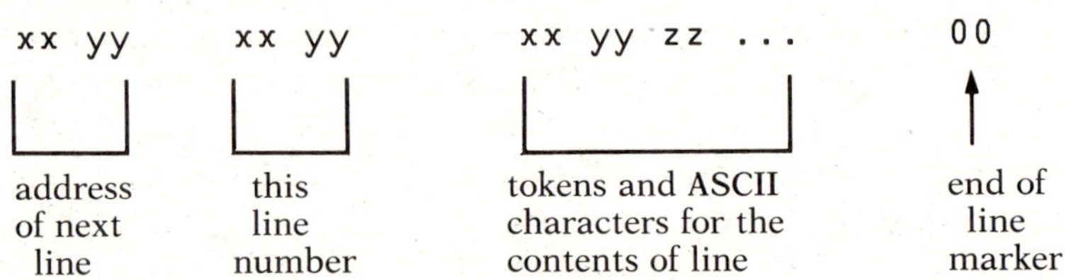

The "address of next line" and "this line number" fields are stored as two bytes, with the least-significant byte coming first. The three bytes of overhead that were mentioned above are made up of the two bytes allocated for the address of the next line and the ØØ byte that marks the end of the line.

Keyword Tokens

We will now take a closer look at what the tokenized part of the line (the part between the line number and end-of-line marker) looks like. We will begin with a description of the tokens used to replace the Applesoft keywords in a program line. These keywords represent the Applesoft commands, functions, and mathematical and logical operators.

Each Applesoft keyword is assigned by the interpreter to a one-byte quantity called a token. This is done for two main reasons: first, to conserve memory space and, second, to improve the execution speed of the program.

The tokens that Applesoft assigns to each of its keywords are presented in Table 4-2 together with the addresses of the subrou-

Table 4-2. Applesoft keyword tokens.

Token	*Keyword*	*Address of Subroutine*
$8Ø	END	$D87Ø
$81	FOR	$D766
$82	NEXT	$DCF9
$83	DATA	$D995
$84	INPUT	$DBB2
$85	DEL	$F331
$86	DIM	$DFD9
$87	READ	$DBE2
$88	GR	$F39Ø
$89	TEXT	$F399
$8A	PR#	$F1E5
$8B	IN#	$F1DE
$8C	CALL	$F1D5
$8D	PLOT	$F225
$8E	HLIN	$F232
$8F	VLIN	$F241
$9Ø	HGR2	$F3D8
$91	HGR	$F3E2
$92	HCOLOR=	$F6E9
$93	HPLOT	$F6FE
$94	DRAW	$F769
$95	XDRAW	$F76F
$96	HTAB	$F7E7
$97	HOME	$FC58
$98	ROT=	$F721
$99	SCALE=	$F727
$9A	SHLOAD	$F775
$9B	TRACE	$F26D
$9C	NOTRACE	$F26F
$9D	NORMAL	$F273
$9E	INVERSE	$F277
$9F	FLASH	$F28Ø
$AØ	COLOR=	$F24F
$A1	POP	$D96B
$A2	VTAB	$F256
$A3	HIMEM:	$F286
$A4	LOMEM:	$F2A6
$A5	ONERR	$F2CB
$A6	RESUME	$F318
$A7	RECALL	$F3BC
$A8	STORE	$F39F
$A9	SPEED=	$F262
$AA	LET	$DA46

Table 4-2. Applesoft keyword tokens (continued).

Token	*Keyword*	*Address of Subroutine*
$AB	GOTO	$D93E
$AC	RUN	$D912
$AD	IF	$D9C9
$AE	RESTORE	$D849
$AF	&	$Ø3F5
$BØ	GOSUB	$D921
$B1	RETURN	$D96B
$B2	REM	$D9DC
$B3	STOP	$D86E
$B4	ON	$D9EC
$B5	WAIT	$E784
$B6	LOAD	$D8C9
$B7	SAVE	$D8BØ
$B8	DEF	$E313
$B9	POKE	$E77B
$BA	PRINT	$DAD5
$BB	CONT	$D896
$BC	LIST	$D6A5
$BD	CLEAR	$D66A
$BE	GET	$DBAØ
$BF	NEW	$D649
$CØ	TAB(	
$C1	TO	
$C2	FN	
$C3	SPC(	
$C4	THEN	
$C5	AT	
$C6	NOT	
$C7	STEP	
$C8	+	
$C9	−	
$CA	*	
$CB	/	
$CC	^	
$CD	AND	
$CE	OR	
$CF	>	
$DØ	=	
$D1	<	
$D2	SGN	$EB9Ø
$D3	INT	$EC23
$D4	ABS	$EBAF
$D5	USR	$ØØØA
$D6	FRE	$E2DE

Table 4-2. Applesoft keyword tokens (continued).

Token	*Keyword*	*Address of Subroutine*
$D7	SCRN(	$D412
$D8	PDL	$DFCD
$D9	POS	$E2FF
$DA	SQR	$EE8D
$DB	RND	$EFAE
$DC	LOG	$E941
$DD	EXP	$EFØ9
$DE	COS	$EFEA
$DF	SIN	$EFF1
$EØ	TAN	$FØ3A
$E1	ATN	$FØ9E
$E2	PEEK	$E764
$E3	LEN	$E6D6
$E4	STR$	$E3C5
$E5	VAL	$E7Ø7
$E6	ASC	$E6E5
$E7	CHR$	$E646
$E8	LEFT$	$E65A
$E9	RIGHT$	$E686
$EA	MID$	$E691

tines within Applesoft that are used to deal with the keyword command or function that they represent (where applicable). You will notice that all of these tokens are greater than or equal to $8Ø. If the tokenized part of a program line contains bytes that are less than $8Ø, then these bytes are simply the ASCII codes for the characters that were typed in when the line was entered (see Appendix I for the ASCII codes used to represent characters). This will include all digits (other than those entered for the line number), all text between quotation marks after a PRINT statement and after DATA and REM statements, and all characters of variable names.

Before you get hopelessly confused, let's look at an example. From Applesoft direct mode, enter NEW, and then enter the following line:

```
100 PI = 4 * ATN (1): PRINT "PI = ";PI: END
```

The bytes used to store this line in memory are as follows:

1D 08	64 00	50	49	D0	34	CA	E1	28	31	29	3A
address of next line	line number	P	I	token for =	4	token for *	token for ATN	(	1	)	:

BA	22	50	49	20	3D	20	22	3B	50	49	3A	80	00
token for PRINT	"	P	I		=		"	;	P	I	:	token for END	end of line marker

(You can see these bytes for yourself by first entering CALL -151 to enter the system monitor, and then entering 8Ø1.81C to display the first few bytes of the program. As we saw earlier, an Applesoft program is usually stored in memory beginning at location $8Ø1.)

Notice that the five keywords in this line, =, *, ATN, PRINT, and END, have been replaced by their tokens, $DØ, $CA, $E1, $BA, and $8Ø, respectively. Also notice that each character that is not part of a keyword is not tokenized and is represented by its ASCII code.

STORAGE OF APPLESOFT VARIABLES

Now that we have seen how an Applesoft program is stored in memory, let's take a more detailed look at how and where the program's variables are stored during program execution. Not only is the knowledge of the data structures used to store variables fundamentally interesting, it will undoubtedly be invaluable to those who wish to manipulate Applesoft variables from within 65Ø2 assembly-language subroutines that are called from Applesoft.

Applesoft supports four fundamental variable types. There are three numeric types, integer, real, and function, and one alphanumeric type, string. Integer numbers are made up of all positive and negative whole numbers and zero, that is, all numbers that have no fractional parts. Real numbers, also called floating-point numbers, are made up of all numbers, including those that do have fractional parts. Strings are simply sequences of ASCII character codes. Functions are special variables that are defined by the Applesoft DEF FN command and that are evaluated using a user-specified mathematical expression. For example, if a function is defined as follows:

```
DEF FN MD(X)=X-256*INT(X/256)
```

then whenever the value of MD(aexpr) is requested (where "aexpr" represents an arithmetic expression) it is evaluated by substituting the value of "aexpr" wherever "X" appears in the "X-256*INT(X/256)" formula and then calculating the result.

The first character of an Applesoft variable name must begin with an upper-case letter from A. . .Z; subsequent characters can be either upper-case letters or a digit from Ø. . .9. The variable name can be up to 239 characters in length, but only the first two char-

Table 4-3. Applesoft variable identifier symbols.

Variable Identifier Symbol	*Variable Type*	*Example*
<none>	real	AB
%	integer	AB%
<none>	function	FN AB ( )
$	string	AB$

acters are significant (the rest are simply ignored). This means that Applesoft considers the variables LESS and LESSEN, for example, to be equivalent.

A variable name cannot be used that contains the names for any of the keywords shown in Table 4-2. For example, the variable name "LETTER" is illegal because it contains the LET keyword.

If an integer or string variable is being defined, a special variable identifier symbol must be added to its name so that Applesoft can properly interpret it and store its value. The variable identifier symbol for integer variables is "%" and for string variables it is "$". No special identifier symbol is needed to identify real or function variables. Table 4-3 sets out the variable identifier symbols used by Applesoft.

When a variable is defined in a program, Applesoft stores its name and value at the end of one of two memory spaces located after the end of the program. One space is reserved for simple variables and functions and is pointed to by VARTAB ($69). The other space is reserved for array variables and is pointed to by ARYTAB ($6B). In the following sections, we will take a look at how variables are represented in these two variable spaces.

Storage of Simple Variables

Whenever Applesoft has to make use of a certain variable, it has to locate it within its variable space. It does this by searching the variable space beginning with the first entry and continuing until it finds a match. Thus, the farther into the space a variable is located, the longer it will take Applesoft to find it. Since Applesoft stores variables in its variable space in the order in which they are encountered when the program is executed, you can improve program execution speed by ensuring that more frequently used variables are defined before less frequently used ones. This is most easily done by defining all the variables in the desired order as soon as the program starts executing. For example, if your program uses four variables, say I, J, K, and L$, but you would like K to be accessed as quickly as possible, then you should execute a line such as

```
10 K=0:I=0:J=0:L$=""
```

before any other line that defines or uses any variables.

Each entry in the simple variable space is exactly seven bytes long and consists of two parts: the name header, which is used to store the variable's name and type, and the data field, which contains the encoded value of the variable or a pointer to its location. The storage format used for each type of variable is summarized in Figure 4-2.

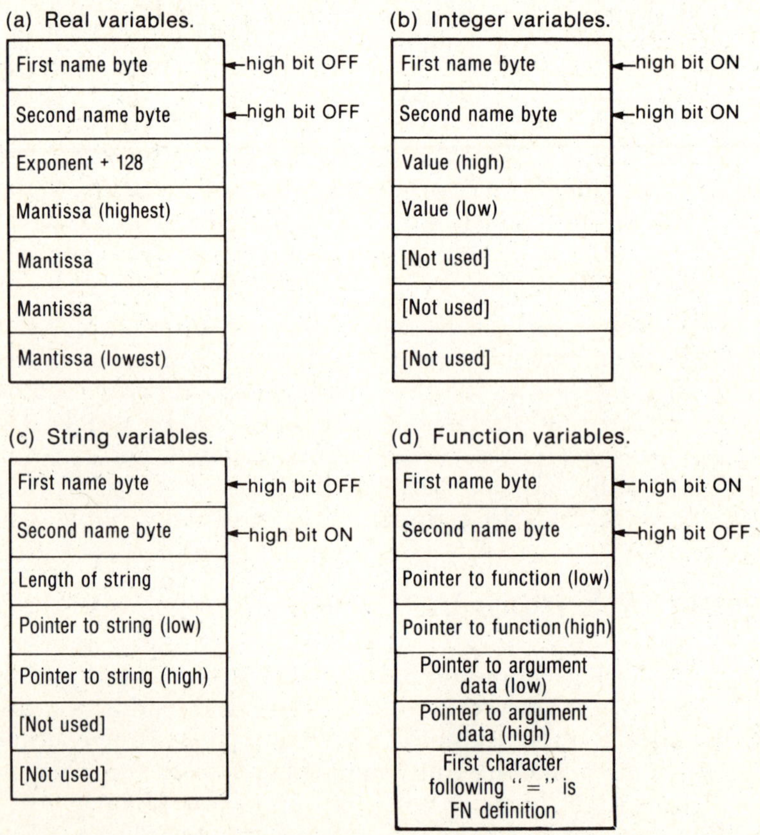

Figure 4-2. Storage formats for Applesoft simple variables.

The Name Header

The name header contains all the information related to the variable's type and name so that it can be quickly located and accessed whenever it is referred to during execution of the Applesoft program. The name header for a simple variable is always exactly two bytes long. Stored in these two bytes are the 7-bit ASCII codes for the the first two characters of the variable's name; if there is only one character used in the name, then the second character is assumed to be the ASCII null character, $ØØ. The high-order bits of each of the two bytes are used to indicate the type of simple variable being referred to. For example, for a string variable, these bits will be OFF (Ø) and ON (1), respectively. For real and integer variables, they will be OFF-OFF and ON-ON, respectively. Lastly, the bits will be ON-OFF if the name refers to a function defined by the DEF FN command.

The Data Field

The encoded data that relates to the value of the simple variable is stored in five bytes just after the end of the two name header bytes. Despite the fact that five bytes are always reserved for data storage, however, only real variables and functions make use of them all. The number of bytes required for the data for each type of variable is as shown in Table 4-4, as are the restrictions on the values for each type of Applesoft variable.

Let's take a look at the storage formats used for each type of variable.

Table 4-4. Storage requirements and limitations for Applesoft variables.

Variable Type	*Number of Data Bytes Required*	*Restrictions on Variable Value*
Integer	2	−32767 . . . +32767
Real	5	2.9E−39 . . . 1.7E+38 (pos. or neg.)
String	3	Length of string is Ø . . . 255
Functions	5	One argument only

INTEGER. The data for integer variables is stored in a signed "two's complement" format and occupies two bytes (most-significant byte followed by least-significant byte). See the section below entitled "REPRESENTATION OF INTEGER NUMBERS" for a detailed description of the two's complement storage format. The high bit of the most-significant byte can be read to determine the sign of the number. If this bit is 1, then the number is negative; if it is Ø, then the number is positive. The last three bytes of the data field are not used.

REAL. The data for real numbers is stored in all five bytes. The first byte is related to the exponent of the number and the next four bytes represent its signed mantissa, most-significant byte first. The sign bit is the high bit of the second byte of the five. See the section below entitled "REPRESENTATION OF REAL NUMBERS" for a detailed description of the method Applesoft uses to store real numbers.

STRING. The data for string variables is really made up of two parts. The first part is stored in the variable table itself and is a three-byte "descriptor" that represents the length of the string (first byte) followed by a two-byte pointer (low-order byte first) to a sequence of ASCII-encoded characters that defines the string itself. The second part is, in fact, made up of those characters that define the contents of the string.

The contents of strings are normally stored in the high end of memory in a string space beginning at a location pointed to by FRETOP ($6F) and ending lower in memory just before the location pointed to by MEMSIZ ($73). Whenever a new string is entered from the keyboard or a diskette file, or an old one is manipulated using any of Applesoft's string-handling commands, it is placed in memory just before the address to which FRETOP points in such a way that the first character in the string is located lowest in memory and the last character is located at the location pointed to by FRETOP. After this is done, FRETOP is adjusted downward so that it points to the byte immediately before the beginning of the string just stored.

When a string variable is redefined using Applesoft's string-handling commands, its new definition is placed in the string space in the upper part of memory as if it were a newly defined variable; however, its former characters are not immediately removed from the string space even though it is no longer used. This means that if strings are continuously being redefined, then a lot of unused information will accumulate in the string space and eventually the address stored in FRETOP will come very close to the address stored in the end-of-variable pointer, STREND ($6D). When this happens, Applesoft initiates a procedure that maximizes its available free space by removing the unused string characters, packing the currently active string characters up to the high end of memory, and resetting FRETOP. This procedure is called "garbage collection" or, more euphemistically, "house-cleaning," and can last anywhere from a few seconds to a few minutes, depending on the number of string variables that have been defined in the program.

Note, however, that if a string is explicitly defined within the program itself, for example, in a program line that looks like this:

```
100 A$="THIS IS A TEST"
```

then the string pointer in the variable table's data field will point to this definition inside the program itself and not to a location within the string space. Such a string will be moved into the string space only if it is operated on by an Applesoft string-handling command.

FUNCTIONS. The data for functions is stored in five bytes. The first two bytes act as a pointer to the body of the function's definition within the program (that is, the part after the "=" sign in the DEF FN definition). The next two bytes contain the address of the data field for the variable representing the function's argument. The last byte contains the first byte in the function definition.

End of Simple Variables

ARYTAB ($6B) points to the Applesoft array variable space located immediately after the end of the simple variable space. Whenever a new simple variable is defined, the whole of the array variable space is moved up in memory by seven bytes to make room for the new simple variable definition and the end-of-variables pointer, STREND ($6D), is adjusted accordingly. The name header and data bytes for the variable are then stored beginning at ARYTAB. ARYTAB is then increased by seven so that it equals the new starting position of the array space.

Storage of Array Variables

Each entry in the array variable space is made up of a name header, special dimensioning bytes that indicate the size of the array and how it is indexed, and a data field. The storage format

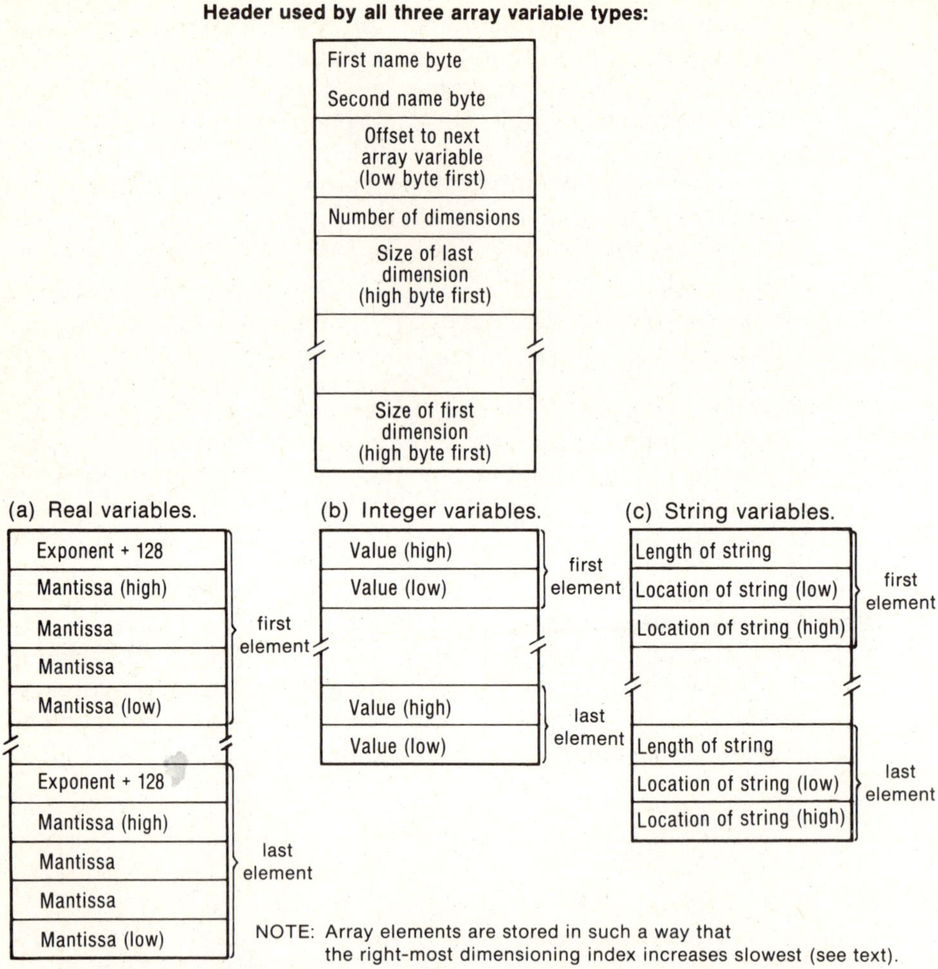

Figure 4-3. Storage formats for Applesoft array variables.

used for each type of array variable is summarized in Figure 4-3. Note that arrays are permitted for each Applesoft variable type except functions.

The Name Header

Just as for simple variables, entries for array variables begin with a name header. The name headers for array variables are identical to those for the corresponding simple variables discussed in the previous section (for example, the header for an array dimensioned as AB(5,6) is the same as for AB).

Dimensioning Bytes

When array variables are stored, a series of bytes that describe the number of dimensions of the array and their sizes are placed in memory just after the header.

First, two bytes are used to store a number that is equal to the number of bytes that the array occupies in the array variable space. This number is simply the offset from the name header of this array to the next array and is stored here so that the address of the next array variable in the array space can be quickly and easily calculated when Applesoft is searching for an array. The number is stored with the low-order byte first.

The next byte is equal to the number of array indexes (or "dimensions") and can be from 1 to 255. For example, an array dimensioned as AB(3,5,2) would have a value of 3 stored in this byte.

Pairs of bytes follow this last byte that indicate the size of the indexes of the array, with the number of elements in the last index being stored in the first pair and the number of elements in the first index being stored in the last pair. The high-order byte is stored first in each pair. The numbers stored here will be one higher than the number used when the array was first dimensioned (using the DIM statement) since it starts counting the elements from one rather than zero.

Let's look at an example. The name header bytes and dimensioning bytes for an array dimensioned as AB(3,5,2) would be as follows:

41 42	73 01	03	00 03	00 06	00 04
name (AB)	offset to next array	# of indexes	size of 3rd index	size of 2nd index	size of 1st index

The Data Field

After the dimensioning bytes come the actual data bytes for each array element. They are stored in exactly the same formats used by the corresponding simple variables except that, in the case of integer and string arrays, the data bytes are packed. This means that the unused bytes that are stored in the simple variable data space for these two types of variables are not stored.

The array elements are stored in memory in such a way that the rightmost dimensioning index ascends most slowly. Thus, if an array is dimensioned as A(1,1), then A(Ø,Ø) is stored first, followed by A(1,Ø), A(Ø,1), and then A(1,1).

End of Array Variables

STREND ($6D) points to one byte past the end of the array variable space. It also points to the beginning of Applesoft free space. When a new array variable is defined, its header and data are stored beginning at this location and then the value STREND is increased by the size of the entry for the array.

REPRESENTATION OF INTEGER NUMBERS

Applesoft stores the data for its integer variables in a special two-byte format called "two's complement." As we will see, the advantage of using this format is that it allows both negative and positive numbers to be represented in a way that greatly simplifies the execution of the two basic signed arithmetic operations, addition and subtraction.

The most-significant byte of the pair of data bytes reserved for an integer is stored first (note that this is just the opposite of how two-byte quantities are usually stored). The high-order bit of this byte is used to indicate the sign of the number. If it is 1, then the number is negative; if it is Ø, then it is positive. The remaining 7 bits of this byte, and the 8 bits of the least-significant byte, are used to represent the magnitude of the integer. For a positive integer, the 15-bit magnitude is simply represented by the standard unsigned binary pattern for the integer. For example,

```
00000001 00000011
```

is used to represent +259 ($Ø1Ø3).

The 15 bits used to represent a negative integer are determined somewhat differently. To determine what they are, you must first take the binary pattern for the absolute value of the integer (that is, its positive counterpart), complement it by changing all its 1 bits to Ø and vice versa, and then add one to the result. The most-significant bit will then be 1, indicating that the number is negative. For example, the representation for the integer −11 would be calculated as follows:

```
  0000000 00001011   (+11)
  1111111 11110100   (complement)
+                1   (add 1)
  ----------------
  1111111 11110101   (−11 in two's complement)
```

Using the two-byte two's complement format, it is possible to hold integers that range from −32768 (10000000 00000000) to +32767 (01111111 11111111). Note, however, that even though the number −32768 can be represented in the two-byte two's complement format, Applesoft does not allow its integer variables to take on this value. The lowest value that is allowed is −32767.

Applesoft stores its integers in this apparently strange format to simplify the way in which binary arithmetic can be performed. By using the two's complement format, positive and negative numbers can be easily added and subtracted without having to perform the complicated adjustments needed to account for the different signs of the numbers if any other representation is used. (Another representation may be the conventional "sign plus magnitude" (S+M), where a positive integer and its negative counterpart are identical except for the value of the sign bit.). When using the two's complement representation, it is only necessary to add the 16-bit representations of the two integers (be they positive or negative) as if they were just two standard unsigned binary numbers. The result, and its sign, will then automatically be correct if the result is viewed as another two's complement integer (which it is).

Let's take a look at an example to see what we mean by this. Consider the problem of adding the integer +8 to the integer −5. If these numbers were stored in their normal binary representations with the sign bit being the most-significant bit, then the calculation to be performed would be

```
  00000000 00001000   (+8)
+ 10000000 00000101   (−5 in S+M binary)
  -----------------
  10000000 00001101   (−13 in S+M binary)
```

This result is, of course, wrong. Thus, if this representation is used, special programs must be written to avoid these erroneous results. On the other hand, if the integers are represented in the two's complement format, then the calculation becomes

```
  00000000 00001000   (+8)
+ 11111111 11111011   (−5 in two's complement)
  -----------------
  00000000 00000011   (+3)
```

This result is, of course, correct. If you experiment with other integers, you will see that the signed result is always correct (unless the result is out of the allowable range).

REPRESENTATION OF REAL NUMBERS

As we have seen, Applesoft real numbers are stored in the simple variable space and array variable space in a binary floating-point format. This special format will be described in detail now.

Knowledge of this format will be of use mainly to those who write 65Ø2 assembly-language programs that access Applesoft numeric variables. However, even if you never intend to write such a program, the following information should prove to be interesting.

Number Theory

Even though numbers are commonly entered into a computer in a "decimal" or "base 1Ø" format, they are generally stored internally in some sort of compressed binary format to reduce data storage space and to make it easy for programs to manipulate them.

Decimal integer numbers can be stored in a binary form without loss of accuracy due to rounding or truncation (provided that the integers are within the numeric range supported by the computer) because they do not contain fractional parts. On the other hand, floating-point numbers (that is, real numbers), which do have fractional parts, can only be *approximated* by a binary representation unless the decimal number is exactly equal to a sum of powers of two. Because approximations have to be made in most cases, you will sometimes find that if you multiply a number by its reciprocal in Applesoft that the number calculated is not equal to one!

Floating-point real numbers are often expressed in "scientific notation" that looks like this:

```
134.56 x 10^6
```

The first part of this representation is called the mantissa and the second part is called the exponent (the exponent is actually the number to which the number base being used has been raised). An understanding of scientific notation is important because it turns out that it is the binary mantissa and exponent that are stored by Applesoft when real numbers are stored in its variable spaces.

Binary Floating-Point Format

Real numbers are stored in the variable spaces of Applesoft in a "binary floating-point" format. As indicated in Figure 4-4, this is a five-byte format in which one byte is reserved for exponent information and four bytes for mantissa information. The mantissa contains the binary representation of the fractional part of the number.

The lowest-addressed byte in the fivesome is the exponent byte. The value stored here is actually not the exponent itself but rather the value of the exponent plus 128. Because this method is used to store the exponent, the exponent is said to be "biased" by 128.

Before a number is stored in the binary floating-point format, it is "normalized." Normalization is the process whereby the binary point of the binary number (as opposed to a decimal point for a decimal number) is adjusted so that there is a "1" to its immediate right and no "1" 's to the left of it. Thus, after normalization, the mantissa of the number will be between Ø.1 and Ø.11111111 . . . (in binary). For each movement of the binary point to the left, the exponent is increased by one; for each movement to the right, the exponent is reduced by one. For example, consider the binary number "11Ø1.11". To normalize this number, the binary point must be moved four places to the left; thus, the initial exponent (Ø) must be increased by four.

In the binary floating-point representation, the high-order bit of the second byte represents the sign of the number. If this bit is 1, then the number is negative; if it is Ø, then the number is positive.

The remaining 7 bits of the second byte and the remaining three bytes are used to represent the mantissa of the number, most-significant byte first. Within a particular byte, the 7th bit is the most significant and the 0th bit the least significant. As has been explained, the mantissa has been normalized so that there is a "1" to the immediate right of the decimal point; this "1" is implicit and is not stored. Thus, a floating-point number has 32-bit precision (about nine decimal digits) even though only 31 bits are actually used to hold the mantissa.

Any number whose exponent byte is equal to zero is considered to be zero by the Applesoft interpreter even though its mantissa bytes may be nonzero.

The decimal range of numbers that is allowed using the five-byte binary floating-point format is as follows:

+/− 2.9387355E−39 to +/− 1.7Ø141183E+38

To calculate a decimal number from its binary format, multiply the value of each mantissa bit by its corresponding binary weight, add the implied Ø.5 (which is the decimal equivalent of binary Ø.1), and then multiply the total by 2 raised to the value of the exponent byte minus 128. The binary weight of a particular mantissa bit is given by (1/2)^(32-BN), where BN is the bit number. The bit numbers range from the most-significant bit 3Ø (bit 6 of byte 2) to the least-significant bit Ø (bit Ø of byte 5).

For example, consider the decimal number '8.67'. It is stored by Applesoft as the following five bytes:

BYTE1	BYTE2	BYTE3	BYTE4	BYTE5
$84	$0A	8B	$51	$EB

and the corresponding binary number is

```
+.10001010  10111000  01010001  11101011  * 2 ($84-$80)
 ↑    byte2     byte3       byte4     byte5         byte1
 |
implicit
```

To convert this binary number to its corresponding decimal number, you must add the implicit 0.5 to the sum of each binary digit multiplied by its binary weight. The resultant calculation is as follows:

```
0.5+(1/2)^5+(1/2)^7+(1/2)^9+(1/2)^11+(1/2)^12+(1/2)^13+(1/2)^18
  +(1/2)^20+(1/2)^24+(1/2)^25+(1/2)^26+(1/2)^27
  +(1/2)^29+(1/2)^31+(1/2)^32
```

If you calculate this quantity, you will get Ø.541875. It then must be multiplied by the exponential part (which is 2^4 or 16) in order to yield the final result: 8.67.

Note that the high bit of BYTE2 in the above example is zero indicating that the number is positive.

If you wish to look at the bytes that Applesoft uses to store other numbers, use the program found in Table 4-5. When you RUN this program, you will be asked to enter a number to be analyzed (X). The program locates the data bytes used to store this number by recognizing the fact that since X is the first simple variable defined in the program, its five data bytes must be stored two bytes from the beginning of the simple variable space (remember that the first two bytes are reserved for the name header). The address of the

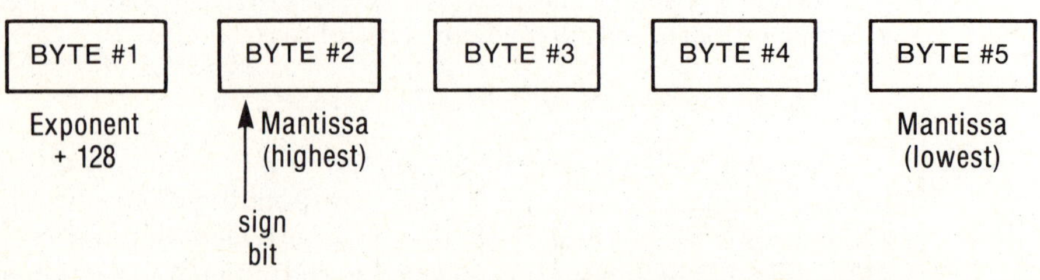

Figure 4-4. Applesoft binary floating-point format.

beginning of this space is simply PEEK(105)+256*PEEK(1Ø6) since the pointer to the beginning of the simple variable space is located at $69 and $6A.

Table 4-5. REAL NUMBER DATA STORAGE. A program to display the data bytes for an Applesoft real variable.

```
]LIST

0  REM "REAL NUMBER DATA STORAGE"

100  TEXT : HOME : PRINT "DECIMAL
      ---> BINARY FLOATING-POINT"

110  VTAB 5
120  INPUT "ENTER NUMBER TO BE CO
     NVERTED: ";X
130  DIM HX$(15) : FOR I = 0 TO 15
     : READ HX$(I) : NEXT
140 XD = PEEK (105) + 256 * PEEK
     (106) + 2: REM LOCATION OF
     DATA FOR X
150  PRINT : PRINT "THE FLOATING-
     POINT REPRESENTATION IS:": PRINT

160  FOR I = XD TO XD + 4
170 D = PEEK (I):D1 = D
180  PRINT "BYTE #";I - XD + 1;":
      ";
190  FOR J = 7 TO 0 STEP - 1
200 T = INT (D / (2 ^ J)) : PRINT
     T;
210 D = D - T * (2 ^ J)
220  NEXT J: PRINT " ($";HX$( INT
     (D1 / 16));HX$(D1 - 16 * INT
     (D1 / 16));") ";
230  READ DS$: PRINT DS$
240  NEXT I: PRINT
250  PRINT "BIT 7 OF BYTE #2 IS T
     HE SIGN BIT": PRINT "(0 -->
     POSITIVE, 1 --> NEGATIVE)"
260  DATA 0,1,2,3,4,5,6,7,8,9,A,B
     ,C,D,E,F
270  DATA EXPONENT + 128,MANTISSA
      HIGH,.,.,MANTISSA LOW
```

HOW AN APPLESOFT PROGRAM RUNS

Right after you enter the RUN command to begin execution of an Applesoft program, at least two important things happen. First, all the pointers to the variable spaces are initialized, effectively destroying any variables that may have been active when the program last stopped running. Then, just before the program starts to be executed, a special pointer, called TXTPTR ($B8/$B9), is initialized so that it contains the address of the beginning of the program. This address is usually $8Ø1.

TXTPTR is an important pointer as far as the interpreter is concerned because it always contains the address of the location within the program that the interpreter is acting on. Whenever the interpreter wants to examine the next byte of the tokenized program, it simply increments this pointer and then reads the new byte to which it points.

The CHARGET Subroutine

Since TXTPTR must be incremented by many different subroutines in the interpreter, one special subroutine is used to take care of it. This subroutine is called CHARGET (for CHARacter GET) and is located in page zero from location $B1 to location $C8. A source listing of CHARGET appears in Table 4-6. Another subroutine, called CHARGOT, is contained within CHARGET; this subroutine reads the current byte being pointed to without incrementing TXTPTR. An image of the CHARGET subroutine is loaded into its page zero locations from the Applesoft ROM area by the Applesoft interpreter when Applesoft is first initialized. It must be placed in a RAM area because, as we will see, it contains self-modifying code.

TXTPTR is actually located within this subroutine at location $B8/$B9 and it forms the operand of an LDA instruction that retrieves the value of the byte pointed to by TXTPTR.

When CHARGET is called, TXTPTR is incremented, the 65Ø2 accumulator is loaded with the byte located at the new address it points to, certain processor flags are set, and then the routine ends. Exactly how the flags are set depends on the value of the byte loaded into the accumulator. If it is an end-of-line marker (Ø) or end-of-statement byte ($3A), then the zero flag (Z) is set; otherwise, it is cleared. In addition, if the byte is a digit (that is, its ASCII code is between $3Ø and $39), then the carry flag (C) will be clear; otherwise, it will be set. The reason for testing for these conditions in the CHARGET subroutine is that many of Applesoft's internal subroutines are constantly checking for end-of-line conditions or for the presence or absence of numbers and this is an efficient way of providing that information. If it wasn't done this way, then

Table 4-6. CHARGET. Applesoft's internal locator subroutine.

```
Page #01

: A S M
                ***********
                * CHARGET *
                ***********

                TXTPTR      EQU   $B8          ; (NOTE: This is CHARGOT+1)

                            ORG   $B1

00B1: E6 B8     CHARGET     INC   TXTPTR       ;Bump the text pointer
00B3: D0 02                 BNE   CHARGOT      ; by one position
00B5: E6 B9                 INC   TXTPTR+1
00B7: AD FF FF  CHARGOT     LDA   $FFFF        ;Get the byte pointed to
00BA: C9 3A                 CMP   #$3A         ; and compare it to ":"
00BC: B0 0A                 BCS   EXIT         ;Branch if >= ":"
00BE: C9 20                 CMP   #$20         ;Is this a blank?
00C0: F0 EF                 BEQ   CHARGET      ;Yes, so get next byte
00C2: 38                    SEC
00C3: E9 30                 SBC   #$30
00C5: 38                    SEC
00C6: E9 D0                 SBC   #$D0         ;If digit, carry will be
                                               ;clear
00C8: 60        EXIT        RTS


--End assembly--

24 bytes

Errors: 0
```

wasteful duplication of code would be required because every subroutine that needed the information would have to perform its own separate testing procedures.

Let's get back to our program, which was just starting to run with TXTPTR set to $8Ø1 when we last left it. Since the first four bytes of the program ($8Ø1 . . . $8Ø3) are simply the line number and the address of the next line, they are skipped over by increasing TXTPTR by four so that the next time CHARGET is called the first byte in the token field of the program line will be read.

The next step, of course, is to call CHARGET and get that first byte and analyze it. This is where Applesoft really starts its interpretation chores. If the byte happens to be an end-of-line marker (Ø), then TXTPTR is bumped by four positions so that it points to the byte just before the token field of the next line. If it's a colon separator ($3A), then CHARGET is called again to load the next byte (which will be the first byte in the token field of the next statement on that line).

If the byte is a keyword token (that is, it is greater than or equal to $8Ø), then, assuming it is not out of context, the appropriate subroutine in the interpreter that handles that command or function to which it refers will be called. That subroutine will, among other things, evaluate numerical or string expressions and perform syntax checking; it will do this by making extensive use of CHARGET to analyze the bytes "surrounding" the keyword. When the keyword has been dealt with, CHARGET will point to the next byte to be interpreted.

If the byte is not a keyword token or an end-of-line or end-of-statement marker, then, depending on the context, it may be considered to be a variable name, a piece of data, or maybe nothing at all (in which case you will see the dreaded SYNTAX ERROR). As long as no syntax errors are detected, TXTPTR will keep being changed and new bytes interpreted until such time as the token for END or STOP is encountered or until the last line in the program has been executed.

Changing Program Flow

Because Applesoft always relies on the value of TXTPTR to determine what part of the program to execute next, you can easily cause Applesoft to skip certain parts of the program and to continue executing elsewhere merely by adjusting TXTPTR. In fact, this is exactly how the Applesoft GOTO and GOSUB commands work. When the interpreter encounters either of these commands, it performs a number of tasks, the most important of which are to determine the target line number, to find that line number in memory, and then to store the address of the line's token field in TXTPTR. Then, when Applesoft continues interpreting the program by calling CHARGET, the commands there will begin to be executed.

Finding Line Numbers

We have just seen how TXTPTR is adjusted when either a GOTO or GOSUB command is executed. What we did not explain is how the interpreter determines where the line to which control is to be passed by either of these commands is located.

There are two different methods Applesoft uses, depending on whether the high-order byte of the destination line number is greater than the high-order byte of the current line number. If it is, then the interpreter starts looking for a line with the proper number beginning with the next line in memory. If it is not, then the interpreter begins with the first line of the program. The interpreter can quickly skip over lines whose numbers don't match by examining the link field address (the first two bytes of the tokenized line) to determine the address of the next line of the program.

What this means is that GOTO and GOSUB commands that transfer control to line numbers just before the current line will execute more slowly than those that transfer control to lines nearer the start of the program or to lines just after the current line.

In should be obvious, then, that to increase program execution speed, "backward" GOTO and GOSUB statements should transfer control to lines that are as close to the beginning of the program as possible. By placing commonly used subroutines near the beginning of a program in decreasing order of activity, program speed can be noticeably increased.

LINKING APPLESOFT TO ASSEMBLY-LANGUAGE SUBROUTINES

The execution speed of an Applesoft program can be improved dramatically by linking it to assembly-language subroutines. This is because the code generated by the assembly process is directly executable by the microprocessor and does not have to be interpreted first. Such subroutines can be accessed from Applesoft by using one of three Applesoft commands: CALL, USR, and & (ampersand). These three commands are summarized in Table 4-7.

Assembly-language subroutines often need to make use of zero

Table 4-7. Applesoft to assembly-language commands.

Command	*Description*
CALL aexpr	Transfers control to the memory location specified by "aexpr".
X = USR (aexpr)	Evaluates "aexpr" and places the result in the floating point accumulator (see text) and then transfers control to $ØØØA. On return, the value of the function is set equal to the value in the FAC.
&	Transfers control to $3F5.

Note: "aexpr" represents an arithmetic expression.

page locations to take advantage of some of the 65Ø2's more powerful addressing modes. As we have seen, however, several locations in zero page are reserved for use by Applesoft pointers. Others are used by Applesoft, the system monitor, or DOS for other purposes. Table 2-5 at the end of Chapter 2 contains a complete list of those zero page locations that are not used and that are available for use by an assembly-language program.

The CALL Command

The CALL command is the one that is usually used to link Applesoft programs with assembly-language subroutines. If such a subroutine begins at a memory location represented by "aexpr", then you would use the command

```
CALL aexpr
```

to invoke the subroutine. The value of "aexpr" that you use must be a literal *decimal* number (not hexadecimal) or, alternately, a mathematical expression that evaluates to a number.

For example, to execute a subroutine from Applesoft that begins at location $3ØØ (768 decimal), you would use the command

```
CALL 768
```

When the subroutine finishes executing, you will normally return to Applesoft and the next statement in the Applesoft program will be executed.

You can try using the CALL command without even writing any assembly-language subroutines simply by accessing subroutines that are already contained in the system monitor ROM. For example, to clear the screen you would use the command CALL 64600 since $FC58 is the address of the screen clear command. As explained in Chapter 3, there are many other subroutines in the monitor, some of which require that data be provided to them first or that registers be set up in certain ways.

If the subroutine that you are calling requires that data be provided to it before it can perform its duties, you would normally precede your CALL with several POKE commands that would place the appropriate information at the locations expected by the subroutine. Similarly, you will usually have to use the PEEK command to examine any numerical results that the program may store in memory.

It is possible, however, using more advanced techniques, to pass the values of named variables to and from your called subroutines. These techniques will be described below in the section entitled "USING APPLESOFT'S BUILT-IN SUBROUTINES."

The & Command

The & (ampersand) command is similar to the CALL command and is used for similar purposes. Whenever the Applesoft interpreter comes across the & command, it immediately causes the system to transfer control to location $3F5, thus causing the subroutine that is located there to be executed. In the usual case, a 6502 JMP (jump) instruction is stored at this location that passes control to some other location where the main body of the subroutine begins.

If you want to use the & command to access assembly-language subroutines, you must first set up the jump at location $3F5 (1013) so that it points to the desired subroutine. This can be done by using the following three POKE commands:

```
POKE 1013,76 : REM 76 ($4C) is the 6502 JMP opcode
POKE 1014,YY : REM YY is the low address of the subroutine
POKE 1015,XX : REM XX is the high address of the subroutine
```

To calculate the high and low halves of the address of the subroutine, you can use the following formulas:

```
XX = INT(ADDRESS/256)
YY = ADDRESS - 256*XX
```

After you install the subroutine at the proper location, you can then execute the & command to access it.

As with the CALL statement, no built-in provisions have been made for the passing of variables to and from & subroutines. However, the program that is called can be written to do this for itself. See the section below entitled "USING APPLESOFT'S BUILT-IN SUBROUTINES."

The USR Function

The USR function can also be used to link Applesoft to assembly-language subroutines. The syntax of the USR function is as follows:

```
Y = USR(aexpr)
```

where "aexpr" represents a mathematical expression that is called the argument of the function. When the USR function is encountered by the interpreter, the formula is evaluated, the result of the evaluation is placed in an internal floating-point accumulator (FAC) in zero page and a jump to location $000A is performed. By setting up a 6502 JMP instruction at $000A, you can transfer control to the beginning of an assembly-language program that has been loaded anywhere in memory.

After the program has finished executing, control will return to Applesoft and the "Y" variable in the above equation will be set equal to the current value of the FAC. This is why USR is called the "user-defined function."

Let's take a look at a specific application involving the USR command. In particular, let's calculate the sine of the argument by using Applesoft's internal sine evaluation subroutine located at $EFF1. As we shall see later in this chapter, this subroutine calculates the sine of the number in the FAC and returns the result there. The subroutine required to perform the conversion is simple: JMP $EFF1. You can install it at location $300 by entering CALL −151 to enter the system monitor, and then entering the command

```
300:4C F1 EF
```

To link this subroutine to the USR command, a JMP $300 instruction must be placed at the USR locations from $A to $C. This can be done by entering the following monitor command:

```
A:4C 00 03
```

where 4C is the JMP opcode and 00 03 represents the address of the subroutine (low-order byte first). Note that you could have also entered all this information using Applesoft POKE statements.

To try out the USR routine, enter and RUN the following short program:

```
100 X = 3
200 PRINT USR (X)
300 PRINT SIN (X)
```

As you will see after the program has stopped RUNning, USR is indeed calculating the sine of X.

USR is not a popular Applesoft function for two main reasons. First, only a single numeric expression can be passed to the USR subroutine. Second, the structure of the internal floating-point accumulator has never been officially described by Apple. However, as we shall see in the section below entitled "USEFUL APPLESOFT BUILT-IN SUBROUTINES," there are many built-in subroutines in Applesoft that can be used to facilitate manipulation of the FAC.

APPLESOFT'S BUILT-IN SUBROUTINES

The Applesoft interpreter is made up of many subroutines that are used to perform many different functions: evaluating functions, performing arithmetic operations, locating variables, handling errors, and so on. Many of them make use of the previously described CHARGET subroutine and the TXTPTR ($B8) pointer to perform their duties. Table 4-8 describes some of the more useful and commonly used Applesoft subroutines. The addresses of these subroutines are called "entry points."

Many of the Applesoft subroutines make use of special locations in the //e's zero page. The locations that are referred to in connection with the subroutines in Table 4-8 are shown in Table 4-9.

Many of the subroutines contained in Table 4-8 deal with floating-point real numbers. Applesoft uses two seven-byte areas in zero page, one from $9D to $A3 and the other from $A5 to $AB, to store binary floating-point numbers whenever mathematical operations are being performed on real numbers or functions are being evaluated. These areas are called the primary floating-point accumulator (FAC) and argument register (ARG), respectively. Note that despite the use of the words "accumulator" and "register," these are not 65Ø2 registers, but merely special data storage areas. Although the format Applesoft uses to store numbers in either FAC is not quite the same as the five-byte format used to store real numbers in the Applesoft simple and array variable spaces, it will not be described here since knowledge of it is not necessary to make use of Applesoft's built-in floating-point mathematical subroutines.

The FAC is used by Applesoft to hold the argument for those calculations that require only one argument (for example, the calculation of a sine). If two arguments are required, however, the first argument is kept in the ARG and the second is kept in the FAC. In either case, the answer is returned in the FAC.

Remember the Applesoft USR command? The argument that is evaluated when this command is executed is stored in the FAC, as is the returned result.

Table 4-8. Applesoft built-in subroutines.

(a) Locating Variables, Data, and Line Numbers

Address Hex	(Dec)	Symbolic Name	Description
$ØØB1	(177)	CHARGET	Increments TXTPTR by one position and returns the next byte in the program in the A-register. Certain flags are also set: if A is a colon (":") or a zero, then the zero flag is set; otherwise, it is cleared. If A is an ASCII digit ("Ø" to "9"), then the carry flag is cleared; otherwise it is set.
$ØØB7	(183)	CHARGOT	Returns the current byte in the program pointed to by TXTPTR in the A register. The flags are set in the same way as for CHARGET.
$DFE3	(57315)	PTRGET	Finds the address of the beginning of the data field within the variable space for any Applesoft variable. On entry, TXTPTR must be pointing to the first character of the variable's name. On exit, the address can be found in VARPNT ($83/$84) and in Y (high) and A (low).
$F7D9	(63449)	GETARYPT	Finds the address of the name header for any array variable. On entry, TXTPTR must be pointing to the first character in the variable's name. On exit, the address can be found in LOWTR ($9B/$9C).
$D61A	(5481Ø)	FNDLIN	Locates the line in the program whose number is in LINNUM ($5Ø/$51). On exit, if the line is found, the carry flag is clear and LOWTR ($9A/$9B) points to the start of the line. If the line was not found, then the carry flag will be set and LOWTR will point to the next higher line.

(b) Evaluating Formulas

Address Hex	(Dec)	Symbolic Name	Description
$DD67	(56679)	FRMNUM	Evaluates a mathematical formula and stores the result in the FAC. On entry, TXTPTR must be pointing to the first character in the formula. On exit, the result is placed in the FAC unless a syntax error is detected in which case an appropriate error message is displayed.
$E6F8	(59128)	GETBYT	Evaluates a mathematical formula that will yield a result in the range Ø . . . 255. On entry, TXTPTR must be pointing to the first character in the formula. On exit, the result is stored in the X-register and FACLO ($A1).
$DD7B	(56699)	FRMEVL	Evaluates a mathematical or string formula and stores the result in the FAC. On entry, TXTPTR must be pointing to the first character in the formula. On exit, if a strong formula is being evaluated, $AØ (low) and $A1 (high) points to the 3-byte string descriptor.

(c) Converting Numbers

Address Hex	(Dec)	Symbolic Name	Description
$E2F2	(58Ø98)	GIVAYF	Converts the 2-byte signed integer in A (high) and Y (low) into floating-point format and stores it in the FAC.
$E6FB	(59131)	CONINT	Converts the number in the FAC to a single-byte integer. On entry, the number to be converted must be in the FAC. On exit, the single-byte integer is contained in the X-register and FACLO ($A1) un-

(continued)

Table 4-8. Applesoft built-in subroutines (continued).

(c) Converting Numbers

Address Hex	(Dec)	Symbolic Name	Description
			less the result is not in the range Ø . . . 255 in which case an "ILLEGAL QUANTITY ERROR" message is displayed.
$E752	(59218)	GETADR	Converts the number in the FAC into an unsigned 2-byte integer (Ø . . . 65535) in LINNUM ($5Ø/$51). If the number is negative, then 65535 is added to its value.
$ED24	(6Ø7Ø8)	LINPRT	Converts the unsigned hexadecimal number in X (low) and A (high) into a decimal number and displays it.
$ED2E	(6Ø718)	PRNTFAC	Prints the number contained in the FAC (in decimal format). The FAC is destroyed by this process.

(d) Applesoft Real-Number Mathematics

Before executing any of the following subroutines, a number must be loaded into the FAC. All of these subroutines first move the number in memory pointed to by Y (high) and A (low) into the ARG and perform the mathematical operation. The result is placed in the FAC.

Address Hex	(Dec)	Symbolic Name	Description
$E7A7	(593Ø3)	FSUB	Subtract the FAC from the ARG.
$E7BE	(59326)	FADD	Add the FAC to the ARG.
$E97F	(59775)	FMULT	Multiply the ARG by the FAC.
$EA66	(6ØØØ6)	FDIV	Divide the ARG by the FAC.

(e) Applesoft String Handling

Address Hex	(Dec)	Symbolic Name	Description
$E452	(5845Ø)	GETSPACE	Reduces the start-of-strings pointer, FRETOP ($6F), by the number specified in the A-register (the string length) and sets up

(e) Applesoft String Handling (continued)

Address Hex	(Dec)	Symbolic Name	Description
			FRESPC ($71) so that it equals FRETOP. After this has been done, A remains unaffected and Y (high) and X (low) point to the beginning of the space. The string can then be moved into place in upper memory by using MOVESTR.
$E484	(58500)	GARBAGE	Clears out old string definitions that are no longer being used and adjusts FRETOP ($6F) accordingly. (Each time that a string is redefined, its old definition is kept in memory but is not used.) This process is called "garbage collection" and is performed automatically whenever the start-of-strings address, FRETOP, comes close to the end-of-variables address, STREND ($6D).
$E5E2	(58850)	MOVESTR	Copies the string that is pointed to by Y (high) and X (low) and that has a length of A to the location pointed to by FRESPC ($71).
$ED34	(60724)	FOUT	Converts the FAC into an ASCII character string that represents the number in decimal form (like Applesoft's STR$ function). The string is followed by a $00 byte and is pointed to by Y (high) and A (low) so that STROUT can be used to print the string.
$DB3A	(56122)	STROUT	Prints the string pointed to by Y (high) and A (low). The string must be followed immediately by a $00 or a $22 byte. All of these conditions are set up by FOUT.
$DB3D	(56125)	STRPRT	Prints the string whose 3-byte descriptor is pointed to by $A0/$A1. FRMEVL sets up such a pointer when calculating string formulas.

(continued)

Table 4-8. Applesoft built-in subroutines (continued).

(f) Applesoft Real-Number Functions

In executing the following subroutines, Applesoft expects the argument to be in the FAC. After the result has been calculated, it will be placed in the FAC.

Address Hex	(Dec)	Symbolic Name	Description
$E941	(59713)	LOG	Calculate the natural logarithm
$EBAF	(6Ø335)	ABS	Calculate the absolute value
$EE8D	(61Ø69)	SQR	Calculate the square root
$EFØ9	(61193)	EXP	Calculate "e to the power of"
$EFEA	(61418)	COS	Calculate the cosine (in radians)
$EFF1	(61425)	SIN	Calculate the sine (in radians)
$FØ3A	(61498)	TAN	Calculate the tangent (in radians)
$FØ9E	(61598)	ATN	Calculate the arctangent (in radians)

(g) Miscellaneous Subroutines

Address Hex	(Dec)	Symbolic Name	Description
$DAØC	(5582Ø)	LINGET	Loads a line number into LINNUM ($5Ø/$51). On entry, TXTPTR must point to the first digit of the line number.
$D412	(5429Ø)	ERROR	Handles any Applesoft error conditions that may occur during the running of a program. The subroutine first checks ERRFLAG ($D8) to see if an ONERR GOTO statement is in effect; if ERRFLAG >=$8Ø, then error handling has been enabled and control passes to the appropriate line number. If ERRFLAG <$8Ø, then an error message is printed (the error-number code is in X) and the program stops.
$DEBE	(57Ø22)	CHKCOM	Checks that TXTPTR ($B8) is pointing to a comma and, if it is, bumps TXTPTR by one. If TXTPTR is not pointing to a comma, then a syntax error will be generated.

(g) Miscellaneous Subroutines (continued)

Address Hex	(Dec)	Symbolic Name	Description
$EØØØ	(57344)	COLD	Performs an Applesoft cold start (the program in memory is destroyed).
$EØØ3	(57347)	WARM	Performs an Applesoft warm start (the program in memory remains intact).

Table 4-9. Some important zero page locations used by Applesoft's built-in subroutines.

Address Hex	(Dec)	Symbolic Name	Description
$5Ø $51	(8Ø) (81)	LINNUM (low) (high)	These are the locations, used by GETADR, that contain the result of the conversion of the FAC to a 2-byte integer.
$71 $72	(113) (114)	FRESPC (low) (high)	This is a temporary pointer, used by GETSPACE and MOVESTR, that contains the address of the location to which a string is to be moved.
$83 $84	(131) (132)	VARPNT (low) (high)	This is a temporary pointer, used by PTRGET, that contains the location of the data bytes for the last variable that was found using PTRGET.
$9B $9C	(155) (156)	LOWTR (low) (high)	A pointer used by FNDLIN and GETARYPT.
$A1	(161)	FACLO	This is a byte in the FAC that contains the result of CONINT and GETBYT.
$B7 $B8	(183) (184)	TXTPTR (low) (high)	This is a pointer to the position within the program that is currently being acted on by the interpreter. It is part of the CHARGET subroutine.
$D8	(216)	ERRFLAG	This is the ONERR GOTO flag. If it's >=$8Ø, then ONERR is active.

USING APPLESOFT'S BUILT-IN SUBROUTINES

Applesoft's built-in subroutines can be used in conjunction with your own assembly-language programs to greatly simplify those programs and to allow you to dispense with having to rewrite programs that have already been written. In most cases, it is not even necessary to understand exactly how the Applesoft subroutine operates as long as you understand what the entry conditions are and what effect the subroutine has on the system.

There are literally hundreds of useful subroutines within the Applesoft interpreter that can be usefully accessed, but only a few of them have been listed in Table 4-8. Three of the more important classes of subroutines will be discussed in detail here: those used to locate variables, those used to evaluate formulas, and those used to convert numbers between different formats.

Locating Variables

We have already seen how Applesoft keeps track of its variables and how it stores them. Using that information, it would be a fairly simple chore to write a program to locate and retrieve any particular one. All you would have to do would be to check the name bytes of each variable in the variable table that begins at the start of simple variable space until a match was found. Applesoft already contains a program to do this, however, so why bother? This program is called PTRGET and begins at $DFE3.

To find the location of a variable, all you must do is adjust TXTPTR ($B8/$B9) so that it points to the first character in the variable name, and then execute a JSR PTRGET instruction. When the subroutine ends, VARPNT ($83/$84) will contain the address of the beginning of the variable's data field.

PTRGET can be used to simplify the passing of Applesoft variables to and from an assembly-language program. Variables are usually passed by tacking their names, separated by commas, on to a CALL or & command. For example, to pass two variables, say F% and L%, to a program starting at $300, you could use the following command:

```
CALL 768,F%,L%
```

Immediately after the CALL 768 command is executed, TXTPTR is pointing to the location occupied by the comma separator. Before we can use PTRGET, TXTPTR must be advanced by one position. This is done at the beginning of the subroutine being called by using a subroutine called CHKCOM ($DEBE) that ensures that the current character is indeed a comma, and then increments TXTPTR. Once this has been done, everything is ready for a call to PTRGET. After it has been called, VARPNT ($83/$84) can be examined to determine where the data for that variable is located. Since the storage format of the data is known, it is a simple matter to read and interpret it. In summary then, the method to be used to locate a variable is as follows:

```
JSR CHKCOM      ;Skip over the "," separator
JSR PTRGET      ;Find the variable and put ptr in VARPNT
LDY #0
LDA (VARPNT),Y ;Get first byte of variable's data
.
.
INY
LDA (VARPNT),Y ;Get second byte of variable's data
.
.
```

After PTRGET has been called, TXTPTR points to the byte after the last character of the variable's name. This means that you would perform another

```
JSR CHKCOM
JSR PTRGET
```

sequence to retrieve the next variable specified after the CALL statement.

Let's look at a complete example to see how to use these subroutines. Table 4-10 shows a program called UPPER that is designed to convert any lower-case characters in a string variable to their corresponding upper-case characters. Once the program has been installed, it can be called from Applesoft as follows:

```
CALL 768,A$
```

where A$ is the string variable to be modified.

Notice how the program works. The first step is to skip over the comma by calling CHKCOM. After that has been done, TXTPTR

Table 4-10. UPPER. A program to convert lower-case strings to upper-case.

```
Page #01

: A S M
                *****************************
                *           UPPER           *
                *                           *
                * CALL 768,A$               *
                * Convert A$ to upper case  *
                *****************************

                STRING    EQU   $6            ;Pointer to string elements
                VARPNT    EQU   $83           ;Pointer to variable's data
                CHKCOM    EQU   $DEBE         ;Check for comma and move on
                PTRGET    EQU   $DFE3         ;Find address of variable

                          ORG   $300

0300: 20 BE DE            JSR   CHKCOM        ;Skip over comma separator
0303: 20 E3 DF            JSR   PTRGET        ;Locate string variable
0306: A0 00               LDY   #0
0308: B1 83               LDA   (VARPNT),Y    ;Get length of string
030A: AA                  TAX                 ; and put it in X
030B: C8                  INY
030C: B1 83               LDA   (VARPNT),Y    ;Get string pointer (low)
```

```
030E: 85 06                 STA   STRING
0310: C8                    INY
0311: B1 83                 LDA   (VARPNT),Y   ;Get string pointer (high)
0313: 85 07                 STA   STRING+1

0315: 8A                    TXA
0316: A8                    TAY                ;Put length in Y
0317: C0 00                 CPY   #0           ;Null string?
0319: F0 16                 BEQ   ALLDONE      ;Yes, so done
031B: 88          SCAN      DEY                ;Move to previous element
031C: C0 FF                 CPY   #$FF         ;At the end?
031E: F0 11                 BEQ   ALLDONE
0320: B1 06                 LDA   (STRING),Y   ;Get string element
0322: C9 61                 CMP   #'a          ;Is it less than "a"?
0324: 90 F5                 BCC   SCAN         ;Yes, so branch
0326: C9 7B                 CMP   #'z+1        ;Is it greater than "z"?
0328: B0 F1                 BCS   SCAN         ;Yes, so branch
032A: 29 DF                 AND   #$DF         ;Convert to u.c.
032C: 91 06                 STA   (STRING),Y   ; and put it into string.
032E: 4C 1B 03              JMP   SCAN
0331: 60          ALLDONE   RTS

--End assembly--

50 bytes
```

will be pointing to the "A" in A$ and PTRGET can be called to locate the three data bytes used to describe the string (one byte for the length and two bytes representing its location). The pointer to the first of these three bytes is automatically stored in VARPNT ($83/$84), so that the three bytes can be examined by using indirect indexed instructions as follows:

```
LDA (VARPNT),Y
```

where Y=Ø,1,2. After the length and pointer have been determined, it is a simple task to scan through the bytes in the string to see whether their ASCII codes are between those for "a" and "z" and, if they are, to convert them to upper-case by performing an AND #$DF operation. (This essentially subtracts 32 from the lower-case ASCII code, thus converting it to the corresponding upper-case ASCII code.) If you print A$ after calling UPPER, you will see that all of its lower-case characters have, indeed, been converted to upper-case.

Evaluating Formulas

Not surprisingly, there are also several built-in Applesoft subroutines that can be used to evaluate mathematical formulas. Again, you could write such programs yourself, but they would need to be exceedingly complex and would be difficult to develop.

The main Applesoft subroutine for evaluating a mathematical formula is called FRMNUM and is located at $DD67. To use it, you must first ensure that TXTPTR is, as usual, pointing to the location of the first character in the formula. Once this has been done, FRMNUM can be called; after this subroutine has finished executing, the result of the calculation will be stored in the FAC. You can then use other built-in subroutines to massage this number as you see fit, for example, to print it out or to convert it to an integer.

Let's look at an example of the use of FRMNUM. The program in Table 4-11, called FORMULA, evaluates any mathematical formula that is passed to it and displays the result. To CALL it from Applesoft, you must enter the command

```
CALL 768,aexpr
```

where "aexpr" represents the Applesoft formula that is to be evaluated.

The first part of the program should look familiar. It is the "standard" JSR CHKCOM instruction that skips over the comma after the CALL statement. Once this has been performed, the formula can be evaluated by a JSR FRMNUM and the result will be placed in the primary FAC. To see the result it is simply necessary to perform a JSR PRINTFAC ($ED2E).

Converting Numbers

Number conversion plays an important role in the Applesoft interpreter. Numbers are normally handled internally in a binary format, but whenever they are to be displayed they must be converted to more recognizable decimal numbers. Conversely, numbers that are inputted, say from the keyboard by a user, are normally inputted in decimal form and must be converted to binary form before they can be processed.

In addition to the above types of conversions, it is often necessary to convert an integer number to a floating-point number and vice versa. This is handled by the Applesoft GIVAYF subroutine and by the CONINT or GETADR subroutines, respectively. The latter two subroutines are especially useful because quite often only integer quantities are being manipulated and, as we have seen, whenever a formula is evaluated by performing a JSR FRMNUM, the result is placed in the FAC, which is difficult to interpret. By using CONINT or GETADR, the FAC can be quickly converted to an easy-to-handle one- or two-byte integer format.

The program in Table 4-12, CONVERT, shows how the CONINT subroutine can be used to convert the contents of the FAC to a one-byte integer in the range Ø . . . 255. As usual, CONVERT is designed to be called from Applesoft, using the command

```
CALL 768,aexpr
```

where "aexpr" represents a mathematical formula that will evaluate into an integer within the Ø . . . 255 range.

The first step is to skip over the comma with a JSR CHKCOM. Then, the formula is evaluated and placed in the primary FAC with a JSR FRMNUM. At this stage, we would like to convert the FAC into an easier format to handle: a one-byte number. This is done by executing a JSR CONINT; after CONINT has been executed, the one-byte number will be found in the X register. CONVERT then stores the value in the X register at location $6 where it can be read with an Applesoft PEEK (6) command.

If the integer result is going to be larger than 255, then GETADR must be used instead of CONINT. After a JSR GETADR, the value of the integer will be contained in LINNUM ($5Ø/$51), so that the decimal result will be PEEK(8Ø) + 256*PEEK(81).

Table 4-11. FORMULA. A program to add two integers together.

```
Page #01

: A S M
                   ******************************
                   *           FORMULA          *
                   *                            *
                   *      CALL 768,[formula]    *
                   * This program evaluates     *
                   * and displays an Applesoft  *
                   * mathematical formula.      *
                   ******************************
                   FRMNUM   EQU  $DD67        ;Evaluate formula
                   CHKCOM   EQU  $DEBE        ;Check for comma and move on
                   PRINTFAC EQU  $ED2E        ;Display the result
                            ORG  $300
0300: 20 BE DE              JSR  CHKCOM       ;Skip over comma separator
```

```
                ********************************
                * Evaluate the fomula and put *
                * it in the FAC.              *
                ********************************
0303: 20 67 DD          JSR FRMNUM

                *****************************
                * Convert the number in FAC *
                * to decimal and display it.*
                *****************************
0306: 20 2E ED          JSR PRINTFAC

0309: 60                RTS


--End assembly--

10 bytes

Errors: 0
```

Table 4-12. CONVERT. A program to evaluate a formula.

```
Page #01

: A S M
                  **********************
                  *       CONVERT      *
                  *                    *
                  * CALL 768,[formula] *
                  **********************

                  RESULT   EQU   $6         ;Store the answer here

                  CHKCOM   EQU   $DEBE      ;Check for comma and move on
                  FRMNUM   EQU   $DD67      ;Evaluate a formula
                  CONINT   EQU   $E6FB      ;Convert FAC to integer

                           ORG   $300

0300: 20 BE DE                     JSR   CHKCOM     ;Skip over comma
0303: 20 67 DD                     JSR   FRMNUM     ;Evaluate the formula
0306: 20 FB E6                     JSR   CONINT     ;Put one-byte answer in X

0309: 86 06                        STX   RESULT     ;Store the answer
030B: 60                           RTS


--End assembly--

12 bytes

Errors: 0
```

FURTHER READING FOR CHAPTER 4

Standard reference works . . .

Applesoft BASIC Programmer's Reference Manual, Volumes 1 and 2, Apple Computer, Inc., 1982.

All About Applesoft, Call -A.P.P.L.E., 1981. A useful source of internal information about Applesoft.

On Applesoft entry points . . .

J. Crossley, "Applesoft Internal Entry Points", *Apple Orchard,* March/April (198Ø). The seminal work on Applesoft entry points. Unfortunately, it contains numerous typographical errors and incorrect addresses — these corrections have been made in a reprint of the article which appears in "All About Applesoft," above.

R.M. Mottola, "Applesoft Floating Point Routines," *Micro,* August 198Ø, p. 53. A detailed look at Applesoft's built-in subroutines that support real-number mathematics.

C. Bongers, "In the Heart of Applesoft," *Micro,* February 1981, p. 31. A comprehensive look at the internals of the Applesoft interpreter.

"Using Applesoft ROMs from Assembly Language," *Apple Assembly Line,* November 1981, pp. 2-13. More on accessing Applesoft's built-in subroutines.

C. Bongers, "Applesoft's CHARGET Routine," *Call -A.P.P.L.E.,* March 1982, p. 21. Suggestions for improvements to CHARGET.

B. Sander-Cederlof, "All About PTRGET & GETARYPT," *Apple Assembly Line,* March 1983, pp. 2-9. A look at two useful entry points to Applesoft.

On Applesoft data storage . . .

V. Golding, "Applesoft From Bottom to Top," *Call -A.P.P.L.E.,* March 1979, p.3. A look at the internal structure of Applesoft.

G.A. Lyle, "Float, Float, Float Your Point (F.P. Representation)," *Apple Orchard,* Winter 198Ø, pp. 37-39. A description of how Applesoft stores real variables.

E.E. Goez, "Real Variable Study," *Call -A.P.P.L.E.,* January 1981, pp. 8-23. A detailed look at how Applesoft deals with real variables.

C.K. Mesztenyi, "Applesoft Internal Structure," *Call -A.P.P.L.E.,* January 1982, p.9

A. Moss, "Playing With Program Pointers," *Nibble,* Vol. 4, No. 3 (1983), pp. 69-81. A look at the various Applesoft pointers.

On linking to assembler language . . .

B. Sander-Cederlof, "Using USR for a WEEK," *Apple Assembly Line,* October 1982, p. 3Ø. A program is presented which uses USR to calculate the value of a two-byte pointer.

D. Lingwood, "The Return of the Mysterious Mr. Ampersand," *Call -A.P.P.L.E.,* May 198Ø, p.26. Examples of uses for the & command.

Source Code for the Applesoft interpreter . . .

Available from:

(1) Roger Wagner Publishing, P.O. Box 582, Santee, CA 92Ø71 (comes with and requires Merlin Assembler).

(2) S-C Software Corporation, P.O. Box 28Ø3ØØ, Dallas, TX 75228 (requires S-C Macro Assembler)

5

Disk Operating System

The first peripheral device that users of the //e add to their systems is invariably a disk drive. There are two main reasons for this. First, the alternative low-cost mass storage device, a cassette recorder, is extremely awkward to use since it is slow, unreliable, and does not allow for random access of information. Second, virtually all commercially available software for the //e is available on diskette only.

Information is passed to and from a diskette by using special disk operating system (DOS) commands that are available for use by an Applesoft program after a DOS diskette is first started up (or "booted"). The purpose of this chapter is not to teach you how to use these commands but rather to explain the methods used by DOS to organize information on diskettes and to provide you with an insight into the internal operation of DOS. The two operating systems used by Applesoft programs will be covered: DOS 3.3 and ProDOS.

Before a diskette can be used by either DOS 3.3 or ProDOS it must be initialized. This is done by using the DOS 3.3 INIT command or a command in the ProDOS FILER program. The initialization process formats the diskette into 35 "tracks" on the diskette (numbered from Ø to 34), each of which can hold 4096 bytes of information. These tracks are arranged in concentric rings around the central hub of the disk, with track Ø being located at the outside edge and track 34 at the inside edge.

Each of the 35 tracks that are formatted on a diskette are subdivided into sixteen smaller units called "sectors." The sectors that make up a track are numbered from Ø to 15 and each can hold exactly 256 bytes of information. If you do the mathematics, you will quickly determine that a diskette can hold 56Ø sectors (14ØK) of information.

Note that although DOS 3.3 and ProDOS both subdivide each track into 256-byte sectors, only DOS 3.3 uses the sector as the basic unit of file storage. That is, the smallest unit of disk space that can be allocated to a file is one sector. ProDOS uses the "block" as the basic unit of file storage; each block is made up of two sectors.

We are now ready to take a look at where DOS 3.3 and ProDOS are loaded into memory and how they organize and store information on a formatted diskette. We will begin with a description of DOS 3.3 and then move on to a description of ProDOS.

THE INTERNAL STRUCTURE OF DOS 3.3

DOS 3.3 Memory Map

DOS 3.3 occupies the upper part of built-in internal RAM memory from locations $9DØØ to $BFFF. However, it also reserves a space just below this for diskette file work areas, called "file buffers." When DOS 3.3 is first activated, three such file buffers are reserved, and they occupy the area from $96ØØ to $9CFF in memory.

To ensure that an Applesoft program does not overwrite the areas used by DOS 3.3, DOS 3.3 ensures that Applesoft's HIMEM pointer at $73/$74 (see Chapter 4) is set equal to the lowest address reserved for the file buffers (usually $96ØØ). Thus, the data for Applesoft string variables will be stored at locations below this memory location and DOS 3.3 and its file buffer areas will be protected.

Note, however, that the starting location of the file buffer area reserved by DOS 3.3 can be changed by using the MAXFILES command. The syntax associated with the MAXFILES command is

```
MAXFILES n
```

where "n" represents an integer from 1 to 16 that is equal to the number of DOS 3.3 files permitted to be open at the same time. Each of these files has associated with it a 595-byte buffer that is used for input/output operations. The first of these buffers begins at location $9AA6 and successive buffers begin every 595 bytes lower in memory than the previous one. Since the default setting for MAXFILES is 3, the lowest file buffer begins at $96ØØ.

Whenever MAXFILES is changed, not only does the start of the file buffer area change, but so also does the Applesoft HIMEM location (in fact, it is set equal to the start of the file buffer area). Because of this, MAXFILES should always be changed at the very beginning of an Applesoft program, before any string variables are defined.

After MAXFILES has been set to the desired value, the Applesoft HIMEM command can be used to set the highest memory location that Applesoft strings can use (this must be lower in memory than the start of the lowest DOS 3.3 file buffer). By moving HIMEM lower in memory, a space can be freed up between HIMEM and the beginning of the DOS 3.3 file buffers that can be used as a safe place to store machine-language programs.

DOS 3.3 Page 3 Vectors

DOS 3.3 also reserves for its own use a block of memory in page 3 of memory beginning at location \$3DØ and ending at location \$3EE. This area contains several subroutines that can be called to transfer control to commonly used DOS 3.3 subroutines; for this reason, these subroutines (most of which are simply 65Ø2 JMP instructions) are called vectors. The reason for placing these vectors at fixed locations in page 3 is to allow a program to automatically maintain compatibility with future versions of DOS 3.3. If a program accesses DOS 3.3 only through these vectors, then it need not be modified even if the absolute locations within DOS 3.3 to which these vectors point are changed.

The memory map of the DOS 3.3 page 3 vector area is set out in Table 5-1.

DOS 3.3 also initializes most of the system vectors that appear in page 3 from \$3FØ . . . \$3FF. This includes the interrupt vectors for BRK, Reset, IRQ, and NMI (see Chapter 2), as well as the vector for the system monitor's <CTRL-Y> USER command (see Chapter 3). Descriptions of the vector addresses set up by DOS 3.3 are given in Table 5-2.

Volume Table of Contents (VTOC)

One of the 56Ø sectors on a DOS 3.3-formatted diskette is reserved for use as the volume table of contents (VTOC). The VTOC is used to hold the following important information:

- The location of the start of the diskette's catalog (see next section)
- Numeric constants that relate to the characteristics of the diskette
- A bit map that is used to indicate which sectors on the diskette are in use.

Table 5-1. DOS 3.3 page 3 vectors.

Address	*Description of Vector*
$3DØ–$3D2	A JMP instruction to the DOS 3.3 warm-start entry point. A call to this vector will reconnect DOS without destroying the Applesoft program in memory. Use the "3DØG" command to move from the system monitor to Applesoft.
$3D3–$3D5	A JMP instruction to the DOS 3.3 cold-start entry point. A call to this vector will initialize DOS 3.3 to the state it was in when it was first loaded and will clear the Applesoft program in memory.
$3D6–$3D8	A JMP instruction to the DOS 3.3 file manager. See Note 1.
$3D9–$3DB	A JMP instruction to the DOS 3.3 RWTS subroutine. See Note 2.
$3DC–$3E2	A subroutine that loads the A register with the high-order address and the Y register with the low-order address of the DOS 3.3 file manager parameter list. See Note 1.
$3E3–$3E9	A subroutine that loads the A register with the high-order address and the Y register with the low-order address of the DOS 3.3 RWTS parameter list (called IOB). See Note 2.
$3EA–$3EC	A JMP instruction to the DOS 3.3 subroutine that causes it to accept new I/O links and reconnect itself. This subroutine must be called to properly install new I/O subroutines without affecting DOS 3.3 (see Chapters 6 and 7).

Note 1. The DOS 3.3 file manager is the intermediary between the DOS 3.3 commands and the fundamental disk I/O subroutine (RWTS). It is responsible for ensuring that the parameters for a DOS 3.3 command have been correctly specified and that the correct disk operations that must be executed for that command are performed.

Note 2. The RWTS subroutine is discussed in detail later in this chapter.

The VTOC is located at track 17, sector Ø on the diskette. Table 5-3 sets out the meaning of each of the 256 bytes in the VTOC sector.

The track bit map that begins at location $38 in the VTOC sector and ends at location $C3 represents the most important part of the VTOC. It is referred to by any DOS 3.3 command that writes information to a diskette so that the command can determine which sectors on the disk are free and which are already in use by a file.

Table 5-2. Initialization of page 3 system vectors by DOS 3.3.

Vector Name	*Address*	*Contents*	*Description*
BRK	$3FØ–$3F1	$FA59	Address of a subroutine to display the 65Ø2 registers and enter the system monitor.
RESET	$3F2–$3F3	$9DBF	Address of the DOS 3.3 reset-handling subroutine (reconnects DOS 3.3).
USER	$3F8–$3FA	"JMP $FF65"	Jump to the system monitor's warm-start entry point.
NMI	$3FB–$3FD	"JMP $FF65"	Jump to the system monitor's warm-start entry point.
IRQ	$3FE–$3FF	$FF65	Address of the system monitor's warm-start entry point.

Note: The addresses stored at each vector location are stored with the low-order byte first.

You will see from Table 5-3 that four bytes in the track bit map are allocated to represent the usage of each track on the diskette; however, it turns out that only the first two are used (the other two bytes are always ØØ). As shown in Figure 5-1, each of the 16 bits in these first two bytes corresponds to one of the 16 sectors that make up the track. Track 15 corresponds to bit 7 of the first byte in the pair, track 14 corresponds to bit 6, track 13 corresponds to bit 5, and so on. Whenever the bit corresponding to a particular sector is Ø, then that sector is in use. Conversely, if that bit is 1, then that sector is free.

Note that when a diskette is first initialized, all of tracks Ø, 1, 2, and 17 are marked "in use" by DOS 3.3. This is because tracks Ø, 1, and part of 2, are used for storage of DOS 3.3 itself and track 17 is used for storage of catalog and VTOC information. When a file is saved to diskette, the sectors it occupies will be marked in use as well. When a file is deleted from the diskette, DOS 3.3 determines which sectors that file was using and changes the zeros in the track bit map corresponding to those sectors to ones.

Table 5-3. Map of the DOS 3.3 Volume Table of Contents (VTOC) sector.

Byte number in VTOC	*Description (Usual values in parentheses)*
$ØØ	<Not used>
$Ø1	Track number of first catalog sector (17)
$Ø2	Sector number of first catalog sector (15)
$Ø3	DOS version number (3 for DOS 3.3)
$Ø4–$Ø5	<Not used>
$Ø6	Volume number of diskette (1 . . . 254)
$Ø7–$26	<Not used>
$27	Maximum number of track/sector pairs in each sector of a file's track/sector list (122)
$28–$2F	<Not used>
$3Ø–$31	Used by DOS 3.3 when allocating sectors
$32–$33	<Not used>
$34	Number of tracks per diskette (35)
$35	Number of sectors per track minus 1 (15)
$36	Number of bytes/sector low (Ø)
$37	Number of bytes/sector high (1)
$38–$3B	Track bit map for track #Ø
$3C–$3F	Track bit map for track #1
$4Ø–$43	Track bit map for track #2
$44–$47	Track bit map for track #3
"	"
"	"
"	"
$BC–$BF	Track bit map for track #33
$CØ–$C3	Track bit map for track #34
$C4–$FF	<Not used>

All manipulations of the track bit map are handled automatically whenever a DOS 3.3 command is entered and it is usually not necessary to deal with it directly. There is one particularly useful utility program, however, that necessitates analyzing the track bit map directly: a program that calculates the free space remaining

Bits of first byte →	7	6	5	4	3	2	1	Ø
Sector number →	$ØF	$ØE	$ØD	$ØC	$ØB	$ØA	$Ø9	$Ø8
Bits of second byte →	7	6	5	4	3	2	1	Ø
Sector number →	$Ø7	$Ø6	$Ø5	$Ø4	$Ø3	$Ø2	$Ø1	$ØØ

Figure 5-1. Correlation of track bit map byte pairs to sectors.

on a diskette. Such a program works by scanning through all the track bit map bytes and counting the number of "1" bits that are detected. A program that will do this will be presented later in this chapter, when we discuss how to read into memory individual sectors of the diskette using the RWTS subroutine.

Diskette Catalog

Up to 1Ø5 files of information can be stored on a diskette. DOS 3.3 keeps track of these files by asking you to assign names to each of them when they are created (the names of all files on the diskette are displayed whenever the CATALOG command is entered). DOS 3.3 reserves 15 sectors in track 17 of the diskette (sectors 15 down to 1) to store these file names; these sectors comprise the diskette catalog. The diskette catalog also holds information relating to the size and type of each file, as well as the locations of the sectors on the disk that contains the list of sectors used to hold the data for each file.

The first catalog sector is actually found at the location stored in byte 1 (track number) and byte 2 (sector number) of the VTOC; the values stored here are 17 and 15, respectively. This first catalog sector at track 17/sector 15 is the first in a linked list of sectors; the next link in the chain is always contained in byte 1 (which contains the track number) and byte 2 (which contains the sector number) of a catalog sector. The last catalog sector will contain zeros in byte positions 1 and 2. If DOS 3.3 has not been modified, the catalog sectors used will be sectors 15 through 1 of track 17.

The layout of a typical catalog sector is shown in Table 5-4. As can be seen, each catalog sector reserves 35 bytes of information for each of seven different files. Since 15 different catalog sectors are used by DOS 3.3, a total of 105 different files can be stored on the diskette.

Each 35-byte catalog entry in a catalog sector contains information relating to the name of a file, its size and type, and the location of its track/sector list (TSL). The structure of the TSL will be discussed in the next section. The meanings of each of the bytes in a catalog entry are set out in Table 5-5.

It may be that a particular catalog entry refers to a file that has been deleted. If this is the case, then byte $ØØ of the catalog entry will be set to $FF and the original value stored there (which represents a track number) will be stored at byte $2Ø.

If a file has been accidentally deleted from a diskette, it is possible to resurrect it *if no other file has been saved to disk since the*

Table 5-4. Map of a DOS 3.3 catalog sector.

Byte number in Catalog Sector	*Description*
$ØØ	<Not used>
$Ø1	track number of next catalog sector
$Ø2	sector number of next catalog sector
$Ø3–$ØA	<Not used>
$ØB–$2D	Catalog entry for file #1
$2E–$5Ø	Catalog entry for file #2
$51–$73	Catalog entry for file #3
$74–$96	Catalog entry for file #4
$97–$B9	Catalog entry for file #5
$BA–$DC	Catalog entry for file #6
$DD–$FF	Catalog entry for file #7

Note: Bytes 1 and 2 are both Ø for the last catalog sector.

deletion. This is done by restoring byte $ØØ in the file's catalog entry to its original value (which is stored in byte $2Ø) and then changing byte $2Ø to an ASCII blank (code $AØ). This can be done using the READ SECTOR program presented later in this chapter. This program allows you to easily modify the contents of any sector on a diskette.

After the modified catalog entry has been saved to the diskette, the deleted program will once again appear in a CATALOG listing. One more important step must be performed, however: the file must be immediately copied to another diskette using the FID program on the DOS 3.3 system master diskette and then deleted from the original diskette once again. It is not enough simply to

Table 5-5. Description of catalog entry.

Relative Byte Number	*Description*
$ØØ	Track number of first TSL sector
$Ø1	Sector number of first TSL sector
$Ø2	File type code (see Table 5-6)
$Ø3–$2Ø	File name (in ASCII with bit 7 = 1)
$21	Number of sectors occupied by file (low)
$22	Number of sectors occupied by file (high)

restore the catalog entry, because the track bit map will not mark as "in use" those sectors used by the accidentally deleted file. Thus, the file could be overwritten the next time any information is saved to the diskette.

File Types

The file type code (relative byte $Ø2 of a catalog entry) can be one of sixteen values, depending on the file type and whether the file is locked or not (a locked file cannot be renamed, deleted, or written to). A code letter for each file type is displayed to the immediate left of the file name whenever a diskette is catalogued and is preceded by an asterisk if the file is locked. Table 5-6 sets out the numeric file type codes and code letters for each permitted DOS 3.3 file type.

Track/Sector List (TSL)

The first two bytes of a catalog entry point to an important sector that is associated with each file. This is the track/sector list (TSL) sector and it contains an ordered list of all those sectors on the diskette that contain the file's data. Without this list, it would be impossible to determine where the contents of a file were stored on the diskette.

The layout of a TSL sector is shown in Table 5-7. Each such sector contains up to 122 track/sector pairs that indicate where on the diskette the file data is located. If more track/sector pairs are used, then another TSL sector is allocated; its location is pointed

Table 5-6. DOS 3.3 file type codes.

File Type	*Code Letter*	*File Type Code Unlocked*	*Locked*
Text	T	$ØØ	$8Ø
Integer BASIC program	I	$Ø1	$81
Applesoft program	A	$Ø2	$82
Binary	B	$Ø4	$84
[Reserved but undefined]	S	$Ø8	$88
Relocatable EDASM	R	$1Ø	$9Ø
[Reserved but undefined]	A	$2Ø	$AØ
[Reserved but undefined]	B	$4Ø	$CØ

Note: EDASM files are created by the Apple 65Ø2 Editor/Assembler.

Table 5-7. Map of a DOS 3.3 Track/Sector List (TSL) sector.

Byte Number	*Description*
$ØØ	<Not used>
$Ø1	Track number of next TSL sector
$Ø2	Sector number of next TSL sector
$Ø3–$Ø4	<Not used>
$Ø5–$Ø6	Number of T/S pairs defined in previous TSL sectors (low byte first)
$Ø7–$ØB	<Not used>
$ØC	Track number of 1st data sector
$ØD	Sector number of 1st data sector
$ØE	Track number of 2nd data sector
$ØF	Sector number of 2nd data sector
"	"
"	"
"	"
$FE	Track number of 122nd data sector
$FF	Sector number of 122nd data sector

to by bytes 1 and 2 in the preceding TSL sector. If these bytes are zero, then no further TSL sectors have been allocated.

If a particular track/sector pair in a TSL is Ø/Ø, then that data sector is undefined. With one exception, the Ø/Ø pair also indicates an end-of-file condition, that is, there are no more track/sector pairs in the TSL that have been allocated to the file.

The only exception arises when random-access textfiles are being used. When these types of files are created, only those track/sector pairs within the TSL that correspond to random-access records that have actually been used will contain track/sector information. A Ø/Ø will be stored at the other TSL locations. Thus, if a high record number is used before any lower ones, several Ø/Ø pairs will appear in the TSL before the one corresponding to the record that was used.

Storing File Data

Generally speaking, the contents of each sector referred to in the TSL for a particular file contains the data that makes up that file: the tokenized program for an Applesoft or Integer BASIC file, the binary data for a binary file, and the ASCII codes (with the high bits set to 1) for the characters in a text file.

In the case of an Applesoft or Integer BASIC file, however, the first two bytes in the first data sector allocated to it are not program tokens but rather the length of the stored program (low-order byte first). The DOS 3.3 LOAD and RUN commands use this information to determine how many bytes in the file are to be transferred into memory.

In the case of a binary file, the first four bytes in the first data sector allocated to it are not part of the binary image that was saved to diskette. The first two bytes represent the default loading address for that image (low-order byte first) and the next two bytes represent the length of that image (low-order byte first). The DOS 3.3 BLOAD and BRUN commands require this information to properly load the image into memory.

Note that every byte in a sequential text file is significant since no overhead bytes are stored with it. The end of the file is indicated by a \$ØØ byte and when this byte is encountered when a READ operation is being performed, no further information is read from the file. For random-access textfiles, the unused portion of each record contains \$ØØ bytes, and there is no end-of-file indicator.

RWTS—Accessing the Diskette Directly

So far, we have only described how information is organized on the diskette and not how DOS 3.3 physically stores it there. It turns out that all diskette I/O operations performed by DOS 3.3 are executed by a single subroutine called RWTS (Read or Write a Track and Sector) that can be invoked by calling the RWTS page 3 vector at location \$3D9 (see Table 5-1). It is this subroutine that is responsible for loading a 256-byte sector into a memory area (called an I/O buffer) and also for storing the contents of an I/O buffer to any particular sector on the diskette.

RWTS expects two data blocks to be set up before control is passed to it. These blocks are called the I/O block (IOB) and the device control table (DCT). The information in these data blocks provides all the information RWTS requires in order to perform its chores: the disk drive slot and drive number, the type of operation to perform, the location of the I/O buffer, and so on. The meanings of each of the bytes in these blocks is shown in Table 5-8.

Just before the RWTS subroutine is called, the accumulator must contain the high-order address of the IOB and the Y register must contain the low-order address. You can set up your own IOB and DCT data blocks or use the ones already set up by DOS 3.3. If

Table 5-8. Map of DOS 3.3 RWTS data blocks—IOB and DCT.

(a) I/O Block (IOB)

Byte Number	Description
$ØØ	Type code of IOB (must be $Ø1)
$Ø1	Slot number × 16 (e.g., $6Ø for slot 6)
$Ø2	Disk drive number ($Ø1 or $Ø2)
$Ø3	Expected volume number ($ØØ will match anything)
$Ø4	Track number (Ø–34)
$Ø5	Sector number (Ø–15)
$Ø6	Address of DCT (low order)
$Ø7	Address of DCT (high order)
$Ø8	Address of data buffer (low order)
$Ø9	Address of data buffer (high order)
$ØA	<Not used>
$ØB	<Not used>
$ØC	Command codes: $ØØ (turn on drive/position head) $Ø1 (read sector into data buffer) $Ø2 (write to sector from data buffer) $Ø4 (initialize the diskette)
$ØD	Error code that is returned: $ØØ (no error) $1Ø (write-protected) $2Ø (wrong volume number) $3Ø (formatting error) $4Ø (disk I/O error)
$ØE	Actual volume number found on diskette
$ØF	Disk slot times 16 last accessed
$1Ø	Drive number last accessed ($Ø1 or $Ø2)

(b) Device Characteristics Table (DCT)

Byte Number	Meaning
$ØØ	Device type (must be $ØØ)
$Ø1	Phases per track (must be $Ø1)
$Ø2–$Ø3	Motor on-time count, low-order byte first (must be $EFD8)

DOS's IOB and DCT blocks are to be used, the accumulator and Y register can be properly set up by a call to the page 3 vector at $3E3.

If you are going to make use of DOS 3.3's own IOB, then all the necessary parameters must be stored in it before calling RWTS.

This can be done by calling $3E3 to get the address of the IOB in Y (low) and A (high), storing this address in two consecutive zero-page locations, and then using the 65Ø2's indirect indexed addressing mode to access the IOB. For example, to locate the IOB and place the value $6Ø (slot 6 times 16) at location $Ø1 and the value $Ø1 (drive number) at location $Ø2, the following program would be used:

```
JSR $3E3          ;Get address of IOB in A/Y
STY $6            ;Put address in zero page
STA $7
LDY #1            ;Set index for slot*16
LDA #$60
STA ($6),Y        ;Store slot*16 at position $01
LDY #2            ;Set index for drive #
LDA #$01
STA ($6),Y        ;Store drive # at position $02
```

After all the applicable parameters have been stuffed into the IOB, another call to $3E3 must be made to ensure that A and Y again contain the address of the IOB, and then RWTS can be called by executing a JSR $3D9 command (RWTS requires that A and Y contain the IOB address). If an error occurs while RWTS is performing diskette I/O, the carry flag will be set when the subroutine ends (otherwise it will be clear). If an error occurs, the type of error can be deduced by looking at byte $ØD of the IOB. The error codes stored here are listed in Table 5-8.

The program in Table 5-9, called DISK FREE SPACE, is a good example of a program that makes use of the RWTS subroutine. DISK FREE SPACE determines the number of free sectors on a diskette by using RWTS to load the VTOC sector into memory (track 17, sector Ø) and then counting the number of "1" bits in the track bit map. Parameters are put into the same IOB that DOS 3.3 uses by setting the Y register equal to that parameter's position within the IOB and then using an indirect-indexed store instruction of the form "STA (IOBPTR),Y", where IOBPTR is the first of two zero page locations containing the address of the IOB.

DISK FREE SPACE stores its two-byte result in zero page locations $8 and $9, low-order byte first. To convert this to a decimal number from Applesoft, it is necessary to calculate the quantity PEEK(8)+256*PEEK(9).

Table 5-9. DISK FREE SPACE. A program to calculate the number of free sectors on a DOS 3.3 diskette.

```
Page #01

: A S M
                  ********************
                  * DISK FREE SPACE *
                  ********************

                  BUFFPTR   EQU  $0          ;Pointer to data buffer
                  IOBPTR    EQU  $6          ;Pointer to location of IOB
                  FREE      EQU  $8          ;Number of free sectors
                  BUFFER    EQU  $200        ;Sector will be loaded here

                  STATUS    EQU  $48         ;Monitor status location
                  RWTS      EQU  $3D9        ;RWTS entry point
                  GETIOB    EQU  $3E3        ;Get DOS 3.3's IOB location in A/Y

                            ORG  $300

0300: 20 E3 03              JSR  GETIOB      ;Find DOS's IOB
0303: 84 06                 STY  IOBPTR      ; and store low address
0305: 85 07                 STA  IOBPTR+1    ; and high address
0307: A0 01                 LDY  #1
0309: A9 60                 LDA  #$60        ;(Slot 6 * 16)
030B: 91 06                 STA  (IOBPTR),Y
030D: C8                    INY
030E: A9 01                 LDA  #1          ;(Drive 1)
0310: 91 06                 STA  (IOBPTR),Y
0312: C8                    INY
0313: A9 00                 LDA  #0          ;(Any volume number will do)
0315: 91 06                 STA  (IOBPTR),Y
0317: C8                    INY
```

```
0318: A9 11                LDA  #17           ;(Track 17)
031A: 91 06                STA  (IOBPTR),Y
031C: C8                   INY
031D: A9 00                LDA  #0            ;(Sector 0)
031F: 91 06                STA  (IOBPTR),Y
0321: A0 08                LDY  #8
0323: A9 00                LDA  #<BUFFER      ;(Low part of buffer address)
0325: 91 06                STA  (IOBPTR),Y
0327: 85 00                STA  BUFFPTR       ;(Set up 0-page pointer too)
0329: C8                   INY
032A: A9 02                LDA  #>BUFFER      ;(High part of buffer address)
032C: 91 06                STA  (IOBPTR),Y
032E: 85 01                STA  BUFFPTR+1     ;(Set up 0-page pointer too)
0330: A0 0E                LDY  #$0C
0332: A9 01                LDA  #1            ;(READ command code)
0334: 91 06                STA  (IOBPTR),Y

0336: 20 E3 03             JSR  GETIOB        ;Get address of IOB in A/Y
0339: 20 D9 03             JSR  RWTS          ; and call RWTS to get VTOC
033C: A9 00                LDA  #0
033E: 85 48                STA  STATUS        ;(Clear monitor status)

Page #02


         * Determine the number of '1' bits in track bit map:
0340: A9 00                LDA  #0            ;Zero the free-space counter
0342: 85 08                STA  FREE
0344: 85 09                STA  FREE+1

0346: A0 38                LDY  #$38          ;Track bit map starts here
0348: A2 08       COUNT    LDX  #8            ;8 bits to examine
034A: B1 00                LDA  (BUFFPTR),Y   ;Get bit map byte
034C: 2A          COUNT1   ROL                ;Put high bit into carry
034D: 90 06                BCC  NEXTBIT       ;Branch if bit was 0
```

(continued)

Table 5-9. DISK FREE SPACE. A program to calculate the number of free sectors on a DOS 3.3 diskette (continued).

```
034F: E6 08                   INC  FREE         ;Bump 2-byte counter by one
0351: D0 02                   BNE  NEXTBIT
0353: E6 09                   INC  FREE+1
0355: CA            NEXTBIT   DEX               ;Decrement bit count
0356: D0 F4                   BNE  COUNT1       ;Branch if not done
0358: C8                      INY               ;Move on to next byte in bit map
0359: C0 C4                   CPY  #$C4         ;At end of bit map?
035B: D0 EB                   BNE  COUNT        ;No, so keep counting
035D: 60                      RTS

--End assembly--

94 bytes

Errors: 0
```

Table 5-10. READ SECTOR. A program to examine sectors on a DOS 3.3 diskette.

```
]LIST

0  REM "READ SECTOR"
1  REM (FOR DOS 3.3 ONLY)
100  FOR I = 768 to 937: READ X: POKE
     I,X: NEXT
110  DEF FN MD(X) = X - 16 * INT
     (X / 16)
120 TS = 15: REM TRACKS/SECTOR
130 TR = 34: REM NUMBER OF TRACKS

140  IN# 0: PR# 0
150  TEXT : HOME : PRINT TAB( 16
     );: INVERSE : PRINT "READ SE
     CTOR": NORMAL : PRINT TAB(
     11);"(C) 1984 GARY LITTLE"
160  VTAB 10: CALL - 958: PRINT
     "ENTER BASE TRACK NUMBER (0
     -";TR;: INPUT "): ";T$: IF T
     $ = ""THEN 160
170 T = INT ( VAL (T$)): IF T =
     0 AND T$ < > "0" THEN 160
180  IF T < 0 OR T > TR THEN 160
190  VTAB 11: CALL - 938: PRINT
     "ENTER BASE SECTOR NUMBER (0
     -";TS;: INPUT "): ";S$: IF S
     $ = "" THEN 190
200 S = INT ( VAL (S$)): IF S =
     0 AND S$ < > "0" THEN 190
210  IF S < 0 OR S > TS THEN 190
220  POKE 0,T: REM TRACK#
230  POKE 1,S: REM SECTOR#
240  POKE 2,1: REM READ=1 WRITE=2

250  CALL 768
260  IF PEEK (8) < > THEN PRINT
     : INVERSE : PRINT "DISK I/O
     ERROR": NORMAL : PRINT "PRES
     S ANY KEY TO CONTINUE: ";: GET
     A$: PRINT A$: GOTO 150
1000  VTAB 4: CALL - 958: PRINT
     "      CONTENTS OF TRACK ";T;
     ", SECTOR ";S: PRINT : POKE
     34,5: HOME
1010  CALL 823: IF PR = 0 THEN GET
     A$
1020  HOME : CALL 924
1030 PR = 0: PR# 0:B = 0:P = 1
```

(continued)

Table 5-1Ø. READ SECTOR. A program to examine sectors on a DOS 3.3 diskette (continued).

```
1040  HTAB 1: VTAB 23: CALL - 95
     8: PRINT "ENTER COMMAND (B,C
     ,D,E,N,P,Q,W,HELP); ";: GET
     A$: IF A $ = CHR$ (13) THEN
     A$ = " "
1050  PRINT A$
1060  IF A$ = "D" AND P = 0 THEN
     P = 1: HOME : CALL 924: GOTO
     1040
1070  IF A$ = "D" AND P = 1 THEN
     P = 0: HOME : CALL 823: GOTO
     1040
1080  IF A$ = "H" THEN 5000
1090  IF A$ = "Q" THEN 1230
1100  IF A$ = "E" THEN 1240
1110  IF A$ = "P" THEN 1190
1120  IF A$ = "N" THEN 1210
1130  IF A$ = "B" THEN 140
1140  IF A$ = "C" THEN VTAB 23: CALL
      - 958: PRINT TAB( 6);: INVERSE
     : PRINT "TURN ON PRINTER IN
     SLOT #1": NORMAL :PR = 1: PR#
     1: PRINT : GOTO 1000
1150  IF A$ <  > "W" THEN 1180
1160  POKE 0,T: POKE 1,S: POKE 2,
     2: VTAB 23: CALL - 958: PRINT
     "PRESS 'Y' TO VERIFY WRITE:
     ";: GET A$: IF A$ = CHR$ (1
     3) THEN A$ = " "
1170  PRINT A$: IF A$ = "Y" THEN
      CALL 768:RW = 1: VTAB 23: CALL
      - 958: PRINT "WRITE COMPLET
     ED. PRESS ANY KEY: ";: GET A
     $: GOTO 1040
1180  GOTO 5000
1190 S = S - 1: IF S = - 1 THEN
     S = 15:T = T - 1: IF T = -
     1 THEN T = TR
1200  GOTO 220
1210 S = S + 1: IF S = 16 THEN S =
     0:T = T + 1: IF T = TR + 1 THEN
     T = 0
1220  GOTO 220
1230  TEXT : HOME : CALL 1002: END

1240  V = 8:H = 3: VTAB 5: PRINT TAB(
     6);: INVERSE : PRINT "I=UP M
     =DOWN J=LEFT K=RIGHT": NORMAL
```

Table 5-1Ø. READ SECTOR. A program to examine sectors on a DOS 3.3 diskette (continued).

```
1250  HTAB 1: VTAB 23: CALL -95
     8: PRINT TAB( 6);"PRESS ";:
      INVERSE : PRINT "ESC";: NORMAL
     : PRINT " TO LEAVE EDITOR"
1260  REM
1270  GOSUB 1410: GET A$
1280 LC = 16384 + 128 * P + 8 * V
      + H:Y = PEEK (LC): X = ASC
     (A$)
1290  IF A$ = CHR$ (27) THEN HTAB
     1: VTAB 5: CALL - 868: GOTO
     1040
1300  IF A$ = "I" THEN B = 0:V =
     V - 1: IF V = - 1 THEN V =
     15: IF P = 1 THEN P = 0: HOME
     : CALL 823: GOTO 1250
1310  IF A$ = "J" THEN B = 0:H =
     H - 1: IF H = - 1 THEN H =
     7
1320  IF A$ = "K" THEN B = 0:H =
     H + 1: IF H = 8 THEN H = 0
1330  IF A$ = "M" THEN B = 0:V =
     V + 1: IF V = 16 THEN V = 0:
      IF P = 0 THEN P = 1: HOME :
      CALL 924: GOTO 1250
1340  IF B = 0 THEN Y = FN MD(Y)
      + 16 * (X - 48) * (X < = 5
     7) + 16 * (X - 55) * (X > =
     65)
1350  IF B = 1 THEN Y = 16 * INT
     (Y / 16) + (X - 48) * (X < =
     57) + (X - 55) * (X > = 65)

1360 X = ASC (A$): IF (X > = 48
      AND X < = 57) OR (X > = 6
     5 AND X < = 70) THEN PRINT
     A$;: POKE ( PEEK (40) + 256 *
      PEEK (41) + 31 + H),Y: POKE
     LC,Y: IF B = 0 THEN CALL 64
     500:B = 1
1370  IF X = 8 AND B = 1 THEN B =
     0
1380  IF X = 21 AND B = 0 THEN B =
     1
1390  GOTO 1270
1400  CALL - 167
1410  VTAB V + 16: HTAB 3 * H + 7 +
     B: RETURN
```

(continued)

Table 5-10. READ SECTOR. A program to examine sectors on a DOS 3.3 diskette (continued).

```
5000  HOME : PRINT TAB( 10);"SUM
     MARY OF COMMANDS": PRINT TAB(
     10);"==================": PRINT

5010  PRINT "B -- RESET BASE TRAC
     K AND SECTOR"
5020  PRINT "C -- COPY SECTOR CON
     TENTS TO PRINTER"
5025  PRINT "D -- DISPLAY THE OTH
     ER 1/2 SECTOR"
5030  PRINT "E -- EDIT THE CURREN
     T SECTOR"
5040  PRINT "N -- READ THE NEXT S
     ECTOR"
5050  PRINT "P -- READ THE PREVIO
     US SECTOR"
5060  PRINT "Q -- QUIT THE PROGRA
     M"
5080  PRINT "W -- WRITE THE SECTO
     R TO DISK"
5090  PRINT : PRINT "PRESS ANY KE
     Y TO CONTINUE: ";: GET A$: PRINT
     A$: GOTO 1020
6000  DATA 169,0,133,8,32,227,3,1
     33,7,132,6,169,0,160,3,145,6
     ,165,0,200,145,6,200,165,1,1
     45,6,169,0,160
6010  DATA 8,145,6,169,64,200,145
     ,6,165,2,160,12,145,6,32,227
     ,3,32,217,3,144,2,102,8,96,1
     69,0,133,25,169
6020  DATA 64,133,26,162,0,160,0,
     169,0,32,218,253,165,25,32,2
     18,253,169,186,32,237,253,16
     9,160,32,237,253,177,25,32
6030  DATA 218,253,169,160,32,237
     ,253,200,192,8,208,241,169,1
     60,32,237,253,160,0,177,25,1
     40,169,3,164,36,145,40,230,3
     6
6040  DATA 172,169,3,200,192,8,20
     8,237,169,141,32,237,253,232
     ,24,165,25,105,8,133,25,165,
     26,105,0,133,26,224,16,208
6050  DATA 170,169,141,76,237,253
     ,169,128,133,25,169,64,133,2
     6,162,0,76,65,3,255
```

DOS 3.3 READ SECTOR Program

Table 5-1Ø shows an extremely useful program called READ SECTOR that can be used to examine any sector on a DOS 3.3 diskette, to edit the contents of a sector, and to write a modified sector back to the diskette. With this program, you can easily look at real examples of the types of sectors we have been discussing in this chapter, for example, the VTOC, the catalog sectors, the TSL sectors, and the file's data sectors themselves. You should be careful when writing a sector to a diskette, however, as it is easy to accidentally render the diskette unreadable.

When READ SECTOR is first run, you will be asked to enter a base track and sector number. After this information has been provided, the sector corresponding to that location on the diskette will be read into memory and displayed on the screen in a special format. Because of 4Ø-column screen size limitations, only one-half of the sector can be represented at once (you have to press the "D" key to display the other half).

The contents of a sector are displayed in 32 rows, each of which contains an offset address from the beginning of a sector followed by the hexadecimal representations of the eight bytes stored from that location onward in the sector. At the far right of each row are the ASCII representations of each of these eight bytes. Note that only the first 16 or last 16 rows are displayed at any one time.

After both halves of the sector have been displayed, you will be asked to enter one of eight commands. The meanings of each of these commands are as follows:

"B"—reset the base track and sector
"C"—copy the contents of the sector to the printer (in slot 1)
"D"—display the other half of the current sector
"E"—edit the current sector
"N"—read and display the next sector on the diskette
"P"—read and display the previous sector on the diskette
"Q"—quit the program
"W"—write the sector back onto the diskette

The functions that most of these commands perform are obvious. The only "tricky" one is the "E" (Edit) command. When the Edit command is entered, the cursor will move into the middle of the 8×16 array of hexadecimal digits that represent the contents of one-half of the sector. To change any of these digits, use the I, J, K, and M keys to move the cursor up, left, right, and down, respectively, and then enter the new two-digit hexadecimal entry for that position. You can leave editing mode at any time by pressing the ESC key. Once you have left editing mode, you can save the changes to diskette by using the "W" (Write) command.

THE INTERNAL STRUCTURE OF ProDOS

ProDOS was first released by Apple in January 1984 as a successor to DOS 3.3. Actually, it does not represent another version of DOS 3.3, but rather a whole new disk operating system for the //e. ProDOS organizes information on a diskette in a completely different way than does DOS 3.3, and so neither DOS can directly use files that have been created by the other. A utility program called CONVERT is included with ProDOS, however, which allows most files to be transferred between DOS 3.3 and ProDOS formatted diskettes so that they can be used by either operating system. Unfortunately, CONVERT will not work properly with random-access textfiles; such files must first be converted to sequential textfiles. ProDOS is compatible with the SOS operating system for the Apple ///, however. This means that files stored on a diskette using ProDOS can be read by SOS and vice versa.

Apple has made great efforts to ensure that virtually all DOS 3.3 commands available to an Applesoft program are also available when ProDOS is being used. ProDOS has enhanced many of these commands, however, and has added several new ones. In addition, ProDOS commands perform disk I/O operations significantly faster than DOS 3.3 commands.

As you might expect, ProDOS supports several useful features that the older DOS 3.3 does not. For example, the CATALOG command displays not only the file name and type, but also the exact size of the file in bytes, the date and time that the file was created and last modified (if a clock card has been installed), the default starting locations of a binary file, and the record length of a random-access textfile.

ProDOS also allows user-defined commands to be added to the standard ProDOS commands that are available to an Applesoft program. In addition, a well-defined group of diskette file I/O subroutines can be easily accessed from a machine-language program by making requests through a special "machine-language interface" handler. This handler can be used to perform all basic diskette file operations: open, read, write, close, and so on.

One useful new feature supported by ProDOS is the ability to use the 64K of auxiliary memory contained on Apple's extended 8Ø-column text card as if it was a disk drive. The volume name given to this "RAM-disk" is /RAM and it is treated as if it were an actual disk drive residing in slot 3, drive 2. The RAM-disk can be used to load and save programs extremely quickly since "disk" I/O operations do not involve using any slow-moving mechanical parts that degrade the data transfer rate considerably. Remember, however, that any information stored in the /RAM volume will disappear as soon as the //e is turned off or when ProDOS is rebooted.

Probably the most noticeable difference between ProDOS and DOS 3.3 is the method used to organize files on a diskette. In DOS 3.3, all files on the diskette are contained within one main catalog that is capable of holding the names of up to 1Ø5 files. ProDOS supports a hierarchical directory structure, however, that allows several separate directories to coexist on the same diskette. Any of these directories can contain standard disk files like those that appear in a DOS 3.3 catalog, but they can also contain files that themselves define directories (called subdirectories). Any nondirectory file in any directory can always be accessed by specifying its unique *pathname*. The pathname is of the form

```
VOLUME/DIRECTORY1/.../DIRECTORYn/FILENAME
```

where VOLUME represents the name of the first directory on the diskette (the *volume* directory), and DIRECTORY1 through DIRECTORYn represent the names of all the directories that must be passed through to reach the file being accessed, FILENAME. Each of the directories in this pathname must be contained within the previously specified directory.

If all files of interest are contained in the same subdirectory, it becomes annoying to have to specify the same chain of directory names leading up to the filename every time one is to be used. To circumvent this problem, ProDOS supports a PREFIX command that can be used to set the chain of directory names to which any name specified in a ProDOS command will be automatically appended. For example, if PREFIX is set by entering the following ProDOS command:

```
PREFIX VOLUME/DIRECTORY1/.../DIRECTORYn/
```

then any file contained in the directory at the end of this path can be referred to by its filename only. (A continuation of the prefix could also be entered to access files in lower-level subdirectories.)

The advantage of subdirectories is often not readily apparent to users of floppy diskettes, but becomes obvious when a hard disk system is used where there is enough room to hold thousands of files. If all the files were held in one directory you might have to wait a long time to spot your file when the disk was catalogued, and even then you could well miss it amidst the multitude of other files. Fortunately, the hierarchical directory structure provided by ProDOS allows related files to be grouped within the same subdirectory for easy access.

As far as organization of files on the diskette is concerned, ProDOS deals with 512-byte blocks rather than 256-byte sectors. An initialized diskette is considered to be made up of 280 blocks (numbered from Ø . . . 279), and it is rarely necessary to know where these blocks are actually located on the diskette since ProDOS performs all necessary conversions.

ProDOS Memory Map

When a ProDOS diskette is first booted, a system file called PRODOS is loaded into memory and executed. This file contains the fundamental I/O subroutines that are used to read and write blocks of data from and to the diskette. PRODOS then loads and executes another system file into memory; the one loaded is in the volume directory and it has a name of the form xxxx.SYSTEM (the first file having such a name when the disk is catalogued will be used). If an Applesoft programming environment is to be supported, this file must be BASIC.SYSTEM (it is found on the ProDOS system diskette). BASIC.SYSTEM contains the subroutines that "add" the standard ProDOS commands to Applesoft. It also takes care of parsing these commands, doing syntax checking, and calling the PRODOS subroutines when required. For convenience, we will be referring to the resultant PRODOS/BASIC.SYSTEM program combination as "ProDOS" even though this is technically not the case.

After ProDOS has been loaded as described, it will occupy the following memory locations:

- $E000-$FFFF in internal bank-switched RAM
- $D000-$DFFF in Bank1 of internal bank-switched RAM
- $9A00-$BFFF in internal RAM
- $D100-$D3FF in Bank2 of internal bank-switched RAM

(See Chapter 8 for a discussion of bank-switched RAM.) In addition, a general-purpose file buffer will be set up from $9600 to $99FF and the Applesoft HIMEM location will be set equal to $9600 (HIMEM refers to the value of the Applesoft end-of-string pointer at $73/$74).

The $400-byte buffer just above Applesoft HIMEM is always used by ProDOS as a buffer for directory blocks whenever the diskette is CATALOGued. This buffer does not always begin at $9600, however, since HIMEM could be changed in the following instances:

- By using the Applesoft HIMEM: command
- By opening and closing diskette files using the ProDOS OPEN and CLOSE commands.

It's obvious how the HIMEM: command affects the position of HIMEM, but why do the OPEN and CLOSE commands affect it? The answer is that whenever a file is opened, ProDOS creates a $400-byte file buffer by moving HIMEM down in memory by that number of bytes and then reserving the $400 byte area beginning at the original HIMEM position for use by the file. Whenever a file is closed, HIMEM is moved up by $400 bytes. While doing all this, ProDOS takes all steps necessary to ensure that Applesoft's string variables are not overwritten.

Earlier in this chapter, we saw how a safe area of memory between HIMEM and the beginning of the DOS 3.3 file buffers could be reserved for use by assembly-language programs. Unfortunately, because ProDOS is forever changing HIMEM when files are opened and closed, it is not possible to use this same technique with ProDOS. There is a way, however, in which a safe area can be reserved *above* ProDOS's file buffers. The steps that must be followed to do this are as follows:

- Close all files using the ProDOS CLOSE command
- Lower HIMEM by a multiple of 256 bytes using the Applesoft HIMEM: command.

These steps must be performed before any Applesoft variables have been defined, since the Applesoft string space will be overwritten. After these two steps have been completed, the area from HIMEM+$400 to $99FF can be used for storage of machine-language programs without danger of having them overwritten by ProDOS operations.

Keep in mind one important restriction that applies when using ProDOS: if HIMEM is being changed (that is, the $73/$74 end-of-string pointer is being changed), it must be changed in multiples of 256 bytes only!

ProDOS Page 3 Vectors

You will recall that DOS 3.3 uses the entire area from $3DØ . . . $3EE to hold several subroutines that can be called to perform special DOS 3.3 functions. Although ProDOS also reserves this entire area, only the first six locations are actually used (at present). As indicated in Table 5-11, these six locations hold two JMP instructions to the warm-start entry point of ProDOS (location $BEØØ).

ProDOS also initializes all of the system vectors that appear in page 3 from $3FØ . . . $3FF. These are the interrupt vectors for

Table 5-11. ProDOS page 3 vectors.

Address	*Description of Vector*
$3DØ–$3D2	A JMP instruction to the ProDOS warm-start entry point. A call to this vector will reconnect DOS without destroying the Applesoft program in memory. Use the "3DØG" command to move from the system monitor to Applesoft.
$3D3–$3D5	Another JMP instruction to the ProDOS warm-start entry point.

BRK, Reset, IRQ, and NMI (see Chapter 2), the vector for the system monitor's <CTRL-Y> USER command (see Chapter 3), and the vector for the Applesoft & command (see Chapter 4). Descriptions of all the vector subroutines installed by ProDOS are given in Table 5-12.

Volume Bit Map

Of the 28Ø blocks on a ProDOS diskette, the first seven (numbered from Ø to 6) are reserved for specific purposes. Blocks Ø and 1 contain a program that is loaded into memory by the ROM subroutine on the disk controller card whenever the system is booted. This program is called the bootstrap loader and is responsible for loading and executing the PRODOS system file. Blocks 2 through 5 represent the four blocks that contain the volume directory information and will be described in the next section. Block 6 contains the volume bit map for the diskette.

The volume bit map is used for the same purpose as DOS 3.3's track bit map, namely, to keep track of which areas of the diskette are in use and which are free. Only the first 35 bytes (28Ø bits) in the volume bit map block are actually used and each bit in each byte corresponds to a unique block number. The byte number (from Ø to 34), and the bit number within that byte (from Ø to 7), that corresponds to any given block number (from Ø to 279) can be calculated using the following Applesoft formulas:

```
BYTENUM = INT(BLOCKNUM/8)
BITNUM = 7- BLOCKNUM - 8 * BYTENUM
```

If the bit associated with a particular block is one, then that block is free. If it is zero, then it is being used by a file on the diskette.

Table 5-12. Initialization of page 3 system vectors by ProDOS.

Vector Name	*Address*	*Contents*	*Description*
BRK	\$3FØ–\$3F1	\$FA59	Address of a subroutine to display the 65Ø2 registers and enter the system monitor.
RESET	\$3F2–\$3F3	\$BEØØ	Address of the ProDOS warm-start entry point (reconnects ProDOS).
&	\$3F5–\$3F7	"JMP \$BEØ3"	Jump to ProDOS's external entry point for command strings (see Apple's *ProDOS Technical Reference Manual*).
USER	\$3F8–\$3FA	"JMP \$BEØØ"	Jump to ProDOS's warm-start entry point.
NMI	\$3FB–\$3FD	"JMP \$FF59"	Jump to the system monitor's cold-start entry point.
IRQ	\$3FE–\$3FF	\$BFEB	Address of the special ProDOS interrupt handler (see Chapter 2).

Note: The addresses stored at each vector location are stored with the low-order byte first.

Diskette Directory

As was explained earlier, ProDOS allows multiple directories to be created on one diskette. With the exception of the volume directory (the one through which all the others must be accessed), these directories can be stored just about anywhere on the diskette since they are treated similarly to standard files. The volume directory, however, is always located in blocks 2 through 5 of the diskette.

Each block used by any directory can hold up to thirteen 39-byte file entries. (This means that the four-block volume directory can hold a total of 52 entries, one of which is the volume name entry.) These entries completely describe the files by specifying the

Table 5-13. Map of a ProDOS directory block.

Byte number in Directory Block	*Meaning of Entry*
$ØØØ–$ØØ1	Block number of the previous directory block (low byte first). This will be zero if this is the first directory block.
$ØØ2–$ØØ3	Block number of the next directory block (low byte first). This will be zero if this is the last directory block.
$ØØ4–$Ø2A	Directory entry for file #1 OR, if this is the first block of the directory (bytes $ØØ and $Ø1 are Ø), the directory header.
$Ø2B–$Ø51	Directory entry for file #2
$Ø52–$Ø78	Directory entry for file #3
$Ø79–$Ø9F	Directory entry for file #4
$ØAØ–$ØC6	Directory entry for file #5
$ØC7–$ØED	Directory entry for file #6
$ØEE–$114	Directory entry for file #7
$115–$13B	Directory entry for file #8
$13C–$162	Directory entry for file #9
$163–$189	Directory entry for file #1Ø
$18A–$1BØ	Directory entry for file #11
$1B1–$1D7	Directory entry for file #12
$1D8–$1FE	Directory entry for file #13
$1FF	<Not used>

name, type, and size of the file. The map of a directory block is shown in Table 5-13.

The first block used by a directory (or subdirectory) is called the *key block* and is configured slightly differently than the others. The 39-byte entry that normally describes the first file in the block is instead used to describe the directory itself. This entry is called the directory header.

The meaning of each of the 39 bytes that make up a directory header are shown in Table 5-14. Notice the differences between the header for a volume directory and the header for a subdirectory.

All directory entries that do not represent directory headers represent either standard data files (for example, binary files, text files, and Applesoft programs) or subdirectory files. The formats of the directory entries for both of these two types of files are virtually identical and are as shown in Table 5-15.

The only way to determine what type of file a particular file

Table 5-14. Map of a ProDOS directory header.

Byte number in Key Block	*Description (usual entries in parentheses)*
\$Ø4	High four bits: storage type –\$ØF for a volume directory –\$ØE for a subdirectory Low four bits: length of directory name
\$Ø5–\$13	Directory name (in ASCII). The length of the name is contained in the low half of byte \$Ø4.
\$14–\$1B	<Reserved>
\$1C–\$1D	The date on which this directory was created (format: MMMDDDDD YYYYYYYM)
\$1E–\$1F	The minute (byte \$1E) and hour (byte \$1F) at which this directory entry was created.
\$2Ø	The version number of ProDOS that created this directory.
\$21	The lowest version of ProDOS that is capable of using this directory.
\$22	Access code for this directory (see Figure 5-2).
\$23	The number of bytes occupied by each directory entry (39).
\$24	The number of directory entries that can be stored on each block (13).
\$25–\$26	The number of active files in this directory (not including the directory header).
\$27–\$28	VOLUME DIRECTORY: The block where the volume bit map is located (6). SUBDIRECTORY: the block in which the entry defining this subdirectory is located (this is in the parent directory of the subdirectory).
\$29–\$2A	VOLUME DIRECTORY: The size of the volume in blocks (28Ø).
\$29	SUBDIRECTORY: The directory entry number within the block given by \$27/\$28 that defines this subdirectory (1 to 13).
\$2A	SUBDIRECTORY: The number of bytes in each directory entry of the parent directory (39).

Table 5-15. Map of a ProDOS directory file entry.

Relative Byte Number	Meaning of Entry
\$ØØ	High four bits: storage type (see text) –\$ØØ for an inactive file –\$Ø1 for a seedling file –\$Ø2 for a sapling file –\$Ø3 for a tree file –\$ØD for a subdirectory file Low four bits: length of file name
\$Ø1–\$ØF	File name (in ASCII with bit 7 = Ø)
\$1Ø	File type code (see Table 5-16)
\$11–\$12	Key pointer. If a subdirectory, the block number of the key block of the subdirectory. If a standard file, the block number of the index block of the file (or the data block if this is a seedling file).
\$13–\$14	Size of the file in blocks.
\$15–\$17	Size of the file in bytes (low-order bytes first).
\$18–\$19	The date on which this file was created (format: MMMDDDDD YYYYYYYM).
\$1A–\$1B	The minute (byte \$1A) and hour (byte \$1B) at which this file was created.
\$1C	The version number of ProDOS that created this file.
\$1D	The lowest version of ProDOS that is capable of using this file.
\$1E	Access code for this file (see Figure 5-2).
\$1F–\$2Ø	For a binary file, the load address of the file; for a random-access textfile, its record length.
\$21–\$22	The date on which this file was last modified (format: MMMDDDDD YYYYYYYM).
\$23–\$24	The minute (byte \$23) and hour (byte \$24) at which this file was created.
\$25–\$26	The block number of the key block of the directory that holds this file entry.

entry corresponds to is to examine the file type code that appears at relative position \$1Ø within the entry. Although 256 different codes are possible, only a few are commonly used by ProDOS, and it is these which are shown in Table 5-16. The three-character mnemonics used to represent these file types in a CATALOG listing

Table 5-16. ProDOS file type codes.

File Type Code	*CATALOG Mnemonic*	*Type of File*
$Ø4	TXT	ASCII text file (with bit 7 = Ø)
$Ø6	BIN	Binary file
$ØF	DIR	Directory file
$FØ	CMD	ProDOS added command file
$FC	BAS	Applesoft program file
$FD	VAR	Applesoft variable file
$FE	REL	Relocatable code file (EDASM)
$FF	SYS	ProDOS system file

are also shown in Table 5-16. For a list of all ProDOS file types, even the obscure ones, refer to the *ProDOS Technical Reference Manual*.

"Protecting" Files

Both DOS 3.3 and ProDOS allow files to be protected using the LOCK command. If a file is locked, then it cannot be altered or renamed unless it is first unlocked. If a file is locked, then an asterisk will appear at the far left of the line in which the file name appears when the directory is catalogued.

ProDOS reserves a one-byte access code in its directory entries to indicate the write status of the file (at relative byte $1E in each directory entry). Four bits in this byte are used to individually control the read, write, rename, and delete status of the file. A fifth bit acts as a flag to indicate whether the file has been modified since the last time it was backed up (it is the backup program's responsibility to clear this bit to Ø when the file is backed up). These bits are described in Figure 5-2.

Unfortunately, there is no ProDOS command that can be used from Applesoft to adjust these bits individually. The LOCK command turns off the write, rename, and delete bits together and the UNLOCK command turns them all back on again. The bits can be changed, however, by directly reading the block that contains the directory entry, changing the access code, and then writing the block back to diskette. The READ.BLOCK program listed in Table 5-18 will allow you to do this (this program will be described later on).

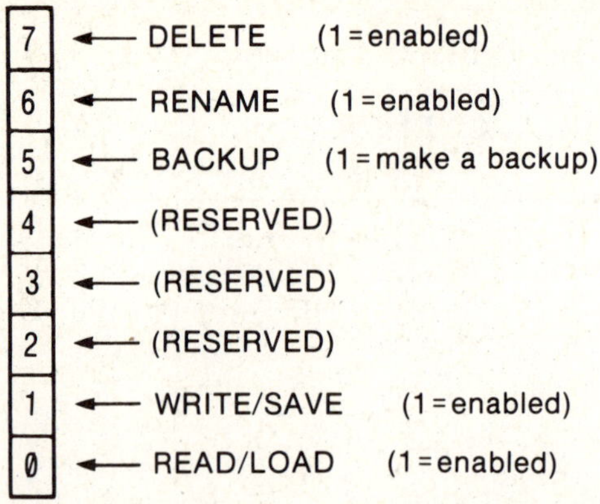

Figure 5-2. ProDOS access codes bit map.

Storing File Data

The method ProDOS uses to keep track of where a standard file's data is stored on the diskette varies depending on the size of the file. ProDOS uses the following "woodsy" file classifications:

Seedling file	: 1 to 512 bytes
Sapling file	: 513 to 131,Ø72 (128K) bytes
Tree file	: 131,Ø73 to 16,777,215 (16M-1) bytes

ProDOS determines what type of file it is dealing with by examining the four highest bits of relative byte $ØØ in the directory entry for the file: the number stored here is 1 for a seedling file, 2 for a sapling file, and 3 for a tree file.

ProDOS uses these three different file structures to reduce the amount of space needed to manage a file on the diskette to the absolute minimum. This permits ProDOS to deal with a file as quickly as possible and frees up valuable disk space for the storage of other files.

The directory entry's key pointer (relative bytes $11 and $12) points to the key block on the diskette for the file. Let's take a look at how ProDOS interprets this key block for each of the three types of files.

SEEDLING FILE. A seedling file, which, by definition, cannot exceed 512 bytes in length, obviously uses only one block on the diskette for data storage. It is this block that is pointed to by the key pointer. This means that the key block is, in fact, also the sole data block for the file.

SAPLING FILE. The key pointer in the directory entry for this type of file points to an index block that contains an ordered list of the block numbers on the diskette that are used to store that file's data. Table 5-17 shows what an index block for a sapling file looks like. Since block numbers can exceed 255, two bytes are needed to store each block number. The low part of the block number is always stored in the first half of the block and the high part is stored 256 bytes further into the block. The maximum size of a sapling file is 128K; it cannot be larger than this since only 256 blocks (of 512 bytes each) can be pointed to by the index block.

TREE FILE. If the file is a tree file, then the key pointer points to a master index block that contains an ordered list of the block numbers of up to 128 sapling-file-type index blocks. The structure of a master index block is shown in Table 5-18. Just as for sapling files, each of the index blocks pointed to by the master index block contains an ordered list of block numbers on the diskette that the file uses to store its data. The maximum size of a tree file is 16 megabytes (less one byte, which is reserved for an end-of-file marker)!

ProDOS takes care of all conversions that might become necessary if a file changes its type because it has either grown or shrunk. All this happens invisibly and it is not necessary to know what type of file is being dealt unless special programs are being used that do not use the standard ProDOS commands to access files.

Table 5-17. Map of the ProDOS index block for a sapling file.

Byte Number	*Meaning*
$ØØØ	Block number of Øth data block (low)
$ØØ1	Block number of 1st data block (low)
$ØØ2	Block number of 2nd data block (low)
"	"
"	"
"	"
$ØFF	Block number of 255th data block (low)
$1ØØ	Block number of Øth data block (high)
$1Ø1	Block number of 1st data block (high)
$1Ø2	Block number of 2nd data block (high)
"	"
"	"
"	"
$1FF	Block number of 255th data block (high)

Table 5-18. Map of the ProDOS master index block for a tree file.

Byte Number	*Meaning*
$ØØØ	Block number of Øth index block (low)
$ØØ1	Block number of 1st index block (low)
$ØØ2	Block number of 2nd index block (low)
"	"
"	"
"	"
$Ø7F	Block number of 127th index block (low)
$1ØØ	Block number of Øth index block (high)
$1Ø1	Block number of 1st index block (high)
$1Ø2	Block number of 2nd index block (high)
"	"
"	"
"	"
$17F	Block number of 127th index block (high)

MLI—Accessing the Diskette Directly

ProDOS supports a special machine-language interface (MLI) protocol that makes it extremely simple for assembly-language programs to perform standard diskette I/O commands. The MLI is explained in detail in Chapter 4 of the *ProDOS Technical Reference Manual*. (In contrast, DOS 3.3 is poorly suited to such use because there is no standard interfacing protocol to allow standard diskette file operations to be performed.)

The same general type of subroutine is used to invoke all MLI commands. The code used to invoke an MLI command looks like this (to review, "DFB" is a BIG MAC assembler directive that causes the byte in the operand to be stored in memory):

```
JSR $BF00         ;Call the MLI
DFB CMDNUM         ; and execute this command #
DFB #<CMDLIST     ;Low part of address
DFB #>CMDLIST     ;High part of address
BCS ERROR         ;Error if carry flag set
```

where $BFØØ represents the entry point to the MLI, CMDNUM is the command number that ProDOS has assigned to the requested command, and CMDLIST is the address of the parameter list associated with the command. (Recall from Chapter 2 that if you are using the Apple 65Ø2 Assembler/Editor rather than BIG MAC, then you should replace "#>" with "#<" and vice versa in the above example.) The parameter list contains the values of variables that the command needs in order to execute properly; result codes are also stored in the parameter list.

After the command is executed, control passes to the code that begins immediately after the three bytes stored after the "JSR $BFØØ" instruction. If an error occurs, then both the carry and zero flags are set and the error code number is placed in the accumulator. You can transfer control to an error-handling subroutine by using a BCS instruction (as shown in the example) or a BNE instruction.

There are two MLI commands that can be used to read from and write to individual blocks on the diskette directly. The command numbers for these commands are $8Ø (READ_BLOCK) and $81 (WRITE_BLOCK). The parameter lists for these commands are identical and are constructed as follows:

1st byte: number of parameters (always $Ø3)
2nd byte: disk slot and drive to be accessed
3rd byte: 512-byte data buffer address (low part)
4th byte: 512-byte data buffer address (high part)
5th byte: block number to be accessed (low part)
6th byte: block number to be accessed (high part)

The second byte in the parameter list contains information relating to the slot and drive number of the diskette to be accessed. The number stored here is equal to 16 times the slot number if the diskette is in drive 1, or 16 times the slot number plus 128 if the diskette is in drive 2.

For example, if a diskette is in slot 6 and drive 2 and you want to read the contents of block number 26Ø on that diskette into a buffer beginning at location $2ØØØ, you would use a program that looks like this:

```
        JSR $BF00
        DFB $80             ;(Code for READ)
        DFB #<CMDLIST
        DFB #>CMDLIST
        BCS IOERROR
        .                   ;(Got it!)
        .
        RTS
IOERROR .                   ;(Didn't get it!)
        RTS
CMDLIST DFB $03
        DFB $E0             ;Slot 6/Drive 2
        DFB $00             ;Buffer address $2000
        DFB $20
        DFB $04             ;Block 260 ($0104)
        DFB $01
```

The same program can be used to write a block to the diskette simply by changing the command code from $8Ø to $81.

ProDOS READ.BLOCK Program

Table 5-19 contains the program listing for the READ.BLOCK program. This program is the ProDOS counterpart of the DOS 3.3 READ SECTOR program in Table 5-10 and can be used to read and display any of the 280 blocks of data on a ProDOS-formatted diskette. It makes use of the MLI READ_BLOCK and WRITE_BLOCK commands and is useful for examining any block on a ProDOS-formatted diskette.

The instructions for using READ.BLOCK are virtually the same as those for READ SECTOR. The two main differences between READ.BLOCK and READ SECTOR are as follows: first, READ.BLOCK asks you to enter block numbers rather than track and sector numbers; second, only one-quarter of the 512-byte block is displayed on the screen at one time. The "D" command can be used to flip between the four display pages.

Table 5-19. READ.BLOCK. A program to read blocks on a ProDOS diskette.

```
]LIST

0  REM "READ BLOCK"
1  REM (FOR PRODOS ONLY)
100  FOR I = 768 TO 892: READ X: POKE
     I,X: NEXT
110  DEF  FN MD(X) = X - 16 * INT
     (X / 16)
120  DEF  FN M2(X) = X - 256 * INT
     (X / 256)
130 D$ =  CHR$ (4)
140 BM = 279: REM NUMBER OF BLOCK
     S
150  TEXT : PRINT  CHR$ (21): HOME
     : PRINT  TAB( 16);: INVERSE
     : PRINT "READ BLOCK": NORMAL
     : PRINT  TAB( 11);"(C) 1984
     GARY LITTLE"
160  VTAB 10: CALL - 958: PRINT
     "ENTER BASE BLOCK NUMBER (0-
     ";BM;: INPUT "): ";T$: IF T$
     = "" THEN 160
170 BL =  INT ( VAL (T$)): IF BL =
     0 AND T$ <  > "0" THEN 160
180  IF BL < 0 OR BL > BM THEN 16
     0
190 RW = 128
200  POKE 782, FN M2(BL): REM BLO
     CK# (LOW)
```

Table 5-19. READ.BLOCK. A program to read blocks on a ProDOS diskette (continued).

```
210   POKE 783, INT (BL / 256): REM
      BLOCK# (HIGH)
220   POKE 771,RW: REM READ=128 /
      WRITE=129
230   CALL 768
240   IF PEEK (8) <  > 0 THEN  PRINT
      : INVERSE : PRINT "DISK I/O
      ERROR": NORMAL : PRINT "PRES
      S ANY KEY TO CONTINUE: ";: GET
      A$: PRINT A$: GOTO 150
1000   VTAB 4: CALL - 958: PRINT
       TAB( 11);"CONTENTS OF BLOCK
       ";BL: PRINT " POKE 34,5
1010  Q = 1
1020   HOME : GOSUB 2000: CALL 794
      :Q = Q + 1: IF Q = 5 THEN 10
      50
1030   IF PR = 0 THEN GET A$: IF
      A$ = CHR$ (27) THEN 1050
1040   GOTO 1020
1050  Q = Q - 1:PR = 0: PRINT D$:"
      PR#0":B = 0
1060   HTAB 1: VTAB 23: CALL - 95
      8: PRINT "ENTER COMMAND (B,C
      ,D,E,N,P,Q,W,HELP): ";: GET
      A$: IF A$ =  CHR$ (13) THEN
      A$ = " "
1070   PRINT A$
1080   IF A$ <  > "D" THEN 1110
1090  Q = Q - 1: OF Q = 0 THEN Q =
      4
1100  HOME : GOSUB 2000: CALL 794
      : GOTO 1060
1110   IF A$ = "H" THEN 5000
1120   IF A$ = "Q" THEN 1260
1130   IF A$ = "E" THEN 1270
1140   IF A$ = "P" THEN 1220
1150   IF A$ = "N" THEN 1240
1160   IF A$ = "B" THEN 150
1170   IF A$ = "C" THEN VTAB 23: CALL
       - 958: PRINT TAB( 6);: INVERSE
      : PRINT "TURN ON PRINTER IN
      SLOT #1": NORMAL :PR = 1: PRINT
      D$;"PR#1": PRINT : GOTO 1000

1180   IF A$ <  > "W" THEN 1210
1190   POKE 782,BL: POKE 771,129: VTAB
      23: CALL - 958: PRINT "PRES
      S 'Y' TO VERIFY WRITE: ";: GET
      A$: IF A$ = CHR$ (13) THEN
      A$ = " "
```

(continued)

Table 5-19. READ.BLOCK. A program to read blocks on a ProDOS diskette (continued).

```
1200  PRINT A$: IF A$ = "Y" THEN
      CALL 768:RW = 128: VTAB 23:
      CALL - 958: PRINT "WRITE C
     OMPLETED. PRESS ANY KEY: ";:
       GET A$: GOTO 1060
1210  GOTO 5000
1220 BL = BL - 1: IF BL = - 1 THEN
     BL = 279
1230  GOTO 190
1240 BL = BL + 1: IF BL > 279 THEN
     BL = 0
1250  GOTO 190
1260  TEXT : HOME : END
1270 V = 8:H = 3: VTAB 5: PRINT TAB(
     6);: INVERSE : PRINT "I=UP M
     =DOWN J=LEFT K=RIGHT": NORMAL

1280  HTAB 1: VTAB 23: CALL - 95
     8: PRINT TAB( 6);"PRESS ";:
      INVERSE : PRINT "ESC";: NORMAL
     : PRINT " TO LEAVE EDITOR"
1290  REM
1300  GOSUB 1500: GET A$
1310 LC = 16384 + 128 * (Q - 1) +
     8 * V + H:Y = PEEK (LC):X =
      ASC (A$)
1320  IF A$ = CHR$ (27) THEN HTAB
     1: VTAB 5: CALL - 868: GOTO
     1060
1330  IF A$ <  > "I" THEN 1370
1340 B = 0:V = V - 1: IF V > = 0
      THEN 1300
1350 V = 15:Q = Q - 1: IF Q < 1 THEN
     Q = 4
1360  GOSUB 2000: HOME : CALL 794
     : GOTO 1280
1370  IF A$ = "J" THEN B = 0:H =
     H - 1: IF H = - 1 THEN H =
     7
1380  IF A$ = "K" THEN B = 0:H =
     H + 1: IF H = 8 THEN H = 0
1390  IF A$ <  > "M" THEN 1430
1400 B = 0:V = V + 1: IF V < 16 THEN
     1300
1410 V = 0:Q = Q + 1: IF Q = 5 THEN
     Q = 1
1420  GOTO 1360
1430  IF B = 0 THEN Y = FN MD(Y)
      + 16 * (X - 48) * (X < = 5
     7) + 16 * (X - 55) * (X > =
     65)
```

Table 5-19. READ.BLOCK. A program to read blocks on a ProDOS diskette (continued).

```
1440  IF B = 1 THEN Y = 16 * INT
     (Y / 16) + (X - 48) * (X < =
     57) + (X - 55) * (X > = 65)

1450 X = ASC (A$): IF (X > = 48
      AND X < = 57) OR (X > = 6
     5 AND X < = 70) THEN PRINT
     A$;: POKE ( PEEK (40) + 256 *
      PEEK (41) + 31 + H),Y: POKE
     LC,Y: IF B = 0 THEN CALL 64
     500:B = 1
1460  IF X = 8 AND B = 1 THEN B =
     0
1470  IF X = 21 AND B = 0 THEN B =
     1
1480  GOTO 1300
1490  CALL - 167
1500  VTAB V + 6: HTAB 3 * H + 7 +
     B: RETURN
2000  IF Q = 1 THEN POKE 795,0: POKE
     799,64
2010  IF Q = 2 THEN POKE 795,128
     : POKE 799,64
2020  IF Q = 3 THEN POKE 795,0: POKE
     799,65
2030  IF Q = 4 THEN POKE 795,128
     : POKE 799,65
2040  RETURN
5000  HOME : PRINT TAB( 10);"SUM
     MARY OF COMMANDS": PRINT TAB(
     10);"==================": PRINT

5010  PRINT "B -- RESET BASE BLOC
     K"
5020  PRINT "C -- COPY BLOCK CONT
     ENTS TO PRINTER"
5030  PRINT "D -- DISPLAY PREVIOU
     S 1/4 BLOCK"
5040  PRINT "E -- EDIT THE CURREN
     T BLOCK"
5050  PRINT "N -- READ THE NEXT B
     LOCK"
5060  PRINT "P -- READ THE PREVIO
     US BLOCK"
5070  PRINT "Q -- QUIT THE PROGRA
     M"
5080  PRINT "W -- WRITE THE BLOCK
      TO DISK"
5090  PRINT : PRINT "PRESS ANY KE
     Y TO CONTINUE: ";: GET A$: PRINT
     A$: GOTO 1100
```

(continued)

Table 5-19. READ.BLOCK. A program to read blocks on a ProDOS diskette (continued).

```
8000  DATA 32,0,191,128,10,3,144,
      8,176,11,3,96,0,64,0,0,169,0
      ,133,8,96,169,1,133,8,96,169
      ,0,133,6
8010  DATA 169,64,133,7,162,0,160
      ,0,56,165,7,233,64,32,218,25
      3,165,6,32,218,253,169,186,3
      2,237,253,169,160,32,237
8020  DATA 253,177,6,32,218,253,1
      69,160,32,237,253,200,192,8,
      208,241,169,160,32,237,253,1
      60,0,177,6,9,128,201,160,176

8030  DATA 2,169,174,32,237,253,2
      00,192,8,208,238,169,141,32,
      237,253,24,165,6,105,8,133,6
      ,165,7,105,0,133,7,232
8040  DATA 224,16,208,168,96
```

FURTHER READING FOR CHAPTER 5

Standard reference works . . .

DOS User's Manual, Apple Computer, Inc., 1983.

DOS Programmer's Manual, Apple Computer, Inc., 1982.

ProDOS Technical Reference Manual, Apple Computer, Inc., 1983.

ProDOS User's Manual, Apple Computer, Inc., 1983.

BASIC Programming with ProDOS, Apple Computer, Inc., 1983.

D. Worth and P. Lechner, *Beneath Apple DOS*, Quality Software, 1981. The definitive work on the "guts" of DOS 3.3.

All About DOS, A.P.P.L.E., 1983. This book contains a lot of interesting information about DOS 3.3 and several useful programs.

On the internal structure of DOS 3.3 and ProDOS . . .

M. Pump, "DOS Internals: An Overview," *Call -A.P.P.L.E.*, February 1981, pp. 8-12. A quick look at some of the important areas within DOS 3.3.

D.J. Black, "Apple DOS Revealed," *Kilobaud Microcomputing*, November 1982, pp. 1Ø2-112. A good analysis of the DOS 3.3 file manager.

B. Sander-Cederlof, "Commented Listing of DOS 3.3," *Apple Assembly Line*:

a. $BØ52-$BØB5, $B35F-$B7FF : October 1981, pp. 18-24

b. $BDØØ-$BEAE : September 1981, pp. 16-2Ø

c. $B8ØØ-$BCFF : June 1981, pp. 1Ø-18

d. $BEAF-$BFFF : April 1981, pp. 14-17

B. Sander-Cederlof, "Commented Listing of DOS 3.3 Boot ROM," *Apple Assembly Line*, August 1981, pp. 17-2Ø.

L. Meador, "DOS Error Trapping from Machine Language," *Apple Assembly Line*, February 1982, pp. 2-1Ø.

D.P. Tuttle and T. Cleaver, "An Overview of DOS," *Micro*, June 1982, pp. 25-33. A good analysis of the internal structure of DOS 3.3.

B. Sander-Cederlof, "Commented Listing of ProDOS," *Apple Assembly Line*:

a. $F9ØC-$F995, $FDØØ-$FE9A, $FEBE-$FFFF : December 1983, pp. 2-11

b. $F8ØØ-$F9ØB, $F996-$FEBD : November 1983, pp. 2-14

On making space for assembly-language programs . . .

G.R. Sogge, "Protecting Memory from DOS," *Micro*, May 1981, p. 81. This article shows how to reserve areas that will not be overwritten by DOS 3.3.

6

Character Input and the Keyboard

The //e, like most other microcomputers, usually deals with information that is delivered to it in one-byte (8-bit) chunks (from a keyboard or a disk drive, for example). This information is commonly referred to as "character input" because the bytes usually represent the encoded representations of letters of the alphabet, numbers, and other printable characters. Although any encoding scheme that the input device cares to use could be dealt with by the //e, it is the American National Standard Code for Information Interchange (ASCII) standard that is usually used to encode characters. Two other incompatible encoding schemes, Extended Binary-Coded Decimal Interchange Code (EBCDIC) and Baudot, are also in widespread use, the first by all large IBM computers and compatibles and the second by some older TeleType machines.

ASCII is a seven-bit code and is used by virtually all microcomputers. A total of 128 (2^7) codes are defined by the ASCII standard. Table 6-1 contains a list of these codes, their standard names or symbols, and the keys on the keyboard (or combination of keys) that must be pressed to enter them.

When the //e performs character input/output operations, the ASCII code for the character is stored in bits Ø through 6 of the byte being inputted or outputted and bit 7 of the byte is normally set equal to "1". Since a "1" in bit 7 is often used to indicate that the value stored in that byte is negative, this "variant" of ASCII is called "negative ASCII"; if bit 7 is Ø, then "positive ASCII" is being used.

Note that all but the first 32 ASCII codes and ASCII code 127 (rubout) are used to represent visible symbols. The first 32 codes are called "control characters" and are usually sent to a video display or a printer controller to cause it to perform some special

Table 6-1. American National Standard Code for Information Interchange (ASCII) character codes.

ASCII Code			
Hex	***Dec***	***Symbol***	***Keys to Press***
$ØØ	ØØØ	NUL (Null)	CONTROL @
$Ø1	ØØ1	SOH (Start of header)	CONTROL A
$Ø2	ØØ2	STX (Start of text)	CONTROL B
$Ø3	ØØ3	ETX (End of text)	CONTROL C
$Ø4	ØØ4	EQT (End of transmission)	CONTROL D
$Ø5	ØØ5	ENQ (Enquiry)	CONTROL E
$Ø6	ØØ6	ACK (Acknowledge)	CONTROL F
$Ø7	ØØ7	BEL (Bell)	CONTROL G
$Ø8	ØØ8	BS (Backspace)	LEFT-ARROW or CONTROL H
$Ø9	ØØ9	HT (Horizontal tabulation)	TAB or CONTROL I
$ØA	Ø1Ø	LF (Line feed)	DOWN-ARROW or CONTROL J
$ØB	Ø11	VT (Vertical tabulation)	UP-ARROW or CONTROL K
$ØC	Ø12	FF (Form feed)	CONTROL L
$ØD	Ø13	CR (Carriage return)	RETURN or CONTROL M
$ØE	Ø14	SO (Shift out)	CONTROL N
$ØF	Ø15	SI (Shift in)	CONTROL O
$1Ø	Ø16	DLE (Data link escape)	CONTROL P
$11	Ø17	DC1 (Device control 1)	CONTROL Q
$12	Ø18	DC2 (Device control 2)	CONTROL R
$13	Ø19	DC 3 (Device control 3)	CONTROL S
$14	Ø2Ø	DC4 (Device control 4)	CONTROL T
$15	Ø21	NAK (Negative acknowledge)	RIGHT-ARROW or CONTROL U
$16	Ø22	SYN (Synchronous idle)	CONTROL V
$17	Ø23	ETB (End of transmission block)	CONTROL W
$18	Ø24	CAN (Cancel)	CONTROL X
$19	Ø25	EM (End of medium)	CONTROL Y
$1A	Ø26	SUB (Substitute)	CONTROL Z
$1B	Ø27	ESC (Escape)	ESC or CONTROL [
$1C	Ø28	FS (Field separator)	CONTROL \
$1D	Ø29	GS (Group separator)	CONTROL]
$1E	Ø3Ø	RS (Record separator)	CONTROL ˆ
$1F	Ø31	US (Unit separator)	CONTROL _
$2Ø	Ø32	(Space)	SPACE BAR
$21	Ø33	!	SHIFT 1
$22	Ø34	″	SHIFT ’
$23	Ø35	#	SHIFT 3
$24	Ø36	$	SHIFT 4

Table 6-1. American National Standard Code for Information Interchange (ASCII) character codes (continued).

ASCII Code *Hex*	*Dec*	*Symbol*	*Keys to Press*
$25	Ø37	%	SHIFT 5
$26	Ø38	&	SHIFT 7
$27	Ø39	'	'
$28	Ø4Ø	(	SHIFT 9
$29	Ø41	)	SHIFT Ø
$2A	Ø42	*	SHIFT 8
$2B	Ø43	+	SHIFT =
$2C	Ø44	,	,
$2D	Ø45	–	–
$2E	Ø46	.	.
$2F	Ø47	/	/
$3Ø	Ø48	Ø	Ø
$31	Ø49	1	1
$32	Ø5Ø	2	2
$33	Ø51	3	3
$34	Ø52	4	4
$35	Ø53	5	5
$36	Ø54	6	6
$37	Ø55	7	7
$38	Ø56	8	8
$39	Ø57	9	9
$3A	Ø58	:	SHIFT ;
$3B	Ø59	;	;
$3C	Ø6Ø	<	SHIFT ,
$3D	Ø61	=	=
$3E	Ø62	>	SHIFT .
$3F	Ø63	?	SHIFT /
$4Ø	Ø64	@	SHIFT 2
$41	Ø65	A	SHIFT A
$42	Ø66	B	SHIFT B
$43	Ø67	C	SHIFT C
$44	Ø68	D	SHIFT D
$45	Ø69	E	SHIFT E
$46	Ø7Ø	F	SHIFT F
$47	Ø71	G	SHIFT G
$48	Ø72	H	SHIFT H
$49	Ø73	I	SHIFT I
$4A	Ø74	J	SHIFT J
$4B	Ø75	K	SHIFT K
$4C	Ø76	L	SHIFT L
$4D	Ø77	M	SHIFT M
$4E	Ø78	N	SHIFT N

(continued)

Table 6-1. American National Standard Code for Information Interchange (ASCII) character codes (continued).

ASCII Code			
Hex	***Dec***	***Symbol***	***Keys to Press***
$4F	Ø79	O	SHIFT O
$5Ø	Ø8Ø	P	SHIFT P
$51	Ø81	Q	SHIFT Q
$52	Ø82	R	SHIFT R
$53	Ø83	S	SHIFT S
$54	Ø84	T	SHIFT T
$55	Ø85	U	SHIFT U
$56	Ø86	V	SHIFT V
$57	Ø87	W	SHIFT W
$58	Ø88	X	SHIFT X
$59	Ø89	Y	SHIFT Y
$5A	Ø9Ø	Z	SHIFT Z
$5B	Ø91	[	[
$5C	Ø92	\	\
$5D	Ø93	]	]
$5E	Ø94	^	SHIFT 6
$5F	Ø95	_	SHIFT –
$6Ø	Ø96	`	`
$61	Ø97	a	A
$62	Ø98	b	B
$63	Ø99	c	C
$64	1ØØ	d	D
$65	1Ø1	e	E
$66	1Ø2	f	F
$67	1Ø3	g	G
$68	1Ø4	h	H
$69	1Ø5	i	I
$6A	1Ø6	j	J
$6B	1Ø7	k	K
$6C	1Ø8	l	L
$6D	1Ø9	m	M
$6E	11Ø	n	N
$6F	111	o	O
$7Ø	112	p	P
$71	113	q	Q
$72	114	r	R
$73	115	s	S
$74	116	t	T
$75	117	u	U
$76	118	v	V
$77	119	w	W
$78	12Ø	x	X
$79	121	y	Y

Table 6-1. American National Standard Code for Information Interchange (ASCII) character codes (continued).

ASCII Code *Hex*	*Dec*	*Symbol*	*Keys to Press*
$7A	122	z	Z
$7B	123	{	SHIFT [
$7C	124	|	SHIFT \
$7D	125	}	SHIFT]
$7E	126	~	SHIFT `
$7F	127	▌(Rubout)	DELETE

action. Some of the more important control characters on the //e are as follows (in negative ASCII):

$87 (bell)—causes the speaker to beep
$88 (backspace)—causes the cursor to move back one position
$8A (line feed)—causes the cursor to move down one line
$8D (carriage return)—causes the cursor to move to the beginning of the current line

Some of the names associated with the other control characters (see Table 6-1) are somewhat archaic in that they refer to various aspects of the operation of old TeleType terminals. Other names relate to the codes used by certain standard data-interchange protocols that the //e does not normally use (for example, Start of Text (STX), End of Text (ETX), and Cancel (CAN)).

In this chapter, we will take a look at how the //e requests and reads character input from any device interfaced to it, including the keyboard. In doing so, we will examine the built-in ROM subroutines that the //e normally uses whenever it requires character input.

You will be able to follow this chapter a lot more easily if you have by your side a copy of the *Apple Reference Manual Addendum: Monitor ROM Listings*. This publication contains the source code listing for all of the ROM subroutines we will be examining.

STANDARD CHARACTER INPUT SUBROUTINES

There are three special, general-purpose character input subroutines in the //e's system monitor that are used to fetch characters so that they can be used and interpreted by other parts of the system, including Applesoft and the system monitor. These routines are usually referred to by the symbolic names of RDKEY, RDCHAR, and GETLN. They, in turn, usually make use of two other subroutines that are used to read information from the keyboard; these are called KEYIN and BASICIN. Each of these subroutines are briefly described in Table 6-2. Let's take a closer look at them.

Reading One Character

RDKEY ($FDØC)

RDKEY is the most important of the three fundamental character input subroutines since it is the one that is eventually called by the other two. This subroutine is used to scan any input device that has been designated as being active (usually, but not necessarily, the keyboard) until a character has been entered, and to return the ASCII code for that character (with its high bit set to one) in the 65Ø2's accumulator. The Applesoft GET command calls RDKEY directly.

As soon as RDKEY is called, it attempts to display a visible cursor by causing the character at the currently active video position (as calculated from the values of CH ($24) and CV ($25), the horizontal and vertical cursor coordinates) to begin to flash. The code that does this looks like this:

```
LDY CH              ;Get horizontal position
LDA (BASL),Y        ;Get the screen byte
PHA                 ; and save it.
AND #$3F            ;Adjust byte for flash video
ORA #$40            ; (see Chapter 7)
STA (BASL),Y        ;Replace screen byte
PLA                 ;Restore the screen byte in A
```

where BASL ($28) is the first of two zero page locations that together contain the base address for the line number held in CV (see Chapter 7). As we will see shortly, this cursor is quickly "removed" by the //e's standard 4Ø-column and 8Ø-column input subroutines and replaced by another one (either a blinking checkerboard or a nonblinking inverse square). This removal is not absolutely necessary when in 4Ø-column mode, but becomes necessary when in 8Ø-column mode because CH no longer contains the true horizontal cursor position (it is held in OURCH ($57B) instead).

Table 6-2. Built-in input subroutines.

Address Hex	(Dec)	Symbolic Name	Description
$FDØC	(6478Ø)	RDKEY	Reads a character from the currently active input device and places its negative ASCII code in the accumulator.
$FD35	(64821)	RDCHAR	Uses RDKEY to read a character from the currently active input device. Handles escape sequences if the 8Ø-column firmware is not being used.
$FD1B	(64795)	KEYIN	Keyboard input routine used when 8Ø-column firmware is not being used. The negative ASCII code for the character is returned in the accumulator.
$C3Ø5	(51446)	BASICIN	Keyboard input routine used when 8Ø-column firmware is being used. The negative ASCII code for the character is returned in the accumulator. This subroutine handles all escape sequences and the right-arrow "pick."
$FD6A	(64874)	GETLN	Reads a line of information into the input buffer at $2ØØ by making repeated calls to RDCHAR.

After the initial blinking cursor is set up, the following code is executed:

```
JMP (KSWL)
```

which effectively passes control to the body of a user-selectable input subroutine whose address is held at KSWL ($38) and KSWH ($39). This input subroutine is responsible for returning the ASCII code for an inputted character as soon as the input device being used makes one available. For the purposes of this discussion, we will assume that the input device is the //e's keyboard. We will see later how other input devices can be linked into the RDKEY subroutine instead by simply storing the address of the input subroutine for the alternate input device at KSWL and KSWH.

The //e's disk operating system (DOS 3.3 or ProDOS) is integrated into the system by storing the address of its special input subroutine at KSWL and KSWH. This input subroutine will read input from either a diskette file or the keyboard, depending on whether a DOS READ command is in effect. It will also cause special disk operations to be performed if a valid DOS command is entered from the keyboard (for example, LOAD a file and CATALOG the diskette). When it reads information from the keyboard, it uses one of the //e's two built-in subroutines available for this purpose.

The keyboard input subroutine that is used will depend on whether the //e's internal 8Ø-column firmware ROM (that uses addresses between \$C3ØØ . . . \$C3FF and \$C8ØØ . . . \$CFFF) is being used. This firmware is not used when you first turn on the //e but can be selected by entering a PR#3 command from Applesoft. (If you do not have an 8Ø-column text card installed, you must enter a POKE 49162,Ø command before entering the PR#3 command — see Chapter 11.) Once you have selected the 8Ø-column firmware in this way, you can flip between an 8Ø-column display and a 4Ø-column display (if you are using an 8Ø-column text card) by using the two-keystroke "escape sequence"

```
ESC 4
```

to go from 8Ø-column mode to 4Ø-column mode and

```
ESC 8
```

to go from 4Ø-column mode to 8Ø-column mode. (An escape sequence is entered by pressing the ESC key, releasing it, and then pressing the second key; the RETURN key must not be pressed.) Note that there is a bug in the 8Ø-column firmware that may cause you to "lose" the cursor and/or overwrite the area reserved for a tokenized Applesoft program if ESC 4 is entered when the cursor is in the right-hand half of the 8Ø-column screen. Because of this, always make sure that the 8Ø-column cursor is in the first forty columns before entering ESC 4.

You can usually tell whether the 8Ø-column firmware is being used by looking at the cursor. If it's a blinking "checkerboard," then the 8Ø-column firmware is not in use; if it's a nonflashing, inverse-video square, then it is. The 8Ø-column firmware can be deactivated by entering an ESC <CTRL-Q> sequence from the keyboard or printing a <CTRL-U> character; this returns you to standard 4Ø-column mode.

We will be looking at the video display modes in considerably more detail in Chapter 7.

Keyboard Input (8Ø-Column Firmware Off)

If the 8Ø-column firmware on the //e is not being used, then the //e usually uses a subroutine called KEYIN ($FD1B) to handle keyboard input. The important part of this subroutine really begins at B.KEYIN ($C288) in the //e's built-in internal ROM space. The first thing that it does is to remove RDKEY's cursor and change it to a blinking checkerboard. This blinking effect is generated totally in software by alternating between the display of the checkerboard character (ASCII code $FF) and the true screen character at fixed intervals. When a key that generates an ASCII code is entered, the screen character is put back on the screen, the ASCII code representing the entered key is placed in the 65Ø2's accumulator (with the high bit set to one), and the subroutine finishes with the X and Y registers preserved.

Keyboard Input (8Ø-Column Firmware On)

If the 8Ø-column firmware has been selected, then another subroutine to handle keyboard input, called BASICIN ($C3Ø5), is used instead. The important part of this subroutine really begins at BINPUT ($C8F6). This subroutine also removes the cursor that RDKEY sets up and changes it to a nonflashing, inverse video block by calling the INVERT ($CEDD) subroutine. INVERT simply reverses the video attribute of the character at the current cursor position (as set by OURCH ($57B) and OURCV ($5FB), the 8Ø-column firmware's horizontal and vertical cursor coordinates). That is, if the screen character is displayed in normal video, it is changed to inverse video, and vice versa. Once this has been done, the subroutine calls GETKEY ($CB15), a subroutine that waits for a key corresponding to an ASCII code to be entered from the keyboard, and then returns that code in the accumulator (with its high bit set to one).

After a key has been entered, BINPUT removes the cursor by calling INVERT once again and then takes one of two paths, depending on whether the ESC key was pressed. If a key other than ESC was pressed, then control passes to NOESC ($C9B7), which performs two main chores. First, it examines the key to see if it was a right arrow (CTRL-U) and, if it was, replaces it with the character on the video display "below" the cursor. This allows the right arrow to be used to "pick" characters off the screen without retyping them. If the key was not a right arrow, then a block of code is executed that takes care of handling the //e's upper-case restrict mode (see the next section). This may involve converting a lower-case character to upper-case if upper-case restrict mode is active. When NOESC finishes, BINPUT does some housekeeping and then returns with the ASCII code for the keyboard character in the accumulator (with the high bit set to one) and with the X and Y registers preserved.

Escape Sequences

If, however, the ESC key is pressed, then BINPUT does something quite different: control passes to ESCAPING ($C918), which causes the cursor to change to an inverse "+" sign and *escape mode* to be turned on. Whenever the //e is in this mode, it reads the keyboard once again and then executes a special function dictated by the key that is read. This two-key combination is commonly referred to as an "escape sequence." A list of all of the valid escape sequences and the functions they perform are listed in Table 6-3.

Most of the escape sequences that have been defined on the //e are used to move the cursor around the screen or to affect the video display in some way and are self-explanatory. Two of them are somewhat unusual, however, and will now be described; they are ESC R and ESC T. ESC R is used to turn on "upper-case restrict" mode, and ESC T is used to turn it off again. When upper-case restrict mode is on, any lower-case alphabetic characters that are entered from the keyboard will automatically be converted to their upper-case equivalents *unless* the characters are entered between successive quotation marks. This feature facilitates the entry of Applesoft programs where all the keyword commands and DOS commands must be in upper-case but any phrases to be displayed with a PRINT command (that appear within quotation marks after the PRINT command) can be in any combination of upper- and lower-case characters.

In general, escape mode ends immediately after the key after ESC has been pressed and, if you want to re-enter escape mode, you must press ESC once again. The I,J,K,M and arrow-key sequences, however, behave a little differently. If you enter any of these sequences, then escape mode remains active until any other key that generates an ASCII code that is not part of an escape sequence is pressed. This means that you can quickly move the cursor around the screen by pressing ESC once and then pressing any combination of cursor-movement keys until the cursor is properly positioned. You can then press another key (the space bar is convenient) to leave escape mode.

Due to a bug in the //e's 80-column firmware, there is one other "unofficial" escape sequence that is supported: ESC <CTRL-L>. When this sequence is entered, control passes to location $4CCE.

Table 6-3. Escape sequences.

Escape Sequence	*Description*
ESC @	Clears the video screen window and places the cursor in the top left-hand corner.
ESC A	Moves the cursor one position to the right.
ESC B	Moves the cursor one position to the left.
ESC C	Moves the cursor down one line.
ESC D	Moves the cursor up one line (if not already at top).
ESC E	Clears the screen from the current cursor position to the end of the line. The cursor position does not change.
ESC F	Clears the screen from the current cursor position to the end of the window. The cursor position does not change.
ESC I ESC ↑	Moves the cursor up one line and keeps escape mode active.
ESC J ESC ←	Moves the cursor one position to the left and keeps escape mode active.
ESC K ESC →	Moves the cursor one position to the right and keeps escape mode active.
ESC M ESC ↓	Moves the cursor down one line and keeps escape mode active.
ESC R*	Turns on upper-case restrict mode. This forces all lower-case alphabetic characters to be displayed in upper-case, except between quotation marks.
ESC T*	Turns off upper-case restrict mode.
ESC 4*	Switches to 4Ø-column mode from 8Ø-column mode.
ESC 8*	Switches to 8Ø-column mode from 4Ø-column mode.
ESC CTRL-Q*	Deselects the 8Ø-column firmware and returns to standard 4Ø-column mode.

*Note: The last five escape sequences are available only when the 8Ø-column firmware is being used.

Unfortunately, this location is right in the middle of the memory area reserved for page2 of the //e's high-resolution graphics screen and could also be within Applesoft's tokenized program space or variable spaces, depending on the size and type of program. If you can ensure that this location (and the few bytes just past it) will not be used by your program, however, you could place a subroutine here that will take control whenever ESC <CTRL-L> is entered. This odd escape sequence is available because the ESCAPING ($C918) subroutine improperly assumes that the table in ROM that contains the valid escape sequences has eighteen entries rather than seventeen.

After escape mode ends, the keyboard is immediately scanned again for another keypress. Thus, BINPUT does not finish until an ASCII code is generated that is not part of an escape sequence. Since ESC is handled internally to BINPUT, the Applesoft GET command cannot be used to detect ESC when the 80-column firmware is being used. Similarly, a right-arrow key (CTRL-U) cannot be detected with GET since it is also processed before BINPUT finishes.

RDCHAR ($FD35)

The RDCHAR subroutine is almost identical to the RDKEY subroutine. In fact, it first calls RDKEY and then, after the inputted character has been entered from the keyboard, it checks to see whether it is the ESC key. If it is, then another escape mode is entered into beginning at ESCNEW ($FBA5), which is similar to the one described above. In fact, the only differences are that the cursor does not change to an inverse "+" sign and that the last five escape sequences set out in Table 6-3 will not be available.

Note, however, that if the 8Ø-column firmware is being used, then a call to RDCHAR turns out to be identical to a call to RDKEY. This is because RDCHAR calls RDKEY to get a keyboard character and it checks for an ESC character only *after* RDKEY has finished. As we have seen, however, when the 8Ø-column firmware is in use, RDKEY itself handles the ESC key and so it will never return the ASCII code for ESC to RDCHAR. Therefore, RDCHAR's escape mode will never be activated unless the 8Ø-column firmware is not in use.

Reading a Line of Characters

RDKEY and RDCHAR read only one character at a time. A much more useful and general subroutine is one that allows you to enter a whole line of information at once (a line being defined as a series of characters that is entered before RETURN is pressed). Such a subroutine does exist on the //e and is called GETLN ($FD6A).

The GETLN subroutine is used by the //e whenever you are entering commands in the system monitor or in Applesoft direct mode. In addition, the Applesoft INPUT command uses this subroutine directly.

As soon as GETLN is called, a special symbol, called a prompt symbol, is displayed. The code for this symbol is always read from PROMPT ($33). This symbol serves two purposes: it tells you what part of the //e is currently active (the system monitor or Applesoft, for example) and it reminds you that the //e is expecting you to enter a line of information. Table 6-4 sets out the various prompt symbols commonly used by the //e.

After the prompt symbol has been displayed, GETLN calls RDCHAR again and again until the RETURN key is pressed. The characters returned by the series of RDCHAR calls are stored in consecutive locations in a 256-byte character input buffer located in page two of memory beginning at IN ($2ØØ). When RETURN is pressed, the subroutine ends and the number of characters in the buffer is returned in the X register.

When a line is entered using GETLN, all those escape sequences that are normally available can be used. In addition, GETLN supports several simple editing commands that can be used when the line is being entered. These editing commands will now be discussed.

LEFT-ARROW KEY. This key allows you to backspace over the previous item in the input buffer and, thus, to remove it from the buffer. The cursor moves one position to the left on the video screen when the left-arrow key is pressed.

Table 6-4. //e prompt symbols.

Prompt Symbol	*Meaning*
*	the system monitor is waiting for a command.
]	Applesoft is waiting for you to enter a command or a program line.
>	Integer BASIC is waiting for you to enter a command or a program line (not available under ProDOS).
?	Applesoft is waiting for you to respond to an INPUT statement.
	Note: The ASCII code for the prompt symbol is kept in PROMPT ($33).

RIGHT-ARROW KEY. This key allows you to copy the character on the video screen beneath the cursor into the input buffer. Note that GETLN itself deals with the right-arrow key only if the 8Ø-column firmware is not being used, because when the 8Ø-column firmware is in use, BASICIN handles the right-arrow key internally (though in much the same way).

CTRL-X. This key allows you to erase everything that is currently in the input buffer. When it is pressed, a backslash ("\") will be displayed after the characters that have already been typed in and the cursor will be placed at the far left of the next line on the screen. Note that the line will automatically be canceled like this if you attempt to enter more than 255 characters before pressing RETURN. Beeps will be sounded after every character entered after the 248th one to remind you that the buffer is almost full.

RETURN. This key indicates to GETLN that the current line is completed and is to be entered.

CHANGING INPUT DEVICES : THE INPUT LINK

The most common source of character input to the //e is the keyboard. It is possible, however, to interface many other sources of such input to the //e through any of the expansion slots located at the rear of the //e's motherboard. A familiar example of such a source is the //e's disk drive.

The //e uses a flexible and powerful method for handling the problems associated with having many possible sources of character input. Even though the source of the input may vary, calls are still always made to the RDKEY subroutine whenever a character from any device, in general, is required. To activate a particular device, the destination of a jump instruction that RDKEY uses to locate the character input subroutine is set to the address of the device's input subroutine. This means that your program's input commands (for example, INPUT and GET in Applesoft) can always be used regardless of the source of input.

Let's take a closer look at the mechanics of this procedure. We saw earlier that whenever RDKEY is called to obtain another character, control ultimately passes to an instruction that looks like this:

```
JMP ($0038)
```

The addressing mode used by the jump instruction here is called "indirect." This means that the destination of the jump is not location $38 itself but rather the address stored at locations $38 (low byte) and $39 (high byte). This address is normally a subroutine within DOS that ultimately calls KEYIN ($FD1B) or BASICIN ($C3Ø5), the system monitor's standard keyboard input routines (unless input is being requested from a diskette file). By simply changing the address stored at $38/$39, however, you can force the //e to execute any subroutine that you want whenever input is requested, including one associated with an alternative input device.

The symbolic name for locations $38/$39 is KSW (for keyboard switch); $38 by itself is called KSWL and $39 is called KSWH. Since these locations are used to incorporate new input routines into the system, KSW is commonly referred to as the "input link" or "input hook."

The address of the input subroutine for a peripheral input device is usually placed in KSWL and KSWH by using the Applesoft "IN#s" command. This command causes the //e to transfer control to a program beginning at location $CsØØ (where "s" is the peripheral slot number) that is the first location in a ROM area reserved for that slot. Typically, the program in the new input device's ROM will modify KSW so that it will point to a new input routine also contained in that ROM. Note that if an IN#Ø command is entered, then the address of KEYIN ($FD1B), the //e's standard 4Ø-column input subroutine, will be stored at KSWL and KSWH.

You can also change the input hook by using the Applesoft POKE command to store the address of the new input routine directly into KSW at $38 and $39; this address can be in a ROM area or a RAM area. Caution should be exercised when carrying out these changes, however, since the slightest error could easily cause the system to crash.

How About Output?

You may well be wondering whether the //e uses the same method to handle its output that it uses to handle its input. The answer is, you guessed it, "yes," but we're going to defer discussion of output until Chapter 7. For those of you who just can't wait, the //e uses an output link called CSW ($36/$37) to point to the output subroutine that is to take control whenever the standard output subroutine, COUT ($FDED), is called. The PR# command can be used to transfer control to a peripheral slot in much the same way that IN# can be.

Designing a KSW Input Subroutine

A KSW input subroutine must be designed carefully to ensure that it adheres to certain rules that restrict its usage of 65Ø2 registers. The most important rule is that when the subroutine ends, the inputted character must be contained in the accumulator with its high-order bit set to one. Furthermore, the X and Y registers must contain the same values they held when the subroutine was first entered. Thus, if X and Y are to be changed by the KSW subroutine, they must first be saved in a safe place (such as the stack) and then restored just before the subroutine ends.

The KSW subroutine must also properly handle the screen cursor. As we saw earlier, before RDKEY ($FDØC) calls the KSW subroutine, it displays a cursor by reading the byte at the current screen position defined by CH ($24) and BASL ($28) and then changing it into its flashing video representation. When the KSW subroutine takes over, the original screen byte is contained in the accumulator and the value in CH ($24) is in the Y register.

If this original cursor is to be "removed" so that it can be replaced by one generated by the KSW subroutine, the contents of the A register must be immediately stored at the address given by BASL+Y. This can be done with a "STA (BASL),Y" instruction. Note that if the 8Ø-column firmware is being used, then you *must* remove the cursor in this way because it will not be properly positioned. This is because CH is not used to store the cursor's horizontal position when the 8Ø-column firmware is being used; instead, it is stored at OURCH ($57B).

Whatever cursor is used, it must be removed just before the KSW subroutine ends.

Replacing the Keyboard Input Subroutine

As we saw earlier, the //e comes with a built-in keyboard input subroutine called KEYIN ($FD1B). This subroutine takes care of setting the cursor flash rate and of scanning the keyboard until a key has been pressed. There is nothing magic about this particular subroutine, however, and you could easily replace it with another program that would still get input from the keyboard, but would do it differently. In fact, this is essentially what is done whenever you enter a PR#3 command to turn on the //e's 8Ø-column display. As we have seen, when this is done, RDKEY uses a new keyboard input routine called BASICIN which changes the type of cursor used and supports more escape sequences.

You can use your own imagination to dream up some useful features that could be added to a keyboard input subroutine. Some interesting ones to think about are as follows:

- The ability to prevent certain characters from being entered
- Allowing additional escape sequences
- Displaying a different cursor
- Allowing for macro keys (a macro key is one that, when pressed, causes a whole string of characters to be entered).

Later in this chapter, after we have seen how to read the keyboard, we will present some examples of modifying the keyboard input subroutine to meet special requirements such as these.

It is simple to redefine the keyboard input subroutine so that it operates properly when standard 4Ø-column mode is active. In fact, only three basic steps need be performed:

1. Wait for a key to be pressed
2. Remove the cursor
3. Return with the key code in the accumulator.

Complications arise, however, when the subroutine is to work when the //e's 8Ø-column firmware is being used. The following seven steps must be performed by such a subroutine:

1. Remove the "RDKEY" cursor
2. Set up a new cursor
3. Wait for a key to be pressed
4. If ESC is pressed, handle any escape sequence and wait for another key
5. If right-arrow (CTRL-U) is pressed, pick character off screen
6. Remove the new cursor
7. Return with the key code in the accumulator.

The input subroutine has suddenly become much more complicated, for two main reasons. First, as we saw in the previous section, the cursor that the RDKEY ($FDØC) subroutine sets up before calling the input subroutine is valid in standard 4Ø-column mode only. Thus, it must be immediately removed (with a "STA (BASL),Y" instruction) and replaced by one that appears in the proper column position on the 8Ø-column screen. A suitable cursor can be set up by calling a subroutine called INVERT ($CEDD) to toggle the video attribute of the character at the cursor position (from normal to inverse or vice versa). Note that since INVERT is located within the //e's internal ROM space (a space shared with peripheral-card

ROM), it can only be used by first activating this ROM area by writing to INTCXROMON ($C007) — see Chapter 8. The cursor can subsequently be removed by calling INVERT once again.

Second, all escape sequences and right-arrow (CTRL-U) entries must be handled within the input subroutine itself. If the ASCII code for an ESC character was permitted to be returned to the subroutine that requested input (which is usually RDCHAR if a line is being read), then RDCHAR would attempt to handle it by calling ESCNEW ($FBA5). Unfortunately, ESCNEW will not properly handle those escape sequences designed to move the cursor left or right. This is because ESCNEW assumes that the horizontal cursor position is stored in CH ($24), whereas it is actually stored in OURCH ($57B) when the 80-column firmware is being used. Writing the subroutines necessary to handle all the 80-column escape sequences is not simple. The chore can be simplified, however, if the standard 80-column firmware subroutines are referred to as models. One simple alternative, which we will use in later examples, is simply to ignore the ESC key and wait for another keypress if an attempt is made to enter it.

The new input subroutine must also handle the right-arrow key internally, because if it doesn't, GETLN ($FD6A), the subroutine that is called to read a line of information, would try to replace it with the character below the flashing cursor that RDKEY ($FD0C) first sets up. As we have already seen, however, this is usually not the proper cursor position and so the "wrong" character would be copied over by the right-arrow key. The new input subroutine can easily handle the right-arrow key itself by loading the current cursor horizontal position stored at OURCH ($57B) into the Y register and then calling PICK ($CF01) to get the character from the screen and put it in the accumulator. You must then set the character's high-order bit to one by executing an "ORA #$80" instruction.

Just before the 80-column input subroutine ends, it must turn off its internal ROM so that the the peripheral-card ROMs will be active once again. This is done by writing to INTCXROMOFF ($C006). See Chapter 8 for a discussion of the INTCXROM switches.

The ideal input subroutine is one that works equally well whether the 80-column firmware is active or not. Unfortunately, there is no definitive way to determine the state of the 80-column firmware. One method, which will be used in later examples, is to read the status of the ALTCHARSET ($C01E) switch. As we will see in Chapter 7, this switch indicates which of two character sets is active and is normally on (greater than 127) when the 80-column firmware is being used and off when it is not. This method is not foolproof, however, and will fail if the state of ALTCHARSET is changed from its expected value.

Table 6-5 lists a simple keyboard input subroutine that demonstrates how to implement some of the techniques referred to above so that it will be usable whether the 8Ø-column firmware is being used or not. To use it, you must BRUN it directly from diskette.

DOS 3.3, ProDOS, and the Input Link

The ability to change the KSW input link is somewhat restricted if either DOS 3.3 or ProDOS is active. (Similar restrictions apply if the CSW output link is to be changed.) When either DOS is first activated, the address stored in the KSW input link is placed in another input link located within DOS itself. A special KSW input subroutine is then installed that is responsible for detecting and executing any DOS commands that are entered (when Applesoft direct mode is active) and for redirecting the source of input to a diskette file if a DOS READ command is in effect. If a READ command is not in effect, then DOS uses the subroutine whose address is stored in its own input link to get input. The address stored here is initially that of one of the standard keyboard input subroutines.

If standard attempts are made to modify KSW, then DOS could be temporarily disconnected. With two exceptions, this means that you must *not* use any of the following methods to install a new input subroutine:

- Using an Applesoft IN# command (as opposed to the DOS IN# command) from within a program
- Using Applesoft POKE commands to place new values directly into KSWL and KSWH
- Using the Applesoft CALL command or the system monitor GO command (as opposed to the DOS BRUN command) to execute an assembly-language program that stores values directly into KSWL and KSWH.

The first exception to these rules applies if you are using DOS 3.3 (but *not* ProDOS). You are permitted to use POKE to store a new address into KSW, or CALL an assembly-language program that modifies KSW, if immediately thereafter (and before any I/O operations are performed) you execute a CALL 1ØØ2 command or a JSR $3EA instruction. At location 1ØØ2 ($3EA) is a subroutine that takes the address stored in KSW, moves it into the DOS 3.3 input link, and then places the address of the standard DOS 3.3 input subroutine back into KSW. This procedure effectively reconnects DOS 3.3 and keeps your new subroutine active at the same time. Although there is no corresponding subroutine at $3EA

Table 6-5. MODIFY KEYBOARD INPUT. A program to illustrate how to modify the keyboard input subroutine.

```
Page #01

: A S M
            **************************
            * MODIFY KEYBOARD INPUT *
            **************************

            * (BRUN this program from disk)

            BASL     EQU $28
            KSWL     EQU $38

            OURCH    EQU $57B           ;Horizontal position (80-column)

            KBD      EQU $C000          ;Keyboard data + strobe
            KBDSTRB  EQU $C010          ;Clear keyboard strobe

            CXROMON  EQU $C007          ;Turn on internal ROM
            CXROMOFF EQU $C006          ;Enable slot ROMs
            ALTCHAR  EQU $C01E          ;>=$80 if 80-column firmware on

            * 80-column firmware subroutines:
            GETKEY   EQU $CB15          ;Get character from keyboard
            INVERT   EQU $CEDD          ;Invert character on screen
            PICK     EQU $CF01          ;Pick character off screen

                     ORG $300

            * Set up new input link:
0300: A9 09          LDA #<NEWIN
0302: 85 38          STA KSWL
0304: A9 03          LDA #>NEWIN
0306: 85 39          STA KSWL+1
```

```
0308: 60                   RTS
                 
                * This is the new input subroutine:
0309: 2C 1E C0  NEWIN      BIT ALTCHAR      ;80-column firmware in use?
030C: 30 0E                BMI NEWIN1       ;Yes, so branch
030E: 2C 00 C0  GETKBD     BIT KBD          ;Key pressed?
0311: 10 FB                BPL GETKBD       ;No, so branch
0313: 91 28                STA (BASL),Y     ;Remove cursor
0315: AD 00 C0             LDA KBD          ;Get the keyboard character
0318: 2C 10 C0             BIT KBDSTRB      ;Clear keyboard strobe
031B: 60                   RTS
                 
031C: 91 28     NEWIN1     STA (BASL),Y     ;Replace RDKEY's cursor
031E: 8D 07 C0             STA CXROMON      ;Turn on internal $C800 ROM
0321: 20 DD CE             JSR INVERT       ;Set up new cursor
0324: 20 15 CB  INPUT      JSR GETKEY       ;Get a keystroke
0327: C9 9B                CMP #$9B         ;Is it an ESC?
0329: F0 F9                BEQ INPUT        ;If so, ignore it
032B: C9 95                CMP #$95         ;Is it a right arrow?

Page #02

032D: D0 08                BNE CLRCURS      ;No, so branch
032F: AC 7B 05             LDY OURCH        ;Get horizontal cursor position
0332: 20 01 CF             JSR PICK         ;Grab character from screen
0335: 09 80                ORA #$80         ; and set its high bit
0337: 20 DD CE  CLRCURS    JSR INVERT       ;Remove the cursor
033A: 8D 06 C0             STA CXROMOFF     ;Re-enable slot ROMs
033D: 60                   RTS

--End Assembly--

62 bytes

Errors: 0
```

that is available when using ProDOS, you can install a new input subroutine by storing its address directly into the ProDOS input links found at $BE32 and $BE33 instead of into KSW.

The second exception relates to the use of the BRUN command and applies to both DOS 3.3 and ProDOS. If an assembly-language program is loaded and executed directly from diskette by using the BRUN command, then the program is permitted to modify the contents of KSW and both DOS and the new input subroutine will still remain active. This is because just before the program which is BRUN ends, DOS checks to see whether the input link has changed. If it has, it moves the link address into its own input link and places the address of its input subroutine back into KSW.

If you want to use an IN# command within an Applesoft program in order to redirect input to a particular slot, you must use the DOS 3.3 or ProDOS "version" of that command by printing a <CTRL-D> character (ASCII code 4), immediately followed by "IN#s" (where "s" is the slot number) and a carriage return. The <CTRL-D> signifies to DOS that a DOS command is about to be presented; it can be generated using the Applesoft CHR$ function. For example, to redirect input to slot 2 when DOS is being used, execute the following statement:

```
PRINT CHR$(4);"IN#2"
```

instead of the Applesoft "IN#2" command. After this is done, both DOS and the new input subroutine will be active.

ProDOS supports a special form of the IN# command that DOS 3.3 does not. This special IN# command can be used to properly install an input subroutine that is located anywhere in memory and not just to pass control to a program located at a slot. The only restriction on its use is that the first byte of the new input subroutine must be a 65Ø2 "CLD" (clear decimal flag) instruction. To install any such input subroutine, you must execute the statement

```
PRINT CHR$(4);"IN# Aaddr"
```

where "addr" represents either the decimal starting address of the new input subroutine or, if preceded by "$", the hexadecimal starting address. For example, if your new input subroutine begins at $3ØØ (decimal 768), then you would execute either of the following two statements:

```
PRINT CHR$(4);"IN# A$300"
```

or

```
PRINT CHR$(4);"IN# A768"
```

and the new input subroutine will be properly installed in the ProDOS input link.

THE KEYBOARD

The keyboard is probably the most important input/output device attached to the //e. It is one of three primary sources of input (the disk drive and the cassette port being the other two) and without it you would not be able to interact conveniently with any program running on the //e.

We are now going to take a close look at the keyboard. We will explain how it is used to enter information and present examples of how to modify the handling of keyboard input to meet special requirements.

Encoding of Keyboard Characters

The //e's keyboard is made up of 62 typewriter-like keys and one special recessed RESET button. These keys include most of the ones that you would see on a standard typewriter as well as a few more special ones. They are spatially arranged in the standard QWERTY configuration familiar to all typists.

All of the keys on the keyboard, except for the RESET button at the far right of the top row and the two "Apple" keys that flank the space bar, are used to generate the ASCII codes that the //e uses to represent the 52 alphabetic characters (26 upper-case and 26 lower-case), 1Ø digits (Ø . . . 9), 34 special symbols, and 32 "control" codes that it recognizes.

Some keys on the keyboard do not generate ASCII codes when pressed by themselves, but are used to affect the code that is normally generated by another key that is pressed at the same time. These keys are the two SHIFT keys, the CONTROL key, and the CAPS LOCK key.

You can probably guess how the SHIFT keys affect the character codes already. Ignoring the effect of the CAPS LOCK key for the moment, if you press any alphabetic key by itself, you will generate an ASCII code for a lower-case character. If either SHIFT key is pressed at the same time, however, the ASCII code for the corresponding upper-case character is generated instead. The SHIFT key is also pressed to select the ASCII code for the top symbol on those keys that have two symbols marked on them.

The CAPS LOCK key, if in the down position, merely causes any lower-case alphabetic character code that is entered to be converted to the code for the corresponding upper-case character.

The CONTROL key acts in a similar way as the SHIFT keys. If you hold the CONTROL key down and then press any of the 26 alphabetic keys, then an ASCII code for a control character will be selected and not the code for the alphabetic key itself. (The remaining six control characters are generated by pressing the CONTROL key together with one of the following special symbols: @, [, \,], ^, and _).

Special Keys

There are several special keys on the //e's keyboard that you probably won't see on a standard typewriter. These are the ESC (for ESCape), TAB, DELETE, UP-ARROW, DOWN-ARROW, LEFT-ARROW, RIGHT-ARROW, OPEN-APPLE, and CLOSED-APPLE keys.

The ESC, TAB, DELETE, and the four arrow keys all generate specific ASCII codes when they are pressed and they are often referred to as "editing" keys. Refer to Table 6-1 for the ASCII codes generated by these keys.

Different programs will perform different tasks when an editing key is pressed. It is hoped, however, that the tasks performed will relate in a meaningful way to the name or the symbol on the keycap. That is, it would be preferable if the ESC key actually caused you to ESCape (or exit) some part of a program and the TAB key caused the cursor to move several spaces to the right, and so on. It would be incredibly annoying, for example, if when you pressed the down-arrow key your cursor moved up or if you pressed the DELETE and the cursor moved five spaces to the right.

The "Apple" Keys

The OPEN-APPLE and CLOSED-APPLE keys that flank the space bar are actually equivalent to push buttons #Ø and #1 on the game I/O connector, respectively. These push buttons will be described in detail in Chapter 1Ø. Although these keys cannot be used to generate ASCII codes, they could be used, with appropriate software, to act as special shift keys. The software, after reading a key, could check to see whether an "Apple" key was being pressed; if one was, then a different action could be taken than if the key were pressed by itself. For example, Apple has issued design guidelines urging software developers to consider the question mark key as a "HELP" key if it is pressed at the same time as the OPEN-APPLE key. Here is how you would implement a help function in an Applesoft program:

```
10 PRINT "Enter a command: ";:GET A$
20 IF A$="?" AND PEEK(49249)>127 THEN 1000
.
.
.
1000 REM PLACE "HELP" CODE HERE
```

Memory location 49249 is the address of the location that holds the state of the OPEN-APPLE key (49250 is used for the CLOSED-APPLE key). If the value read from this location is greater than 127 (that is, bit 7 is on), then OPEN-APPLE is being pressed.

The OPEN-APPLE and CLOSED-APPLE keys can also be used to modify the effect of resetting the //e. This is discussed in the last section of this chapter.

KEYBOARD I/O LOCATIONS

The Apple //e reserves two I/O memory locations for use by the keyboard I/O device. These two locations are $C000 and $C010 and their meanings are summarized in Table 6-6.

KBD ($C000) is used to hold the 7-bit ASCII code for any key-

Table 6-6. Keyboard I/O locations.

Address Hex	*(Dec)*	*Symbolic Name*	*Meaning*
$C000	(49152)	KBD	Keyboard data and strobe. Keyboard data is stored in bits 0 . . . 6. Bit 7 represents the keyboard strobe and will be 1 if keyboard data is ready to be read.
$C010	(49168)	KBDSTRB or AKD	Clear keyboard strobe and read any-key-down status. Reading or writing this location will clear the keyboard strobe bit at $C000. Bit 7 indicates whether a key is being pressed; if it is 1, then a key is being pressed.

board character that is entered as well as a 1-bit "strobe" flag. The strobe flag is held in bit 7 of KBD and indicates whether a key has been pressed and is ready to be presented to the system. If the bit is set to 1, then keyboard data is ready to be read; if it is cleared to Ø, then no keyboard character has yet been entered since the last time the strobe was cleared. The lower 7 bits of KBD always contains the ASCII code of the last key entered.

The second keyboard I/O location is KBDSTRB ($CØ1Ø). This location is used for two purposes. First, if any read or write operation is performed on this location, such as a PEEK or a POKE, then the keyboard strobe bit (in KBD) will be cleared to zero. This tells the //e's built-in keyboard input subroutines that the keyboard data has already been dealt with and that no further information should be read from the keyboard until the strobe flag becomes set once again.

Second, bit 7 of KBDSTRB ($CØ1Ø), also called AKD ($CØ1Ø), indicates the status of the "any-key-down" flag. If it is 1, then a key is being pressed; if it is Ø, then no key is being pressed. This flag is not the same as the strobe flag because, as we will see later on, there are times when even though a key is being pressed, it has not yet been officially strobed into the system.

Here is a simple assembly-language program to read data from the keyboard:

```
WAITFORKEY LDA $C000        ;Get keyboard data + strobe
           BPL WAITFORKEY   ;Loop until strobe is set
           STA $C010        ;Clear keyboard strobe
```

The branch-on-plus (BPL) instruction will cause this program to loop until KBD becomes "negative," that is, until bit 7 of KBD (the strobe bit) becomes 1.

In Applesoft, this program would be written as follows:

```
100 IF PEEK(49152)<128 THEN 100 : REM WAIT FOR STROBE
110 POKE 49168,0 : REM CLEAR KEYBOARD STROBE
```

It is important that the keyboard strobe be cleared after reading data from the keyboard. If it isn't, the program will keep thinking that a key has just been pressed whenever it checks for more keyboard data.

Let's look at a simple program, called TYPING TIMER, that makes use of the AKD ($CØ1Ø) flag; it is shown in Table 6-7. This program analyzes your typing speed by displaying the length of time your finger stays on each key that you press and the time delay between successive keystrokes. It does this by simply monitoring the status of the AKD flag and keeping track of the elapsed time using a software counter. In a fully developed program of this sort, you would be able to quickly pinpoint a typist's problem areas.

After you enter the program, you can run it by entering CALL 768 from Applesoft direct mode. After you do this, type in four characters from the keyboard as fast as you can. After you have done this, a set of five times (in units of 2Ø microseconds) will be displayed. The meanings of each of these times are as follows:

First : ON time for first key
Second : delay between first and second keys
Third : ON time for second key
Fourth : delay between second and third keys
Fifth : ON time for third key
Sixth : delay between third and fourth keys

To convert the displayed numbers into milliseconds, simply divide them by fifty. You should take note of how the decimal values for these times are displayed. The program makes use of an Applesoft subroutine called LINPRT ($ED24); this subroutine takes a binary number that is in X (low byte) and A (high byte) and displays it as an unsigned decimal number.

MODIFYING THE KEYBOARD INPUT SUBROUTINE

Earlier in this chapter, we saw how it was possible to replace the subroutine that the //e uses in order to obtain character input by simply changing the input link at KSW ($38/$39). At that time, we indicated that it would be possible to install a wide variety of subroutines that would still obtain input from the keyboard but would do it in different, more useful, ways.

Look at the program called MACRO ENTRY in Table 6-8. It must be installed by using the BRUN command to execute it directly from diskette. This program allows you to automatically enter a commonly used command phrase from the keyboard simply by pressing the OPEN-APPLE key at the same time as one of three other keys, C, H, or L. These keys will generate the following sequences of characters:

C → CATALOG,D1 (followed by RETURN)
H → HOME (followed by RETURN)
L → LOAD (followed by SPACE)

A key that is used to enter a whole string of other characters is called a macro key. With MACRO ENTRY installed, it is a simple matter to catalog the disk, clear the screen, or to "type in" LOAD before specifying the name of a program. All you must do is press OPEN-APPLE and the appropriate macro key.

Table 6-7. TYPING TIMER. A program to demonstrate how AKD($C010) works.

```
Page #01

: A S M

                    ****************
                    * TYPING TIMER *
                    ****************

                    CHARS    EQU 3           ;Number of chars. to be typed

                    AKD      EQU $C010       ;Any-key-down flag

                    HEXDEC   EQU $ED24       ;Hex-to-decimal conversion
                    CROUT    EQU $FD8E       ;Send a CR

                             ORG $300

0300: A2 00                  LDX #0
0302: 20 41 03               JSR RELEASE
0305: 20 2C 03      NEXTKEY  JSR PRESS       ;Get a keystroke
0308: E8                     INX
0309: E8                     INX
030A: E8                     INX
030B: E8                     INX
030C: E0 0C                  CPX #CHARS*4
030E: D0 F5                  BNE NEXTKEY

                    * Display the results:
0310: A0 00                  LDY #0
0312: B9 58 03      TIMEDSP  LDA TIMEON,Y
0315: AA                     TAX
0316: B9 59 03               LDA TIMEON+1,Y
0319: 8C 57 03               STY YSAVE
031C: 20 24 ED               JSR HEXDEC      ;Display in decimal
031F: 20 8E FD               JSR CROUT
0322: AC 57 03               LDY YSAVE
```

```
0325: C8                    INY
0326: C8                    INY
0327: C0 0C                 CPY #CHARS*4
0329: D0 E7                 BNE TIMEDSP
032B: 60                    RTS

             * (Loop time is ~20 microsec.)
032C: A9 00     PRESS       LDA #0
032E: 9D 59 03              STA TIMEON+1,X   ;Initialize "ON" timer
0331: 9D 58 03              STA TIMEON,X
0334: FE 58 03  KEYWAIT     INC TIMEON,X     ;Bump the time count
0337: D0 03                 BNE KEYWAIT1
0339: FE 59 03              INC TIMEON+1,X
033C: 2C 10 C0  KEYWAIT1    BIT AKD          ;Is key still pressed?
033F: 30 F3                 BMI KEYWAIT      ;Yes, so wait

0341: A9 00     RELEASE     LDA #0

Page #02

0343: 9D 5B 03              STA TIMEOFF+1,X ;Initialize "OFF" timer
0346: 9D 5A 03              STA TIMEOFF,X
0349: FE 5A 03  RELWAIT     INC TIMEOFF,X    ;Bump the time count
034C: D0 03                 BNE RELWAIT1
034E: FE 5B 03              INC TIMEOFF+1,X
0351: 2C 10 C0  RELWAIT1    BIT AKD          ;Has key been released?
0354: 10 F3                 BPL RELWAIT      ;No, so wait
0356: 60                    RTS

                YSAVE       DS  1

                TIMEON      DS  2            ;Duration of keypress
                TIMEOFF     DS  2            ;Duration of key release
                            DS  CHARS*4-4    ;Data for other keystrokes

--End assembly--

100 bytes

Errors: 0
```

Table 6-8. MACRO ENTRY. A program to define macro keys.

```
Page #01

: A S M

                ****************
                * MACRO ENTRY *
                ****************
                * (BRUN this program from disk)
                MTOTAL   EQU 3           ;Number of macro keys in MACROKEY
                BASL     EQU $28         ;Base address for video line
                KSW      EQU $38         ;Input "link"
                OURCH    EQU $57B        ;Horizontal position (80-column)
                KBD      EQU $C000       ;Keyboard data + strobe
                CXROMOFF EQU $C006       ;Select slot ROMs
                CXROMON  EQU $C007       ;Select internal ROM
                KBDSTRB  EQU $C010       ;Clear keyboard strobe
                ALTCHAR  EQU $C01E       ;Status of character set
                OPENAPL  EQU $C061       ;OPEN-APPLE switch
                INVERT   EQU $CEDD       ;Invert character on screen
                PICK     EQU $CF01       ;Pick character off screen
                         ORG $300
                * Set up new input link:
0300: A9 09              LDA #<NEWIN
0302: 85 38              STA KSW
0304: A9 03              LDA #>NEWIN
0306: 85 39              STA KSW+1
0308: 60                 RTS
```

```
                  * This is the new input routine:

0309: 2C 1E C0    NEWIN     BIT ALTCHAR     ;80-column firmware active?
030C: 10 08                 BPL NEWIN1      ;No, so branch
303E: 91 28                 STA (BASL),Y    ;Replace RDKEY's cursor
0310: 8D 07 C0              STA CXROMON     ;Turn on internal $Cx ROM
0313: 20 DD CE              JSR INVERT      ;Set up new cursor
0316: 8E AE 03    NEWIN1    STX XSAVE
0319: 8C AF 03              STY YSAVE
031C: 8D AD 03              STA ASAVE
031F: 2C B1 03              BIT MACROFLG    ;Are we processing a macro?
0322: 30 67                 BMI GETMAC      ;Yes, so branch
0324: 2C 00 C0    NEWIN2    BIT KBD         ;Anything at keyboard?
0327: 10 FB                 BPL NEWIN2      ;Branch until there is
0329: 2C 1E C0              BIT ALTCHAR     ;80-column firmware active?
032C: 30 02                 BMI NEWIN3      ;Yes, so branch
032E: 91 28                 STA (BASL),Y    ;Replace screen character

Page #02

0330: AD 00 C0    NEWIN3    LDA KBD         ;Get the keystroke
0333: 2C 10 C0              BIT KBDSTRB     ; and clear the strobe.
0336: 2C 1E C0              BIT ALTCHAR     ;80-column firmware active?
0339: 10 16                 BPL NEWIN4      ;No, so branch
033B: C9 9B                 CMP #$9B        ;ESC pressed?
033D: F0 E5                 BEQ NEWIN2      ;Yes, so ignore and branch
033F: C9 95                 CMP #$95        ;Right arrow?
0341: D0 08                 BNE CLRCURS
0343: AC 7B 05              LDY OURCH
0346: 20 01 CF              JSR PICK        ;Get character from screen
0349: 09 80                 ORA #$80
034B: 20 DD CE    CLRCURS   JSR INVERT      ;Remove cursor
034E: 8D 06 C0              STA CXROMOFF    ;Re-enable slot ROMs
0351: 2C 61 C0    NEWIN4    BIT OPENAPL     ;Is OPEN-APPLE being pressed?
0354: 10 53                 BPL EXIT        ;No, so exit
0356: A2 00                 LDX #0
```

(continued)

Table 6-8. MACRO ENTRY. A program to define macro keys (continued).

```
0358: DD B3 03    ORIGSCAN CMP MACROKEY,X   ;Is this a command key?
035B: F0 07                BEQ FINDMAC      ;Yes, so branch
035D: E8                   INX              ;Go on to next item in table
035E: E0 03                CPX #MTOTAL      ;At end of table?
0360: D0 F6                BNE ORIGSCAN     ;No, so keep looking
0362: F0 45                BEQ EXIT
0364: A9 80       FINDMAC  LDA #$80
0366: 8D B1 03             STA MACROFLG     ;Set "macro in effect" flag
0369: 8E B0 03             STX CMDNUM
036C: A2 00                LDX #0
036E: 8E B2 03             STX MACROPOS
0371: A0 00                LDY #
0373: CC B0 03    FINDMAC1 CPY CMDNUM       ;Have we found the macro?
0376: F0 13                BEQ GETMAC       ;Yes, so branch
0378: AE B2 03    SKIPMAC  LDX MACROPOS
037B: BD B6 03             LDA PHRASES,X    ;Get macro character
037E: F0 05                BEQ FINDMAC2     ;Branch if past end
0380: EE B2 03             INC MACROPOS     ; else move to next position
0383: D0 F3                BNE SKIPMAC
0385: EE B2 03    FINDMAC2 INC MACROPOS
0388: C8                   INY              ;Increment macro count
0389: D0 E8                BNE FINDMAC1
0388: AE B2 03    GETMAC   LDX MACROPOS
038E: BD B6 03             LDA PHRASES,X    ;Get new character
0391: EE B2 03             INC MACROPOS     ;Update position within macro
0394: C9 00                CMP #0           ;At the end?
0396: D0 07                BNE EXIT1        ;No, so exit
0398: A9 00                LDA #0
039A: 8D B1 03             STA MACROFLG     ;Clear "macro in effect" flag
039D: F0 85                BEQ NEWIN2       ; and get a keystroke
039F: 48          EXIT1    PHA
03A0: AD AD 03             LDA ASAVE
03A3: AC AF 03             LDY YSAVE
03A6: 91 28                STA (BASL),Y
03A8: 68                   PLA
```

```
Page #03

03A9: AE AE 03  EXIT      LDX XSAVE
03AC: 60                  RTS

                ASAVE     DS  1
                XSAVE     DS  1
                YSAVE     DS  1
                CMDNUM    DS  1
03B1: 00        MACROFLG  DFB 0              ;0=no macro / $80=macro
03B2: 00        MACROPOS  DFB 0

                * Table of macro keys:
                * (high bit must be on)
03B3: C3        MACROKEY  ASC "C"
03B4: C8                  ASC "H"
03B5: CC                  ASC "L"

                * Table of macro phrases:
                * (each entry must end with a 0)
03B6: C3 C1 D4  PHRASES   ASC "CATALOG,D1"
03B9: C1 CC CF C7 AC C4 B1
03C0: 8D 00               DFB $8D,0
03C2: C8 CF CD            ASC "HOME"
03C5: C5
03C6: 8D 00               DFB $8D,0
03C8: CC CF C1            AC  "LOAD"
03CB: C4 A0
03CD: 00                  DFB 0


--End assembly--

206 bytes

Errors: 0
```

The first part of MACRO ENTRY simply sets up the new input link so that it points to NEWIN, the start of the new input routine. This means that every time a program requests input from the //e by calling the standard RDKEY ($FDØC) input subroutine, control will eventually pass to NEWIN instead of the standard keyboard input subroutine.

When NEWIN is entered, some registers that will be used are first saved and then a location (called MACROFLG) is checked to see whether a macro entry is currently being processed. If not, the program enters a tight loop until a keypress is detected. After a key has been pressed, the character is loaded into the accumulator and the status of the OPEN-APPLE key is examined with a BIT OPENAPL instruction. If it is not being pressed, then the following BPL instruction will succeed (because bit 7 of OPENAPL will be Ø) and control will return to the calling program as usual.

However, if OPEN-APPLE is being pressed, then the MACROKEY table is scanned to see whether it contains the keyboard character that has been entered. If it doesn't, then control returns to the calling program. If it does, then the high-order bit of MACROFLG is set and the first character of the entry in the PHRASES table is returned to the calling program. Each time that input is requested after this, the next character in the macro phrase will be returned to the calling program. This will continue until all characters have been returned, at which time MACROFLG is cleared.

If you want to change the macro commands and associated entries, then you must modify the MACROKEY and PHRASES tables. The ASCII code for each command key must be stored in the MACROKEY table with the high bit on. The corresponding macro phrases for each key must be stored, in order, in the PHRASES table; each phrase must be terminated by a ØØ byte. In addition, you must set MTOTAL equal to the number of macro keys in the MACROKEY table before reassembling the program.

Recall that only locations $3ØØ through $3CF are available for use in page three of memory. You must ensure that your macro tables are short enough that you do not spill over the $3CF boundary.

KEYBOARD AUTO-REPEAT

When you enter a key that corresponds to a particular ASCII code, that code will begin to repeat after you have kept the key pressed for longer than about 9ØØ milliseconds. (This time could be shorter, but heavy-handed typists might then encounter difficulties.) Once this "pre-repeat" period has elapsed, the code will begin to repeat itself 15 times per second (that is, once every 66.7 milliseconds). The auto-repeat phenomenon is generated by circuitry on the //e's motherboard.

The auto-repeat feature is useful if you are editing programs or if are you are using word-processing programs. In both cases, it is often necessary to repeat character sequences or use an arrow key several times in succession to move the cursor to a new position. These tasks can be done easily merely by pressing the appropriate key and holding it down until the key is repeated as many times as is required.

The timing diagram for the keyboard's auto-repeat function is shown in Figure 6-1. As soon as a key is first pressed, the AKD ($CØ1Ø) flag is turned on and, a few microseconds later, the keyboard strobe is turned on. The keyboard strobe will then stay on until it is cleared by accessing KBDSTRB ($CØ1Ø). This is done right after the keyboard is read by the standard keyboard input subroutines. Note, however, that if the key is still being pressed, the AKD flag will remain on even after the strobe has been cleared.

After the strobe is cleared, and if the key is still being pressed, there is a short delay of about 9ØØ milliseconds (called the "pre-repeat" delay) and then the keyboard strobe is turned on again.

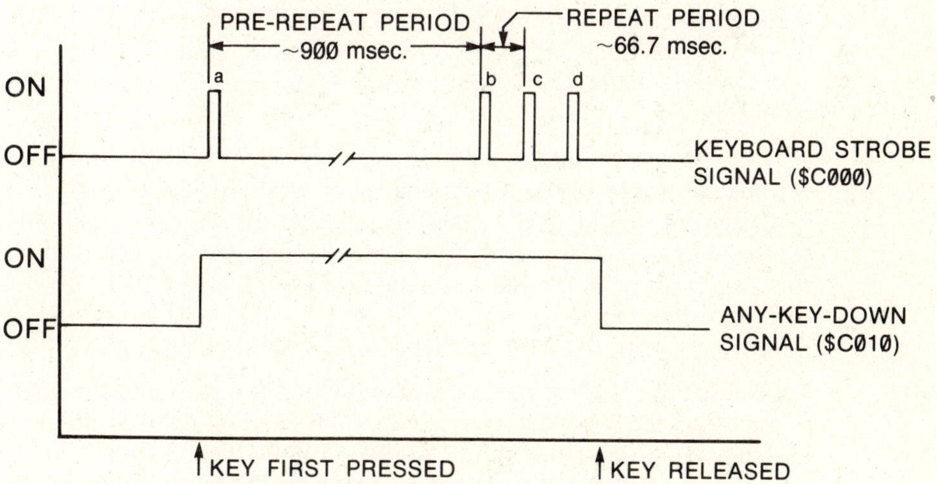

NOTE: The keyboard strobe is cleared at points "a", "b", "c", and "d" by accessing KBDSTRB ($CØ1Ø).

Figure 6-1. Keyboard auto-repeat timing diagram.

As usual, it will stay on until KBDSTRB is accessed once again. The width of the strobe pulse will depend on how rapidly the strobe is cleared after the strobe is turned on. Figure 6-1 was prepared by assuming that this is happening soon after the strobe is high and certainly much faster than the rate at which the key repeats.

At this stage, the keyboard strobe will automatically be turned on once every 66.7 milliseconds after it has been cleared and until the key is finally released. Even while the keyboard strobe is being turned on and off, however, the AKD flag remains on; in fact, AKD is turned off only when the key is finally released. Thus, there are substantial periods of time when even though the AKD flag is on (that is, a key is being pressed), the keyboard strobe is not on.

Since most keyboard input subroutines, including the standard ones used in the //e, rely on the keyboard strobe to detect the presence or absence of a valid key code, the key code will be repeated at the same rate that the strobe is turned on (this is fixed by the //e's internal circuitry). If, however, an alternate input subroutine is used that examines the AKD flag and returns a key code if it is on continuously for a given time period (even though, at the end of the period, the keyboard strobe may not be on), then a different repeat rate can be generated in software.

The SOFTWARE AUTO-REPEAT program in Table 6-9 shows you how to adjust the auto-repeat rate in software. This program must be installed by using the BRUN command to load and execute it directly from diskette. SOFTWARE AUTO-REPEAT modifies the input link so that it points to the code beginning at NEWIN. After this has been done, all requests for keyboard input will be processed by this subroutine and a much faster auto-repeat rate will be observed.

The first thing the new input subroutine does when it is called is to determine whether a new character was entered the last time it was called (RPTFLAG = $ØØ) or whether an old one was being repeated (RPTFLAG = $8Ø). If a new character was entered, then the accumulator is loaded with the number given by PREDELAY (the pre-repeat delay time); if not, it is loaded with the smaller number given by RPTDELAY (the auto-repeat time interval).

A delay loop is then entered during which the status of the AKD flag is repeatedly checked. If the flag is turned off (that is, the key is released) at any time before the loop finishes, then RPTFLAG is set equal to $ØØ (to indicate that repeating has ended) and then keyboard input is requested in the standard way (by waiting for the keyboard strobe to be turned on). After a keyboard character is received, it is stored in OLDKEY.

If a key remains pressed until the timing loop finishes, then the keyboard data is immediately read from KBD ($CØØØ), even though the strobe may not actually be on. This data will usually equal the code stored in OLDKEY (the previous key strobed in). If at some time during the loop, however, another key was pressed before the previous one was released, it will be different. If the key code is the same (the usual case), RPTFLAG is set equal to $8Ø. This indicates that an auto-repeat sequence is in effect so that the next time input is requested, the shorter "RPTDELAY" delay loop will be selected. Otherwise, RPTFLAG is set to $ØØ. In either case, the key code is stored in OLDKEY before the subroutine finishes.

The important point to note here is that the keyboard data will *always* be read after the key has been pressed for the length of time set by the loop counter (PREDELAY or RPTDELAY). Thus, we can select both the auto-repeat rate and the predelay time simply by changing the RPTDELAY and PREDELAY constants. You may want to try out different repeat rates and predelay times by changing these constants in the program. Be warned, however, that if you set RPTDELAY too low, your reflexes may not be fast enough to control the speeding cursor! You should also be careful not to set PREDELAY too low or else you may not be able to press and release a key before it starts to repeat!

KEYBOARD TYPE-AHEAD

As we have seen, whenever the //e wants to receive a character from the keyboard it calls a subroutine that continually scans the keyboard strobe line until it goes high and then reads KBD. This technique is called "polling" because the software is continually directly "asking" the keyboard whether it has a character available. One consequence of using the polling method is that if you try to enter characters from the keyboard when the //e is not actually polling the keyboard, then all those characters will be "missed" except for the last one entered.

Some computer systems, notably the IBM Personal Computer, handle keyboard input in a different way. They allow the keyboard to interrupt the microprocessor whenever a key has been strobed into the system. The keyboard interrupt-handling routine then gets this character from the keyboard and stores it in a small buffer, typically 16 bytes in length. When a program wants a character from the keyboard, it does not poll the keyboard itself but rather reads it from this buffer.

Table 6-9. SOFTWARE AUTO-REPEAT. A program to alter the auto-repeat rate.

```
Page #01

: A S M

************************
* SOFTWARE AUTO-REPEAT *
************************

* (BRUN this program from disk)

PREDELAY EQU 150           ;Delay before repeating begins
RPTDELAY EQU 20            ;Delay between repeats

BASL     EQU $28           ;Base address for video line
KSW      EQU $38           ;Input "link"

OURCH    EQU $57B          ;Horizontal position (80-column)

KBD      EQU $C000         ;Keyboard data + strobe
KBDSTRB  EQU $C010         ;Clear keyboard strobe
AKD      EQU $C010         ;Any-key-down flag

CXROMOFF EQU $C006         ;Select slot ROMs
CXROMON  EQU $C007         ;Select internal ROM
ALTCHAR  EQU $C01E         ;Character set status

INVERT   EQU $CEDD         ;Invert character on screen
PICK     EQU $CF01         ;Pick character off screen

         ORG $300

* Install new input subroutine:

```

```
0300: A9 09               LDA #<NEWIN
0302: 85 38               STA KSW
0304: A9 03               LDA #>NEWIN
0306: 85 39               STA KSW+1
0308: 60                  RTS

0309: 48        NEWIN     PHA               ;Save screen character
030A: 8C 82 03            STY YSAVE         ;Save Y-register
030D: 2C 1E C0            BIT ALTCHAR       ;Using 80-column firmware?
0310: 10 08               BPL NEWIN1        ;No, so branch
0312: 91 28               STA (BASL),Y      ;Remove RDKEY cursor
0314: 8D 07 C0            STA CXROMON       ;Turn on internal $Cx ROM
0317: 20 DD CE            JSR INVERT        ;Set up new cursor

                * Wait before repeating:

031A: A9 14     NEWIN1    LDA #RPTDELAY     ;Get auto-repeat counter
031C: 2C 81 03            BIT RPTFLAG       ;Are we repeating?
031F: 30 02               BMI WAIT          ;Yes, so branch
0321: A9 96               LDA #PREDELAY     ;Use pre-repeat counter instead

Page #02

0323: 38        WAIT      SEC
0324: A0 80     WAIT1     LDY #128
0326: 2C 10 C0  WAIT2     BIT AKD           ;Key still being pressed?
0329: 10 20               BPL RPTOFF        ;No, so go to standard input
032B: 88                  DEY
032C: D0 F8               BNE WAIT2
032E: E9 01               SBC #1
0330: D0 F2               BNE WAIT1

                * If we've reached here, we are repeating (unless another
                * key was pressed before releasing the first one). The
                * following code reads the keyboard (before its code
```

(continued)

Table 6-9. SOFTWARE AUTO-REPEAT. A program to alter the auto-repeat rate (continued).

```
                   * has been strobed in) and sets the high bit as per
                   * the standard input protocol:

0332: AD 00 C0               LDA KBD          ;Get key code
0335: 2C 10 C0               BIT KBDSTRB      ;Clear strobe (just in case)
0338: 09 80                  ORA #$80         ;Set high bit
033A: CD 80 03               CMP OLDKEY       ;Same as previous key?
033D: F0 04                  BEQ RPTON        ;Yes, so we're repeating
033F: A0 00                  LDY #0           ;Repeat off
0341: F0 02                  BEQ FIXRPT       ;(always taken)
0343: A0 80          RPTON   LDY #$80         ;Repeat on
0345: 8C 81 03       FIXRPT  STY RPTFLAG      ;Adjust the repeat flag
0348: 4C 58 03               JMP GETKEY1

                   * Key was lifted, so wait for standard keypress:

034B: A9 00          RPTOFF  LDA #0
034D: 8D 81 03               STA RPTFLAG      ;Repeat off

0350: AD 00 C0       GETKEY  LDA KBD          ;Has a key been strobed in?
0353: 10 FB                  BPL GETKEY       ;No, so branch
0355: 2C 10 C0               BIT KBDSTRB      ;Clear keyboard strobe
0358: 8D 80 03       GETKEY1 STA OLDKEY       ;Save key code for next time

035B: 2C 1E C0               BIT ALTCHAR      ;80-column firmware active?
035E: 10 16                  BPL CLRCURS1     ;No, so branch
0360: C9 9B                  CMP #$9B         ;Is it an ESC?
0362: F0 B6                  BEQ NEWIN1       ;Yes, so ignore
0364: C9 95                  CMP #$95         ;Is it a right arrow?
0366: D0 08                  BNE CLRCURS      ;No, so branch
0368: AC 7B 05               LDY OURCH        ;Get screen position
036B: 20 01 CF               JSR PICK         ;Grab character from screen
036E: 09 80                  ORA #$80         ; and set its high bit
```

```
0370: 20 DD CE    CLRCURS   JSR INVERT      ;Remove 80-column cursor
0373: 8D 06 C0              STA CXROMOFF    ;Re-enable slot ROMs
0376: 68          CLRCURS1  PLA             ;Get old screen character
0377: AC 82 03              LDY YSAVE       ;Restore Y-register
037A: 91 28                 STA (BASL),Y    ;Remove 40-column cursor
037C: AD 80 03              LDA OLDKEY      ;Get the key code

Page #03

037F: 60                    RTS

0380: 00          OLDKEY    DFB 0           ;Last key pressed
0381: 00          RPTFLAG   DFB 0           ;0=not repeating / $80=repeating
                  YSAVE     DS  1           ;Temporary storage area for Y


--End assembly--

131 bytes

Errors: 0
```

The advantage of using the keyboard interrupt technique should be obvious: unless the interrupts are turned off by the software (using something like a SEI instruction), all characters entered from the keyboard will be recorded in the buffer (assuming that it is not full) and will be available to the system even if the program is not, at the time of the keypress, reading the keyboard. Thus, you can "type ahead" of the program and wait for it to read your already entered input later, when it is ready to receive it.

It is not possible to use the keyboard interrupt technique on the //e without making major hardware changes to the system. We can simulate such a technique in software, however, by using a program such as SOFTWARE TYPE-AHEAD, listed in Table 6-1Ø.

This program maintains a 16-byte first-in, first-out (FIFO) type-ahead buffer that can be used to store up to 15 characters. Two pointers are used to keep track of the information contained in this buffer: BUFFHEAD is always equal to the position, less one, of the first character placed in the buffer and not yet read; and BUFFTAIL is always equal to the position of the last character placed in the buffer. If BUFFHEAD and BUFFTAIL are equal, then the buffer is empty.

Because we can't take advantage of a keyboard interrupt to signal us whenever a character has been entered from the keyboard, we will have to do the next best thing and call, as often as possible, a subroutine called GETCHAR that checks the keyboard for the presence of input. GETCHAR takes care of scanning the keyboard and, if a keypress is detected, of placing its ASCII code in the buffer. If it turns out that the buffer is full, then you will hear a beep and the character will not be placed in the buffer. If it is placed in the buffer, you will hear a more pleasant-sounding click.

Two convenient times to call GETCHAR are whenever the //e is performing input or output operations. If you look at the program listing in Table 6-1Ø you will see that the input link (and the output link that will be discussed in Chapter 7) have been adjusted so that they point to INPUT and OUTPUT, respectively. The INPUT subroutine executes a loop where it continually calls GETCHAR and, at the same time, keeps checking the keyboard buffer to see whether a character is available. If a character is available, it is taken from the buffer and BUFFHEAD is incremented.

OUTPUT is almost identical to the //e's standard output routine at COUT1 ($FDFØ). In fact, the only difference is that it first calls GETCHAR to buffer a keyboard character, if one has been entered.

Table 6-10. SOFTWARE TYPE-AHEAD. A program that provides a keyboard type-ahead buffer.

```
Page #01

: A S M
         *************************
         *   SOFTWARE TYPE-AHEAD *
         *************************

         * (BRUN this program from disk)

         BASL      EQU   $28          ;Base address of video line
         CSWL      EQU   $36          ;Output link
         CSWH      EQU   $37
         KSWL      EQU   $38          ;Input link
         KSWH      EQU   $39
         RNDL      EQU   $4E          ;Random number seed
         RNDH      EQU   $4F
         CHRGET    EQU   $BA          ;Applesoft line parsing routine
         RETCHR    EQU   $BE
         OURCH     EQU   $57B         ;Horizontal position (80-column)

         KBD       EQU   $C000        ;Keyboard data + strobe
         CXROMOFF  EQU   $C006        ;Select slot ROM
         CXROMON   EQU   $C007        ;Select internal ROM
         KBDSTRB   EQU   $C010        ;Clear keyboard strobe
         ALTCHAR   EQU   $C10E        ;Character set status
         SPEAKER   EQU   $C030        ;I/O address for speaker

         BASICOUT  EQU   $C307        ;Standard 80-column output
         INVERT    EQU   $CEDD        ;Invert character on screen
         PICK      EQU   $CF01        ;Pick character off screen
         WAIT      EQU   $FCA8
```

(continued)

Table 6-10. SOFTWARE TYPE-AHEAD. A program that provides a keyboard type-ahead buffer (continued).

```
                BELL      EQU  $FF3A        ;Sound the bell
                COUT1     EQU  $FDF0        ;Video output

                BUFFSIZE  EQU  16           ;Size of type-ahead buffer

                          ORG  $2DB

                 ***************************
                 * Initialize the buffer   *
                 * read and write pointers.*
                 ***************************
02DB: A9 00                LDA  #0
02DD: 8D AC 03             STA  BUFFHEAD
02E0: 8D AD 03             STA  BUFFTAIL

                 *******************************
                 * Overlay Applesoft CHRGET    *
                 * routine with a JMP PARSECHK *
                 * to allow type-ahead to work *
                 * during line parsing.        *
                 *******************************

Page #02

02E3: A9 4C                LDA  #$4C        ;JMP opcode
02E5: 85 BA                STA  CHRGET
02E7: A9 A1                LDA  #<PARSECHK
02E9: 85 BB                STA  CHRGET+1
02EB: A9 03                LDA  #>PARSECHK
02ED: 85 BC                STA  CHRGET+2

                 *************************
                 * Set up new I/O links. *
                 *************************
```

```
02EF: A9 5A                 LDA  #<OUTPUT
02F1: 85 36                 STA  CSWL
02F3: A9 03                 LDA  #>OUTPUT
02F5: 85 37                 STA  CSWH
02F7: A9 00                 LDA  #<INPUT
02F9: 85 38                 STA  KSWL
02FB: A9 03                 LDA  #>INPUT
02FD: 85 39                 STA  KSWH
02FF: 60                    RTS

                ********************************
                * This is the new input        *
                * routine that takes a         *
                * character from the buffer    *
                * instead of the keyboard.     *
                ********************************
0300: 2C 1E C0  INPUT       BIT  ALTCHAR      ;80-column firmware active?
0303: 10 0B                 BPL  INPUT1       ;No, so branch
0305: 91 28                 STA  (BASL),Y     ;Replace RDKEY's cursor
0307: 8D 07 C0              STA  CXROMON      ;Turn on internal $Cx ROM
030A: 20 DD CE              JSR  INVERT       ;Set up new cursor
030D: 4C 11 03              JMP  INPUT2
0310: 48        INPUT1      PHA               ;Save video character
0311: 20 68 03  INPUT2      JSR  GETCHAR      ;Buffer a character (if possible)
0314: E6 4E                 INC  RNDL         ;(Random number generator)
0316: D0 02                 BNE  INPUT3
0318: E6 4F                 INC  RNDH
031A: AD AC 03  INPUT3      LDA  BUFFHEAD     ;If buffer head = buffer tail,
031D: CD AD 03              CMP  BUFFTAIL     ; then buffer is empty
0320: F0 EF                 BEQ  INPUT2
0322: 2C 1E C0              BIT  ALTCHAR      ;80-column firmware active?
0325: 30 03                 BMI  INPUT4       ;Yes, so branch
0327: 68                    PLA
0328: 91 28                 STA  (BASL),Y     ;Restore video character
032A: AC AC 03  INPUT4      LDY  BUFFHEAD
032D: 20 52 03              JSR  PTRBUMP
```

(continued)

Table 6-1Ø. SOFTWARE TYPE-AHEAD. A program that provides a keyboard type-ahead buffer (continued).

```
0330: 8C AC 03              STY   BUFFHEAD
0333: B9 AE 03              LDA   BUFFER,Y    ;Get next character in buffer
0336: 2C 1E C0              BIT   ALTCHAR     ;80-column firmware active?
0339: 10 16                 BPL   EXIT        ;No, so branch
033B: C9 9B                 CMP   #$9B        ;ESC pressed

Page #03

033D: F0 D2                 BEQ   INPUT2      ;Yes, so ignore
033F: C9 95                 CMP   #$95        ;Is it a right arrow?
0341: D0 08                 BNE   CLRCURS     ;No, so branch
0343: AC 7B 05              LDY   OURCH
0346: 20 01 CF              JSR   PICK        ;Get character off screen
0349: 09 80                 ORA   #$80
034B: 20 DD CE    CLRCURS   JSR   INVERT      ;Turn off cursor
034E: 8D 06 C0              STA   CXROMOFF    ;Re-enable slot ROMs
0351: 60          EXIT      RTS

                  *****************************
                  * Increment buffer pointer. *
                  *****************************
0352: C8          PTRBUMP   INY
0353: C0 10                 CPY   #BUFFSIZE
0355: D0 02                 BNE   NOWRAP
0357: A0 00                 LDY   #0          ;Wrap-around to beginning
0359: 60          NOWRAP    RTS

                  *****************************
                  * This is the new output    *
                  * routine that allows       *
                  * characters to be buffered *
                  * during video output       *
                  * operations.               *
                  *****************************
```

```
035A: 20 68 03     OUTPUT    JSR   GETCHAR     ;Buffer a character (if possible)
035D: 2C 1E C0               BIT   ALTCHAR     ;80-column firmware active?
0360: 30 03                  BMI   OUTPUT1     ;Yes, so branch
0362: 4C F0 FD               JMP   COUT1       ;Standard output (40-column)
0365: 4C 07 C3     OUTPUT1   JMP   BASICOUT    ;Standard output (80-column)

                   *******************************
                   * This routine will put a     *
                   * character in the type-ahead *
                   * buffer if a key has been    *
                   * pressed. If the buffer is   *
                   * full, however, a bell will  *
                   * be sounded and the          *
                   * character will be ignored.  *
                   *******************************
0368: 48           GETCHAR   PHA               ;Save A,P,Y
0369: 08                     PHP
036A: 98                     TYA
036B: 48                     PHA
036C: AD 00 C0               LDA   KBD         ;Check keyboard
036F: 10 1D                  BPL   NOPRESS     ;Branch if nothing there
0371: 2C 10 C0               BIT   KBDSTRB
0374: AC AD 03               LDY   BUFFTAIL
0377: 20 52 03               JSR   PTRBUMP
037A: CC AC 03               CPY   BUFFHEAD    ;Is the buffer full?

Page #04

037D: D0 06                  BNE   NOTFULL     ;No, so branch
037F: 20 3A FF               JSR   BELL        ;Yes, so sound bell
0382: 4C 8E 03               JMP   NOPRESS     ; and exit
0385: 8C AD 03     NOTFULL   STY   BUFFTAIL    ;Store new buffer write pointer
0388: 99 AE 03               STA   BUFFER,Y    ;Store character in buffer
038B: 20 93 03               JSR   CLICK       ;Click speaker when key entered
038E: 68           NOPRESS   PLA               ;Restore Y,P,A
038F: A8                     TAY
0390: 28                     PLP
0391: 68                     PLA
```

(continued)

Table 6-10. SOFTWARE TYPE-AHEAD. A program that provides a keyboard type-ahead buffer (continued).

```
0392: 60                      RTS

                 ***********************
                 * Click the speaker. *
                 ***********************
0393: A0 03      CLICK    LDY   #3
0395: A9 0F      CLICK1   LDA   #$0F
0397: 20 A8 FC            JSR   WAIT
039A: AD 30 C0            LDA   SPEAKER
039D: 88                  DEY
039E: D0 F5               BNE   CLICK1
03A0: 60                  RTS

                 *********************
                 * Patch to CHRGET. *
                 *********************
03A1: 20 68 03   PARSECHK JSR   GETCHAR     ;Buffer a character (if possible)
03A4: C9 3A               CMP   #$3A        ;Continue with CHRGET routine
03A6: B0 03               BCS   NULL
03A8: 4C BE 00            JMP   RETCHR
03AB: 60         NULL     RTS

03AC: 00         BUFFHEAD DFB   0
03AD: 00         BUFFTAIL DFB   0
                 BUFFER   DS    BUFFSIZE


--End assembly--

227 bytes

Errors: 0
```

There can be long periods of time, however, when the //e is performing neither input nor output. Unless calls are made to GETCHAR during these periods, keystrokes could be missed. If you are running an assembly-language program, then you can avoid missing keystrokes by making repeated explicit JSRs to GETCHAR.

If you are running an Applesoft program, then the problem is a bit more difficult to solve. The brute-force solution would be to place CALL statements to the GETCHAR subroutine at the beginning of every line in the program. This is not only highly inconvenient, however, it is also wasteful of space and makes it awkward should you wish to use the program *without* the type-ahead feature installed.

A much more elegant solution is to make a modification to the Applesoft CHARGET subroutine. This subroutine was discussed in detail in Chapter 4. In summary, it is responsible for examining and interpreting Applesoft program lines whenever an Applesoft program is being executed. By overlaying CHARGET with a JSR GETCHAR instruction, an attempt will be made to buffer a character every time an Applesoft line is being examined (which happens very often).

To use the SOFTWARE TYPE-AHEAD program, load and execute it directly from diskette by using the BRUN command from Applesoft direct mode. To see that is working properly, enter and run the following program:

```
100 FOR I = 1 TO 2000: NEXT
```

and then start typing madly away at the keyboard. When the program finishes, all the keystrokes that you entered should be displayed after the Applesoft prompt symbol!

Potential Problems with SOFTWARE TYPE-AHEAD

Even with SOFTWARE TYPE-AHEAD installed and operating, there may be occasions on which characters will be missed. This will occur in situations where you are calling time-consuming machine language routines from Applesoft or when Applesoft itself invokes a rather time-consuming ROM routine (such as the string-data garbage collection subroutine) or when DOS commands are being executed. The problem is that while such routines are executing no attempts are made to call the GETCHAR subroutine until the routine is finished. To overcome these problems, keep pressing the key that you want to enter until you hear the click that is produced each time a character is placed in the buffer.

RESETTING THE APPLE //e

The RESET button on the //e should really be called a "panic" button since it is usually used to interrupt the running of a program when all else fails. After a reset signal is generated, the //e generally returns to Applesoft direct mode from where you can easily examine the program that was just running or you can load and run another one.

Actually, the RESET button does nothing really important if you press it by itself. If you press it while you are also holding down the CONTROL key, however, then the RESET pin on the 65Ø2 microprocessor will be held in a low state, causing the 65Ø2 to begin its standard reset procedure. This procedure was described in Chapter 2.

Special RESET Procedures

There are two special reset procedures that can be selected by pressing either of the two "Apple" keys on the keyboard at the same time that CONTROL and RESET are pressed. Both of these reset procedures are unconditional and both will destroy any program that may be in memory when they are requested.

If the OPEN-APPLE key is held down when CONTROL-RESET is pressed, then a "cold" reset procedure will be started that will always allow you to restart the //e. If you are using a disk drive, then the cold reset will cause the diskette to boot up just as it did when the power was first turned on.

If the CLOSED-APPLE key is held down when CONTROL-RESET is pressed, then the Apple will begin a self-test procedure that involves the execution of a program that begins at location $C4Ø1 in the system monitor and that performs several diagnostic tests on the //e. If every test is passed, then the following message will be displayed:

```
KERNEL OK
```

If a diagnostic test fails, then an error message will be displayed. After the self-test procedure has been completed, you will have to press CONTROL-RESET to restart the system.

Trapping "Soft" RESETs

The two reset procedures just mentioned cannot be avoided using software techniques because they are wholly contained within the

//e's ROM area. It is possible, however, to redirect a standard "soft" reset (invoked by pressing CONTROL-RESET by itself) to any routine that you want to use to trap such a condition.

When CONTROL-RESET is pressed, the 65Ø2 microprocessor jumps to a location stored at locations $FFFC/$FFFD (low byte first). On the //e, these locations are stored either in the system monitor ROM area or in the bank-switched RAM area that shares the same address space as the system monitor, depending on which one was enabled when the reset signal occurred (see Chapter 8 for a discussion of bank-switched RAM). The ROM locations always hold the address of RESET ($FA62) in the system monitor but *any* address can be stored in bank-switched RAM. If ProDOS is being used, the address stored is $FFCB, which is the start of a ProDOS subroutine that re-enables the system monitor ROM and then passes control to the standard reset handler at RESET ($FA62).

The subroutine that begins at $FA62 takes care of some general-purpose housekeeping chores (like setting normal video, selecting the keyboard and video screen for I/O, and so on), checks for one of the two special "Apple" resets, and then, if no special reset has been requested, checks to see whether a user-defined reset handling routine should be executed.

If the result of the logical exclusive-OR of the value stored at SOFTEVH ($3F3) with the constant $A5 is stored at PWREDUP ($3F4), the //e will jump to a subroutine whose address is contained in SOFTEV ($3F2/$3F3) (low-order byte first). If this test fails, then the //e will begin a sequence that is identical to the one performed when you press the OPEN-APPLE key at the same time as CONTROL-RESET; that is, if you are using a disk drive, it will be rebooted. The important reset locations are summarized in Table 6-11.

Thus, to trap a RESET condition, two things must be done:

1. The address of the subroutine that is to take control after a RESET must be stored at SOFTEV.
2. The byte stored at $3F3 must be logically exclusive-ORed with $A5, and the result stored at $3F4. This can be done by executing the following instructions:

```
LDA $3F3
EOR #$A5
STA $3F4
```

Right after the //e is turned on, SOFTEV is initialized to $EØØØ, the cold start for Applesoft, and then, after CONTROL-RESET has been pressed once, to $EØØ3, the warm start for Applesoft. If DOS 3.3 or ProDOS is being used, then SOFTEV will later be adjusted

Table 6-11. Reset interrupt locations.

Address Hex	(Dec)	Symbolic Name	Description
$FFFC $FFFD	(65532) (65533)	RESETV (low) (high)	Reset vector. These locations contain the address of the subroutine that is called when a reset signal occurs.
$Ø3F2 $Ø3F3	(1Ø1Ø) (1Ø11)	SOFTEV (low) (high)	User-defined reset vector. These locations contain the address of a user-installed subroutine to which control is passed when a reset signal occurs (if PWREDUP is set up properly).
$3F4	(1Ø12)	PWREDUP	Powered-up byte. If the value stored here is the same as the result of the logical exclusive-OR of the value at $3F3 with $A5, then control will pass to the user-defined subroutine specified by SOFTEV.

so that it points to a reset handler within DOS itself. This handler takes care of reconnecting DOS after reset is pressed and of entering Applesoft direct mode. (When reset is pressed, the addresses of the standard keyboard input and output subroutines are stored in the input and output links, thus effectively "removing" DOS from the system.)

By the way, the reason for storing the "funny" number at PWREDUP is to allow the //e to detect whether or not it has just been turned on. If it has been, then it is highly likely that PWREDUP will not be properly "related" to SOFTEVH, and the //e will interpet this to mean that the diskette must be automatically booted.

Trapping RESET from Assembly Language

If an assembly-language program is being executed, any reset condition that may occur can be easily trapped by setting up SOFTEV and PWREDUP as indicated above as soon as the program begins. The error-handling routine to which SOFTEV points must handle the reset in an orderly manner; its main duty will be to ensure that the data areas of the program still make sense and to take appropriate action if they do not. For example, if reset is pressed after one byte of a two-byte pointer has been set up, then the reset handler had better detect this and fix it or else the next time that the program uses this (incomplete) pointer it will disappear into outer space.

It is also important to ensure that the reset-handling routine adjusts the stack pointer to a suitable value. Remember that reset can be pressed at any time, including times when there are several bytes of information stored on the stack. If you don't adjust the stack pointer downward in these situations, it might eventually "overflow," allowing you to overwrite important information stored on the stack. A simple way of handling this problem is to always reset the stack pointer to its value when the program was first entered. To do this, execute the following two instructions when beginning your assembly-language program:

```
TSX
STX STACKSV
```

where STACKSV refers to a memory location. In the reset-handling routine, the original stack pointer can be restored by executing the following instructions:

```
LDX STACKSV
TXS
```

and then the remainder of the reset-handling routine can be executed.

Another important chore for the reset-handling routine to perform is to reconnect DOS (recall that DOS is deactivated whenever the //e is reset). This is most easily done by initially saving the DOS addresses stored in the input and output links (at $36 . . . $39) in safe locations so that the links to DOS can be restored when reset is trapped.

Trapping RESET from Applesoft

Reset can be trapped while running an Applesoft program by using Applesoft's built-in error-handling subroutine. If this is done properly, then every time the //e is reset, the program can be caused to go to the line number that is specified in the currently active ONERR GOTO statement.

The following steps must be performed by the subroutine that traps reset when Applesoft is active:

- The DOS I/O addresses must be stored in the I/O links to reactivate DOS.

- The 8Ø-column MODE ($4FB) byte must be set to Ø to indicate to the 8Ø-column firmware that Applesoft is active.
- The 8Ø-column video display must be turned on (but only if it was on before the //e was reset).
- A subroutine at $D683 must be called to properly configure the 65Ø2 stack.
- The program should put an error code number in the X register and then execute a "JMP $D412" to pass control to the Applesoft ONERR GOTO handler. (The handler will place the error code number in location 222).

To install such a subroutine, its starting address must be stored in SOFTEV (low-order byte first) and PWREDUP must be properly adjusted as discussed above.

You can reactivate DOS using the technique mentioned at the end of the last section: save the values of the I/O links when the reset-handling subroutine is first installed and then restore them when reset is pressed.

Two special steps must be performed if reset is pressed when the 8Ø-column display is on. These steps are necessary because the 4Ø-column display will be automatically turned on and the 8Ø-column firmware's MODE ($4FB) byte will be destroyed. First, a $ØØ value must be stored in MODE; this indicates to the 8Ø-column firmware that Applesoft is being used and will cause the video output routines to continue to work as expected. Second, the 8Ø-column display must be turned on; as we will see in the next chapter, this is done by writing to 8ØCOLON ($CØØD). Note, however, that this last step is only to be performed if the 8Ø-column display was active when reset was pressed. The only way for the reset handler to determine this is to examine a flag which contains the contents of the 8ØCOL ($CØ1F) status location immediately before the //e was reset. This flag can be initialized in the subroutine that sets up the reset vector, but it must be changed whenever the display mode is changed.

The subroutine at $D683 must be called in order to fix a bug in Applesoft which arises when an error (which is not handled by the Applesoft RESUME command) occurs within a FOR/NEXT loop or a GOSUB/RETURN subroutine. This bug causes incorrect information to be left on the 65Ø2 stack after the error is processed.

Applesoft, DOS 3.3, and ProDOS all store error code numbers in location $DE (222) whenever an error occurs. The ONERR GOTO error-handling routine can then examine this location using a PEEK(222) command to determine what kind of error occurred. (See the *Applesoft BASIC Programmer's Reference Manual* and the

Table 6-12. TRAPPING RESET. A program to trap reset when an Applesoft program is running.

```
Page #01

: A S M
                 ******************
                 * TRAPPING RESET *
                 ******************
                           ORG  $300
                 CSW       EQU  $36          ;Output Link
                 KSW       EQU  $38          ;Input Link
                 SOFTEV    EQU  $3F2         ;RESET soft entry vector
                 PWREDUP   EQU  $3F4         ;Power-up byte
                 MODE      EQU  $4FB         ;80-column firmware mode flag
                 COL80ON   EQU  $C00D        ;Turn on 80-column mode
                 COL80     EQU  $C01F        ;Read status of 80COL
                 ERRFN     EQU  $D412        ;Applesoft ONERRGOTO handler
                 FIXSTACK  EQU  $D683        ;Fix stack "bug"
                 * Set up RESET vector:
0300: A9 2A                LDA  #<ERRHNDL
0302: 8D F2 03             STA  SOFTEV
0305: A9 03                LDA  #>ERRHNDL
0307: 8D F3 03             STA  SOFTEV+1
030A: 49 A5                EOR  #$A5         ;Adjust the power-up byte
030C: 8D F4 03             STA  PWREDUP      ; to prevent rebooting
030F: AD 1F C0             LDA  COL80        ;Get video status
```

(continued)

Table 6-12. TRAPPING RESET. A program to trap reset when an Applesoft program is running (continued).

```
0312: 8D 57 03            STA  FLAG80       ; and save it.

0315: A5 38               LDA  KSW          ;Save current DOS links
0317: 8D 53 03            STA  KSWTEMP
031A: A5 39               LDA  KSW+1
031C: 8D 54 03            STA  KSWTEMP+1
031F: A5 36               LDA  CSW
0321: 8D 55 03            STA  CSWTEMP
0324: A5 37               LDA  CSW+1
0326: 8D 56 03            STA  CSWTEMP+1
0329: 60                  RTS

               * RESET handler:
032A: AD 53 03 ERRHNDL    LDA  KSWTEMP      ;Restore DOS input link
032D: 85 38               STA  KSW
032F: AD 54 03            LDA  KSWTEMP+1
0332: 85 39               STA  KSW+1
0334: AD 55 03            LDA  CSWTEMP      ;Restore DOS output link
0337: 85 36               STA  CSW
0339: AD 56 03            LDA  CSTEMP+1
033C: 85 37               STA  CSW+1


Page #02


033E: A9 00               LDA  #0           ;Set "BASIC" flag for
0340: 8D FB 04            STA  MODE         ; 80-column firmware

0343: 2C 57 03            BIT  FLAG80       ;Was 80-column mode active?
0346: 10 03               BPL  ERRHNDL1     ;No, so branch
0348: 8D 0D C0            STA  COL80ON      ;Yes, so turn it on again
```

```
034B: 20 83 D6   ERRHNDL1  JSR  FIXSTACK     ;Fix stack bug
034E: A2 FD                LDX  #253         ;RESET = error code #253
0350: 4C 12 D4             JMP  ERRFN        ;Go to ONERRGOTO handler

                 KSWTEMP   DS   2            ;DOS input hook
                 CSWTEMP   DS   2            ;DOS output hook
                 FLAG80    DS   1            ;>=$80 if 80-column mode


--End assembly--

88 bytes

Errors: 0
```

DOS Programmer's Manual for a list of error code numbers.) Several error code numbers are not used by either Applesoft, DOS 3.3, and ProDOS, including number 253. Thus, if the X register is loaded with 253 just before calling $D412, the Applesoft error-handling subroutine will be able to detect a reset "error" by determining whether PEEK(222)=253.

Table 6-12 contains a program that will set up the reset vector so that it points to a subroutine that traps reset when an Applesoft program is being run. To use it effectively, an ONERR GOTO statement must always be active, that is, error-trapping should never be turned off with a POKE 216,Ø command. The error-trapping subroutine must be installed by loading into memory and then executing a CALL 768 command. It must not be BRUN directly from diskette.

FURTHER READING FOR CHAPTER 6

On changing the input link . . .

G. Little, "Zoom and Squeeze," *Micro*, July 1980, pp. 37-38. This article shows how the input link can be changed to control keyboard input.

On ProDOS and the input link . . .

C. Fretwell, "Setting I/O Hooks in ProDOS," *Call -A.P.P.L.E.*, April 1984, p.39

On modifying the keyboard input device . . .

L.A. Tomlinson, "Type-Ahead Keyboard Buffer for the Apple II," *Nibble*, Vol. 4, No. 8 (1983), pp. 101-107. This article shows you how to create a hardware type-ahead buffer on an Apple II Plus.

P. Schwejda and G. Vanderheiden, "Adaptive-Firmware Card for the Apple II," *Byte*, September 1982, pp. 276-314. This article gives an example of how to substitute an alternate input device for the keyboard.

7

Character and Graphic Output and Video Display Modes

In this chapter, we will be discussing the primary output device supported by the //e: the video display monitor. This will include an analysis of how both text and graphic information are generated and how alternate output devices can be easily integrated into the system.

The //e is capable of controlling the video display in such a way as to support three general classes of output modes:

- Text mode
- Low-resolution graphics mode
- High-resolution graphics mode

Text mode is used whenever the standard character symbols represented by ASCII codes are to be displayed on the screen. Both graphics modes are used to illuminate distinct blocks (low-resolution graphics) or points (high-resolution graphics) on the screen so that a variety of shapes can be generated. Whereas text can be displayed in black-and-white only, both graphics modes can be used to generate colored images if a color monitor or television set is connected to the //e. All of these modes can exist in a standard single-width format or, with an 8Ø-column text card installed, in a special double-width format (which includes an 8Ø-column text mode).

The //e uses a *memory-mapped* video display technique. This means that the display of information on the video screen can be controlled simply by storing bytes of information in special memory locations that make up part of the 65Ø2's 64K address space; these locations are mapped to unique positions on the screen display.

Similarly, information shown on the video screen can be retrieved by reading the contents of these memory locations. These memory locations are connected to the //e's video display support circuitry in such a way that the bytes stored are converted into appropriate pictorial representations on the video display monitor.

TEXT MODE

A standard //e is capable of displaying text in a 40-column-by-24-row mode only. However, if an 80-column text card is installed in the //e's auxiliary slot, then an 80-column-by-24-row mode can also be selected.

There are actually two versions of 40-column text mode supported by the //e. The "standard" 40-column mode is the one that is usually in effect and is easily identified by its characteristic "checkerboard" cursor that is displayed whenever keyboard information is being requested. The other version is the "special" 40-column mode that is available when the //e's 80-column firmware is being used; in this mode the cursor is an inverse block that does not flash. If an 80-column text card is installed in the //e's auxiliary slot, you can enter this mode only from 80-column mode (see below).

The 80-column text mode is invoked (assuming that you have an 80-column text card installed) by entering a PR#3 command from Applesoft direct mode or by executing a

```
PRINT CHR$(4);"PR#3"
```

command from within an Applesoft program. This command activates the //e's special internal 80-column firmware, which is capable of displaying information properly on the 80-column text screen. This is done by changing the addresses stored in the //e's input and output links.

Once you are in 80-column mode, you can switch between the 80-column mode and the special 40-column mode whenever keyboard information is being requested by using the two special escape sequences discussed in Chapter 6: ESC 4 and ESC 8. For example, if you are in 80-column mode and you want to enter the special 40-column mode, enter the sequence

```
ESC 4
```

If you want to go in the opposite direction, enter the sequence

```
ESC 8
```

To leave either the special 4Ø-column mode or 8Ø-column mode and go back to the standard 4Ø-column mode, you can do one of two things (apart from resetting the system). First, you can enter ESC <CTRL-Q> from the keyboard or you can print a <CTRL-U> character (by using a PRINT CHR$(21) command).

Note that you cannot leave 8Ø-column mode by entering a PR#Ø and a IN#Ø command. Although these commands do, indeed, reconnect the standard 4Ø-column input and output subroutines, KEYIN ($FD1B) and COUT1 ($FDFØ), they do not turn off the 8Ø-column screen display.

In the following sections, we will be taking a closer look at the memory-mapped video RAM areas, the standard character output subroutines that are built into the //e, and the soft switches used to select the video display mode.

Turning on the Text Display

The //e uses several input/output (I/O) memory locations as soft switches to control various aspects of the video display as well as several locations that can be read to determine the states of these switches. These locations are summarized in Table 7-1 and we will be referring to them throughout this chapter. Notice that the soft switches are arranged in pairs of locations, one of which turns the switch on and the other that turns it off.

To activate a particular soft switch, other than those from $CØ5Ø . . . $CØ57, you must *write* to its location using an Applesoft POKE command or a STA assembler instruction. You can activate any of the switches from $CØ5Ø . . . $CØ57 by either reading or writing. Each pair of ON/OFF soft switches is associated with a status location that can be read to determine the state of the switch. The status is kept in bit 7 (that has a binary weight of 128), which means that the associated switch will be on if the value read from the status location is greater than or equal to 128.

The //e uses the TEXT and 8ØCOL switches to select the video display mode to be used. The TEXT switches are used to select either a graphics mode or a text mode. To select text mode, the TEXTON ($CØ51) switch must be accessed (by a read or write operation). This can be done by executing a PEEK(49133) command from Applesoft or a LDA $CØ51 command from assembler language. Alternately, you can use just the Applesoft TEXT command.

Table 7-1. Video display soft switch and status locations.

Address Hex	(Dec)	Usage	Symbolic Name	Action Taken	Note
$CØØØ	(49152)	W	8ØSTOREOFF	Allow PAGE2 to switch between video page1 and page2	1
$CØØ1	(49153)	W	8ØSTOREON	Allow PAGE2 to switch between main and aux. video memory	1
$CØ18	(49176)	R7	8ØSTORE	1 = PAGE2 switches main/aux. Ø = PAGE2 switches video pages	1
$CØØC	(49164)	W	8ØCOLOFF	Turn off 8Ø-column display	
$CØØD	(49165)	W	8ØCOLON	Turn on 8Ø-column display	
$CØ1F	(49183)	R7	8ØCOL	1 = 8Ø-column display is on Ø = 4Ø-column display is on	
$CØ5Ø	(49232)	RW	TEXTOFF	Select graphics mode	
$CØ51	(49233)	RW	TEXTON	Select text mode	
$CØ1A	(49178)	R7	TEXT	1 = a text mode is active Ø = a graphics mode active	
$CØ52	(49234)	RW	MIXEDOFF	Use full-screen for graphics	2
$CØ53	(49235)	RW	MIXEDON	Use graphics with four lines of text	2

$CØ1B	(49179)	R7	MIXED	1 = mixed graphics and text Ø = full screen graphics	2
$CØ54	(49236)	RW	PAGE2OFF	Select page1 display (or main video memory)	1
$CØ55	(49237)	RW	PAGE2ON	Select page2 display (or aux. video memory)	1
$CØ1C	(4918Ø)	R7	PAGE2	1 = video page2 selected OR aux. video page selected	1
$CØ56	(49238)	RW	HIRESOFF	Select low-resolution graphics	1,2
$CØ57	(49239)	RW	HIRESON	Select high-resolution graphics	1,2
$CØ1D	(49181)	R7	HIRES	1 = high-resolution graphics Ø = low-resolution graphics	1,2

The "Usage" column in this table indicates how a particular location is to be accessed:
"W" means "write to the location."
"RW" means "read from or write to the location."
"R7" means "read and check bit 7 to determine the status."

Notes:

1. If 8ØSTORE is ON, then PAGE2OFF activates main video RAM ($4ØØ-$7FF) and PAGE2ON activates auxiliary video RAM. If HIRES is also ON, then PAGE2OFF also activates main high-resolution video RAM ($2ØØØ-$3FFF) and PAGE2ON also activates auxiliary high-resolution video RAM.
   If 8ØSTORE is OFF, then PAGE2OFF turns on text page1 mode and PAGE2 turns on text page2 mode. If HIRES is also ON, then PAGE2OFF also selects high-resolution page1 mode and PAGE2ON selects high-resolution page2 mode.
2. The HIRES and MIXED switches are meaningful only if the TEXT switch is OFF (i.e., a graphics mode is active).

The //e uses the 80COLOFF ($C00C) and 80COLON ($C00D) soft switches to control whether a 40- or 80-column text screen is to be displayed. If you write to 80COLOFF, then the 40-column display will be turned on. To turn on the 80-column display instead, write to 80COLON. These writes can be performed by an Applesoft POKE command or an assembler STA instruction. A program can always deduce which display mode is currently active by reading the 80COL ($C01F) status location. If the number read is greater than 127 (that is, bit 7 is on), then the 80-column display is on.

Of course, the PR#3 command that is usually used to enter 80-column mode automatically takes care of properly setting the 80COL switches. Hence, you will usually not have to deal with them directly.

You can see for yourself how the 80COL soft switches work by entering the system monitor so that you can easily access them. Before doing this, make sure that the standard 40-column mode is active by resetting the //e. Then enter CALL −151 from Applesoft and wait for the monitor's "*" prompt to appear. To tell the //e's internal hardware to display an 80-column screen, store any number at 80COLON ($C00D) by entering the command

```
C00D:0
```

As you will recall from Chapter 3, this command causes a 0 to be stored at $C00D. (Any other number could also have been stored.) As soon as you do this, the 80-column display will be turned on. Since the special 80-column firmware required to fully support this display mode is not being used, however, the system monitor's video output subroutine will not function properly and only odd-numbered columns in the display will be used when information is sent to it. To return to a normal 40-column display, enter the command

```
C00C:0
```

to activate the 80COLOFF ($C00C) switch. Again, any number, not just 0, can be stored at a soft switch location in order to activate the switch.

Text Mode Memory Mapping

There are significant differences in the method the //e uses to display 40-column and 80-column text. We will begin with a discussion of the 40-column text display and then move on to explain how the 80-column text display differs.

4Ø-Column Text Mode

In the 4Ø-column text mode, the screen can be considered to be a matrix of 4Ø columns by 24 rows. The video subroutines within the system monitor number the rows starting with Ø at the top and ending with 23 at the bottom; the columns are numbered starting with Ø at the left and ending with 39 at the right. Unfortunately, the Applesoft cursor positioning commands, VTAB and HTAB, start numbering the rows and columns with 1. We shall be using the system monitor's numbering system in this section.

In 4Ø-column text mode, the //e translates the contents of one of two 1Ø24-byte blocks of memory (called video RAM) into appropriate images on the video display. The first of these two blocks extends from $4ØØ . . . $7FF and is referred to as page1 of text; the other block extends from $8ØØ . . . $BFF and is referred to as page2 of text. Note that the word "page" in this context means a block of 1Ø24 bytes of video RAM.

Each character that appears on the 4Ø-column video display screen is defined by one byte in the currently active video page. This means that 64 of the bytes in the 1Ø24-byte block are not used because there are only 96Ø (4Ø×24) screen locations to be displayed. These unused locations are called "screenholes" and are reserved for data storage by devices interfaced to the //e's expansion slots (see Chapter 11).

To makes things as simple as possible, it would be nice if the memory locations used by the video display were mapped linearly to their corresponding coordinates on the video display. If this were the case, then the memory location corresponding to any screen location would be given by BASE+(4Ø×LINE)+COLUMN, where BASE is the starting address of the video page, LINE is the line number (Ø . . . 23), and COLUMN is the column number (Ø . . . 39). Unfortunately for all programmers, this is not how the //e handles its mapping of the video display.

Instead, the //e assigns a unique base address to each line on the video screen that is not simply forty positions further into the video memory area from the start of the previous line. The byte at this address and the thirty-nine bytes that immediately follow it in memory are used to represent the forty characters on that video line. Table 7-2 shows the base addresses that are used for the page1 video display and shows how to calculate the address of the byte corresponding to any position on the video display (add 1Ø24 to these addresses to calculate the corresponding page2 addresses).

Table 7-2. Text screen video RAM addresses.

Line Number	*Base Address*	*Line Number*	*Base Address*
Ø	$4ØØ	12	$628
1	$48Ø	13	$6A8
2	$5ØØ	14	$728
3	$58Ø	15	$7A8
4	$6ØØ	16	$45Ø
5	$68Ø	17	$4DØ
6	$7ØØ	18	$55Ø
7	$78Ø	19	$5DØ
8	$428	2Ø	$65Ø
9	$4A8	21	$6DØ
1Ø	$528	22	$75Ø
11	$5A8	23	$7DØ

(a) 4Ø-COLUMN SCREEN (columns Ø . . . 39). The address corresponding to a position on the screen is equal to the base address for the line plus the column number.
(b) 8Ø-COLUMN SCREEN (columns Ø . . . 79). The address corresponding to a position on the screen is equal to the base address for the line plus *one-half* of the column number. If the column number is even, then this address on the 8Ø-column Text Card is used; if it is odd, then the address in main memory is used.

In general terms, if the video line number (Ø . . . 23), in binary notation, is given by

```
000abcde
```

where a . . . e represent bit values, then the 2-byte base address is given by

```
000001cd eabab000
```

for page1 addresses or

```
000010cd eabab000
```

for page2 addresses.

The base address for the line in which the cursor is currently located is always stored in two zero page locations, called BASL ($28) and BASH ($29). To calculate the decimal value of the base address for a given line on the page1 video display from Applesoft, simply move the cursor to the line and then calculate the quantity PEEK(4Ø)+256*PEEK(41). You can add 1Ø24 to this result to convert it to a page2 base address. Table 7-3 shows a short program that does just this. It positions the cursor with the VTAB command

Table 7-3. TEXT SCREEN BASE ADDRESSES. A program to calculate the base addresses for each line on the text screen.

```
]LIST

0  REM "TEXT SCREEN BASE ADDRESSE
     S"
50  TEXT : HOME
60  DIM RW(24)
100  FOR I = 1 TO 24
200  VTAB I
300 RW(I) = PEEK (40) + 256 * PEEK
     (41)
400  NEXT I
500  HOME
600  PRINT "THE BASE ADDRESSES FO
     R EACH LINE ARE:": PRINT
700  FOR I = 1 TO 24 STEP 2
800  PRINT "LINE #";I -1;":"; TAB(
     11);RW(I);
900  PRINT TAB( 20);"LINE #";I;"
     :"; TAB( 31);RW(I)
1000  NEXT : PRINT
```

and then calculates the base address using the method just described.

If you want to calculate the base address for a line from assembly language, then use the following instructions:

```
LDA #LINENUM     ;LINENUM=0...23
JSR BASCALC      ;BASCALC = $FBC1 (standard 40-column)
                          = $CB51 (special 40-column)
```

BASCALC is a subroutine within the system monitor ($FBC1) or 8Ø-column firmware ($CB51) that does the base address calculation for you. The result will be stored in BASL/BASH ($28/$29) and will be equal to the *page1* base address. To convert it to the corresponding page2 base address, add $Ø4 to BASH.

Why does the //e use this strange video mapping scheme? Well, back when the original Apple II was being designed, the main concern was not simplicity of software but rather simplicity of hardware. By changing to this mapping scheme, several chips from the original hardware design could be eliminated, thus making the Apple II less expensive and easier to manufacture. Six years later the new and improved //e was released but, for the sake of compatibility, the video mapping scheme was not changed.

80-Column Text Mode

Since the 80-column screen displays twice as many characters as its 40-column counterpart, another 1024-block of video memory is required to support it. It turns out that this additional block is not located in the //e's main built-in memory; if this were the case, then the //e would be unacceptably incompatible with the Apple II and Apple II Plus. Instead, a 1K block of memory that is contained in an auxiliary memory area on the 80-column text card is used.

This "extra" 1K block actually shares the same addresses used by the main display page, $400 . . . $7FF, but, as we have just said, it is in a different physical location. When the //e's 80-column display is active, the video circuitry maps the standard page1 video page locations in main memory to the odd-numbered column positions on the 80-column screen and the auxiliary memory locations to the even-numbered positions. So for any given line on the screen, the contents of columns 0,2,4, . . . ,78 are found in auxiliary memory and the contents of columns 1,3,5, . . . ,79 are found in main memory. The base addresses for each line are the same as for the 40-column screen, however. The mapping scheme used by the 80-column screen is explained in Table 7-2.

You should now be able to see why only odd-numbered columns were used when you experimented with the 80COLON switch earlier. The standard system monitor video output subroutine presumes that a 40-column display is being used and so it accesses the $400 . . . $7FF area in main memory only. When 80COL is ON, these locations correspond to odd-numbered columns on the video display; the locations corresponding to even-numbered columns are never accessed by this monitor subroutine.

It is not permissible, of course, to have two physical memory locations, which share the same logical address, active at the same time. The //e uses soft switches to control which of the two $400 . . . $7FF areas is to be active so that data can be stored to or read from any 80-column screen position directly. The switches used are PAGE2OFF ($C054) and PAGE2ON ($C055). They are used to select the main memory video RAM block and the auxiliary memory video RAM block, respectively, provided that the 80STORE switch is ON. If 80STORE is not ON, then, as we will see below, the PAGE2 switches are used to select between the two different 40-column video pages.

The procedure to follow to store any value to a particular 80-column screen location is as follows:

1. Turn off 65Ø2 interrupts by executing a SEI instruction. This will prevent an interrupt routine from taking over when the video screenholes (which are in main memory only) are not available to a peripheral card.
2. Select the proper mode for the PAGE2 switches by storing any number at 8ØSTOREON ($CØØ1).
3. Determine the base address for the line required.
4. Divide the required horizontal position (Ø . . . 79) by two and add it to the base address.
5. If the horizontal position is odd, then turn on the main $4ØØ . . . $7FF video page by storing any number at PAGE2OFF ($CØ54). If the position is even, then turn on the auxiliary $4ØØ . . . $7FF video page by storing any number at PAGE2ON ($CØ55).
6. Store the byte at the address calculated in step 4.
7. Reselect main memory by accessing PAGE2OFF ($CØ54). This ensures that the main memory screenholes will be available for use by devices interfaced to the expansion slots.
8. Re-enable interrupts by executing a CLI instruction.

This is a fairly elaborate procedure but it is handled automatically if you are using the 8Ø-column firmware for video output. It must be followed strictly, however, if you want to POKE data directly into the video screen from your own programs. Table 7-4 shows an Applesoft program called POKE8Ø that uses this technique to display information on the video screen. Note that this program turns off interrupts by calling a two-byte program that begins at $3ØØ. This program is simply made up of the two one-byte instructions for SEI ($78) and RTS ($6Ø). The corresponding program to turn interrupts on begins at $3Ø2 and is made up of the instructions for CLI ($58) and RTS ($6Ø).

Using Page2 of Text

We have seen how the PAGE2 switches can be used to select between main and auxiliary memory if 8ØSTORE is ON. If 8ØSTORE is OFF, then PAGE2 behaves in quite a different way. That is, it is used to select which of the two available 4Ø-column text pages is to be displayed, the one from $4ØØ . . . $7FF (page1) or the one from $8ØØ . . . $BFF (page2).

To select page1, the PAGE2OFF ($CØ54) switch must be accessed and to select page2 — you guessed it — the PAGE2ON ($CØ55)

Table 7-4. POKE80. A program to write data directly to the 8Ø-column screen.

```
]LIST

0  REM "POKE80"
100  HOME
110  FOR I = 768 TO 771
120  READ X: POKE I,X
130  NEXT
140  INPUT "ENTER LINE # (0...23)
     : ";L
150  INPUT "ENTER COLUMN # (0...7
     9): ";C
160  INPUT "ENTER VALUE OF BYTE T
     O BE POKED TO SCREEN (0...25
     5): ";BY
170  CALL 768: REM DISABLE INTERR
     UPTS
180  VTAB L + 1: REM MOVE CURSOR
     TO PROPER LINE
190 BA = PEEK (40) + 256 * PEEK
     (41): REM GET BASE ADDRESS
200 BA = BA + INT (C / 2): REM A
     DD HORIZ/2
210  IF 2 * INT (C / 2) <  > C THEN
      POKE 49236,0: PRINT A: GOTO
     230
220  POKE 49237,0: REM SELECT AUX
      MEMORY IF EVEN
230  POKE BA,BY
240  POKE 49236,0: REM SELECT MAI
     N MEMORY
250  CALL 770: REM ENABLE INTERRU
     PTS
260  VTAB 22: END
270  DATA 120,96: REM "SEI","RTS"

280  DATA 88,96: REM "CLI","RTS"
```

switch must be accessed. You can always tell which page has been selected by reading the PAGE2 ($CØ1C) status location. If the number read is greater than 127, page2 is active.

Page1 of the video display is the one that is invariably used by programs, especially if those programs are written in Applesoft. There are two good reasons for this. First, the //e's standard video output subroutines always write screen information to the page1 memory area; if you wanted to send output in the usual way to page2, you would have to write your own subroutines to do this. Second, Applesoft programs are normally stored beginning at location $8Ø1, that is, within page2, which means that your program will be overwritten when the screen display changes. Although it is possible to load an Applesoft program so that it starts beyond page2 at $CØ1, this involves using an awkward "preloading" program that looks something like this:

```
100 POKE 103,1:POKE 104,12:POKE 3072,0
200 PRINT CHR$(4);"RUN YOUR.PROGRAM"
```

where YOUR.PROGRAM is the name of the program that you want loaded above page2. Line 1ØØ in the above program stores $CØ1 in the Applesoft beginning-of-program pointer, TXTTAB ($67), and puts a $ØØ byte at $CØØ (a zero byte must always be stored immediately before the start of a tokenized Applesoft program). See Chapter 4 for a discussion of TXTTAB and other Applesoft pointers.

Page2 does have its uses, however. For example, while page1 is being displayed, a program can be busily writing information on page2 and then, when page2 is complete, the PAGE2ON switch can be accessed to immediately display page2. Then, while page2 is being displayed, page1 can be modified and later switched in by accessing PAGE2OFF. If this process is repeated, extremely good animation effects can be achieved and pages of written information can be displayed very smoothly.

Note that the second 8Ø-column text page (from $8ØØ . . . $BFF in main and auxiliary memory) can be selected using PAGE2ON with 8ØSTORE set to OFF and 8ØCOL set to ON. Use the RAMRD and RAMWRT switches to access the appropriate half of the secondary page (see Chapter 8).

Video Display Attributes : Normal, Inverse, Flash

The //e text screens support three fundamental video display attributes:

1. Normal video (white characters on a black background)
2. Inverse video (black characters on a white background)
3. Flash video (blinking characters)

Every printable ASCII character (that is, those with negative ASCII codes greater than $9F) can be displayed in normal video without restriction. There are restrictions, however, on what characters can be displayed in inverse and flash video, and these restrictions will depend on which of two possible characters sets available for the //e is currently active.

The two characters sets that the //e supports are called the "primary" character set and the "alternative" character set. When the

//e's primary character set is in effect, it is not possible to display flashing or inverse lower-case characters. On the other hand, when the alternative character set is in effect, you will be able to display inverse lower-case characters but you will not be able to display flashing characters.

One character set or the other can be selected by writing to one of the following two soft switch memory locations:

ALTCHARSETOFF ($C00E) to select the primary character set

or

ALTCHARSETON ($C00F) to select the alternative character set

When the //e is in its standard 40-column mode, the default setting of ALTCHARSET is off; when the 80-column firmware is active, the default setting is on. The setting of ALTCHARSET can easily be changed at any time, however, in order to allow either character set to be used in both text modes.

You can determine which character set is currently active by reading the ALTCHARSET status location at $C01E. If this location is greater than 127 (that is, bit 7 is on), then the alternative set is currently active; otherwise, the primary set is active. The soft switch and status locations that relate to the //e's character sets are summarized in Table 7-5.

The //e examines the two most-significant bits (bits 7 and 6) of each byte that has been stored within the video RAM area in order to determine which attribute is to be used to display the character that it represents.

If these two bits are "10" or "11", then the character will be displayed in normal video. If they are "00", the character will be

Table 7-5. Character set soft switches and status location.

Address *Hex*	*(Dec)*	*Symbolic Name*	*Description*
$C00E	(49166)	ALTCHARSETOFF	Select primary character set
$C00F	(49167)	ALTCHARSETON	Select alternative character set
$C01E	(49182)	ALTCHARSET	Status of character set switch (>=$80 if alternative set is active)

Table 7-6. Video attribute control bits.

Bit 7	*Bit 6*	*Video Attribute*
1	1	Normal
1	Ø	Normal
Ø	1	Flash (primary character set) Inverse (alternate character set)
Ø	Ø	Inverse

displayed in inverse video. Finally, if they are "Ø1", then the character will be displayed either in flash video, if the primary character set is active, or in inverse video, if the alternative character set is active. These rules are summarized in Table 7-6.

Table 7-7 sets out how the //e interprets each of the 256 possible values that can be stored in its video display memory area, for both the primary and alternative character sets. You can see that the only difference between the two sets is that codes $4Ø . . . $7F represent flashing alphabetic characters and special symbols when the primary set is active, whereas they represent inverse upper- and lower-case alphabetic characters when the alternative set is active.

The program in Table 7-8 will show you visually how the //e's video system interprets each of the 256 possible bytes that might be stored in a video RAM memory location. When you run this program, the name of the currently active character set will be shown at the top of the screen and then eight rows of 32 characters will be displayed, which represent bytes $ØØ through $FF. You can easily select the character set that you want to view by pressing "P" for primary or "A" for alternative after the symbols corresponding to each of the 256 bytes have been displayed. Notice how fast the display changes after you change the character set — this is indicative of a hardware-controlled change rather than a software-controlled change.

Standard Character Output Subroutines

There is just one standard output subroutine that is used when a program running on the //e wants to send a character to the currently active output device; it is called COUT ($FDED). The Applesoft PRINT command makes uses of this subroutine. If the active output device is the video display screen, however, then

Table 7-7. Text screen character display and attributes.

<table>
<tr><th>Value of Bytes in Video Page</th><th>Symbols Displayed</th><th>Display Attribute</th></tr>
<tr><td>$00-$1F</td><td>@ABCDEFGHIJKLMNOPQRSTUVWXYZ[\]^_</td><td>Inverse</td></tr>
<tr><td>$20-$3F</td><td>!"#$%&'()*+,-./0123456789:;<=>?</td><td>Inverse</td></tr>
<tr><td>$40-$5F</td><td>@ABCDEFGHIJKLMNOPQRSTUVWXYZ[\]^_</td><td>Flash (primary)</td></tr>
<tr><td>$60-$7F</td><td>!"#$%&'()*+,-./0123456789:;<=>?</td><td>Flash (primary)</td></tr>
<tr><td>$40-$5F</td><td>@ABCDEFGHIJKLMNOPQRSTUVWXYZ[\]^_</td><td>Inverse (alternative)</td></tr>
<tr><td>$60-$7F</td><td>`abcdefghijklmnopqrstuvwxyz{|}~█</td><td>Inverse (alternative)</td></tr>
<tr><td>$80-$9F</td><td>@ABCDEFGHIJKLMNOPQRSTUVWXYZ[\]^_</td><td>Normal</td></tr>
<tr><td>$A0-$BF</td><td>!"#$%&'()*+,-./0123456789:;<=>?</td><td>Normal</td></tr>
<tr><td>$C0-$DF</td><td>@ABCDEFGHIJKLMNOPQRSTUVWXYZ[\]^_</td><td>Normal</td></tr>
<tr><td>$E0-$FF</td><td>`abcdefghijklmnopqrstuvwxyz{|}~█</td><td>Normal</td></tr>
</table>

Table 7-8. APPLE //e CHARACTER SETS. A program to display the primary and alternative character sets.

```
0  REM "APPLE //e CHARACTER SETS
   "
100  PRINT  CHR$ (21): TEXT : HOME

110  GOSUB 500
120  FOR I = 0 TO 255
130  HTAB 1 + I - 32 * ( INT (I /
    32))
140  VTAB 3 + I / 32
150 SL = PEEK (40) + 256 *  PEEK
     (41) + PEEK (36)
160  POKE SL,I
170  NEXT
180  GOSUB 500
190  VTAB 20: HTAB 1: CALL  - 95
    8
200  PRINT "(P)RIMARY OR (A)LTER
    NATIVE? ";: GET A$: PRINT A$

210  IF A$ = "P" OR A$ = "p" THEN
     POKE 49166,0: GOTO 180
220  IF A$ = "A" OR A$ = "a" THEN
     POKE 49167,0: GOTO 180
230  IF A$ =  CHR$ (27) THEN  HOME
    : END
240  GOTO 180
500  VTAB 1: HTAB 1: CALL  - 868
    : PRINT "THE ";
510  IF  PEEK (49182) > 127 THEN
    PRINT  "ALTERNATIVE";: GOTO
    530
520  PRINT "PRIMARY";
530  PRINT " CHARACTER SET IS:"
540  RETURN
```

COUT usually makes use of two other built-in subroutines called COUT1 ($FDFØ), and BASICOUT ($C3Ø7) to display the character at the proper position on the screen. All of these subroutines are summarized in Table 7-9.

As soon as COUT is called, the following code is executed:

```
JMP (CSWL)
```

which causes the //e to jump to a subroutine that begins at the address stored at CSWL ($36) and CSWH ($37). This subroutine is responsible for properly handling the character to be outputted (which is in the accumulator). If the current output device being

Table 7-9. Built-in output subroutines.

Address Hex	(Dec)	Symbolic Name	Description
$FDED	(65ØØ5)	COUT	Sends a character to the currently active output device. The negative ASCII code for the character is in the accumulator.
$FDFØ	(65ØØ8)	COUT1	Video output routine used when standard 4Ø-column mode is active.
$C3Ø7	(49927)	BASICOUT	Video output routine used when the 8Ø-column firmware is being used (this includes 8Ø-column mode and the special 4Ø-column mode).

used is the video display, then this usually means displaying the character on the screen at the current cursor position and advancing the cursor (and scrolling when necessary). If a special control character is being outputted, then special video control subroutines may be invoked instead (see below). Note that by simply changing the address stored at CSWL/CSWH, any output subroutine can be installed on the //e. We will see how to do this in greater detail later on.

When DOS 3.3 or ProDOS is being used, the address stored at CSWL and CSWH is actually that of a special DOS output subroutine. This subroutine will either store information on diskette or display it on the video screen, depending on whether a diskette file is being written to. It also continuously checks to see whether a valid DOS command has been printed so that it can execute it immediately. DOS commands are easily identified because they are always preceded by a <CTRL-D> character.

If the DOS output subroutine needs to display the output on the video screen, then one of two built-in video output subroutines is used. One is called COUT1 ($FDFØ), which is used when in standard 4Ø-column mode. The other is called BASICOUT ($C3Ø7) and is used when the 8Ø-column firmware is being used. Before calling either of these subroutines, the 65Ø2 accumulator must be loaded with the ASCII code for the character to be printed (usually with the high bit set to one). If the high bit is zero, the character will be displayed with a special display attribute (either inverse or flashing).

Let's take a closer look at both of these subroutines right now.

Video Output (8Ø-Column Firmware Off)

As we have seen, if the //e is in its standard 4Ø-column mode, then COUT will normally pass control (through DOS) to a subroutine called COUT1 ($FDFØ) to handle the task of displaying a character on the screen. Before COUT1 actually deals with the character, however, it calls a subroutine called VIDWAIT ($FB78) that will (if an $8D carriage return code is being printed) check the keyboard to see whether a <CTRL-S> has been entered. If it has, then VIDWAIT pauses until another ASCII code is entered from the keyboard before passing control to VIDOUT ($FBFD), the subroutine that actually handles the printed character.

If the character being printed is not a control character (that is, its ASCII code is not between $8Ø and $9F), then VIDOUT stores its code in the video RAM page at the currently active cursor position. This position is defined by the values stored at CH ($24) and CV ($25), the horizontal and vertical cursor coordinates, respectively. It then advances the cursor and finishes.

If the character is a control character, VIDOUT will either ignore it or perform a special action that usually affects some aspect of the video screen display, depending on the control character involved. VIDOUT reacts in a special way to four control characters only: <CTRL-G>, <CTRL-H>, <CTRL-J>, and <CTRL-M>. The actions that are taken when any of these control characters is encountered are listed in Table 7-1Ø. After a control character is handled, VIDOUT finishes.

Video Output (8Ø-Column Firmware On)

If the 8Ø-column firmware is being used, then COUT passes control (through DOS) to BASICOUT ($C3Ø7). After doing some basic housekeeping, this subroutine passes control to BPRINT ($C8A1). The first part of BPRINT is similar to the VIDWAIT subroutine, that is, a pause will be generated if a <CTRL-S> is entered from the keyboard when a carriage return is being printed.

BPRINT then examines the character to be printed to see whether it is a control character. If it isn't, then a subroutine called BPNCTL ($C8CC) is called that stores the character code in the video RAM

Table 7-1Ø. Special control codes used by COUT1 and BASICOUT.

Control Code	*Description*
<CTRL-G> $87	Bell. Beep the speaker.
<CTRL-H> $88	Backspace. Move the cursor one position to the left or to the end of the previous line if already at left edge.
<CTRL-J> $8A	Line feed. Move the cursor down one line.
<CTRL-M> $8D	Carriage return. Initiates a carriage return/line feed sequence that moves the cursor to the left position of the next line.

memory location defined by the currently active cursor position. This position is defined by the values stored at OURCH ($57B) and OURCV ($5FB), the horizontal and vertical cursor coordinates, respectively. After this is done, the cursor is advanced by one position by updating OURCH and OURCV, and then BASICOUT finishes.

If BPRINT encounters a control character, control passes to a subroutine called CTLCHAR ($CB99) that is responsible for processing it. As with the corresponding 4Ø-column VIDOUT subroutine, CTLCHAR reacts only to certain control characters; however, it reacts to a lot more. The control characters that cause special effects are listed in Tables 7-1Ø and 7-11. After a control character is dealt with, BASICOUT finally finishes.

Video Screen Windowing

When the //e is first turned on, the standard output subroutines will automatically use the entire video screen for text display. It is possible to define a smaller "window," however, into which all output is to be confined. The advantage of defining such a window is that information outside the window will not usually be overwritten. When it becomes necessary to perform a scrolling operation, only the contents of the window will be moved; the information outside of the window will stay put.

The dimensions of the text window can be set by adjusting four locations in zero page, described in Table 7-12. These locations are used to set the leftmost column position of the window (WNDLFT), the first line number used by the window (WNDTOP), the bottom

Table 7-11. Special control codes used by BASICOUT (80-column firmware only).

<CTRL-K>	$8B	Clear to end of screen. Clear from the current cursor position to the end of the screen.
<CTRL-L>	$8C	Form feed. Clear the screen and move the cursor to the home position (top left-hand corner).
<CTRL-N>	$8E	Normal. Turn on normal video display.
<CTRL-O>	$8F	Inverse. Turn on inverse video display.
<CTRL-Q>	$91	40-column. Keep 80-column firmware active, but move to a 40-column display.
<CTRL-R>	$92	80-column. Move to an 80-column display.
<CTRL-U>	$95	80-off. Turn off the 80-column firmware and return to 40-column format.
<CTRL-V>	$96	Scroll down. Scroll the display down one line leaving the cursor where it is.
<CTRL-W>	$97	Scroll up. Scroll the display up one line leaving the cursor where it is.
<CTRL-Y>	$99	Home. Move the cursor to the home position.
<CTRL-Z>	$9A	Clear line. Clear the entire line on which the cursor is positioned.
<CTRL-\>	$9C	Forward. Move the cursor forward one space with wraparound.
<CTRL-]>	$9D	Clear to end of line. Clear the screen from the current cursor position to the end of the line.
<CTRL-_>	$9F	Move cursor up one line (in the same column). If the cursor is already at the top, it will not move.

line number used by the window plus one (WNDBTM), and the width of the window (WNDWDTH).

You can change the window parameters with simple Applesoft POKE statements. If you do change them, however, keep in mind the following two rules:

1. WNDBTM must always be greater than WNDTOP.
2. WNDWDTH + WNDLFT must not exceed the maximum display width (40 or 80).

You should note that if 80-column text mode is being used, the window width, WNDWDTH ($21), should be an even number. If

Table 7-12. Text window parameters.

Address Hex	(Dec)	Symbolic Name	Description
$2Ø	(32)	WNDLFT	Left side of window (4Ø column: Ø . . . 39) (8Ø column: Ø . . . 79)
$21	(33)	WNDWDTH	Width of window (4Ø column: 1 . . . 4Ø) (8Ø column: 2, 4, . . . 8Ø)
$22	(34)	WNDTOP	Top of window (Ø . . . 23)
$23	(35)	WNDBTM	Bottom of window +1 (1 . . . 24)

an odd number is specified, then the 8Ø-column firmware that controls the screen display will automatically assume that the next lower (even) width has actually been selected.

After the window parameters have been changed, you can quickly and easily restore them to their initial default values by entering the Applesoft TEXT command.

How COUT1 and BASICOUT Set the Video Attribute

As we have seen, a character is normally displayed on the video screen by loading the 65Ø2 accumulator with its ASCII code (with the high bit on) and then calling COUT ($FDED). COUT, in turn, calls either COUT1 ($FDFØ), if the standard 4Ø-column mode is active, or BASICOUT ($C3Ø7), if the 8Ø-column firmware is being used. These subroutines take care of displaying the character at the proper position on the screen.

How, then, does the //e determine whether to display the character in normal, inverse, or flash video? The answer depends on whether COUT1 or BASICOUT is being used.

If COUT1 is being used, then just before a printable ASCII code (that is, everything above $9F) is sent on to the main part of the video output routine, it is logically ANDed with the number stored at INVFLG ($32). The purpose of doing this is to adjust bits 6 and 7 of the outgoing character code so that they are equal to the values needed to select the required video attribute (see Table 7-6). The value stored at INVFLG is called a "mask" because it will hide (clear to Ø) those bits in the character code that are Ø in the INVFLG

Table 7-13. INVFLG mask values.

Value of INVFLG	*Video Attribute*	*Effect on Character Code*
$FF	Normal video	No effect
$7F	Flash video	Clears bit 7
$3F	Inverse video	Clears bits 7 and 6

INVFLG is at location $32.

byte, but will leave unaffected those bits that are 1 in the INVFLG byte. The three values for INVFLG, which are used to select the normal, flash, and inverse attributes, respectively, are set out in Table 7-13.

If you take any printable ASCII code and logically AND it with each of the three values for INVFLG, you will see that the bits will be set in accordance with the rules set out in Table 7-6.

If BASICOUT is being used, then INVFLG is still examined before storing the character code in the video RAM area, but only bit 7 is used. If it is one, the character will be displayed in normal video; if it is zero, it will be displayed in inverse video. Although it is possible to display a flashing character on the 8Ø-column screen, the 8Ø-column firmware does not support this attribute.

The Applesoft NORMAL, FLASH, and INVERSE commands are all used to select the value stored at INVFLG. Keep in mind, however, that the 8Ø-column firmware is being used, the FLASH command will only cause an inverse video display; if you want to display flashing characters, you will have to POKE bytes directly to the video RAM area.

Changing Output Devices : The OUTPUT Link

Character output on the //e is usually sent to built-in system monitor subroutines that control the //e's 4Ø-column or 8Ø-column video display screens. It is possible, however, to interface many other output devices to the //e through its expansion slots and it will be necessary to control these as well. Examples of such devices are a disk drive and a serial interface card connected to a printer or a modem.

The //e uses the same general method to handle output to such peripheral devices that it uses to handle input. This method was discussed in detail in Chapter 6 in the section describing the //e's input link.

We mentioned earlier that the first instruction in the standard COUT character output routine looks like this:

```
JMP ($0036)
```

As we explained when discussing the input link, this is called an "indirect jump" instruction and it will cause the //e to transfer control to the address stored at location $36 (low byte) and location $37 (high byte). If you are using the standard 4Ø-column output routine, $36/$37 will contain the address of a subroutine in DOS that in turn usually calls COUT1 ($FDFØ). (It could also call another subroutine to write information to a diskette file instead.) By changing the address stored at $36/$37, you can redirect the //e to any other output subroutine that you care to execute, including one used by an alternative output device.

The symbolic name for locations $36/$37 is CSW (for character switch); $36 by itself is called CSWL and $37 is called CSWH. CSW is commonly referred to as the "output link" or "output hook."

You will recall from Chapter 6 that the Applesoft "IN#s" command can be used to redirect input to slot "s". In a similar way, you can use "PR#s" to redirect output to slot "s". When "PR#s" is entered, a program beginning at location $CsØØ (where s is the expansion slot number), which is the first location in a ROM area dedicated to that slot (see Chapter 11), is executed. Typically, the program in the new output device's ROM will modify CSW so that it will point to a new output routine also contained in its ROM. Note that if a PR#Ø command is entered, then the address of COUT1 ($FDFØ), the //e's standard 4Ø-column output subroutine, will be stored at CSW.

Subject to complications that arise whenever DOS 3.3 or ProDOS is being used (see below), you can also change the output link directly by using the Applesoft POKE command or the assembler's STA command to store the address of the new input routine directly into CSW at $36 and $37. This address can be in either ROM or RAM.

Designing a CSW Output Subroutine

Any CSW output subroutine that will be used to replace the standard ones used by the //e must adhere to certain rules relating to the usage of 65Ø2 registers. First of all, the output subroutine must examine the accumulator to determine which character code is being passed to it. Second, the subroutine must end with the A, X, and Y registers unaffected. If it is necessary to change the contents of these registers in the body of the subroutine, the registers must first be saved and then restored just before the subroutine ends.

Replacing the Video Output Subroutine

One common reason for changing the CSW output subroutine is simply to modify the manner in which character output to the video display is handled. For example, you may want to perform one of the following tasks:

- Redefine the effect of control characters on the video display or define special actions to be performed by previously unused control characters.
- Prevent certain characters from being displayed.
- Translate character codes from one encoding system to another.

For relatively minor changes such as these, it is not necessary to rewrite all the underlying code that takes care of positioning the cursor and displaying characters on the video display. What can be done instead is to install a new output subroutine that performs its special chores and then, if necessary, passes control to the standard output subroutine that can then handle the relatively complex chores of displaying a character on the screen and executing special video-control commands.

Here is an example of a short input subroutine that preprocesses character output before passing it on (if necessary) to the standard output subroutine:

```
NEWOUT     CMP #$87       ;Is this a bell?
           BNE NOCHANGE   ;No, so branch
           RTS            ;Yes, so do nothing
NOCHANGE   JMP COUT1      ;Perform normal output
                          ;(JMP BASICOUT if 80-column
                          ; firmware is being used.)
```

This subroutine will prevent a bell character from ever being sent to the standard output subroutine (meaning that you won't hear that annoying beep when you make an error). It works by continually comparing each character code that is printed with the ASCII "bell" code (code $87) and by simply executing an RTS instruction if one is found. If the character code is not a bell, control passes directly to the standard video output subroutine (either COUT1 or BASICOUT).

DOS 3.3, ProDOS, and the Output Link

The same restrictions referred to in Chapter 6 that apply when changing the input link while either DOS 3.3 or ProDOS is active also apply when changing the output link. When DOS is first activated, the address stored in CSW is copied to an internal DOS output link location and then the address of a special DOS output subroutine is placed in CSW. This subroutine is responsible for detecting and handling any DOS commands that are printed (they are preceded by a <CTRL-D> character) and for writing information to a diskette file if a DOS WRITE or APPEND command is in effect. If DOS is not currently writing to a file, then it will send output to the subroutine whose address is stored in the DOS output link. This is initially one of the standard video output subroutines.

Normal attempts to store new addresses directly to CSW will obviously lead to a disconnection of DOS. Rather than repeating the explanations given in Chapter 6, we shall simply state how the output link must be changed to ensure that both DOS and the new output subroutine will be active. Any one of the following procedures may be used:

- Use the PR# command while in Applesoft direct mode (not within a program) or use the command

  ```
  PRINT CHR$(4);"PR#s"
  ```

  from within a program (where "s" represents the slot number).
- Use the BRUN command to load and execute an assembly-language program that stores the new output address into CSW.
- DOS 3.3 only: execute a CALL 1002 command or a "JSR $3EA" instruction immediately after using the POKE command to put a new address into CSW or after using CALL to execute a subroutine that changes CSW (this must be done before performing any further I/O operations).
- ProDOS only: use the POKE command to store the new input address directly into the ProDOS output link locations at $BE30 and $BE31. Alternately, use the Applesoft CALL command or the system monitor GO command to execute an assembly-language program that stores the address directly into $BE30 and $BE31.

If you are using ProDOS, you can also use a special form of the PR# command to properly install an output subroutine that is located anywhere in memory and not just in the slot ROM area. The output subroutine must, however, begin with a 6502 "CLD" (clear decimal) instruction. To install the output subroutine, execute a statement of the form

```
PRINT CHR$(4);"PR# Aaddr"
```

from within an Applesoft program, where "addr" represents either the decimal starting address of the new output subroutine or, if preceded by "$", the hexadecimal starting address.

LOW-RESOLUTION GRAPHICS MODE

The //e also supports two general graphic display modes called low-resolution graphics and high-resolution graphics. These modes are primarily used to present nontext information such as pictures, graphs, and maps and will now be described in detail, beginning with low-resolution graphics mode.

Turning on the Low-Resolution Graphics Display

The easiest way to activate the //e's low-resolution graphics display is to enter the Applesoft GR command from Applesoft direct mode. This command, however, selects only one of four possible versions of low-resolution graphics (namely, page1 with mixed graphics/text). As we will see later, other versions must be activated by directly setting some of the //e's video soft switches.

When low-resolution graphics mode is in effect, colored "blocks" are displayed on the screen instead of text symbols. The dimensions of the screen are 4Ø blocks wide by 48 blocks deep (or 4Ø blocks deep if a special mixed mode is in effect—see below). Column positions range from Ø on the left to 39 on the right; row positions range from Ø on the top to 47 on the bottom.

There are two possible pages of low-resolution graphics that can be displayed on the //e. The video RAM area that defines the first display screen (page1) extends from $4ØØ . . . $7FF, and the area that defines the second (page2) extends from $8ØØ . . . $BFF. These are the same video RAM areas used to support the two pages of text mode.

To turn on either page of standard low-resolution graphics, you must first ensure that the PAGE2 switches (PAGE2OFF and PAGE2ON) can be used to select which of the two graphics pages is to be used rather than to select whether main memory or auxiliary memory is to be used. This can be done by writing to 8ØSTOREOFF ($CØØØ). In addition, to ensure that double-width

Table 7-14. Low-resolution graphics display modes.

Page1 of Low-Resolution Graphics (full-screen mode)		*Page2 of Low-Resolution Graphics (full-screen mode)*	
TEXTOFF	($CØ5Ø)	TEXTOFF	($CØ5Ø)
HIRESOFF	($CØ56)	HIRESOFF	($CØ56)
MIXEDOFF	($CØ52)	MIXEDOFF	($CØ52)
PAGE2OFF	($CØ54)	PAGE2ON	($CØ55)
Page1 of Low-Resolution Graphics (mixed mode)		*Page2 of Low-Resolution Graphics (mixed mode)*	
TEXTOFF	($CØ5Ø)	TEXTOFF	($CØ5Ø)
HIRESOFF	($CØ56)	HIRESOFF	($CØ56)
MIXEDON	($CØ53)	MIXEDON	($CØ53)
PAGE2OFF	($CØ54)	PAGE2ON	($CØ55)

low-resolution graphics are not accidentally enabled, you must read from or write to CLRAN3 ($CØ5F) in order to turn off annunciator 3 on the //e's game I/O connector (see Chapter 1Ø). As we shall see in the next section on double-width low-resolution graphics, this will disable the circuitry that enables this special graphics mode.

To turn on page1 of low-resolution graphics, the following switches must be "thrown" by reading from or writing to all of the following soft switch memory locations:

TEXTOFF ($CØ5Ø)—selects a graphics mode
HIRESOFF ($CØ56)—selects low-resolution graphics
PAGE2OFF ($CØ54)—selects page1

To turn on page2, throw the following switches by reading from or writing to all of the following locations:

TEXTOFF ($CØ5Ø)
HIRESOFF ($CØ56)
PAGE2ON ($CØ55)—selects page2

In addition, it will be necessary to throw one of two other switches that control whether full screen graphics will be displayed or whether four lines of text will be "mixed in" at the bottom of the screen with 4Ø lines of low-resolution graphics above them. The switches that control this are MIXEDON ($CØ53), which enables mixed graphics and text, and MIXEDOFF ($CØ52), which enables full-screen graphics. Simply read from or write to these memory locations to activate these switches.

The switches that must be accessed to turn on the four different combinations of low-resolution graphics display modes are summarized in Table 7-14.

Low-Resolution Graphics Screen Memory Mapping

Each block on the low-resolution graphics screen is defined by one-half of a byte (four bits) that is stored within the currently active video RAM area ($4ØØ . . . $7FF for page1 or $8ØØ . . . $BFF for page2). The number stored in this half byte is the color code for the block (see the next section). Table 7-15 shows the mapping scheme for each block on page1 of the low-resolution graphics

Table 7-15. Low-resolution graphics video RAM screen addresses.

Line Number	*Base Address*	*Line Number*	*Base Address*
Ø,1	$4ØØ	24,25	$628
2,3	$48Ø	26,27	$6A8
4,5	$5ØØ	28,29	$728
6,7	$58Ø	3Ø,31	$7A8
8,9	$6ØØ	32,33	$45Ø
1Ø,11	$68Ø	34,35	$4DØ
12,13	$7ØØ	36,37	$55Ø
14,15	$78Ø	38,39	$5DØ
16,17	$428	49,41	$65Ø
18,19	$4A8	42,43	$6DØ
2Ø,21	$528	44,45	$75Ø
22,23	$5A8	46,47	$7DØ

(a) STANDARD LOW-RESOLUTION GRAPHICS (columns Ø . . . 39). The address corresponding to a position on the screen is equal to the base address for the line plus the column number. If the line number is even, then the lower 4 bits of the byte stored at this address are used to store the color code; if it is odd, the upper 4 bits are used.

(b) DOUBLE-WIDTH LOW-RESOLUTION GRAPHICS (columns Ø . . . 79). The address corresponding to a position on the screen is equal to the base address for the line plus *one-half* of the column number. If the column number is even, then this address on the 8Ø-column text card is used; if it is odd, the address in main memory is used. If the line number is even, then the lower 4 bits of the byte stored at this address are used to store the color code; if it is odd, the upper 4 bits are used.

screen; page2 addresses can be calculated by adding 1Ø24 to the corresponding addresses for page1. Note that the base addresses for each pair of lines in the graphics screen (that is, Ø/1, 2/3, 4/5, . . . ,46/47 are the same as those for text lines Ø, 1, 2, . . . ,23.)

Low-Resolution Graphics Colors

A special color code is stored in 4 bits of the byte in the video RAM page that corresponds to a particular block position. As Table 7-15 indicates, these 4 bits are found in the top half of the byte (bits 4 . . . 7) or the bottom half (bits Ø . . . 3), depending on the block's position on the screen. Table 7-16 contains a list of the color codes that can be stored in the byte in video RAM in order to generate the sixteen different colors that the low-resolution graphics mode supports.

Double-Width Low-Resolution Graphics

The //e is also capable of supporting a special double-width low-resolution graphics mode that was not available on the earlier Apple II and Apple II Plus models. Unfortunately, this mode cannot

Table 7-16. Low-resolution graphics color codes.

Color Code	*Color*
$ØØ	Black
$Ø1	Magenta
$Ø2	Dark blue
$Ø3	Purple
$Ø4	Dark green
$Ø5	Gray1
$Ø6	Mcdium bluc
$Ø7	Light blue
$Ø8	Brown
$Ø9	Orange
$ØA	Gray2
$ØB	Pink
$ØC	Light green
$ØD	Yellow
$ØE	Aquamarine
$ØF	White

Note: These codes relate to bytes in main memory only (see Table 7-17 for the corresponding codes for bytes in auxiliary memory when using double-width low-resolution graphics).

be controlled by the standard Applesoft low-resolution graphics commands or the associated system monitor subroutines. It is necessary to develop entirely new subroutines from scratch to use this mode efficiently. The references at the end of the chapter provide sources of such subroutines.

Unlike standard low-resolution graphics, only one page of double-width graphics is available. Just as for 8Ø-column text mode, the PAGE2 switches normally used to flip between display pages are instead used to select whether the part of the double-width graphics video page within main memory or auxiliary memory is to be used.

There are two important prerequisites to using this special double-width graphics mode. First, you must be using an Apple //e with a Revision-B motherboard (the revision marking can be found at the back of the //e's motherboard, behind the expansion slots). Second, you must have an 8Ø-column text card installed in the auxiliary slot (ideally the "extended" version) that has pins 5Ø and 55 connected to one another.

If you are using the extended 8Ø-column text card, you can easily connect pins 5Ø and 55 together by properly installing the jumper plug that comes with the card. If you are using the standard 8Ø-column text card (the one without the extra 64K of memory), then you will have to solder a wire between pins 5Ø and 55 yourself (CAUTION: This will undoubtedly void your //e's warranty). Once the necessary connection has been made, the //e will be capable of displaying double-width graphics.

Turning on Double-Width Low-Resolution Graphics

Once the 8Ø-column text card has been properly configured, the double-width low-resolution graphics can be displayed by first setting the TEXTOFF ($CØ5Ø) soft switch to select a graphics mode, HIRESOFF ($CØ56) to select low-resolution graphics, and either MIXEDOFF ($CØ52) to select full-screen graphics or MIXEDON ($CØ53) to select 4Ø lines of graphics with 4 lines of text. This can be done by executing the following assembly-language instructions:

```
STA $C050
STA $C056
STA $C052 (or STA $C053)
```

If you do this while you are in standard 4Ø-column mode, the normal-width low-resolution graphics screen will be displayed. To enable the double-width graphics, two further soft switches must be set: 80COLON ($CØØD) and SETAN3 ($CØ5E). As we saw when discussing 8Ø-column text mode, the 8ØCOLON switch is used to turn on the double-width display mode. We haven't come across the SETAN3 switch before—it is usually used to turn on annunciator 3 on the //e's game I/O connector (see Chapter 1Ø). It is also connected to the 8Ø-column text card in such a way as to allow you to turn on and off the double-width graphics support circuitry. Annunciator 3 can be turned off by accessing CLRAN3 ($CØ5F). To select 8ØCOLON and SETAN3 from an assembly-language program, you would use the following two instructions:

```
STA $C00D
STA $C05E
```

An easier way to turn on the double low-resolution graphics screen is to use standard Applesoft commands. To throw the same series of switches that we have just outlined from Applesoft, you would use this program segment:

```
100 PRINT CHR$(4);"PR#3": REM THIS SETS 80COLON
200 GR : REM THIS SETS LOW-RES GRAPHICS SWITCHES
300 POKE 49246,0: REM TURN ON AN3
```

Of course, you will *not* be able to use the standard low-resolution graphics commands to properly plot points and draw lines on the screen because they assume you are using the standard low-resolution screen. If you try using these graphics commands, you will notice that only the odd-numbered columns will be affected. As we shall see next, these columns relate to physical memory locations used by standard low-resolution graphics only.

Double-Width Low-Resolution Graphics Screen Memory Mapping

The //e displays double-width low-resolution graphics in much the same way that it displays its 8Ø-column text screen. That is, the region of memory from $4ØØ . . . $7FF that resides on the 8Ø-column text card (auxiliary memory) is interleaved with the same region of memory on the motherboard (main memory). For a given low-resolution graphics screen line, all even locations are mapped to locations in auxiliary memory and all odd locations are mapped to locations in main memory. This mapping scheme is described in Table 7-15.

You can select which area of screen memory is to be accessed by first ensuring that the 8ØSTORE switch is on (by writing to location $CØØ1). This allows the PAGE2 switches to be used to select between main and auxiliary memory rather than page1 and page2 of graphics. PAGE2OFF ($CØ54) is used to select main memory and PAGE2ON ($CØ55) is used to select auxiliary memory. As you can see, writing to the double low-resolution graphics screen is done in exactly the same way as writing to the 8Ø-column text screen. Keep in mind that if you do write directly to the auxiliary memory part of the screen, then interrupts should first be turned off with a SEI instruction. After auxiliary memory has been written to, interrupts can be re-enabled with a CLI instruction and PAGE2 must be turned off by accessing PAGE2OFF ($CØ54). This will ensure that the main memory screenholes will still be available to peripheral cards.

Note that there is a second page of double-width low-resolution graphics that occupies $8ØØ . . . $6FF in main and auxiliary memory. (It can be selected by setting 8ØSTOREOFF, 8ØCOLON and PAGE2ON.) Use the RAMRD and RAMWRT switches to access the appropriate half of the secondary page (see Chapter 8).

Double-Width Low-Resolution Graphics Colors

Because of timing differences in interpreting auxiliary memory, the color codes stored in auxiliary memory to set the color of the low-resolution graphics blocks are different from the standard ones set out in Table 7-16. These new color codes are set out in Table 7-17 in the standard color order of Table 7-16.

Table 7-17. Low-resolution graphics color codes for auxiliary memory locations.

Color Code	*Color*
$ØØ	Black
$Ø8	Magenta
$Ø1	Dark blue
$Ø9	Purple
$Ø2	Dark green
$ØA	Gray1
$Ø3	Medium blue
$ØB	Light blue
$Ø4	Brown
$ØC	Orange
$Ø5	Gray2
$ØD	Pink
$Ø6	Light green
$ØE	Yellow
$Ø7	Aquamarine
$ØF	White

Table 7-18. Applesoft low-resolution graphics commands.

Command	*Description*
GR	Turns on page1 of low-resolution graphics in mixed mode and clears the display.
COLOR=	Selects a low-resolution color number.
PLOT	Plots a block on the screen.
HLIN	Draws a horizontal line on the screen.
VLIN	Draws a vertical line on the screen.
SCRN	Gets the color code at a given screen position.

Built-In Support for Low-Resolution Graphics

The easiest way to manipulate the standard low-resolution graphics screen is to use the Applesoft commands designed for this purpose. These commands are briefly summarized in Table 7-18.

Support for low-resolution graphics is also afforded by a series of subroutines contained within the //e's system monitor. These subroutines are described in Table 7-2Ø and the zero page locations that they use are set out in Table 7-19. Note that some zero page locations must be properly set up before calling these subroutines. In particular, COLOR ($3Ø) must contain the desired 4-bit color code (in both halves of the byte), H2 ($2C) must contain the destination location of a horizontal line before HLINE ($F819) is called, and V2 ($2D) must contain the destination location of a vertical line before VLINE ($F828) is called.

Remember that these commands and subroutines can be used for single-width page1 low-resolution graphics only.

HIGH-RESOLUTION GRAPHICS MODE

Of the two main graphics modes that the //e supports, high-resolution graphics mode is probably the most useful and exciting. This is because, as the name of this mode suggests, the points that can be plotted on the screen (called "pixels", for picture elements) are much smaller than low-resolution graphics blocks, thus allowing you to draw much finer shapes. This allows you not only to place easily recognizable images on the screen but also to place more images on the screen. No wonder that virtually all popular games now being released for the //e use high-resolution graphics.

Table 7-19. Zero page locations used by low-resolution graphics subroutines.

Address Hex	(Dec)	*Symbolic Name*	*Description*
\$26	(38)	GBASL	Low byte of graphics screen line base address.
\$27	(39)	GBASH	High byte of graphics screen line base address.
\$2C	(44)	H2	Horizontal destination location for drawing a horizontal line.
\$2D	(45)	V2	Vertical destination location for drawing a vertical line.
\$2E	(46)	MASK	Contains \$FØ or \$ØF and is used to clear out the proper 4-bit area before setting the color for a low-resolution block.
\$3Ø	(48)	COLOR	Contains the color code for the low-resolution block in the upper 4 bits and the lower 4 bits.

Turning on the High-Resolution Graphics Display

The //e supports two pages of high-resolution graphics, each of which are defined by a block of 8192 bytes. Page1 of high-resolution graphics is mapped to the area from \$2ØØØ . . . \$3FFF and page2 is mapped to \$4ØØØ . . . \$5FFF.

The dimensions of the full-size high-resolution screens are 280 pixels wide by 192 pixels high. A mixed mode can also be defined, however, where the bottom 32 lines of pixels are replaced by 4 lines of text so that the dimensions of the graphics screens become 28Ø × 16Ø. Numbering of both the pixel rows and the pixel columns begins at Ø and the (Ø,Ø) position is at the top left-hand corner of the screen.

Each pixel on the display screen is controlled by one bit of a byte in the 8K area associated with that screen and can be made to appear as one of eight colors, with some restrictions. If that bit is off, then a black dot will be displayed on the screen; if it is on, one

Table 7-2Ø. System monitor low-resolution graphics subroutines.

Address Hex	*(Dec)*	*Symbolic Name*	*Description*
$F8ØØ	(63488)	PLOT	Plot a block using the current color at the position given by A (vertical) and Y (horizontal).
$F819	(63513)	HLINE	Draw a horizontal line beginning from the position given by A (vertical) and Y (horizontal). The ending horizontal position is stored at H2 ($2C).
$F828	(63528)	VLINE	Draw a vertical line beginning from the position given by A (vertical) and Y (horizontal). The ending vertical position is stored at V2 ($2D).
$F832	(63538)	CLRSCR	Clear the full low-resolution graphics screen to black.
$F836	(63542)	CLRTOP	Clear the top 4Ø lines of the low-resolution graphics screen to black.
$F847	(63559)	GBASCALC	Put the base address for the line number contained in the accumulator (Ø . . . 47) into GBASL ($26) and GBASH ($27).
$F864	(63558)	SETCOL	Set up the color mask at location COLOR ($3Ø). On entry, A contains the color code (Ø . . . 15).
$F871	(636Ø1)	SCRN	Determine the color code stored at the location given by A (vertical) and Y (horizontal).

of the five other colors (white, green, violet, orange, or blue) will be displayed. The two other colors are a duplicate white and black. We'll take a closer look at how to generate colored images later in this chapter.

You can quickly turn on the two high-resolution screens from

Applesoft by using the HGR and HGR2 commands. HGR turns on mixed-mode page1 high-resolution graphics, and HGR2 turns on full-screen page2 high-resolution graphics. Let's take a closer look at how the //e's video soft switches can be used directly to select the various high-resolution graphics display modes.

To turn on either page of standard high-resolution graphics, you must first ensure that the PAGE2 switches (PAGE2OFF and PAGE2ON) can be used to select which of the two graphics pages is to be used rather than to select whether main memory or auxiliary memory is to be used. This can be done by writing to 8ØSTOREOFF ($CØØØ). In addition, to ensure that double-width high-resolution graphics are not accidentally enabled, you must read from or write to CLRAN3 ($CØ5F) to turn off annunciator 3 on the game I/O connector. As we shall see in the next section on double-width high-resolution graphics, this will disable the circuitry that enables this special graphics mode.

The high-resolution graphics displays are turned on in much the same way as the low-resolution displays. In fact, the only difference is that the HIRESON ($CØ57) soft switch must be accessed instead of the HIRESOFF ($CØ56) soft switch. To turn on page1, read from or write to the following locations (with 8ØSTORE in the off position):

TEXTOFF ($CØ5Ø)—selects a graphics mode
HIRESON ($CØ57)—selects high-resolution graphics
PAGE2OFF ($CØ54)—selects page1

To turn on page2, simply access PAGE2ON ($CØ55) instead of PAGE2OFF.

You can also control whether full screen graphics are to be displayed or whether four lines of text are to appear at the bottom of the screen instead of the last 32 lines of the graphics page. The switches to use to control these two options are MIXEDON ($CØ53), which selects the graphics-text combination, and MIXEDOFF ($CØ52), which selects full-screen graphics.

Table 7-21 summarizes the switches that must be set to select each of the four possible combinations of high-resolution display modes.

High-Resolution Graphics Screen Memory Mapping

The //e uses 4Ø consecutive bytes in the applicable high-resolution screen video RAM memory area ($2ØØØ . . . $3FFF, page1, or

Table 7-21. High-resolution graphics display modes.

Page1 of High-Resolution Graphics (full-screen mode)		*Page2 of High-Resolution Graphics (full-screen mode)*	
TEXTOFF	($CØ5Ø)	TEXTOFF	($CØ5Ø)
HIRESON	($CØ57)	HIRESON	($CØ57)
MIXEDOFF	($CØ52)	MIXEDOFF	($CØ52)
PAGE2OFF	($CØ54)	PAGE2ON	($CØ55)

Page1 of High-Resolution Graphics (mixed mode)		*Page2 of High-Resolution Graphics (mixed mode)*	
TEXTOFF	($CØ5Ø)	TEXTOFF	($CØ5Ø)
HIRESON	($CØ57)	HIRESON	($CØ57)
MIXEDON	($CØ53)	MIXEDON	($CØ53)
PAGE2OFF	($CØ54)	PAGE2ON	($CØ55)

$4ØØØ . . . $5FFF, page2) to define the contents of each 28Ø-pixel graphics line. The most-significant bit of each of these bytes, however, is not used for display purposes (it is used to select which of two sets of four colors can be displayed). Each of the 4Ø×7=28Ø active bits in these 4Ø bytes corresponds to a unique column position. The seven pixels corresponding to each byte in memory are displayed on the screen in reverse order of their positions within the byte. That is, the first pixel displayed on the screen (the one farthest to the left) corresponds to bit Ø, the next one corresponds to bit 1, and so on. If a bit is set to "1", then the pixel will be illuminated; if it is cleared to "Ø", it will be turned off.

As with the text screen, the high-resolution page1 and page2 memory areas are not mapped linearly to the video screen. To determine the memory address corresponding to a particular pixel, it is first necessary to calculate the base address for the line in which it appears. Reverting to binary notation for a moment, if the line number (Ø . . . 191) is given by

```
abcdefgh
```

(where a . . . h represent values of bits 7 . . . Ø, respectively), then the base address for that line is given by the two bytes

```
0ppfghcd eabab000
```

where

```
pp = 01 for page1
pp = 10 for page2
```

The base addresses for each line of the high-resolution display are set out in Table 7-22. To convert these addresses to the corresponding page2 addresses, add $2ØØØ (8192).

The byte position number (Ø . . . 39) for a particular pixel column (remember that 7 columns are defined by one byte) is given by the quotient of

```
X/7
```

where X is the column number (Ø . . . 279). To access this byte, the 65Ø2 indirect-indexed addressing mode, "(zp),Y", can be used ("zp" refers to any zero page location that contains the low half of the base address for the line; zp+1 contains the high half). The bit number within this byte that is mapped to the column is given by

Table 7-22. High-resolution graphics video RAM screen addresses.

Line Number	*Base Address*	*Line Number*	*Base Address*
Ø–7	$2ØØØ + $4ØØ × RLN	96–1Ø3	$2228 + $4ØØ × RLN
8–15	$2Ø8Ø + $4ØØ × RLN	1Ø4–111	$23A8 + $4ØØ × RLN
16–23	$21ØØ + $4ØØ × RLN	112–119	$2328 + $4ØØ × RLN
24–31	$218Ø + $4ØØ × RLN	12Ø–127	$23A8 + $4ØØ × RLN
32–39	$22ØØ + $4ØØ × RLN	128–135	$2Ø5Ø + $4ØØ × RLN
4Ø–47	$228Ø + $4ØØ × RLN	136–143	$2ØDØ + $4ØØ × RLN
48–55	$23ØØ + $4ØØ × RLN	144–151	$215Ø + $4ØØ × RLN
56–63	$238Ø + $4ØØ × RLN	152–159	$21DØ + $4ØØ × RLN
64–71	$2Ø28 + $4ØØ × RLN	16Ø–167	$225Ø + $4ØØ × RLN
72–79	$2ØA8 + $4ØØ × RLN	168–175	$22DØ + $4ØØ × RLN
8Ø–87	$2128 + $4ØØ × RLN	176–183	$235Ø + $4ØØ × RLN
88–95	$22A8 + $4ØØ × RLN	184–191	$23DØ + $4ØØ × RLN

RLN = relative line number. This number is equal to the actual line number minus the first line number in the group of eight within which it falls in the above table. For example, RLN for line #83 is 3 (83 − 8Ø).

(a) STANDARD HIGH-RESOLUTION GRAPHICS (columns Ø. . .279). The address of the byte corresponding to a pixel position is equal to the base address for the line plus the horizontal pixel position divided by 7. The bit position within this byte corresponding to the pixel is the horizontal pixel position modulo 7.

(b) DOUBLE-WIDTH HIGH-RESOLUTION GRAPHICS (columns Ø. . .559). The address of the byte corresponding to a pixel position is equal to the base address for the line plus the horizontal pixel position divided by 14. If the horizontal pixel position modulo 14 is between Ø–6, this address on the 8Ø-column text card is used; if it is between 7–13, this address in main memory is used. The bit position within the byte corresponding to the pixel is the horizontal pixel position modulo 7.

the remainder generated by the X/7 calculation (that is, X modulo 7). This is the bit that can be set to 1 to illuminate a pixel on the screen or cleared to 0 to turn it off.

High-Resolution Graphics Colors

Pixels on the high-resolution graphics screen can be one of eight colors: black1, black2, white1, white2, green, orange, violet, and blue. These are the eight colors that can be set using the Applesoft HCOLOR= command. Because of the way the high-resolution graphics circuitry works on the //e, however, you cannot display all colors at all positions on the high-resolution screen. For example, green and orange pixels can appear only in odd-numbered columns, and violet and blue pixels can appear only in even-numbered columns. In addition, in some circumstances that we will refer to in a moment, you cannot display blue and orange pixels close to green and violet pixels, and vice versa.

If you are plotting points in a particular color, you must ensure that, even if a particular column is selected, you do not illuminate pixels in that column if it is a restricted column for that color, or else the color will be wrong. This is handled automatically by the Applesoft high-resolution graphics commands and can be done from assembly language by logically ANDing the byte that is to be stored in the video page with the appropriate color mask. This mask will ensure that no "1"s can appear in restricted columns. Table 7-23 sets out the column restrictions and color masks for each of the eight allowed high-resolution graphics colors.

Not all colors can be used at the same time. The most- significant bit of the byte that defines the pixel must be cleared to Ø in order to have a '1' in the byte displayed as green/violet or set to 1 to have it displayed as orange/blue (for an odd/even column). A side effect of this phenomenon is that it is not possible to generate green and violet pixels if they are defined by bits in the same byte as orange and blue pixels.

To get white displayed on the screen, two horizontally adjacent pixels on the screen must be set to 1. If this is done, then both pixels will be displayed as white. Note that there are two different types of white, white1 and white2. The only difference between these two colors is the status of the high-order bit within the byte that defines the two adjacent pixels. Note, also, that it is not possible to get a single white dot surrounded by black because an isolated '1' bit will be interpreted as either green/violet or orange/blue.

Table 7-23. High-resolution screen display information.

Color	*Applesoft HCOLOR=*	*Value of High-Order Bit of Display Byte*	*Display Byte Mask Even Byte*	*Display Byte Mask Odd Byte*	*Column Restriction*
Black1	Ø	Ø	$ØØ	$ØØ	None
Green	1	Ø	$2A	$55	Odd only
Violet	2	Ø	$55	$2A	Even only
White1	3	Ø	$7F	$7F	None
Black2	4	1	$8Ø	$8Ø	None
Orange	5	1	$AA	$D5	Odd only
Blue	6	1	$D5	$AA	Even only
White2	7	1	$FF	$FF	None

In summary, the standard high-resolution screen looks at each horizontally adjacent pair of bits to determine which of four colors is to be displayed: black1 (ØØ), white1 (11), green (Ø1), or violet (1Ø), if bit 7 in the byte in which they are contained is off; or black2 (ØØ), white2 (11), orange (Ø1), or blue (1Ø), if bit 7 is on.

It should now be clear that because of the column restrictions on colors other than black and white, the effective screen resolution is only 14Ø × 192 for color graphics even though it is possible to control the states of all 28Ø horizontal pixels individually.

Animation with High-Resolution Graphics

One of the primary reasons for including two high-resolution graphics pages on the //e was to allow you to generate high-quality animation effects. Animation is typically simulated on a computer by first drawing a shape, pausing, erasing the original shape, and then redrawing it at its new position. By repeating this procedure, the effect of motion is created.

If this procedure is used in connection with one display screen only, then the problem of "flickering" can arise and the first shape will not appear to change smoothly into the next. This effect is observed because the screen is continually being "redrawn" by the electronic circuitry within the video display unit before the first shape has been completely erased and redrawn. If the shape is complex enough, a partially erased or partially redrawn shape will be displayed for discernible periods of time.

One way of getting around this problem is to draw the next shape in an animation sequence on the graphics page that is *not* being displayed and then, after it has been so drawn, to throw the switch that activates that page of graphics. Then, while that page is being displayed, the shape on the other page can be erased and repositioned, and then that page can be displayed again. The net effect is that all erasing and redrawing is done on the screen that is not being displayed and so flickering will be eliminated. If Applesoft graphics commands are being used, the page that is being written to can be controlled simply by adjusting the value of the byte located at $E6. To write to page1, this byte must be set equal to $2Ø; to write to page2, it must be set equal to $4Ø.

One problem with using the two pages of high-resolution graphics in this way, however, is that another 8K of memory must be devoted for use by the display screen and is unavailable for use by the program. For larger programs, this can be a major limitation indeed.

Fortunately, there is an alternative method that can be used to achieve flicker-free animation: moving a shape while the video display unit is not actually refreshing the screen. This method is available on the //e only and not on the earlier Apple II and Apple II Plus models.

The video display unit is continually "refreshing" the screen by redrawing all the scan lines that define the display screen. It does this by moving an electron beam in a zig-zag motion across the display screen from top to bottom. After all of the video scan lines have regenerated in this way, there is a synchronization delay during which the electron beam is repositioned to the upper left-hand corner of the screen awaiting the arrival of the next video frame.

The delay between the end of one zig-zag scan and the beginning of the next one is called the vertical blanking interval, and during this time the screen display is not being altered in any way. Thus, if during this vertical blanking interval we could change the data bytes that define the screen display image in such a way as to cause the shape being animated to be erased and repositioned, there would be no discernible flickering.

How do we tell when the video display unit is performing a vertical blanking operation? By examining another I/O memory location, that's how. This location is called VERTBLANK and is located at $CØ19. If the value read from this location is greater than 127, then the video display unit is performing a retrace; if it is less than 128, it is not. Table 7-24 summarizes how the VERTBLANK status location is used.

Table 7-25 lists a short assembly-language program that can be

Table 7-24. Vertical blanking status location.

Address *Hex*	*(Dec)*	*Symbolic Name*	*Meaning*
$CØ19	(49177)	VERTBLANK	If this location is >=$8Ø, then the video display is performing a vertical blanking operation.

used to tell you how long the vertical blanking interval lasts in terms of 65Ø2 machine cycles. If you load this program into memory and then enter CALL 768 to activate it, a number will be displayed that should be either 52Ø or 521. This number is equal to the number of 24 machine-cycle periods that occur during one vertical blanking interval. Thus, the vertical blanking interval is somewhere between 12,48Ø and 12,5Ø4 machine cycles. If you can erase and redraw your animated shape in less than this number of cycles, then you can achieve the goal of flicker-free animation.

Just before you draw a shape to be animated using the vertical blanking technique, you should call a subroutine that looks something like this:

```
WAITVBL    LDA VERTBLANK      ;Wait for end of retrace
           BMI WAITVBL        ; currently in progress
WAITVBL1   LDA VERTBLANK      ;Wait for retrace to begin
           BPL WAITVBL1
           RTS
```

This subroutine will end at the beginning of the next vertical blanking interval and will allow you to maximize the time available to erase and redraw your animated shape.

Double-Width High-Resolution Graphics

The //e also supports an impressive double-width high-resolution graphics display mode if an extended 8Ø-column text card has been installed in a //e with a Revision-B motherboard and the jumper plug on the text card has been installed. The extended 8Ø-column text card contains the additional memory required to support the other "half" of the double-width graphics screen. As with the double-width low-resolution graphics mode, however, neither Applesoft nor the system monitor contains any commands or subroutines that allow you to use this mode directly. Programs are available, however, that will allow you to take advantage of the power of this

Table 7-25. VERTICAL BLANKING. A program to determine the time needed to perform a vertical blanking operation.

```
Page #01

: A S M
                ********************
                * VERTICAL BLANKING *
                ********************
                VBLANK   EQU  $C019       ;Vertical blanking signal
                HEXDEC   EQU  $ED24       ;Hex-to-decimal conversion
                CROUT    EQU  $FD8E       ;Send a carriage return
                         ORG  $300
0300: A9 00              LDA  #0
0302: 8D 32 03           STA  TIMECNT
0305: 8D 33 03           STA  TIMECNT+1
0308: AD 19 C0  ENDWAIT  LDA  VBLANK      ;Wait for end of retrace
030B: 30 FB              BMI  ENDWAIT     ; currently in progress
030D: AD 19 C0  STRTWAIT LDA  VBLANK      ;Wait for retrace to begin
0310: 10 FB              BPL  STRTWAIT
```

```
                  * (Loop time is 24 microsec.):
0312: EE 32 03    TIMEIT   INC  TIMECNT     ;(Incremented during retrace)
0315: D0 05                BNE  TIMEIT1
0317: EE 33 03             INC  TIMECNT+1
031A: D0 04                BNE  TIMEIT2
031C: EA          TIMEIT1  NOP              ;Even out the loop time
031D: EA                   NOP
031E: EA                   NOP
031F: EA                   NOP
0320: AD 19 C0    TIMEIT2  LDA  VBLANK
0323: 30 ED                BMI  TIMEIT      ;Loop until retrace finished

0325: AE 32 03             LDX  TIMECNT
0328: AD 33 03             LDA  TIMECNT+1
032B: 20 24 ED             JSR  HEXDEC      ;Display result in decimal
032E: 20 8E FD             JSR  CROUT       ;Send a CR
0331: 60                   RTS

                  TIMECNT  DS   2


--End assembly--

52 bytes

Errors: 0
```

graphics mode; some of them are listed in the references at the end of this chapter.

The double-width high-resolution graphics mode has a pixel resolution of 560 × 192, rather than the standard 280 × 192, and allows a total of sixteen colors! These colors are the same ones that can be displayed when using standard low-resolution graphics.

Turning on Double-Width High-Resolution Graphics

Assuming that you have installed the jumper on the extended 80-column text card, it is relatively simple to activate the double-width high-resolution graphics mode. The first step is to turn on page1 of high-resolution graphics mode as you would normally. This can be done by executing the following sequence of instructions:

STA $C050—TEXTOFF (enables graphics)
STA $C057—HIRESON (high-resolution)
STA $C053—MIXEDON (mixed graphics/text)

The next step is to enable the double-width mode by setting the 80COLON ($C00D) switch and then setting the SETAN3 ($C05E) switch to enable the double-width graphics circuitry. As mentioned earlier, SETAN3 turns on annunciator 3 on the //e's game I/O connector. You can set these switches by executing these two instructions:

STA $C00D—80COLON (sets double-width switch)
STA $C05E—SETAN3 (enables double-width graphics)

You can also turn on the same series of switches from Applesoft by running the following program:

```
100 PRINT CHR$(4);"PR#3": REM THIS SETS 80COLON
200 HGR : REM THIS SETS HIGH-RES GRAPHICS SWITCHES
300 POKE 49246,0: REM TURN ON AN3
```

Once the double-width graphics screen has been activated, the next step is to draw something on it. This is easier said than done, however, because the Applesoft high-resolution graphics commands work only with the standard 280-column screen. If you attempt to use them, you will see rather strange effects, since only the screen area in main memory will be used. For example, try entering the Applesoft commands

```
HCOLOR=3
HPLOT 0,0 TO 279,0
```

If you were to do this for normal-width high-resolution graphics you would see a horizontal white line drawn across the top of the screen. With double-width graphics enabled, however, the white line is "broken" at forty different positions. The data bytes for these positions are contained in auxiliary memory and are not dealt with by Applesoft.

See the references at the end of this chapter for sources of programs that support double-width high-resolution graphics.

Double-Width High-Resolution Graphics Screen Memory Mapping

You will recall that when the //e is displaying double-width text (that is, 8Ø columns of text) or double-width low-resolution graphics, it interleaves the video RAM bytes in main memory with those contained at the same addresses in auxiliary memory. Well, double-width high-resolution graphics works in exactly the same way. The region of memory from $2ØØØ ... $3FFF in main memory is interleaved with an 8K block of memory having the same addresses on the extended 8Ø-column text card in such a way that of the 8Ø consecutive bytes used to define the contents of one line (recall that only 4Ø were required for standard high-resolution graphics), the even ones (Ø, 2, 4, . . . ,78) are found in auxiliary memory and the odd ones in main memory. The mapping scheme used is summarized in Table 7-22.

Just as in standard high-resolution graphics mode, each of the 80 bytes corresponds to seven consecutive pixels on the screen. The first pixel is controlled by bit Ø, the next one by bit 1, and so on. Bit 7 is not used.

The 8ØSTORE switch enables you to select which of the two $2ØØØ . . . $3FFF blocks you want to read from or write to. By setting 8ØSTOREON (by writing to location $CØØ1), the PAGE2 switches can be used to select either the 8K block in main memory, by accessing PAGE2OFF ($CØ54), or the 8K block in auxiliary memory, by accessing PAGE2ON ($CØ55). As we have warned before, always ensure that interrupts are disabled before reading from or writing to auxiliary memory like this, and always access PAGE2OFF ($CØ54) after you have finished doing so. This will prevent peripheral cards from gaining control when the screenholes in main memory are not available.

Note that there is a second page of double-width high-resolution graphics that occupies a $4ØØØ ... $5FFF in main and auxiliary memory. It can be selected by setting 8ØSTOREOFF, 8ØCOLON and PAGE2ON. Use the RAMRD and RAMWRT switches to access the appropriate half of the secondary page (see Chapter 8).

Table 7-26. Bit patterns for the sixteen double-width high-resolution graphics colors.

Color	*Bit Pattern*
Black	ØØØØ
Dark red	1ØØØ
Dark blue	Ø1ØØ
Purple	11ØØ
Dark green	ØØ1Ø
Gray1	1Ø1Ø
Medium blue	Ø11Ø
Light blue	111Ø
Brown	ØØØ1
Orange	1ØØ1
Gray2	Ø1Ø1
Pink	11Ø1
Green	ØØ11
Yellow	1Ø11
Light green	Ø111
White	1111

Table 7-27. Applesoft high-resolution graphics commands.

Command	*Description*
HGR	Turns on page1 of high-resolution graphics in mixed mode and clears the screen.
HGR2	Turns on page2 of high-resolution graphics in full-screen mode and clears the screen.
HCOLOR=	Selects the high-resolution color number.
HPLOT	Plots pixels and draws lines on the screen.
DRAW	Draws a shape on the screen in the color set by HCOLOR=.
XDRAW	Draws a shape on the screen using the complement of the color already existing at each plotted point.
SHLOAD	Loads a shape table from cassette tape.
ROT=	Sets the rotation factor used when drawing shapes.
SCALE=	Sets the scale factor used when drawing shapes.

Double-Width High-Resolution Graphics Colors

When we discussed normal high-resolution graphics, we saw how the //e interprets two adjacent pixels as one of four colors. Not surprisingly, when *double-width* graphics are used, the //e interprets *four* adjacent pixels as one of sixteen different colors (2^4=16). The 4-bit pixel patterns that give rise to these colors are set out in Table 7-26. Since pixels are displayed on the video screen in the reverse order that they appear in the video RAM data bytes, these patterns must be reversed to obtain the corresponding bit patterns that must be stored in memory to generate them.

Note that the high bit of each of the 8Ø bytes that is used to store information for each line of double-width graphics is not used at all—not even to affect the colors generated by the bits within that byte (as it is in normal high-resolution graphics).

Built-In Support for High-Resolution Graphics

Applesoft contains several commands that are used to control various aspects of the two standard high-resolution graphics screens. These commands are summarized in Table 7-27.

The //e's system monitor does not support high-resolution graphics at all. The Applesoft ROM itself does, however, contain several

Table 7-28. Zero page locations used by the Applesoft high-resolution graphics subroutines.

Address Hex	(Dec)	Symbolic Name	Description
$EØ	(224)	HHORIZ (low) (high)	Horizontal coordinate (Ø . . . 279).
$E2	(226)	HVERT	Vertical coordinate (Ø . . . 191).
$E4	(228)	HMASK	High-resolution color mask.
$E6	(23Ø)	HPAG	High-resolution page designation. Set this byte to $2Ø for page1 and to $4Ø for page2.
$E7	(231)	SCALE	Applesoft SCALE= factor for shapes.
$F9	(249)	ROT	Applesoft ROT= factor for shapes.

built-in subroutines that can be used from an assembly-language program in order to draw points, lines, and shapes. These subroutines are set out in Table 7-29 and the zero page locations that they use are set out in Table 7-28.

Note that these commands and subroutines do not support double-width high-resolution graphics at all.

Table 7-29. Applesoft ROM high-resolution graphics subroutines.

Address Hex	*(Dec)*	*Symbolic Name*	*Description*
$F3D8	(62424)	HGR2	Turns on high-resolution page2 (full-screen) and clears it to black.
$F3E2	(62434)	HGR	Turns on high-resolution page1 (with 4 lines of text) and clears it to black.
$F457	(62551)	HPLOT	Plots a colored dot at the position given by A (vertical), Y (horizontal high) and X (horizontal low).
$F53A	(62778)	HLIN	Draws a line from the last plotted dot to the position given by Y (vertical), X (horizontal high), and A (horizontal low).
$F6Ø1	(62977)	DRAW	Draws the shape whose data area is pointed to by Y (high) and X (low) using the rotation factor in A. The shape is drawn by inverting the existing screen bits that are used by the shape.
$F65D	(63Ø69)	XDRAW	Same as DRAW except that when the shape is plotted, the existing screen bits and the shape bits are logically exclusive-ORed with each other to determine the new value of the screen bit.
$F6EC	(63212)	SETHCOL	Sets the active code to the value of X (Ø . . . 7). These are the eight colors defined by the Applesoft HCOLOR= command.

FURTHER READING FOR CHAPTER 7

Standard reference works . . .

80-Column Text Card Manual, Apple Computer, Inc., 1982.

Extended 80-Column Text Card Supplement, Apple Computer, Inc., 1982.

On changing the output link . . .

G. Little, "Paged Printer Output for the Apple," *Micro*, October 1980, pp. 47-48. This article demonstrates how to change the output link so that the format of printed output can be controlled.

On ProDOS and the output link . . .

C. Fretwell, "Setting I/O Hooks in ProDOS," *Call -A.P.P.L.E.*, April 1984, p.39

On high-resolution graphics . . .

B. Bishop, "Apple II Hires Picture Compression," *Micro*, November 1979, p. 17.

L. Spurlock, "Understanding Hi-Res Graphics," *Call -A.P.P.L.E.*, January 1980, p.6. An analysis of the high-resolution mapping scheme.

B. Bishop, "Apple II Hi-Res Graphics: Resolving the Resolution Myth," *Apple Orchard*, Fall 1980, pp. 7-10. Discussion of the mapping of the high-resolution graphics screen.

E.C. So, "Picture Compression," *Call -A.P.P.L.E.*, May 1982, p. 21.

R.T. Simoni, Jr., "A New Shape Subroutine for the Apple," *Byte*, August 1983, pp. 292-309. A new method for drawing high-resolution shapes that leads to flicker-free animation.

On double-width graphics . . .

R. Moore, "80-Column //e Low-Res Graphics," *Call -A.P.P.L.E.*, July 1983, pp. 9-13. A set of subroutines supporting double-width low-resolution graphics is presented in this article.

D. Worth, "Hi-Res Double Play," *Softalk*, July 1983, pp. 120-126. A description of the //e's double-width high-resolution graphics.

P. Baum and L. Roddenberry, "Applesoft Brushes for Double Hi-Res Art," *Softalk*, September 1983, pp. 82-99. Programs are presented which support double-width high-resolution graphics.

A. Watson III, "True Sixteen-Color Hi-Res," *Apple Orchard*, January 1984, pp. 26-46. An excellent discussion of the theory of double-width high-resolution graphics. A set of assembly language driver programs are also presented which can be called from Applesoft.

Extended 8Ø-Column Text Card Supplement, Apple Computer, Inc., 1982.

R.R. Devine, "Double Hi-Res Graphics I," *Nibble*, May 1984, pp. 81-96. Another detailed discussion of the double-width display mode.

On hardware for alternate output devices . . .

S. Ciarcia, "High-Resolution Sprite-Oriented Color Graphics," *Byte*, August 1982, pp. 57-8Ø. This article describes how to use sprite graphics on an Apple II.

R. Dahlby, "Polish Your Apple With a Luminance Board," *Computers & Electronics*, November 1982, pp. 42-52. This article presents construction details for a special video board for the Apple II.

On video display theory . . .

J. Hockenhull, "Video Interfacing," *Call -A.P.P.L.E.*, June 1982, pp. 9-13. A good discussion of the theory of video display technology.

J. Mazur, "Hardtalk," *Softalk*, April 1983, pp. 215-225. A technical analysis of the Apple II video display system.

J. Mazur, "Hardtalk," *Softalk*, May 1983, pp. 91-98. A technical analysis of the Apple II video display system.

R.H. Sturges, Jr., "Double the Apple II's Color Choices," *Byte*, November 1983, pp. 449-463. A good explanation of how the Apple II generates colored images.

8

Memory Management

As we saw in Chapter 2, the 65Ø2 microprocessor that controls the //e is capable of addressing only 65536 (64K) different logical memory locations. These locations have addresses that range from $ØØØØ to $FFFF. A standard //e, however, contains much more built-in internal physical memory locations than this and even more can be added.

A detailed memory map of the //e was presented at the end of Chapter 2. In summary, the memory that is internal to a "standard" //e is as follows:

- 64K of RAM memory on the motherboard
- 1ØK of ROM memory for Applesoft
- 2K of ROM memory for the standard system monitor
- Ø.25K of I/O memory.
- 3.75K of ROM memory that contains extensions to the standard system monitor, self-test subroutines, and 8Ø-column support subroutines

To this memory can be added an additional 1K if the standard 8Ø-column text card is being used or 64K if the extended 8Ø-column text card is being used.

Finally, each peripheral card that is interfaced to the //e typically adds another 2.25K of memory to the system (although some special memory cards can add much more than this). See Chapter 11 for a discussion of the memory used by peripheral cards.

Assuming that all the peripheral slots are being used and that each peripheral card uses 2.25K of memory, a "fully loaded" Apple //e system with an extended 8Ø-column text card contains a total of 159.75K of memory!

But hold on, we just said that the //e's 65Ø2 microprocessor is capable of addressing only 64K locations. How is all that extra memory accessed? To answer this, you must first realize that you can install as much memory in the //e as you want, as long as you can provide a way to ensure that there will never be more than 64K physical memory locations active at the same time and that no two active memory locations will be associated with the same address. Several soft switches are available on the //e that allow you to easily select which one of those duplicated memory areas is to be active. The technique used to select memory in this way is called "bank-switching."

In this chapter, we will be looking at the soft switches that the //e uses to control usage of its duplicated ROM and RAM areas, and we will show how they can be used to take advantage of all of the memory available on the //e.

BANK-SWITCHED ROM AREAS

The //e contains an internal ROM space that is mapped to addresses $C1ØØ . . . $CFFF. These same addresses are used by memory that is installed on peripheral cards plugged into one of the //e's seven standard expansion slots (see Chapter 11). A memory map of these alternate ROM areas is shown in Figure 8-1.

There are several soft switches that can be used to select which of these different ROM areas is to be active at any given time. These switches, and their corresponding status locations, are summarized in Table 8-1. In the next two sections, we will explain in detail how to use these switches.

The INTCXROM Switches : Switching the $C1ØØ . . . $CFFF Memory Space

The seven 256-byte pages of memory from $C1ØØ to $C7FF on the //e are normally reserved for use by memory contained on peripheral cards that are connected to expansion slots 1 through 7, respectively (see Chapter 11). The memory associated with these addresses is usually contained in ROMs located on the interface cards themselves. For example, a typical printer card that is connected to slot 1 will contain a ROM chip that occupies the area of memory from $C1ØØ . . . $C1FF.

Each card that is connected to an expansion slot can also make use of a 2K memory space from $C8ØØ . . . $CFFF to hold programs or data. This is called the peripheral-card expansion ROM space and the memory needed to support it is also contained on the peripheral card itself. Before a card can use its own expansion

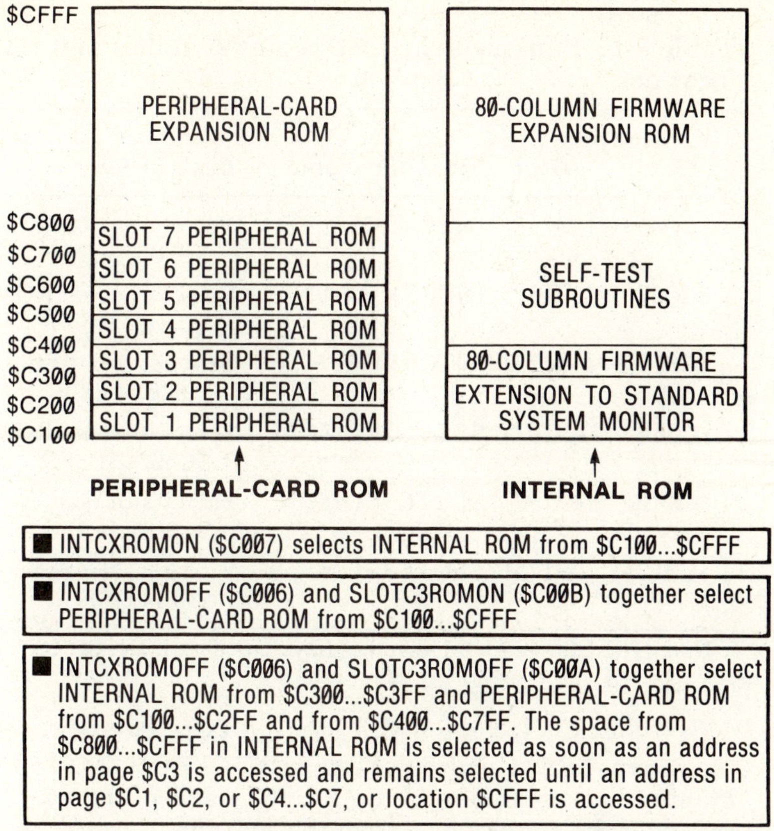

Figure 8-1. Alternate ROM areas from $C1ØØ . . . $CFFF.

ROM, it must first turn off all expansion ROMs and then turn its own on; it can do this by first accessing memory location $CFFF and then any address within its 256-byte ROM space. This procedure must be followed to ensure that only the one expansion ROM space on the card being used is active.

The //e also contains built-in ROM memory that shares the same addresses used by memory residing on the peripheral cards: $C1ØØ . . . $CFFF. This ROM contains extensions to the system monitor, self-test subroutines, and subroutines that support the 8Ø-column text display and is usually referred to as the //e's "internal ROM" to distinguish it from peripheral-card ROM.

The INTCXROM switches are used to control whether the internal ROM area from $C1ØØ . . . $CFFF is to be selected for use or whether the ROMs on any peripheral cards installed are to be selected instead. If you write to INTCXROMOFF ($CØØ6), the peripheral card ROM areas will be selected (subject to the state of the SLOTC3ROM switches that control the two spaces from $C3ØØ

Table 8-1. Bank-switched ROM soft switches and status locations.

Address Hex	(Dec)	Symbolic Name	Description
$CØØ6	(49158)	INTCXROMOFF	Select slot ROM from $C1ØØ–$CFFF
$CØØ7	(49159)	INTCXROMON	Select internal ROM from $C1ØØ–$CFFF
$CØ15	(49173)	INTCXROM	Status: >=$8Ø is ON, <$8Ø is OFF
$CØØA	(49162)	SLOTC3ROMOFF	Select internal ROM from $C3ØØ–$C3FF
$CØØB	(49163)	SLOTC3ROMON	Select slot ROM from $C3ØØ–$C3FF
$CØ17	(49175)	SLOTC3ROM	Status: >=$8Ø is ON, <$8Ø is OFF

Note: The SLOTC3ROM switches have no effect if INTCXROM is ON.

. . . $C3FF—see below). If you write to INTCXROMON ($CØØ7), the internal ROM will be selected. INTCXROM ($CØ15) can be examined at any time to determine the status of the INTCXROM switch. If the number read from this location is greater than 127, then internal ROM is enabled; otherwise, peripheral-card ROM is enabled.

If you want to call any of the subroutines that reside in internal ROM or if you simply want to disassemble them using the monitor's "L" command, you must first enable internal ROM by setting the INTCXROMON switch. You can easily do this by entering the system monitor from Applesoft with a CALL −151 command, and then entering the command

```
C007:0
```

To deactivate internal ROM, enter the command

```
C006:0
```

When internal ROM is deactivated, the peripheral-card ROM will be enabled, allowing you to examine or use the ROMs residing on peripheral cards.

The internal ROM from $C1ØØ . . . $CFFF is normally used only when performing standard input/output operations with routines contained in the system monitor that make use of subroutines contained in the internal ROM. These routines automatically turn on INTCXROM just before calling the subroutines and usually turn it off right after the subroutine finishes. (INTCXROM will not be turned off if, for whatever reason, it was already on when the subroutine was called.)

The SLOTC3ROM Switches : Switching the $C3ØØ . . . $C3FF Memory Space

When the INTCXROM switch is OFF, the SLOTC3ROM switches can be used to control which of two ROM areas is to occupy the memory space from $C3ØØ . . . $C3FF. There are two choices: the ROM that is contained on a peripheral card plugged into slot 3, or the internal ROM that contains subroutines that support the Apple 8Ø-column text card.

SLOTC3ROMON ($CØØB) is used to turn on the peripheral-card ROM memory, and SLOTC3ROMOFF ($CØØA) is used to select internal ROM instead. The status of the switch is contained at SLOTC3ROM ($CØ17). If the number read from this location is greater than 127, then the peripheral-card ROM is currently active; otherwise, the internal ROM is active.

The default setting of the SLOTC3ROM switch (that is, its setting when the //e is first turned on or when it is reset) depends on whether an 8Ø-column text card is installed in the auxiliary slot. If the auxiliary slot is being used, then SLOTC3ROM will initially by turned off so that the internal 8Ø-column firmware will be available. If the auxiliary slot is vacant, however, SLOTC3ROM will initially be turned on and the ROM on a peripheral card in slot 3 will be available. Thus, SLOTC3ROM automatically takes on the setting that is most appropriate in the circumstances.

Since SLOTC3ROM is usually off when an 8Ø-column text card is installed, internal ROM from $C3ØØ . . . $C3FF will be selected, and so the ROM on a peripheral-card installed in slot 3 will not be active. If, however, SLOTC3ROM is turned on by writing to SLOTC3ROMON ($CØØB), then the peripheral-card ROM will be activated and a PR#3 command can be used to pass control to it instead of the firmware that supports the 8Ø-column text card. Similarly, if no 8Ø-column text card is installed, then even though SLOTC3ROM is initially on, the internal 8Ø-column firmware can be activated by writing to SLOTC3ROMOFF ($CØØA) and then entering a PR#3 command. This allows you to enter the special 4Ø-column mode supported by the 8Ø-column firmware even if the 8Ø-column text card is not installed.

16K BANK-SWITCHED RAM AREAS

The //e comes with 64K of internal RAM memory built in to its motherboard. This memory, however, is not mapped to one contiguous area of memory encompassing the entire 64K space that the 65Ø2 is capable of addressing. The first 48K of this memory space corresponds to the contiguous block of memory from $ØØØØ . . . $BFFF but the remaining 16K of memory, which is called "bank-switched RAM," corresponds to one 8K region of memory from $EØØØ . . . $FFFF and two 4K regions of memory from $DØØØ . . . $DFFF. The addresses used by bank-switched RAM are exactly the same as those used by the internal Applesoft ROM and the standard system monitor ROM. A memory map of the alternate internal memory areas from $DØØØ . . . $FFFF is shown in Figure 8-2.

The 16K bank-switched RAM on the //e traces its roots to the earlier Apple II or Apple II Plus models. On those models, the 16K of bank-switched RAM was introduced to the system by inserting a special 16K memory expansion card into slot Ø of those systems (the //e does not have a slot Ø). The original reason for adding this memory was to provide needed space for the extremely large Apple Pascal Operating System. The extra memory, however, can also be used for conventional data and program storage. In fact, ProDOS occupies much of bank-switched RAM.

As usual, the //e reserves several I/O memory locations for use as soft switches to control whether bank-switched RAM or the

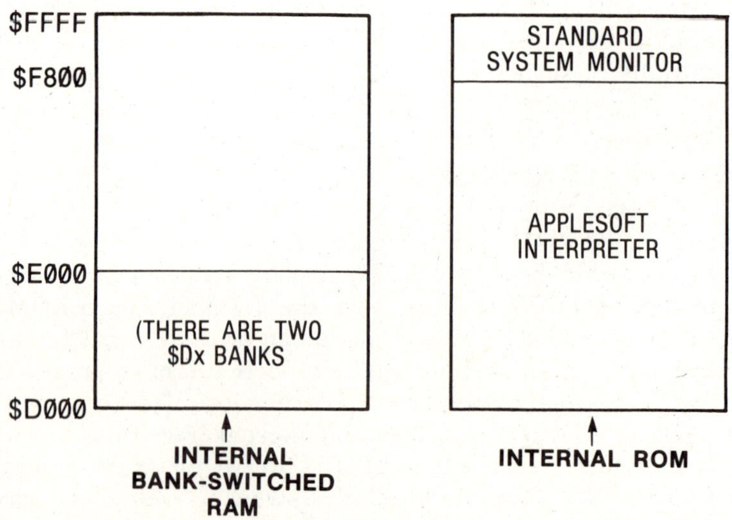

Figure 8-2. Alternate internal memory areas from $DØØØ . . . $FFFF.

corresponding internal ROM space is to be active. As we will see in the following section, we can even set these switches in such a way that the RAM area will be active for write operations at the same time that the corresponding ROM area is active for read operations, and vice versa.

Using Bank-Switched RAM

As we have seen, the 16K of bank-switched RAM on the //e's motherboard is made up of one 8K area that is mapped to the addresses $EØØØ . . . $FFFF and two different 4K areas that are mapped to the addresses $DØØØ . . . $DFFF. These 4K areas are commonly referred to as "banks."

Unfortunately, there are two schools of thought on how to refer to these two 4K memory banks: sometimes they are referred to as banks 0 and 1 and sometimes as banks 1 and 2. For our purposes, we will use the latter nomenclature.

The sixteen I/O addresses in the range $CØ8Ø. . . . $CØ8F are used as soft switches to control the operation of the bank-switched RAM. Switches are available to select which of the two 4K banks is to be used, to enable the bank-switched RAM for reading, for writing, or for both reading and writing. Note that the bank-switched RAM does not have to be enabled for reading and writing at the same time. This means that you can be writing to the RAM area while running a program that uses subroutines in the ROM that occupies the same memory locations (that is, subroutines in Applesoft and the system monitor).

To activate the particular mode of operation that is desired, it is necessary to select the appropriate soft switch address and then perform any kind of *read* operation at that address, for example, an LDA, LDY, LDX, or BIT instruction in assembly language or a PEEK from Applesoft.

The addresses that are to be used to control the operation of bank-switched RAM are of the form $CØ8X, where X represents the four least-significant bits of the address. Figure 8-3 indicates the general function of each of these bits; only three of these bits are used.

The functions of each of the three active bits are as follows:

BANK-SELECT BIT (bit 3). This bit indicates which of the two $DØØØ-$DFFF memory banks is to be used. If the bit is set to 1, then bank 1 will be selected; if it is cleared to Ø, then bank 2 will be selected.

I/O Address: $CØ8X

X =	BANK—SELECT bit 3	UNUSED bit 2	READ—SELECT bit 1	WRITE—SELECT bit Ø	
	1 = bank 1		1	1	→ read RAM/write RAM
	Ø = bank 2		Ø	1	→ read ROM/write RAM
			1	Ø	→ read ROM/write ROM
			Ø	Ø	→ read RAM/write ROM

Figure 8-3. Bank-switched RAM control bits.

READ-SELECT BIT (bit 1). This bit, in conjunction with the write-select bit, indicates the read status of bank-switched RAM. If the bit is set equal to the value of the write-select bit, then locations in bank-switched RAM will be read from when an address in the range $DØØØ . . . $FFFF is specified; otherwise, the corresponding locations in ROM will be used.

WRITE-SELECT BIT (bit Ø). This bit indicates the write status of bank-switched RAM. If the bit is 1, *and the I/O address is read twice in succession*, then locations in bank-switched RAM will be written to when an address in the range $DØØØ . . . $FFFF is specified; otherwise, the corresponding locations in ROM will be used.

There are eight different ways of turning on and off these three control bits, and each of the eight different addresses generated controls bank-switched RAM in a unique way. The function of each of the eight unique bank-switched RAM soft switches is summarized in Table 8-2.

Reading the Status of Bank-Switched RAM Soft Switches

Any program that changes the soft switches that control the state of bank-switched RAM should properly restore them to their original states when the program ends. (If it doesn't, the next program executed may not perform properly.) This can easily be done on the //e because there are two I/O status locations, called BSRBANK2 ($CØ11) and BSRREADRAM ($CØ12), that can be read to determine the current state of the bank-switched RAM switches. These two locations are summarized in Table 8-3.

Table 8-2. Bank-switched RAM soft switches.

Address	Symbolic Name	Active $Dx Bank	Read From	Write to RAM?
$CØ8Ø	READBSR2	2	RAM	No
$CØ81	WRITEBSR2	2	ROM	Yes*
$CØ82	OFFBSR2	2	ROM	No
$CØ83	RDWRBSR2	2	RAM	Yes*
$CØ88	READBSR1	1	RAM	No
$CØ89	WRITEBSR1	1	ROM	Yes*
$CØ8A	OFFBSR1	1	ROM	No
$CØ8B	RDWRBSR1	1	RAM	Yes*

Note: Addresses $CØ84. . .$CØ87 and $CØ8C. . .$CØ8F duplicate the functions of addresses $CØ8Ø. . .$CØ83 and $CØ88. . .$CØ8B, respectively.

* These locations must be read twice in succession to write-enable bank-switched RAM.

Table 8-3. Bank-switched RAM status locations.

Address Hex	(Dec)	Symbolic Name	Description
$CØ11	(49169)	BSRBANK2	If this location is >=$8Ø, then Bank2 of bank-switched RAM has been selected; if not, Bank1 has been selected.
$CØ12	(4917Ø)	BSRREADRAM	If this location is >=$8Ø, then bank-switched RAM has been read-enabled; if not, the corresponding ROM locations are enabled.

A program that saves the two bank-switched RAM status values and then uses them to restore the original state of bank-switched RAM would look something like this:

```
LDA BSRBANK2       ;Save bank status
STA BANKSAVE
LDA BSRREADRAM     ;Save read-enable status
```

```
         STA READSAVE
         .
         <the program fiddles with
         bank-switched RAM here>
         .
         LDA BANKSAVE      ;Get bank status
         BPL SETBANK1      ;Branch if bank1 selected
         LDA BSRREADRAM    ;Get read-enable status
         BPL SETROM        ;Branch if ROM selected
         LDA $C083         ;Read RAM, bank2
         LDA $C083         ; (write-enable)
         RTS
SETROM   LDA $C081         ;Read ROM, bank2
         LDA $C081         ; (write-enable)
         RTS
SETBANK1 LDA BSRREADRAM    ;Get read-enable status
         BPL SETROM1       ;Branch if ROM selected
         LDA $C08B         ;Read RAM, bank1
         LDA $C08B         ; (write-enable)
         RTS
SETROM1  LDA $C089         ;Read ROM, bank1
         LDA $C089         ; (write-enable)
         RTS
```

Since there is no status location available for determining the write-enable status of bank-switched RAM, you always have to "guess" what it was. The best guess is that it was write-enabled because even if your guess is wrong, no program should be trying to write to bank-switched RAM without first write-enabling it anyway. In keeping with this, those soft switches that write-enable bank-switched RAM were used in the above example (remember that they must be read twice in succession).

Auxiliary Bank-Switched RAM

If you have an extended 8Ø-column text card installed in the //e, then another 16K bank-switched RAM area is available to the system. This time, however, the memory resides in auxiliary memory on the card itself and not in the //e's internal memory.

The same soft switches that are used to control the bank-switched RAM area on the motherboard are used to control the bank-switched RAM area in auxiliary memory. Before you can read to or write from this part of auxiliary memory, however, you will also have to use another set of switches that control, among other things, which of the two bank-switched RAM areas is to be used. These switches are ALTZPOFF ($CØØ8) and ALTZPON ($CØØ9) and are described in Table 8-4. The status of the switch is held in ALTZP ($CØ16).

Table 8-4. Auxiliary bank-switched RAM soft switches.

Address *Hex*	*(Dec)*	*Symbolic Name*	*Description*
$CØØ8	(4916Ø)	ALTZPOFF	Enable the main bank-switched RAM + main zero page/stack
$CØØ9	(49161)	ALTZPON	Enable auxiliary bank-switched RAM + auxiliary zero page/stack
$CØ16	(49174)	ALTZP	States: >=$8Ø is ON, <$8Ø is OFF

The ALTZP switches are used not only to select which of the two bank-switched RAM areas is to be used, but also to select which of two 65Ø2 zero pages ($Ø . . . $FF) and stacks ($1ØØ . . . $1FF) are to be used. As you might expect, the //e keeps its "spare" zero page and stack in auxiliary memory and the "original" ones in main memory. This means that as soon as the ALTZPON switch is set, the main zero page and stack are disengaged and unless the program that is running realizes this and adjusts for it, it might just end up in the twilight zone.

To avoid such problems, the program must always set ALTZPOFF as soon as it is finished dealing with auxiliary bank-switched RAM but *after* it has returned from all subroutines that it has called since it first set ALTZPON. The return addresses for these subroutines are stored in the auxiliary stack and not the main stack and will be lost when the main stack is restored. For similar reasons, the program must *never* return from a subroutine that was called before ALTZPON was set until ALTZPOFF is restored. Furthermore, before setting ALTZPON, the program should move to a safe part of memory all zero page locations that it will be using while ALTZP is ON. Once ALTZP is ON, it can move them into the same locations in the auxiliary zero page. It should repeat this process when going in the other direction (that is, from ALTZPON to ALTZPOFF) so that no zero page information is lost.

Using Bank-Switched RAM

If you want to store information (programs or data) in bank-switched RAM, then you must first write-enable the portion of bank-switched RAM that you want to write to, store the information at the desired locations in the $DØØØ . . . $FFFF address space, and then write-protect bank-switched RAM. The programming sequence to use to do this would be as follows:

```
LDA $C081                ;Two accesses will write-enable
LDA $C081                ; Bank-switched RAM (bank 2)
<store information>
LDA $C082                ;Write-protect and set ROM read
```

To read information (programs or data) contained in bank-switched RAM, or to execute programs that reside there, you must first enable bank-switched RAM for reading, read the information or execute the program, and then re-enable reading of the ROMs. The programming sequence would be as follows:

```
LDA $C080           ;read-enable bank-switched RAM (bank 2)
⟨read information⟩
LDA $C082           ;re-enable ROM read
```

The latter method can be used to execute machine-language programs only. The reason that Applesoft programs cannot be made to execute while residing in bank-switched RAM is that the place where the program is stored and the Applesoft ROM area must be active at the same time and this just isn't possible because bank-switched RAM and the Applesoft interpreter use the same addresses.

Note that if you are running assembly-language programs that reside in bank-switched RAM, you must make absolutely sure that those programs do not use subroutines contained in the internal ROMs (that is, those contained in Applesoft or the system monitor). The reason is simple: as far as the //e is concerned, as soon as you read-enable bank-switched RAM, the //e doesn't think the ROMs exist and so the system will "hang" when it attempts to execute a ROM subroutine. If you really must use these ROM subroutines, you must first execute a JSR instruction to a location in normal RAM that contains code that first deselects bank-switched RAM for reading and selects the ROMs ($CØ82), calls the ROM subroutine, and then read-enables bank-switched RAM ($CØ80) and executes an RTS instruction to return to the program in bank-switched RAM.

To avoid these software complexities, you could move the ROM code that you need to use into bank-switched RAM by write-enabling bank-switched RAM and then performing a memory move from the ROMs to the same memory locations in bank-switched RAM. When this is done, the program can call the "pseudo-ROM" locations directly. For example, to move the system monitor to bank-switched RAM, you would execute the following commands, starting from Applesoft direct mode:

```
CALL -151           ;Enter the monitor
C081                ;Two accesses will write-enable
C081                ; the RAMcard (Read ROM)
F800<F800.FFFFM     ;Move the monitor to the BSR
C082                ;Write-protect and set ROM read
3D0G                ;Return to Applesoft
```

By the way, you can easily customize the system monitor by first saving it to disk by entering the DOS command "BSAVE MONITOR,A$F8ØØ,L$8ØØ" and then BLOADing it into normal RAM (say beginning at location $8ØØ), making the desired changes, and then moving the "new" monitor to bank-switched RAM using the method just described (except that the monitor move command will now be "F800<8ØØ.FFFM"). In a similar manner, you could even modify Applesoft to suit your requirements!

You should bear in mind one more important consideration when using bank-switched RAM. Do not attempt to deselect bank-switched RAM for reading while running a program that is contained in bank-switched RAM. If you try to do this, the motherboard ROMs will immediately be enabled and your program, which is still executing at the same address in RAM, will suddenly enter limbo because its code has been "replaced" by the internal ROM code. Any deselection of bank-switched RAM must be done by a program segment that resides in "normal" RAM (from $ØØØØ . . . $BFFF).

Bank-Switched RAM and ProDOS

If you are using ProDOS, as opposed to DOS 3.3, then you should not try to use the main bank-switched RAM area for data or program storage. The reason for this is simple: ProDOS uses this area of memory to hold its operating system subroutines. If you overwrite this area, you will almost certainly crash the system.

AUXILIARY RAM MEMORY AREA

"Auxiliary" memory is that memory contained on an 8Ø-column text card that has been inserted into the //e's auxiliary connector. There are currently two such cards available for the //e, the standard 8Ø-column text card and the extended 8Ø-column text card. As we saw in Chapter 7, both of these cards contain a special 1K area of memory that is needed to support the //e's special 8Ø-column text display. The extended 8Ø-column text card, however, also contains an additional 63K of memory; the entire 64K of RAM memory on the extended card is mapped to addresses in exactly the same way as main RAM memory. In the following sections, we will be describing in detail how to use the auxiliary memory on the extended 8Ø-column text card.

There are several soft switches that are used to control auxiliary memory. We have already discussed some of these in Chapter 7, when we looked at how to control the 8Ø-column text display and double-width graphics displays. In addition, in the previous section, we saw that the upper 16K of auxiliary memory is functionally identical to main memory's bank-switched RAM and can be selected or deselected by making use of the ALTZPON and ALTZPOFF switches.

In this section, we will examine all the other soft switches that control auxiliary memory and elaborate further on the ones that have previously been discussed.

Using Auxiliary Memory

There are three main groups of switches that control the status of auxiliary memory. These are the ALTZP switches ("ALTernate Zero Page"), the RAMRD ("RAM ReaD") switches, and the RAMWRT ("RAM WRiTe") switches; they are summarized in Table 8-5.

The ALTZP Switch

We briefly discussed ALTZP earlier in this chapter when we looked at the bank-switched RAM contained in auxiliary memory. The ALTZP switches control two blocks of memory that are duplicated in main and auxiliary memory. First, they are used to select whether the 65Ø2 zero page and stack areas ($ØØØØ . . . $Ø1FF) in main internal memory or in auxiliary memory are to be used. Second, they are used to select whether main-memory bank-switched RAM or auxiliary-memory bank-switched RAM is to be used.

The ALTZPON ($CØØ9) switch is used to select auxiliary memory and the ALTZPOFF ($CØØ8) switch is used to select main memory. The current status of this switch can be determined by reading ALTZP ($CØ16); if the value read from this location is greater than 127, then ALTZP is ON; otherwise it is OFF. Note that you must *write* to the ALTZPON and ALTZPOFF switches in order to use

Table 8-5. Auxiliary memory soft switch and status locations.

Address Hex	(Dec)	Symbolic Name	Description
$CØØ2	(49154)	RAMRDOFF	Read main memory from $2ØØ–$BFFF
$CØØ3	(49155)	RAMRDON	Read aux. memory from $2ØØ–$BFFF
$CØ13	(49171)	RAMRD	Status: >=$8Ø is ON, <$8Ø is OFF
$CØØ4	(49156)	RAMWRTOFF	Write main memory from $2ØØ–$BFFF
$CØØ5	(49157)	RAMWRTON	Write aux. memory from $2ØØ–$BFFF
$CØ14	(49172)	RAMWRT	Status: >=$8Ø is ON, <$8Ø is OFF
$CØØ8	(4916Ø)	ALTZPOFF	Select main memory from $Ø–$1FF and enable main 16K bank from $DØØØ–$FFFF
$CØØ9	(49161)	ALTZPON	Select aux. memory from $Ø–$1FF and enable aux. 16K bank from $DØØØ–$FFFF
$CØ16	(49174)	ALTZP	Status: >=$8Ø is ON, <$8Ø is OFF

them. Figure 8-4 indicates which memory areas are switching whenever the ALTZP switches are written to.

As was mentioned earlier, great care must be taken when using the ALTZP switches to ensure that vital zero page and stack information is not "lost." All 65Ø2 operations that affect the stack (this includes PHA, PLA, PHP, PLP, JSR, and RTS instructions) use the stack that is currently selected by ALTZP, which is not necessarily the stack in main memory. So, if ALTZP is on and information is stored on the stack in auxiliary memory, don't expect it to be on the stack in main memory when ALTZP is turned off.

Keep in mind that it is extremely important that the value of the 65Ø2 stack pointer be saved before changing ALTZP and then restored when ALTZP is changed to its original state. If this is not done and the stack pointer is changed while in the other state, then

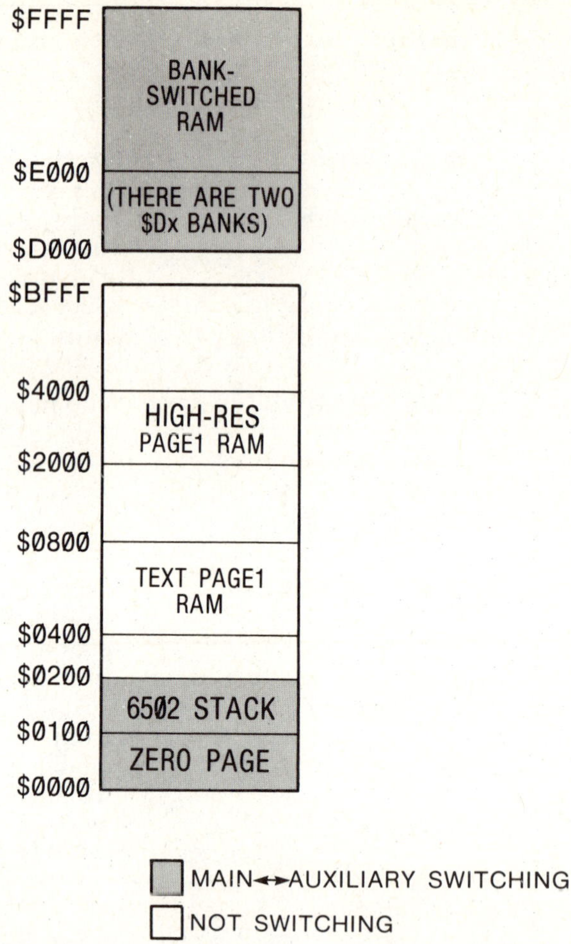

Figure 8-4. The effect of switching ALTZP.

the program will become hopelessly confused and will crash. The following program segment will do the trick:

```
TSX                    ;Put stack pointer in X
STX SAVESP             ; and save it somewhere in memory.
STA ALTZPON            ;Turn on ALTZP
.
<execute instructions>
.
STA ALTZPOFF           ;Turn off ALTZP
LDX SAVESP             ;Get original stack pointer in X
TXS                    ; and restore it.
```

Any zero page locations that need to be used after ALTZP has been changed will have to be duplicated in the other portion of memory before they can be properly used. To do this, it is necessary to move the contents of zero page into a part of memory that the ALTZP switches do not affect, say $200 ... $2FF, set the appropriate ALTZP switch, and then move this area of memory back down into the new zero page. This process should be repeated when setting ALTZP back to its original position.

The RAMRD and RAMWRT Switches

The RAMRD switches are used to control whether read operations are to use the memory locations from $200 ... $BFFF in main memory or the same locations in auxiliary memory. The RAMWRT switches control write operations for the same area of memory.

If RAMRDON ($C003) or RAMWRTON ($C005) is selected, and the 80STOREOFF ($C000) switch is active, then the entire block of auxiliary memory from $200 ... $BFFF will be selected for reading or writing, respectively. If RAMRDOFF ($C002) or RAMWRTOFF ($C004) is selected, then main memory will be selected for reading or writing, respectively, instead. The memory areas that are switched by RAMRD or RAMWRT in each of three different situations are summarized in Figure 8-5.

The area of memory that is affected when the RAMRD and RAMWRT switches are used is slightly different if the switching occurs when 80STOREON ($C001) is active. As you will recall from Chapter 7, the 80STORE switches are used to define the effect of the //e's PAGE2 switches. If 80STORE is ON, then PAGE2ON ($C055) and PAGE2OFF ($C054) are used to select whether the text screen video RAM page ($400 ... $7FF) in auxiliary or main memory is to be selected. In addition, if HIRESON ($C057) is active, then the PAGE2 switches will also select whether the high-resolution graphics screen video RAM page ($2000 ... $3FFF) in auxiliary or main memory is to be selected. The important point to note is that whenever 80STORE is ON, the PAGE2 switches take priority over the RAMRD and RAMWRT switches and so these latter two switches cannot be used to control which of the video RAM areas are active. The effect of switching PAGE2 with 80STOREON is summarized in Figure 8-6.

Auxiliary Memory Support Subroutines

The //e has two useful subroutines contained in its system monitor ROM area that facilitate the use of auxiliary memory. These subroutines are called AUXMOVE ($C311) and XFER ($C314).

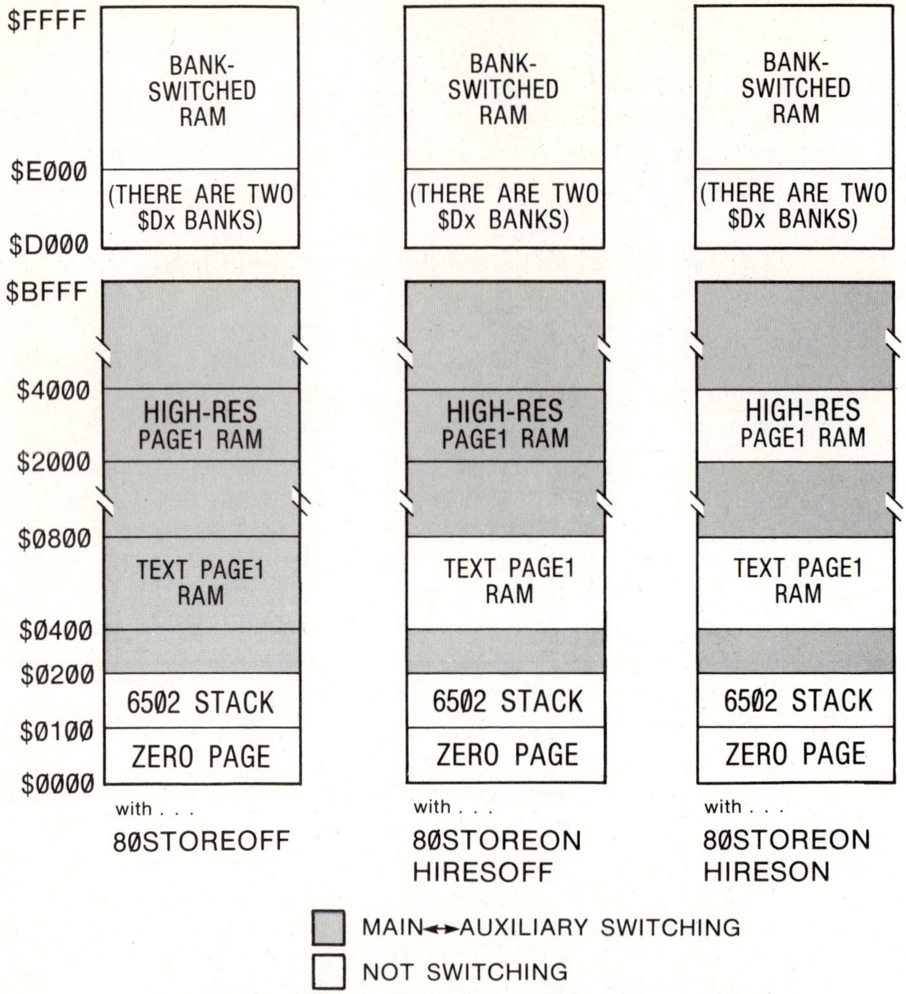

Figure 8-5. The effect of switching RAMWRT or RAMRD.

AUXMOVE ($C311)—Transferring data to and from auxiliary memory

AUXMOVE is used to transfer blocks of data contained within the memory range $200 . . . $BFFF from main memory to auxiliary memory or vice versa. Before using this subroutine, six locations in zero page must be set so that they hold the parameters of the block move. These are summarized in Figure 8-7.

The beginning address of the block to be moved must be stored at locations A1L ($3C) and A1H ($3D) and the ending address at

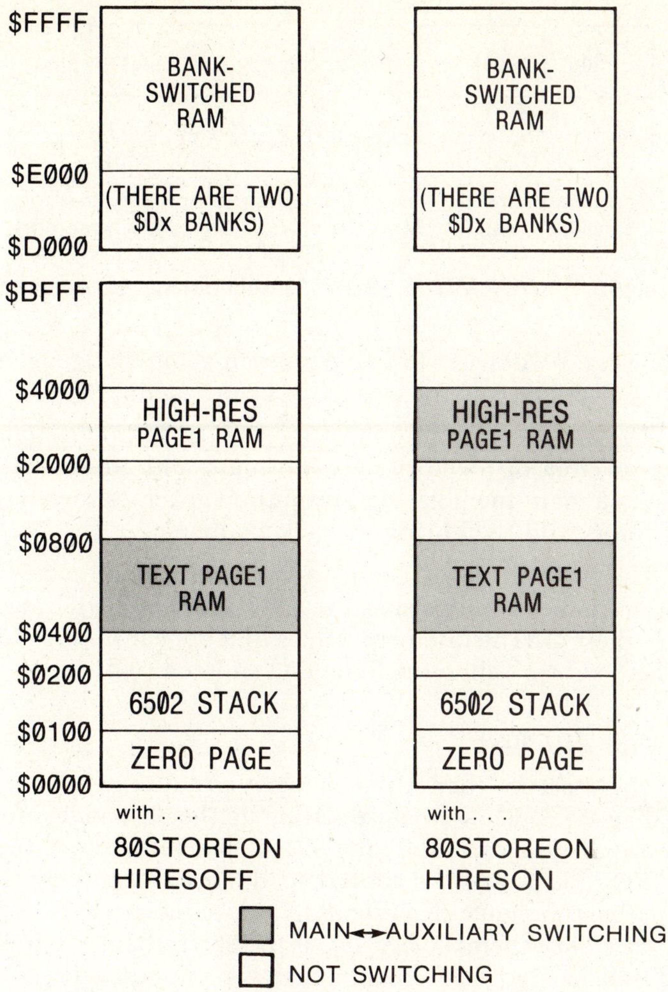

Figure 8-6. The effect of switching PAGE2.

A2L ($3E) and A2H ($3F). Finally, the destination address must be stored at A4L ($42) and A4H ($43). As is usually the case on the //e, the low-order part of each address is stored in the first byte of each zero-page pair.

The state of the 6502 carry flag is used to tell AUXMOVE the direction of the block move. If the carry flag is set, then the move will be performed from main memory to auxiliary memory. If it is clear, the move will take place in the opposite direction. The state of the carry flag can be set by using the 6502's CLC (clear carry) and SEC (set carry) instructions. There is no simple way, however, of setting these flags using Applesoft commands; the best

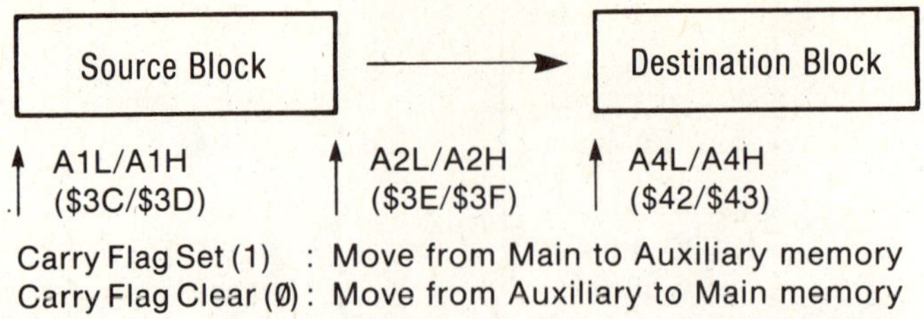

Figure 8-7. AUXMOVE ($C311) subroutine parameters.

that can be done is to call a short machine-language subroutine that clears or sets the carry flag before calling AUXMOVE.

The Applesoft program in Table 8-6 shows how you might transfer an area of memory between main and auxiliary memory. It saves a main-memory high-resolution graphics screen to auxiliary memory and then brings it back again.

The program first installs a short four-byte machine-language program beginning at location 768 ($3ØØ) by POKEing into memory those DATA statement values that appear in lines 12Ø and 13Ø. These values define the following simple program:

```
SEC
JMP AUXMOVE
```

The program then turns on high-resolution graphics and draws a diagonal line on it before setting up the parameters for the block move. In this case, the area of memory to be moved is $2ØØØ . . . $3FFF and it will be moved to the area beginning at $4ØØØ in auxiliary memory. (You shouldn't try to move it to $2ØØØ . . . $3FFF in auxiliary memory because if the 8ØSTORE switch is ON—and it will be if the 8Ø-column firmware is being used—and high-resolution graphics are being displayed, then the RAMRD and RAMWRT switches that AUXMOVE uses when performing the transfer will not affect this area of memory and no transfer will take place.)

After the screen has been saved to auxiliary memory, you can press a key to clear the screen, and then press another key to restore the line that was drawn on the screen. The line is restored by simply moving the 8K of screen memory that was saved in auxiliary memory back into main memory and not simply by redrawing the line.

To transfer a block of memory in the opposite direction, the first instruction in the four-byte machine-language subroutine must be changed from SEC to CLC. This is done in line 27Ø by POKEing 24 into location 768. The number 24 is the value of the CLC instruction.

Table 8-6. AUXMOVE. A program to move data between main and auxiliary memory.

```
0  REM "AUXMOVE" DEMO
100  PRINT  CHR$ (4);"PR#3"
110  FOR I = 768 TO 771: READ X: POKE
     I,X: NEXT
120  DATA 56: REM "SEC"
130  DATA 76,17,195: REM "JMP $C3
     11"
140  HGR : HCOLOR= 3: HPLOT 10,10
      TO 150,150
150  HOME : VTAB 22: PRINT  TAB(
     17);"MAIN <--->  AUXILIARY ME
     MORY TRANSFER DEMO"
160  HTAB 2: VTAB 23
170  PRINT "PRESS ANY KEY TO SAVE
      THE SCREEN IN AUXMEM: ";: GET
     A$
180  REM SET UP THE PARAMETERS OF
      THE MOVE:
190  POKE 60,0: POKE 61,32: REM F
     ROM $2000
200  POKE 62,255: POKE 63,63: REM
     THROUGH $3FFF
210  POKE 66,0: POKE 67,64: REM T
     O $4000 (AUX)
220  CALL 768: REM PERFORM THE MO
     VE
230  HTAB 2: VTAB 23: CALL  - 958
240  PRINT "PRESS ANY KEY TO CLEA
     R THE SCREEN: ";: GET A$: HGR
250  HTAB 2: VTAB 23; CALL  - 958
260  PRINT "PRESS ANY KEY TO REST
     ORE THE SCREEN FROM AUXMEM:
     ";: GET A$
270  POKE 768,24: REM PUT IN A "C
     LC"
280  REM SET UP THE PARAMETERS OF
      THE MOVE:
290  POKE 60,0: POKE 61,64: REM F
     ROM $4000
300  POKE 62,255: POKE 63,95: REM
     THROUGH $5FFF
310  POKE 66,0: POKE 67,32: REM T
     O $2000 (MAIN)
320  CALL 768: REM PERFORM THE MO
     VE
```

XFER ($C314)—Transferring control to a program from main or auxiliary memory

XFER is used to transfer control to a program in either main or auxiliary memory and, at the same time, to select which stack and zero page is to be used when the new program takes over. This is done by setting up certain parameters and executing a JMP (jump) instruction to XFER at $C314.

As with AUXMOVE, certain parameters and 65Ø2 flags must be set up before XFER is called. These are summarized in Table 8-7. First of all, the address of the program that is going to take control must be placed at locations $3ED and $3EE (low-order byte first). Then, the carry flag must be adjusted to indicate the direction of transfer: it must be set (1) if control is being transferred from a program in main memory to a program in auxiliary memory and clear (Ø) if transferring control in the reverse direction. Finally, the 65Ø2 overflow flag must be adjusted to indicate which of the two zero pages and stacks the new program is to use: if it is set (1), then the auxiliary zero page and stack will be used and if it is clear (Ø), then the main zero page and stack will be used.

The CLV (clear overflow) instruction can be used to clear the 65Ø2 overflow flag to zero. There is no similar command, however, that can be used to set the overflow flag to one. One method of forcing the overflow flag to one is to use the BIT instruction to test any memory location that holds a byte that has a "1" in bit 6. A convenient location to use is $FF58 because there is an RTS instruction located there and it has an opcode value of $6Ø.

Of course, before you transfer control to a program in the other

Table 8-7. XFER ($C314) subroutine parameters.

Parameter	*Description*
Transfer address	$3ED/$3EE (low-order byte first). This contains the starting address of the program to which control is to be transferred.
Carry flag	Carry set (1) means "transfer from main to auxiliary memory." Carry clear (Ø) means "transfer from auxiliary to main memory."
Overflow flag	Overflow set (1) means "use auxiliary stack and zero page." Overflow clear (Ø) means "use main stack and zero page."

memory area, you had better make sure that the program has been loaded there. This is easily done for programs residing in main memory but is a bit more tricky for those residing in auxiliary memory. The easiest way to load a program into auxiliary memory is to use the AUXMOVE subroutine.

Note that the same concerns that were raised about the stack and the stack pointer when discussing the ALTZP switches apply to the use of XFER. It is good practice to save the stack pointer immediately before jumping to XFER and then to restore it if and when a reverse transfer is made. In addition, if the two programs are both using the same stack, care must be taken to avoid overwriting any information that the other program has left on the stack. This is most easily done by saving the whole stack when control is transferred and then restoring it just before returning to the calling program. Alternately, the two programs should each use a different stack; however, this cannot be done without using two zero pages as well and this may be inconvenient.

Running Co-Resident Programs

As we have seen, the 64K of RAM memory on the //e's extended 8Ø-column text card is virtually a mirror image of the 64K of RAM on the motherboard. Both of these memory spaces span exactly the same logical addresses, each has its own 65Ø2 stack and zero page, and each has a 16K area of bank-switched RAM. One important area of difference, however, lies in the use of locations $4ØØ . . . $7FF. When in 4Ø-column text mode, only these locations in main memory are used to define the video display; the same locations in auxiliary memory have no effect on the video display. When the 80-column display is active, locations $4ØØ . . . $7FF in main memory define the odd-numbered columns in the display while the same locations in auxiliary memory define the even-numbered columns.

The similarities between these two 64K spaces are great enough, however, that it is conceivable that different programs could be loaded into each space and then run independently of one another (well, *almost* independently of one another). After all, since each program can have its own stack and zero page, there is not a strong temptation for either program to interfere with the other's use of these important areas of memory. The video display will have to be shared, however, for the reasons just given.

Table 8-8. CONCURRENT. A program to control two Applesoft programs in memory at the same time.

```
Page #01

: A S M

**************
* CONCURRENT *
**************

* (BRUN this program from disk)

SPSAVE    EQU  $6            ;Stack pointer save area
OLDCSW    EQU  $7            ;Initial value of CSW (aux, only)

CSW       EQU  $36

* Parameter locations for AUXMOVE:
A1        EQU  $3C
A2        EQU  $3E
A4        EQU  $42

* Memory switches:
STOR80ON  EQU  $C001         ;Don't switch $400...$7FF
RAMRDOFF  EQU  $C002         ;Read main from $200...$BFFF
RAMRDON   EQU  $C003         ;Read auxiliary from $200...$BFFF
RAMWRTOF  EQU  $C004         ;Write main from $200...$BFFF
RAMWRTON  EQU  $C005         ;Write auxiliary from $200...$BFFF

ALTZPOFF  EQU  $C008         ;Select main zero page+stack
ALTZPON   EQU  $C009         ;Select auxiliary zero page+stack
ALTZP     EQU  $C016         ;ALTZP status: on if >=$80

AUXMOVE   EQU  $C311         ;AUX <--> MAIN move subroutine
```

```
                APPLSOFT EQU  $E000-1     ;Cold start to Applesoft (less 1)
                * Monitor initialization subroutines:
                INIT     EQU  $FB2F
                HOME     EQU  $FC58
                SETNORM  EQU  $FE84
                SETVID   EQU  $FE93
                SETKBD   EQU  $FE89
                         ORG  $2B3
                * Copy SWITCH to auxiliary memory:
02B3: A9 00              LDA  #<SWITCH
02B5: 85 3C              STA  A1
02B7: 85 42              STA  A4
02B9: A9 03              LDA  #>SWITCH
02BB: 85 3D              STA  A1+1
02BD: 85 43              STA  A4+1
02BF: A9 4A              LDA  #<SWLAST
02C1: 85 3E              STA  A2


Page #02

02C3: A9 03              LDA  #>SWLAST
02C5: 85 3F              STA  A2+1
02C7: 38                 SEC              ;(Move to aux. mem)
02C8: 20 11 C3           JSR  AUXMOVE
02CB: 8D 09 C0           STA  ALTZPON     ;Select aux. zero page + stack
                * Initialize the monitor's auxiliary zero-page usage:
02CE: D8                 CLD
```

(continued)

Table 8-8. CONCURRENT. A program to control two Applesoft programs in memory at the same time (continued).

```
02CF: 20 84 FE              JSR   SETNORM     ;Set normal video
02D2: 20 2F FB              JSR   INIT        ;Set full-screen text mode
02D5: 20 93 FE              JSR   SETVID      ;Set for standard 40-column output
02D8: 20 89 FE              JSR   SETKBD      ;Set for standard 40-column input
02DB: 20 58 FC              JSR   HOME        ;Clear the screen

                   * Redefine output link to keep 80STOREON:
02DE: A5 36                 LDA   CSW
02E0: 85 07                 STA   OLDCSW
02E2: A5 37                 LDA   CSW+1
02E4: 85 08                 STA   OLDCSW+1

02E6: A9 44                 LDA   #<NEWOUT
02E8: 85 36                 STA   CSW
02EA: A9 03                 LDA   #>NEWOUT
02EC: 85 37                 STA   CSW+1

                   * Initialize auxiliary memory stack:
02EE: A9 DF                 LDA   #>APPLSOFT ;Set up a return to the cold
02F0: 8D FF 01              STA   $1FF        ; start entry point for
02F3: A9 FF                 LDA   #<APPLSOFT ; Applesoft the first time
02F5: 8D FE 01              STA   $1FE        ; you enter auxiliary memory
02F8: A2 FD                 LDX   #$FD        ;Set up initial stack pointer
02FA: 86 06                 STX   SPSAVE      ; and save it in aux. memory

02FC: 8D 08 C0              STA   ALTZPOFF    ;Select main zero page + stack

02FF: 60                    RTS

                   * SWITCH is used to move between aux. and main:
0300: 8E 41 03     SWITCH   STX   XSAVE       ;Save X, Y, A, P, S
0303: 8C 42 03              STY   YSAVE
```

```
0306: 8D 40 03                STA   ASAVE
0309: 08                      PHP
030A: 68                      PLA
030B: 8D 43 03                STA   PSAVE
030E: BA                      TSX
030F: 86 06                   STX   SPSAVE
0311: 8D 01 C0                STA   STOR80ON     ;Don't switch video RAM
0314: AD 16 C0                LDA   ALTZP        ;Check ALTZP status
0317: 30 1B                   BMI   TOMAIN       ;Go to main if in aux.
0319: 8D 09 C0                STA   ALTZPON      ;Turn on aux. ZP+stack

Page #03

031C: 8D 03 C0                STA   RAMRDON      ;Turn on aux. memory
031F: 8D 05 C0                STA   RAMWRTON
0322: A6 06         RESTORE   LDX   SPSAVE       ;Restore all registers
0324: 9A                      TXS
0325: AE 41 03                LDX   XSAVE
0328: AC 42 03                LDY   YSAVE
032B: AD 43 03                LDA   PSAVE
032E: 48                      PHA
032F: AD 40 03                LDA   ASAVE
0332: 28                      PLP
0333: 60                      RTS
0334: 8D 08 C0      TOMAIN    STA   ALTZPOFF     ;Turn on main ZP+stack
0337: 8D 02 C0                STA   RAMRDOFF     ;Turn on main memory
033A: 8D 04 C0                STA   RAMWRTOF
033D: 4C 22 03                JMP   RESTORE

                    ASAVE     DS    1
                    XSAVE     DS    1
                    YSAVE     DS    1
                    PSAVE     DS    1
```

(continued)

Table 8-8. CONCURRENT. A program to control two Applesoft programs in memory at the same time (continued).

```
                * The following new input subroutine is really needed only
                * when Applesoft is first initialized. When Applesoft is
                * initialized, it writes to $C000, thus turning 80STOREOFF
                * and preventing the program in auxiliary memory from
                * using the 40-column video RAM (in main memory).
0344: 8D 01 C0  NEWOUT   STA  STOR80ON
0347: 6C 07 00           JMP  (OLDCSW)

                SWLAST   EQU  *


--End assembly--

151 bytes

Errors: 0
```

The CONCURRENT program in Table 8-8 is a short assembly-language program that allows you to run one of two Applesoft programs that can be loaded into memory at the same time, one in main memory and the other in auxiliary memory, and to easily switch between the two programs. It must be activated by using the BRUN command to load and execute it directly from diskette; you must be in standard 4Ø-column mode before doing this.

The first thing that CONCURRENT does is to copy its SWITCH and NEWOUT subroutines from main to auxiliary memory by using the AUXMOVE subroutine. The SWITCH subroutine is responsible for transferring control from main to auxiliary memory and vice versa, and so a copy of it must be stored in both these memory areas to ensure that it is always available. There is one other important reason for duplicating SWITCH in this way. Part way through the subroutine, the area of memory (main or auxiliary) that is currently active will be turned off and replaced by the other, thus causing the current copy of SWITCH to temporarily vanish. This would normally cause the system to hang because the instruction at the next address at which SWITCH resumes executing after switching would no longer be available and the program would behave unpredictably. If SWITCH is present at exactly the same locations in the other area of memory, however, then one copy will always be active and no problems will be encountered.

After CONCURRENT has moved SWITCH to auxiliary memory, it enables the zero page and stack in auxiliary memory (ALTZPON) and then calls five system monitor initialization routines (SETNORM, INIT, SETVID, SETKBD, and HOME) that will cause the auxiliary zero page to be properly initialized so that system monitor I/O subroutines will work properly.

The next task that CONCURRENT performs is to redefine the standard character output subroutine by storing the address of the NEWOUT subroutine at the CSWL/CSWH ($36/$37) output link in auxiliary memory. The NEWOUT subroutine must be used to handle output because of a complication that arises when Applesoft is first initialized in auxiliary memory.

When Applesoft is first initialized, it determines how much RAM memory is installed in the //e by storing and reading numbers at the first location of each memory page (beginning with page $Ø8) until it finds that the number read is not the same as the number stored. When such a discrepancy occurs, then a non-RAM location must have been reached.

On the //e, the first non-RAM address written to will be $CØØØ, which is the first address in the //e's I/O memory space. Unfortunately, this has the side effect of turning off the 8ØSTORE soft switch that resides at that location. This means that if the RAMRD and RAMWRT switches are on (that is, auxiliary memory from \$2ØØ . . . \$3FF and \$8ØØ . . . \$BFFF is active), then the auxiliary memory space from \$4ØØ . . . \$7FF will be active as well. (Remember that this same space in main memory—which represents the video RAM for the 4Ø-column text screen—will remain active if 8ØSTORE is on.) This auxiliary memory space has no effect on the 4Ø-column screen display, however, and so the screen display will not change when attempts are made to update it by calling the standard video subroutines (that only affect the currently active \$4ØØ . . . \$7FF space).

If we could turn the 8ØSTORE switch on before Applesoft tries to perform its first video operation after initialization (the displaying of its "]" prompt symbol), then we could avoid the problem of having the "wrong" \$4ØØ . . . \$7FF space active. This is done by replacing the standard output subroutine with the nearly identical NEWOUT subroutine. In fact, the only difference is that NEWOUT first writes to 8ØSTOREON (\$CØØ1) to ensure that the video RAM area from \$4ØØ . . . \$7FF in main memory will be active.

Initialization of the Auxiliary Stack

After the new output link address is set up in auxiliary memory, CONCURRENT initializes the auxiliary stack by placing the address, less 1, of the cold start entry point to Applesoft (\$EØØØ) at the first two stack locations, \$1FF and \$1FE. The high-order part of this address is stored at \$1FF and the low-order part at \$1FE. After this has been done, the value \$FD is stored at SPSAVE, a temporary storage location. The first time that auxiliary memory is enabled by calling SWITCH, the 65Ø2 stack pointer register will be loaded from SPSAVE, meaning that when the RTS is executed at the end of the SWITCH subroutine, control will be returned to \$EØØØ, the Applesoft cold start entry point. The subroutine at \$EØØØ takes care of initializing Applesoft in auxiliary memory by setting up all its program and data pointers that are contained in zero page.

The last thing that CONCURRENT does is re-enable zero page and the stack in main memory and then end. At this point the //e is configured in such a way as to allow you to easily switch between programs in main and auxiliary memory.

Using CONCURRENT

CONCURRENT is simple to use. Whenever you want to leave main memory and resume running the program in auxiliary memory, or vice versa, you must activate the SWITCH subroutine by entering a CALL 768 command. This subroutine determines which bank of memory is active (by examining the status of the ALTZP switch) and then enables the other bank of memory from $ØØØØ . . . $BFFF (except for the $4ØØ . . . $7FF video RAM area) for reading and writing by adjusting the ALTZP, RAMRD, and RAMWRT switches accordingly. The $4ØØ . . . $7FF video RAM area in main memory is kept active by writing to 8ØSTOREON ($CØØ1) before accessing the RAMRD and RAMWRT switches.

When the SWITCH subroutine ends it executes an RTS instruction that instructs the 65Ø2 to return to the address (plus 1) that is stored on the top of the stack. Unless some tricky programming is being done, this address is that of the instruction immediately following the JSR instruction that called the subroutine. Such is not the case, however, when calling SWITCH because just before its RTS instruction is executed, the other stack is reactivated and its stack pointer is set equal to the value it had when SWITCH was last called. What this means is that as soon as SWITCH is called, the //e begins executing those instructions right after the CALL 768 that activated the switch in the first place.

To see a simple example of how CONCURRENT works, first install SWITCH by executing CONCURRENT. Then enter the following Applesoft program:

```
100  IF  PEEK (49152) = 155 THEN
      POKE 49168,0: CALL 768
200  PRINT "MAIN MEMORY": GOTO 100
```

and RUN it. This program doesn't do much but continuously print out "MAIN MEMORY" on the screen. However, the program is constantly monitoring the keyboard for an ESC character in line 1ØØ. If ESC is pressed, then the keyboard strobe is cleared (POKE 49168,Ø) and then SWITCH is called by executing a CALL 768 command.

When SWITCH is called for the first time, you will be put into Applesoft direct mode in *auxiliary* memory. While you are there for the first time, enter this program:

```
100  IF  PEEK (49152) = 155 THEN
      POKE 49168,0: CALL 768
200  PRINT "AUXILIARY MEMORY": GOTO 100
```

This is the same as the previous program, except that it prints out "AUXILIARY MEMORY." Now type RUN to start this program and then press the ESC key. As soon as ESC is pressed, you will switch back to main memory and the program there will resume executing right where it left off and will start printing "MAIN

MEMORY." By pressing ESC again and again, you can see that you are indeed switching between the two programs!

Limitations of CONCURRENT

The major limitation of CONCURRENT is that the program running in auxiliary memory cannot use any DOS commands. Although a copy of DOS could be transferred to auxiliary memory and used by the program running there, several problems could arise that would be difficult to solve in software. For example, special "lockout" flags would have to be used to prevent one program from modifying a file until the other had finished using it. If this was not done, then the data in the file could easily become scrambled. Rather than complicate the CONCURRENT program and obscure its usefulness as an example of how to use main and auxiliary memory, no attempt has been made to allow the program in auxiliary memory to use DOS.

Other problems arise because the two programs must share the same video screen. This means that information placed on the screen by one program could easily be overwritten by the other. One solution to this problem is to define nonoverlapping text windows for each program by modifying the window parameters held in zero page (see Chapter 7).

Since auxiliary memory is initialized by installing the standard 4Ø-column input and output subroutines (by calling SETVID and SETKBD), you should not enter auxiliary memory when 8Ø-column mode is active. If you wish to use CONCURRENT with an 8Ø-column display, the "JSR SETVID" and "JSR SETKBD" instructions should be replaced by a "JSR $C3ØØ" instruction; the latter instruction takes care of installing the I/O subroutines that support the 8Ø-column display.

Finally, you should note that you must not write to 8ØSTOREOFF ($CØØØ) while in auxiliary memory. If this is done, then the auxiliary memory space from $4ØØ . . . $7FF will become active and, as explained above, you will not be able to display anything on the video screen.

FURTHER READING FOR CHAPTER 8

Standard reference works . . .

80-Column Text Card Manual, Apple Computer, Inc., 1982.

Extended 80-Column Text Card Supplement, Apple Computer, Inc., 1982.

On uses for auxiliary memory . . .

D.C. Johnson, "Using Auxiliary Memory in the //e," *Apple Assembly Line*, August 1983, pp. 2-12. Another program to switch between main and auxiliary memory.

On uses for bank-switched RAM . . .

C. Bongers, "Loading DOS 3.3 on the Language Card," *Call -A.P.P.L.E.*, July/Aug 1981, pp. 9-21. Putting DOS 3.3 in bank-switched RAM frees up a lot more room for Applesoft. See follow-ups in *Call -A.P.P.L.E.*, Nov/Dec 1981, pp. 81-85, and in "All About DOS," *Call -A.P.P.L.E.*, 1983, pp. 5-17.

D.W. Miller, Jr., "Painting the Ramcard," *Call -A.P.P.L.E.*, April 1983, p. 51. How to store high-resolution pictures in bank-switched RAM.

K. Manly and F. Manly, "RAM Disk," *Nibble*, Vol. 4, No. 8 (1983), pp. 25-37. How to use bank-switched RAM as a "fake" disk drive.

9

The Speaker and the Cassette Port

In this chapter, we will examine two more built-in I/O devices that the //e supports: the speaker and the cassette port.

The //e's speaker can be used to add the dimension of sound to programs. In many cases, this simply means that you will hear a short (but suitably aggravating) beep whenever you make an error. However, some programs, notably educational software and games, exercise the speaker in much more dramatic ways to generate complex sound effects and recognizable musical patterns that tend to dramatically liven up these types of programs. We will look at the techniques used to generate music later in this chapter.

With the advent of low-cost and reliable disk drives, the cassette port has probably become the least used built-in I/O device on the //e. This is because its prime function has always been to store programs or data on standard audio cassette tape and to read them back again into the computer, a chore that the disk drive performs much more conveniently, quickly, and reliably. Nevertheless, many users still use cassette tape for archival storage of information. In this chapter, we will describe a particularly interesting application involving the cassette port: the digitization of voice input.

THE SPEAKER

As was indicated above, the speaker on the //e serves several purposes, the most common of which is to emit a harsh "beeeep!!" whenever some kind of error occurs while entering or operating a program. This sound is generated by entering or printing the ASCII "bell" character (ASCII code 7). This can be done by pressing <CTRL-G> on the keyboard or by printing CHR$(7) from Applesoft. With appropriate software, the speaker can also be used to generate music and sound effects and even to reproduce (though crudely) the human voice.

The sounds that the speaker generates are caused by the in and out movement of the speaker cone; the frequency (also called the pitch) of a sound is the same as the frequency of the cone's movement. The position of the cone is controlled by a voice coil and a permanent magnet located near the base of the cone. When this coil is turned on, the cone moves out and when it is turned off, the cone moves in. Thus, you can select the frequency of the tone to be emitted merely by switching this coil on and off at the desired frequency.

There is one special I/O memory location reserved for the speaker that allows you to control it in this way. As indicated in Table 9-1, this is SPEAKER ($CØ3Ø). This is yet another soft switch location; each time that it is read (using Applesoft's PEEK or an assembler's LDA) the state of the speaker changes from off to on (if it was last off) or from on to off (if it was last on).

Generating Musical Notes

Let's take a close look at how you can use the //e to generate musical notes. First recognize that the sound wave generated by a single musical note is merely a smoothly varying sine wave, as shown in Figure 9-1 (a). Since, however, we can only turn the //e's speaker on or off (that is, we cannot smoothly vary the amplitude of its output), we can only generate square waves like the one shown in Figure 9-1 (b). It turns out, however, that for most frequencies, this square wave is an acceptable approximation of its sine wave equivalent and the sound that is generated is close to what you would normally expect to hear.

Before a specific note can be generated, you will have to know its frequency (or "pitch"). Table 9-2 contains a list of two octaves of musical notes from Low "C" through Middle "C" to High "C",

Table 9-1. Speaker I/O memory location.

Address Hex	*(Dec)*	*Symbolic Name*	*Description*
$CØ3Ø	(492ØØ)	SPEAKER	Speaker output. Reading this location toggles the state of the speaker.

(a) Sine wave for pure tone.

(b) Square wave approximation of pure tone.

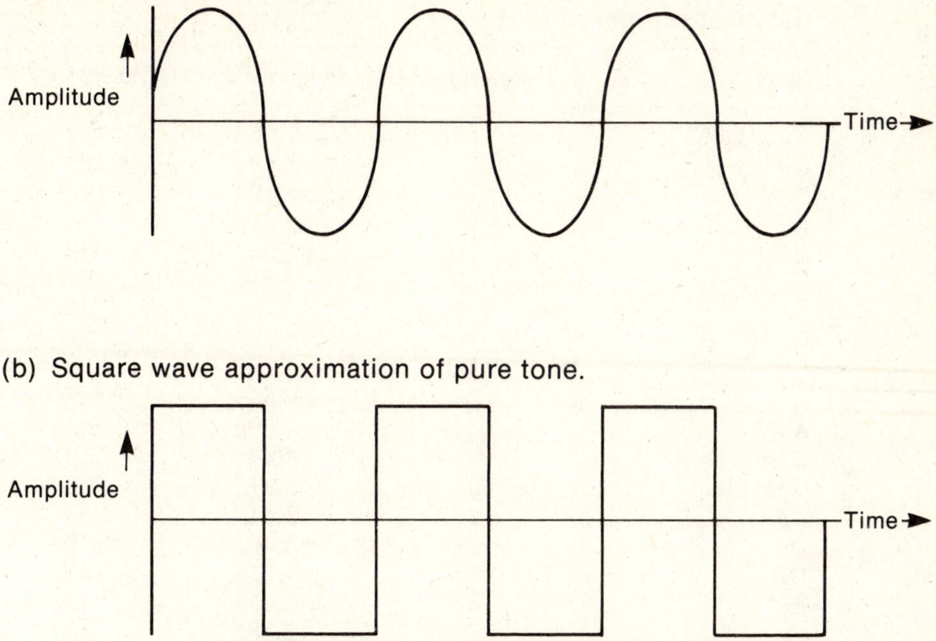

Figure 9-1. Sine waves and square waves.

their frequencies on the standard Even-Tempered Scale in hertz (cycles/second), and their periods. The period is equal to the time it takes to finish one complete sinusoidal cycle and is equal to the reciprocal of the frequency.

To generate the waveform for any note, the speaker must be turned on for one-half of its period and off for the other half. Given this information, the procedure to follow for generating a note is as follows:

1. Turn the speaker on
2. Wait one-half period
3. Turn the speaker off
4. Wait one-half period
5. Return to step 1

Since the status of the speaker toggles between on and off every time you access its soft switch at SPEAKER ($CØ3Ø), you can simplify this flowchart by removing steps 3 and 4.

The above procedure must be repeated for the duration of the note; if you are playing a note from a piece of music, this duration

Table 9-2. Frequencies and periods of musical notes on the even-tempered scale.

Note	*Frequency (Hz)*	*Period (μsec)*	*HALFTIME**
C (low "C")	131	7,634	112
C#	139	7,194	106
D	147	6,803	100
D#	156	6,410	94
E	165	6,061	89
F	175	5,714	84
F#	185	5,405	80
G	196	5,102	75
G#	208	4,808	71
A	220	4,545	67
A#	233	4,292	63
B	247	4,049	60
C (Middle "C")	262	3,817	56
C#	277	3,610	53
D	294	3,401	50
D#	311	3,215	47
E	330	3,030	45
F	349	2,865	42
F#	370	2,703	40
G	392	2,551	38
G#	415	2,410	35
A (Concert "A")	440	2,273	33
A#	466	2,146	32
B	494	2,024	30
C (High "C")	523	1,912	28

* See text.

will depend on the type of note that is being played (a whole note, half-note, quarter-note, and so on) and the tempo of the music.

Table 9-3 shows the NOTE program, which is capable of using the //e's speaker to produce a note of a specified frequency and duration. This program toggles the speaker whenever the X register, which at the beginning of every tone cycle contains a code number related to the period of the note, is reduced to zero by successive DEX instructions. The X register is reduced by one unit every 34*HALFTIME microseconds, where HALFTIME is this code number and 34 happens to be the length of an internal software delay loop that has been used. The code number is simply equal to the number of 34-microsecond loops that must be performed before one-half of the period of the note elapses. It can be calculated by dividing one-half of the period time (in microseconds) by 34. For example, the value of HALFTIME for an "A" note (440 Hz) would be equal to 1136 (one-half its period in microseconds) divided by 34, which is equal to 33. In this way, you can easily calculate the HALFTIME values for all the other notes that you may wish to generate; they are listed in Table 9-2 for your convenience.

NOTE also allows you to specify the duration of the note to be played by adjusting the LENGTH constant. A temporary value of LENGTH, called LTEMP, is decremented each time the program executes 255 of the aforementioned 34-microsecond loops, that is, once every 867Ø microseconds. Thus, to play a note for one second (1,ØØØ,ØØØ microseconds), LENGTH would be set equal to 1,ØØØ,ØØØ/867Ø, or 115.

The loop time in the NOTE program has been calculated by determining exactly how many 65Ø2 machine cycles take place between successive reductions of the loop counters (that control the frequency and duration of the note) and multiplying that number by the period of the 65Ø2 microprocessor's clock. Since the //e's clock is operating at about 1 MHz, it turns out that the loop time (in microseconds) is simply equal to the number of machine cycles needed to perform the instructions in the loop. To calculate the total number of machine cycles being performed in the loop, you must first determine what instructions are being executed in the loop and then add up their individual cycle times. The cycle times for each 65Ø2 instruction are listed in Appendix II. Note that the number of cycles depends not only on the particular instruction being executed but also on the addressing mode that is being used by that instruction.

It should be obvious by now that because of the meticulous timing loops that music programs require to produce precise frequencies, it is really not possible to create quality music by directly accessing SPEAKER ($CØ3Ø) using the Applesoft PEEK statement and FOR/NEXT loops. Applesoft delay times simply cannot be adjusted as finely as can assembler delay times and, even if they could be, they could actually change depending on the location of the loop in the program. So stick to assembly language if you want to create music. Applesoft programs can be used, however, to POKE frequency and duration information into an assembly-language program's data area and to CALL the assembly-language program. We will see how to do this next.

Generating Music

Now that we have written a program to generate one musical note, it will be almost trivial to develop a program that actually

Table 9-3. NOTE. A program to play a musical note.

```
Page #01

: A S M
                   1     ********
                   2     * NOTE *
                   3     ********
                   4
                   5     SPEAKER  EQU  $C030      ;Speaker I/O location
                   6
                   7              ORG  $300
                   8
0300: 21           9     HALFTIME DFB  33         ; = (1/frequency)/(2*34)
0301: 1D          10     LENGTH   DFB  29         ;Duration in units of 34*255 usec
                  11
0302: A0 FF       12     NOTE     LDY  #255       ;The program starts here
0304: AD 01 03    13              LDA  LENGTH
0307: 8D 2F 03    14              STA  LTEMP
030A: AE 00 03    15     NOTE1    LDX  HALFTIME   ;X contains the length of the note
030D: AD 30 C0    16              LDA  SPEAKER    ;Toggle the speaker
0310: 4C 1A 03    17              JMP  STALL1
0313: EA          18     STALL    NOP             ;These NOPs compensate for
0314: EA          19              NOP             ; branches to NOTE1 from line 37
0315: EA          20              NOP             ;They ensure that the overall loop
0316: EA          21              NOP             ; times are the same so that the
0317: EA          22              NOP             ; units of "length" don't vary
0318: EA          23              NOP             ; with the frequency
```

```
0319: EA         24            NOP
031A: 88         25   STALL1   DEY            ;Loop time is 34 cycles
031B: D0 07      26            BNE   STALL2
031D: CE 2F 03   27            DEC   LTEMP    ;Reduce this every 34*255 cycles
0320: F0 0C      28            BEQ   EXIT
0322: D0 05      29            BNE   STALL3
0324: EA         30   STALL2   NOP            ;These NOPs compensate even
0325: EA         31            NOP            ; out the loop time when the code
0326: EA         32            NOP            ; in lines 27-29 is not executed
0327: EA         33            NOP
0328: EA         34            NOP
0329: CA         35   STALL3   DEX            ;Loop time is 34 cycles
032A: D0 E7      36            BNE   STALL
032C: F0 DC      37            BEQ   NOTE1
032E: 60         38   EXIT     RTS
                 39
                 40   LTEMP    DS    1
                 41

--End assembly--

48 bytes

Errors: 0
```

plays a short tune. All we have to do is link single notes together in the orders, and for the durations, dictated by the sheet music for the tune.

Consider the Applesoft SONG program in Table 9-4. This program contains several DATA statements that contain the HALFTIME and LENGTH values needed by NOTE for each of the notes in the first part of the theme from the television series "M*A*S*H." The LENGTH values have been calculated by assuming that a whole note has a duration of one second; if this is the case, then LENGTH=115, as explained earlier. To play the tune defined by the DATA statements, first ensure that the NOTE program has been saved to diskette and then enter the Applesoft RUN command. SONG plays the tune by executing an Applesoft FOR/NEXT loop that reads the HALFTIME and LENGTH values for a note, POKEs them into the NOTE program data area, and then CALLs the NOTE program to generate the tone. After all the notes have been played in this way, the program ends.

You can easily play your own favorite song by translating its notes into HALFTIME and LENGTH values and placing these values into the DATA statements of the SONG program. The last pair of values in the DATA statements must be zeros so that SONG will know when all the notes have been read.

You may well be wondering whether you can play chords of music, that is, more than one note at once, in order to improve the quality of the sound that is generated. The short answer is "yes, you can!" but the software required to do this is much more complex. For example, to play two notes at once, you would have to intertwine two timing loops, one for each note, and you would have to ensure that the speaker was being toggled at the proper rate for each note. This is not an impossible feat to be sure, but it is left as an exercise for the more interested reader.

THE CASSETTE PORT

The cassette port is primarily used to store programs and data on cassette tape and to read this information back again. Externally, the port is made up of two miniature phone jacks, called the input and output jacks, that are located on the //e's back panel right next to the video connector. To connect up a cassette recorder to the //e, you need only acquire a pair of miniature phone plug cables and connect them between the input jack (marked with a picture of an arrow coming from a cassette tape) and the recorder's earphone jack and the output jack (marked with a picture of an

Table 9-4. PLAYTUNE. A program to play a song.

```
]LIST

0  REM "PLAYTUNE"
100  PRINT  CHR$ (4);"BLOAD NOTE"

110  READ HT: READ LN: REM READ
     HALFTIME AND LENGTH
120  IF HT = 0 AND LN = 0 THEN 16
     0
130  POKE 768,HT: POKE 769,LN
140  CALL 770: REM PLAY THE TONE
150  GOTO 110: REM AND GET NEXT N
     OTE
160  END
1000  REM NAME THAT TUNE!!
1010  DATA 63,29,67,29,63,29,67,2
     9,63,29,67,29,75,58
1020  DATA 67,29,75,29,67,29,75,2
     9,67,29,75,29,84,29,67,29,75
     ,29,84,29,75,29,84,29
1030  DATA 75,29,84,29,89,29,75,2
     9,84,29,89,29,84,29,89,29,84
     ,29,75,29,67,58
1040  DATA 67,58,56,29,50,29,56,2
     9,50,29,56,29,50,29,56,58,56
     ,29
1050  DATA 50,29,56,29,50,29,56,2
     9,50,29,56,58,56,29,67,29,56
     ,29,50,29,42,29
1060  DATA 38,29,42,29,50,29,56,2
     9
1070  DATA 50,115,50,58,50,29,56,
     29,67,29,56,29,50,29,42,29
1080  DATA 38,29,42,29,50,29,56,2
     9,50,115,50,58
1090  DATA 0,0: REM END OF DATA
      MARKER
```

arrow pointing toward a cassette tape) and the recorder's microphone jack.

The //e devotes two I/O memory locations for use by the cassette port; these locations allow you to control the signal that is sent to the output jack and to monitor the signal that is received through the input jack. These memory locations are described in Table 9-5.

The cassette output jack transmits audio voltage levels to a cassette recorder that are compatible with the levels that the recorder would normally receive through a microphone. For this output to

Table 9-5. Cassette port I/O memory locations.

Address Hex	(Dec)	Symbolic Name	Description
$CØ6Ø	(49248)	CASSIN	Cassette input. The status of the cassette input port is contained in bit 7.
$CØ2Ø	(49184)	CASSOUT	Cassette output. Reading this location will toggle the state of the cassette output port.

be saved to tape, all you have to do is put the recorder into record mode by simultaneously pressing its RECORD and PLAY buttons. Two discrete levels of output (high and low) can be generated by using a soft switch at CASSOUT ($CØ2Ø). Whenever this location is read, the output level will toggle from high to low or from low to high, depending on its prior state. The timing of these transitions can easily be controlled by software, thus allowing you to generate audible frequencies and to store them on tape. This procedure should sound familiar: it's the same one used to generate sound on the //e's speaker (except that in that case, of course, the speaker's soft switch is read).

The cassette input jack is designed to be compatible with the audio voltage levels sent by a cassette recorder to its earphone jack. When a miniature phone plug cable is connected between the cassette input jack and this earphone jack, the signal from the recorder can be interpreted and dealt with by the //e instead of your ear. This signal will typically fluctuate between a positive and negative voltage at a rate that is dictated by the sound being played.

The status of the cassette input port can be determined by examining the status of bit 7 of I/O memory location CASSIN ($CØ6Ø). When this bit is "on" (1), the input voltage of the audio signal is positive; when it is "off" (Ø), the voltage is negative. When bit 7 changes from 1 to Ø or from Ø to 1, the signal is said to have performed a "zero-crossing."

Since the //e can only detect signals that are either on or off, it is not possible to determine the amplitude of the audio input or its waveform. This is fine if you are simply reading binary data stored on the tape, because in such a case amplitude is largely irrelevant (we're concerned only with whether the signal is on or off) and the waveform can be considered to be a square wave. If you are attempting to read anything else, however, such as voice data, then this important information will not be available to you. More on this later, when we examine how to digitize and play back a voice signal.

DIGITIZING VOICE

Now that we've covered the basics of the cassette port, let's embark on a seemingly complex (but actually straightforward) software project that makes use of both the cassette port and the speaker. What we want to be able to do is to play a voice recording into the cassette input port, sample the incoming waveform, and save it as a series of bits that represent whether the signal was on or off (a process called "digitization"), and then play the voice back through the //e's speaker by using these bits to reconstruct the audio waveform.

As we have seen, all we can tell about a signal that appears at the cassette input jack is how long it is in the "on" state and how long it is in the "off" state. It turns out, however, that for our purposes, the square-wave defined by the pattern of on times and off times is an acceptable representation of the actual voice signal being monitored. There will be significant distortion, to be sure, but not enough to prevent us from understanding what is being said.

A typical voice signal has a complex waveform that is quite unlike the perfect sine wave generated by a pure tone; it is made up of a combination of many, many sine waves. To be able to ultimately reconstruct such a signal, we will have to periodically sample the signal at a fixed rate and record the values that are detected. The sampling rate to be used will obviously be an important factor if the signal is to be reconstructed properly. For example, if the sampling rate is too low then we could well miss several zero-crossings that might occur between consecutive samples; if this happens, the signal we detect will not be the true one (it is said to be an *alias* signal).

Even though a voice signal does have a complex, and apparently nonrepetitive, waveform, mathematicians have proved that it can be considered the sum of a series of periodic sine waves of varying frequencies and amplitudes. As we have just seen, the higher frequencies that make up this signal are going to be troublesome if the sampling rate is not fast enough to keep up with them. Just how fast does the sampling rate have to be to allow us to detect a particular frequency?

To answer this question, we must resort to the theoretical mathematicians once again. There is a theorem, called the Fundamental Sampling Theorem, that states that in order to be able to properly reconstruct a signal, it must be sampled at a rate that is at least twice the frequency of the highest frequency component present in the signal. For example, if the highest frequency present in a signal is 1,ØØØ Hz, then to be able to reconstruct it, you would have to sample it at least 2,ØØØ times per second. One-half of the sampling rate is often referred to as the "Nyquist frequency."

If the incoming signal contains frequencies that are higher than the Nyquist frequency (that is, you are sampling too slowly to detect them), then erroneous frequencies will be detected. As we saw earlier, these frequencies are called "aliases." This aliasing effect will cause the signal to be distorted when it is ultimately reconstructed.

The human voice can generate sound frequencies anywhere between 2Ø Hz and 1Ø,ØØØ Hz (approximately). Thus, to detect the highest frequency of 1Ø,ØØØ Hz, we would have to sample the cassette input status at least 2Ø,ØØØ times per second, or once every 5Ø microseconds.

Whenever you are sampling a signal, however, there is a tradeoff between the quality of the reconstructed signal and memory availability. As we have seen, to be able to precisely digitize any signal, including voice, you have to sample it quickly in order to detect all the zero-crossings. The more sampling data that is collected, however, the faster your computer's memory is used up and the shorter the voice sample that can be stored. You can decrease the sampling rate to conserve memory, but as soon as you do this you will not, according to the Fundamental Sampling Theorem, be able to detect some of the higher frequencies that make up the signal. A sampling rate has to be selected that allows you to digitize the voice for a significant time period without sacrificing voice quality when it is ultimately reconstructed.

The program in Table 9-6, called GETVOICE, takes care of sampling the cassette input port, assembling eight successive one-bit samples into a byte, and storing this byte in a "voice buffer" extending from $1ØØØ to Applesoft HIMEM (normally $96ØØ). To run GETVOICE, load it into memory, press the PLAY button on the recorder to begin sending your voice sample, and then start GETVOICE by entering CALL 768 from Applesoft direct mode or by entering 3ØØG from the system monitor.

Table 9-6. GETVOICE. A program to digitize a voice sample.

```
Page #01

: A S M
                ************
                * GETVOICE *
                ************
                VPOINT   EQU $6          ;Pointer to current pos. in buffer
                VDATA    EQU $1000       ;Beginning of voice buffer
                HIMEM    EQU $73         ;Top of memory pointer
                KEYBOARD EQU $C000
                KBSTROBE EQU $C010
                CASSIN   EQU $C060       ;Cassette input port
                         ORG $300
0300: A9 00              LDA #<VDATA     ;Set up pointer to the beginning
0302: 85 06              STA VPOINT      ; of the voice data area
0304: A9 10              LDA #>VDATA
0306: 85 07              STA VPOINT+1
0308: A2 08              LDX #8          ;Set bit counter
                * Loop time is 76 + 5*(STALLNUM-1) cycles
030A: AC 53 03  READTAPE LDY STALLNUM
030D: 88        STALL    DEY
030E: D0 FD              BNE STALL
0310: EA                 NOP
0311: EA                 NOP
```

(continued)

Table 9-6. GETVOICE. A program to digitize a voice sample (continued).

```
0312: EA                    NOP
0313: EA                    NOP
0314: AD 60 C0              LDA CASSIN      ;Read the cassette port
0317: 2A                    ROL             ;Put result into carry bit
0318: 2E 52 03              ROL VBYTE       ;Move result into current byte
031B: CA                    DEX             ;Decrement bit counter
031C: D0 25                 BNE DELAYADJ    ;Branch until 8 bits done

031E: A2 08                 LDX #8          ;Reinitialize bit counter
0320: AD 00 C0              LDA KEYBOARD    ;Has a key been pressed?
0323: 30 1A                 BMI EXIT        ;Branch if so
0325: A0 00                 LDY #0
0327: AD 52 03              LDA VBYTE       ;Get the voice byte
032A: 91 06                 STA (VPOINT),Y  ; and store it in buffer
032C: E6 06                 INC VPOINT      ;Move to the next buffer position
032E: D0 05                 BNE FULLCHK
0330: E6 07                 INC VPOINT+1
0332: 4C 39 03              JMP FULLCHK1
0335: EA           FULLCHK  NOP
0336: EA                    NOP
0337: D0 00                 BNE FULLCHK1    ;(Kill 3 cycles)

Page #02

0339: A5 07        FULLCHK1 LDA VPOINT+1    ;Get the page we're in
033B: C5 74                 CMP HIMEN+1     ;At HIMEM yet?
033D: D0 CB                 BNE READTAPE    ;No, so keep on digitizin'

033F: 2C 10 C0     EXIT     BIT KBSTROBE    ;Clear the keyboard strobe
0342: 60                    RTS

                   * Kill 43 cycles to equalize loops
0343: 20 51 03     DELAYADJ JSR DUMMY       ; (12)
```

```
0346: 20 51 03               JSR DUMMY      ; (12)
0349: 20 51 03               JSR DUMMY      ; (12)
034C: EA                     NOP            ; (2)
034D: EA                     NOP            ; (2)
034E: 4C 0A 03               JMP READTAPE   ; (3)

0351: 60           DUMMY     RTS

                   VBYTE     DS  1          ;Contains 8 cassette input samples
0353: 10           STALLNUM  DFB 16         ;(Change to adjust sampling rate)


--End assembly--

84 bytes

Errors: 0
```

To digitize the voice signal, GETVOICE samples CASSIN ($CØ6Ø) once every 76+5*(STALLNUM-1) microseconds, where STALLNUM is a constant. In the sample program, STALLNUM is set equal to 16 so that the sampling rate is 151 microseconds. This period corresponds to a sampling rate of 1/(151 × 1Ø^ – 6) = 6,623 Hz and a Nyquist frequency of 3,311 Hz.

Every time that CASSIN ($CØ6Ø) is read, the cassette input status (bit 7 of $CØ6Ø) is moved into the next available bit in a data byte called VBYTE. After eight bits have been stored in VBYTE in this way, VBYTE is stored in the voice buffer and another eight bits are assembled. This process continues until the buffer becomes full or until any key is pressed on the keyboard. When GETVOICE ends, we will be left with a series of bits in the buffer that represents the status of the cassette input port every 151 microseconds. This is precisely the information required to simulate the voice using square-waves generated by the //e's speaker.

The period of the loop used in GETVOICE has been carefully selected to allow you to digitize as long a voice sample as possible without sacrificing intelligibility when the voice is eventually played back through the speaker. It has been calculated by adding up the number of machine cycles required to execute each instruction within the loop (see Appendix II for machine-cycle times for each 65Ø2 instruction). If you shorten the loop time, then, although the voice quality will improve, the voice buffer will be filled more quickly. Conversely, if the loop time is longer, then a less accurate digitization of the voice will occur because higher frequency tones in the voice will cause aliasing and, therefore, distortion in the reconstructed signal. As it stands now, all frequencies in the voice that are above the 3,311-Hz Nyquist frequency will cause problems; however, in most voice samples, these frequencies are not abundant. The bulk of voice information is usually contained in the 2ØØ-Hz to 3,ØØØ-Hz range, especially in male voices.

If you are thinking of modifying GETVOICE in any way, then you must be careful to ensure that its loop time (the time between taking successive samples of the cassette input port) remains the same no matter which of two main paths the program follows. The program spends most of its time in the main loop, which comprises all of the code from $3ØA (READTAPE) to $31C and then from $343 (DELAYADJ) to $34E. If, however, the branch at $31C (BNE) to $343 is not performed, and it won't after all eight bits of VBYTE are assembled, then the program will fall through into another portion of the code beginning at $31E and ending at $33D. This portion is responsible for storing VBYTE in the voice buffer and incrementing the pointer to the end of the buffer. To compensate

Table 9-7. PLAYVOICE. A program to play back a digitized voice sample.

```
Page #01

: A S M
                 *************
                 * PLAYVOICE *
                 *************

                 VPOINT   EQU  $6
                 VDATA    EQU  $1000

                 HIMEM    EQU  $73          ;Top of memory pointer

                 KEYBOARD EQU  $C000
                 KBSTROBE EQU  $C010
                 SPEAKER  EQU  $C030        ;Speaker output port

                          ORG  $300

0300: A9 00               LDA  #<VDATA      ;Set up pointer to beginning
0302: 85 06               STA  VPOINT       ; of voice data area
0304: A9 10               LDA  #>VDATA
0306: 85 07               STA  VPOINT+1

0308: A9 00               LDA  #0
030A: 8D 60 03            STA  LASTSPKR     ;Assume speaker was last off
030D: 4C 43 03            JMP  GETVDATA

                 * Loop time is 76+5*(STALLNUM-1) cycles
0310: AC 61 03   PLAYIT   LDY  STALLNUM
0313: 88         STALL    DEY
0314: D0 FD               BNE  STALL
```

(continued)

Table 9-7. PLAYVOICE. A program to play back a digitized voice sample (continued).

```
0316: 4D 60 03            EOR   LASTSPKR     ;This bit same as previous one?
0319: 30 03               BMI   SPKRHIT      ;No, so hit speaker
031B: EA                  NOP
031C: 10 03               BPL   SPKRMISS
031E: AC 30 C0  SPKRHIT   LDY   SPEAKER      ;Toggle speaker
0321: 4D 60 03  SPKRMISS  EOR   LASTSPKR     ;Restore current bit
0324: 8D 60 03            STA   LASTSPKR     ; and save it
0327: 2A                  ROL                ;Move next bit into high bit
0328: CA                  DEX                ;Decrement bit counter
0329: D0 25               BNE   DELAYADJ

032B: AD 00 C0            LDA   KEYBOARD     ;Has a key been pressed?
032E: 30 1C               BMI   EXIT         ;Yes, so done
0330: E6 06               INC   VPOINT       ;Move to next buffer position
0332: D0 05               BNE   FULLCHK
0334: E6 07               INC   VPOINT+1
0336: 4C 3D 03            JMP   FULLCHK1
0339: EA        FULLCHK   NOP
033A: EA                  NOP
033B: D0 00               BNE   FULCHK1      ;(Kill 3 cycles)


Page #02

033D: A5 07     FULLCHK1  LDA   VPOINT+1     ;Get current page
033F: C5 74               CMP   HIMEM+1      ;At HIMEM yet?
0341: F0 09               BEQ   EXIT         ;If so, stop

0343: A0 00     GETVDATA  LDY   #0
0345: B1 06               LDA   (VPOINT),Y   ;Get the next byte in buffer
0347: A2 08               LDX   #8           ;Reinitialize bit count
0349: 4C 10 03            JMP   PLAYIT
```

```
034C: 2C 10 C0     EXIT      BIT  KBSTROBE    ;Clear the keyboard strobe
034F: 60                     RTS

                   * Kill 42 cycles to equalize loops
0350: 20 5F 03     DELAYADJ  JSR  DUMMY       ; (12)
0353: 20 5F 03               JSR  DUMMY       ; (12)
0356: 20 5F 03               JSR  DUMMY       ; (12)
0359: 4C 5C 03               JMP  D1          ; (3)
035C: 4C 10 03     D1        JMP  PLAYIT      ; (3)

035F: 60           DUMMY     RTS

                   LASTSPKR  DS   1           ;High bit is state of speaker
0361: 10           STALLNUM  DFB  16          ;(Change to adjust sampling rate)


--End assembly--

98 bytes

Errors: 0
```

for the additional time required to execute this code, the main loop is routed through the portion of the code beginning at DELAYADJ that the second loop never sees. This code simply kills time for the number of microseconds required to execute the code between $31E and $33D. As a result, the cassette input port is always sampled at the same rate, no matter which path through the program is taken.

Once a voice sample has been digitized using GETVOICE, the next step is to play it back through the speaker. The program for reconstructing the digitized voice on the //e's speaker is called PLAYVOICE and is listed in Table 9-7. It performs a tedious chore. It repeatedly executes a loop in which it gets a byte from the voice buffer, examines each bit, and then toggles the speaker whenever two consecutive bits are different. This process is repeated for each byte in the buffer in such a way that the processing time between two consecutive bits is always the same. Although there are two main paths through the main program loop, careful programming has ensured that the overall loop time is always kept the same. To ensure that the voice is reconstructed at its normal speech rate, this loop time has been adjusted so that it is identical to the loop time of the GETVOICE program.

Note that the speaker is toggled only when the voice data indicates that the cassette input has changed from 1 to Ø or vice versa, because it is only then that the voice signal changes. To detect these changes, a variable called LASTSPKR is used that contains (in bit 7) the last voice data bit read. The current bit is compared to the last one by performing an EOR LASTSPKR instruction at $316. If the two bits are the same, then the BMI instruction that follows will fail and the speaker will not be toggled. If they are different, then the BMI instruction will succeed and the speaker will be toggled.

By using GETVOICE and PLAYVOICE, you can easily add the dimension of voice to your own programs. By digitizing short phrases and words and storing the data on diskette (using DOS's BSAVE command), you can quickly build up an extensive voice library that can be easily accessed and replayed when required.

FURTHER READING FOR CHAPTER 9

On the speaker . . .

"Apple Noises and Other Sounds," *Apple Assembly Line*, February 1981, pp. 2-9. Generating sound effects using the speaker.

B.C. Detterich, "Apple Free Speech," *Call -A.P.P.L.E.*, September 1981, pp. 9-14. Using the Apple II speaker to generate voice and sound.

J.H. Bender, "Pitch and Rhythm on the Apple," *Call -A.P.P.L.E.*, June 1982, p. 15. More on music for the Apple.

B. Sander-Cederlof, "Your Apple Can Talk," *Apple Assembly Line*, November 1982, pp. 2-9.

M. Eve, "Apple Talker," *Nibble*, Vol. 4, No. 8 (1983), pp. 72-75. Digitization and playback of voice.

On the cassette . . .

C.C. Foster, *Real Time Programming—Neglected Topics*, Addison-Wesley Publishing Company, Inc., 1981. There is a great chapter in this book on digital sampling theory.

Apple Computer, Inc., "The Apple II Cassette Interface," *Apple Orchard*, Spring 1981, pp. 57-58. The method used to store programs and data on tape is discussed.

10

The Game I/O Connector

The game I/O connector is a 16-pin socket located in the right-hand back corner of the //e's motherboard (as viewed from the keyboard end). Some of the signals from that socket are duplicated in an external 9-pin D-type miniature game I/O connector located on the back panel of the //e. Pinout diagrams for both connectors are shown in Figure 1Ø-1.

The external connector has been provided to permit you to connect and disconnect game paddles and joysticks without having to remove the //e's lid. In addition, there are screw holes on the external connector that can be used to securely fasten the incoming male connector. This means that even during the most exciting video game, you won't inadvertently yank the plug out of the connector.

For the remainder of this chapter we will be considering the internal game I/O connector only. You can refer to Figure 1Ø-1, however, to relate pin numbers on that connector to those on the external connector.

The game I/O connector is a versatile interface. As its name suggests, it is primarily used to interface devices that allow you to play video games: devices such as paddles, joysticks, and push buttons. When interfaced to the appropriate supporting circuitry, however, it can also be used to control circuits that turn on indicator lights, detect light levels, measure the temperature, and perform many other interesting and useful feats.

Of the 16 pins on the main game I/O connector, two are not used, two are used for the power supply connections (+5 volts and electrical ground), seven are used for one-bit inputs (3 switch inputs and 4 analog inputs), and five for one-bit outputs (4 annunciators and 1 strobe). All of these inputs and outputs will be discussed in detail in the following sections.

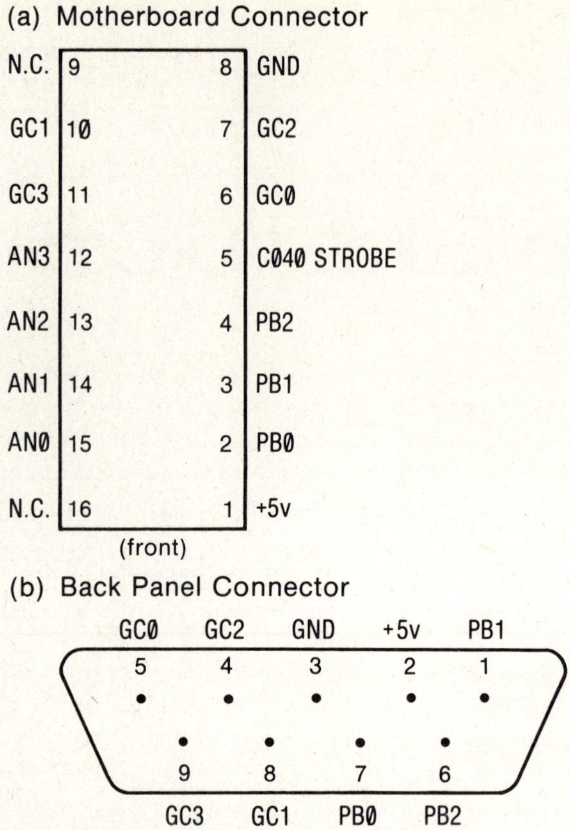

NOTE:
AN = annunciator output
PB = push button input
GC = game controller input
GND = electrical ground
+5v = +5 volt power supply
N.C. = no connection

Figure 10-1. Pinout diagrams for the game I/O connectors.

GAME I/O CONNECTOR EXPERIMENTS

In this chapter, you are going to be encouraged to perform some simple, yet instructive, experiments in electronics. To make these experiments as simple as possible, you should first obtain the experimenter's "protoboard" and special 16-pin dual-inline-package (DIP) jumper cable shown in Figure 10-2. These are readily obtainable from most Radio Shack dealers; the relevant part numbers are 276-1395 (protoboard) and 276-1976 (jumper cable).

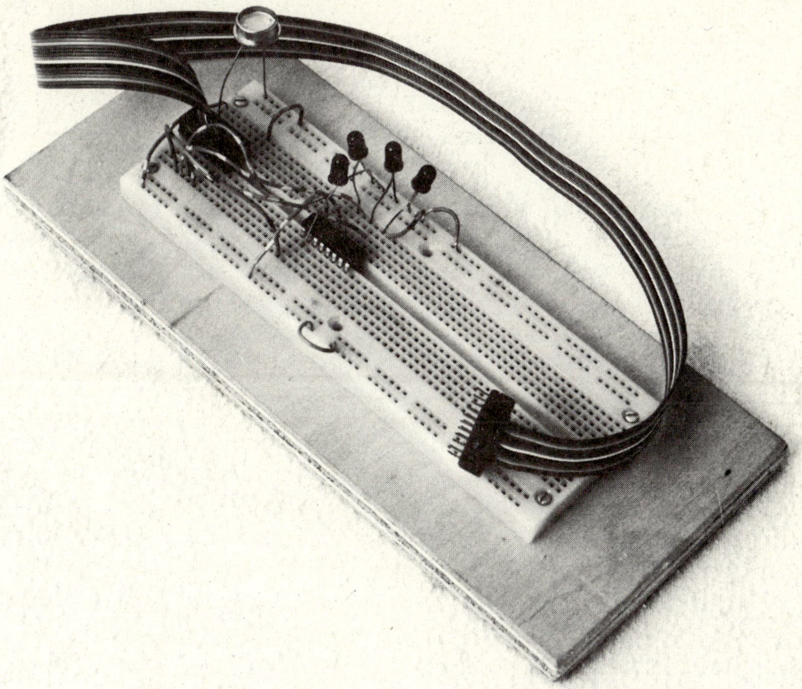

Figure 10-2. Protoboard and DIP jumper cable.

The protoboard is an extremely handy device to use if you are going to build circuits that make use of the game I/O connector. If you use the protoboard, you can easily construct simple circuits without doing any soldering at all, thus making troubleshooting and disassembly a relatively simple task.

The jumper cable is used to extend the game I/O connector interface to the protoboard where it is a lot more convenient to deal with. This is done by plugging one end of the jumper cable into the game I/O connector and the other end into the protoboard in such a way that the two rows of pins on the plug straddle the protoboard's longitudinal center line. (Check the orientation of the DIP plug so that you can tell which pin on the plug on the protoboard corresponds to which pin on the plug in the game I/O connector.) Once this is done, each pin on the jumper cable plug will be connected in parallel to four other pinholes right next to it on the protoboard. When a wire must be connected to a particular pin on the game I/O connector, all you have to do is plug the wire into one of these parallel pinholes instead.

Now that you have your protoboard set up and ready to go, let's take a close look at the game I/O connector and the signals that it supports.

GAME CONTROLLER INPUTS

There are four game controller input pins on the game I/O connector (GCØ, GC1, GC2, and GC3), which are normally used to interface game paddles or joysticks to the //e. These inputs are also often referred to as the analog inputs. The GC inputs are each associated with a unique I/O memory location, as shown in Table 1Ø-1. Only bit 7 of these locations is meaningful as we will see shortly.

The game controller inputs are designed to be used with analog devices capable of changing their internal resistances in the range Ø-15ØK ohms in response to a physical phenomenon that is to be measured (such as the position of a game paddle or joystick, the temperature, or air pressure). Such devices are called "transducers" because they are converting a physical phenomenon into an electrical quantity (resistance) that can be quantified by a digital computer like the //e.

Each GC input is part of an analog-to-digital (A/D) conversion circuit that allows an analog resistance value to be converted (by software) into a digital quantity the //e can handle. The resistor forms part of a simple "RC" (resistor-capacitor) timing circuit that sets the time constant of a special integrated circuit called a 558 Timer. When this timer is reset, by accessing GCRESET ($CØ7Ø), bit 7 of each GC I/O memory location becomes high (1) but will eventually become low (Ø) when the timer "times out," that is, the period of time equal to the time constant for each of the four "RC" circuits has elapsed.

Table 1Ø-1. Game controller I/O memory locations.

Address *Hex*	*(Dec)*	*Symbolic Name*	*Description*
$CØ64	(49252)	GCØ	Status of game controller Ø (bit 7).
$CØ65	(49253)	GC1	Status of game controller 1 (bit 7).
$CØ66	(49254)	GC2	Status of game controller 2 (bit 7).
$CØ67	(49255)	GC3	Status of game controller 3 (bit 7).
$CØ7Ø	(49264)	GCRESET	Reset the game controllers.

To interface a variable-resistor device, all you need to do is connect one of its leads to +5v (pin 1) and the other to one of the GC input pins. A simplified diagram for one such circuit is presented in Figure 10-3. Since the maximum "R" value recommended by Apple is 150,000 ohms and the "C" value is 0.022 microfarad, the maximum time constant for this circuit is 0.022 x 150,000 ohms = 0.0033 second. That is, when the resistance is at its maximum, the time required for the 558 Timer to bring bit 7 of the GC I/O memory location low (0) is about 3.3 milliseconds. The time required to do this will change whenever the resistance of the device changes because the RC time constant will also change.

By setting up a program that periodically checks to see whether the 558 Timer has timed out (by examining bit 7 of the GC I/O memory location) and increments a counter if it has not, you can easily convert the resistance to a numerical value that varies linearly with resistance. In fact, Applesoft's built-in paddle-reading functions, PDL(0), PDL(1), PDL(2), and PDL(3), do this for you automatically—the counter value they return is an integer between 0 and 255. (You can examine the assembly-language subroutine that these functions use by looking at the PREAD ($FB1E) subroutine located in the system monitor; it checks for a timeout condition every 11 microseconds.) You should note, however, that the PDL functions assume that your input resistance is in the range 0-150K ohms. This translates to a time constant that ranges from 0 to about 2.8 milliseconds and to PDL readings between 0 and 255. (Remember that the PDL subroutine's counter increments every 11 microseconds until the timer has timed out. This means that the maximum allowable time constant is 255*11 microseconds, or 2.8 milliseconds.) If the upper limit of the resistance is higher than 150K ohms, then there will be a "dead area" where the resistance may change but the value calculated stays at 255; if it is lower, then the highest PDL value that can be generated will be less than 255.

The GCRESET ($C070) signal initiates the A/D conversion procedure for all four game controller circuits at the same time. Since the 558 Timer will time out at different times for each game controller (unless their resistances are identical), it is possible that after reading one PDL value that certain of the other game controllers will still be timing out. If an attempt is made to read one of these controllers immediately after reading the first controller, then only the time needed to complete the timing-out process from the first GCRESET will be measured. This leads to a spurious game controller signal that is lower than expected. To avoid this "cross-talk" between paddles, you should wait about 3 milliseconds before reading another game controller; this delay gives all of the

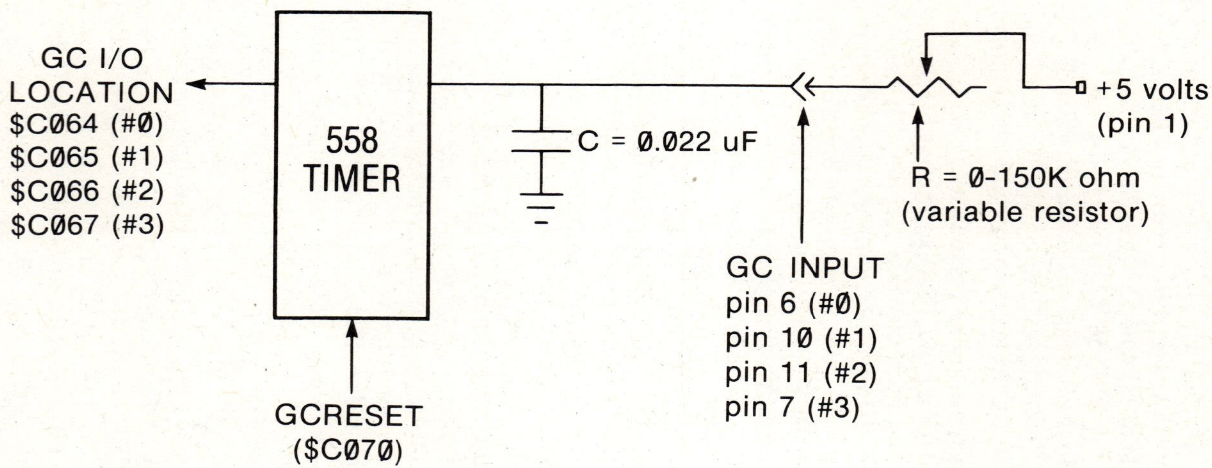

NOTE: the RC time constant varies from Ø to 3.3 milliseconds.

Figure 1Ø-3. Block diagram of game controller circuitry.

game controllers a chance to time out. This can be done in Applesoft by placing a short FOR/NEXT loop between the two PDL functions. Here is an example of how to do this:

```
100 X=PDL(0):FOR I=1 TO 10:NEXT: Y=PDL(1)
```

Two devices that are commonly interfaced to the game controller inputs are the game paddle and the joystick. A game paddle is a device that controls the signal at one GC input only; it typically takes the form of a knob that you can rotate with your hand. As the knob is rotated, the resistance value changes linearly. A joystick allows you to control two GC inputs at once in such a way that the two-dimensional position of the joystick can be easily detected by reading two game controller values.

There is no reason to restrict the game controller inputs for use with game paddles and joysticks, however. Any device that provides a fluctuating resistance value within the Ø-15ØK range could also be interfaced and its resistance converted to a value between Ø and 255 using the Applesoft PDL() commands or their assembly-language equivalents.

Examples of two such useful devices are a thermistor and a photoresistor. A thermistor is a device that changes resistance with temperature. Several types of thermistors are available, including types that will generate resistances within the Ø-15ØK ohm range for most temperatures that you would want to measure.

Unfortunately, most thermistors are not sensitive to small temperature changes, such as those that might occur in a home, so the range of PDL values read may not be large. In addition, the values generated may not vary linearly with temperature. Nevertheless, you can calibrate the thermistor by preparing a table of actual temperatures (measured with a standard thermometer) and their associated paddle readings. This will at least allow you to estimate the temperature from a given "paddle" reading.

A photoresistor is a device that changes resistance with the amount of light shining on it. The greater the light intensity, the lower the resistance. You would calibrate this device by preparing a table of light intensities (as measured by a light meter) and their associated "paddle" readings.

Let's wire up a photoresistor to the game I/O connector to show you how it works. A handy photoresistor to use is a cadmium sulfide one that is readily available from Radio Shack (part number 276-116). All you have to do to interface it to a game controller input, say GC3, is to connect one leg of the photoresistor to +5 volts (pin 1) and the other leg to GC3 (pin 11). Once you have done this, you can read its current setting by using the Applesoft PDL(3) command. Enter the following program and then run it:

```
100 PRINT PDL(3)
200 GOTO 100
```

While the program is running, turn off the room lights to verify that the "paddle" value increases when there is less light. If you have a dimmer light switch, slowly turn the light intensity up and see how the value slowly decreases until it goes to Ø in very bright light.

PUSH BUTTON INPUTS

There are three one-bit input ports on the game I/O connector that are normally used to read the state of external switches connected to them. These are the so-called "push-button" input ports. These ports, and the switches themselves, are usually referred to by their descriptive names: PBØ, PB1, and PB2.

The //e assigns one I/O memory location to each of the push-button input ports, but only bit 7 at that location is actually used. These locations are shown in Table 1Ø-2. By reading the memory location for a particular push-button input (using an Applesoft PEEK or an assembler LDA) and examining bit 7, you can determine whether a switch is being pressed or not. By convention, if the bit is set to 1, then the switch is considered to be on (that is, pressed); if it is cleared to Ø, the switch is considered to be off (that is, released). You should note, however, that it is possible for a switch to be connected in such a way that exactly the opposite result is observed. More on this later.

A switch is a simple electrical component. It is typically used to allow you to complete an electrical circuit between its two contacts in order to turn something on and to break this circuit in order to turn something off. (Some switches can have more than two contacts, but we'll ignore them for the moment.) There are many va-

Table 1Ø-2. Push button I/O memory locations.

Address Hex	Address (Dec)	Symbolic Name	Description
$CØ61	(49249)	PBØ	Status of push button Ø (bit 7).
$CØ62	(4925Ø)	PB1	Status of push button 1 (bit 7).
$CØ63	(49251)	PB2	Status of push button 2 (bit 7).

rieties of switches, but the variety that is commonly connected to the push button inputs is, you guessed it, the push button. This is because they are ideally suited as triggers for such video game weaponry as laser cannons, machine guns, and so on.

Switches can be classified into one of two categories: "momentary contact" or "fixed contact." A momentary-contact switch is one that returns to its initial "resting" position immediately after you take your finger off it. All of the keys on the //e's keyboard (except the CAPS LOCK key) are examples of such a switch.

A fixed-contact switch is one that can be turned on or off and that will stay on or off, as the case may be, after you have taken your finger off it. Examples of fixed-contact switches are the CAPS LOCK key on the //e's keyboard, a standard light switch, and a toggle switch.

Two other special terms are used to describe the operation of momentary-contact switches: "normally open" and "normally closed." A switch is said to be normally open if, when it is not being pressed, no connection is made between its contacts. Conversely, a normally closed switch is one in which the contacts are closed when it is not pressed.

It is important to know whether the momentary-contact switch that you wish to interface to the game I/O connector is normally open or normally closed, because the interface circuit that you must build will be different for each type of switch. Figure 1Ø-4 sets out the two alternate circuits. These circuits have been designed in such a way that if the switch is not being pressed, then the input to the push button pin is grounded and when it is being pressed, it is connected to 5 volts. This ensures compatibility with Apple's on/off push-button convention referred to earlier.

It is easy to install your favorite type of switch, be it momentary contact or fixed contact, normally open or normally closed, to the game I/O connector. You must install it, however, when the power to the //e is off! Let's assume you have a normally open push button switch and you want to install it as PB2. Following Figure 1Ø-4 (a), connect a wire from one switch contact to the +5v line (pin 1 on the game I/O connector), another wire from the other contact to PB2 (pin 4), and then connect a 1,ØØØ-ohm resistor between PB2 (pin 4) and ground (pin 8). (This resistor ensures that the input to the connector will not "float" between 1 and Ø when the switch is not pressed and will also prevent a short-circuit when the switch is pressed.)

You can easily determine whether or not a push button is being pressed by examining bit 7 of the I/O memory location that the

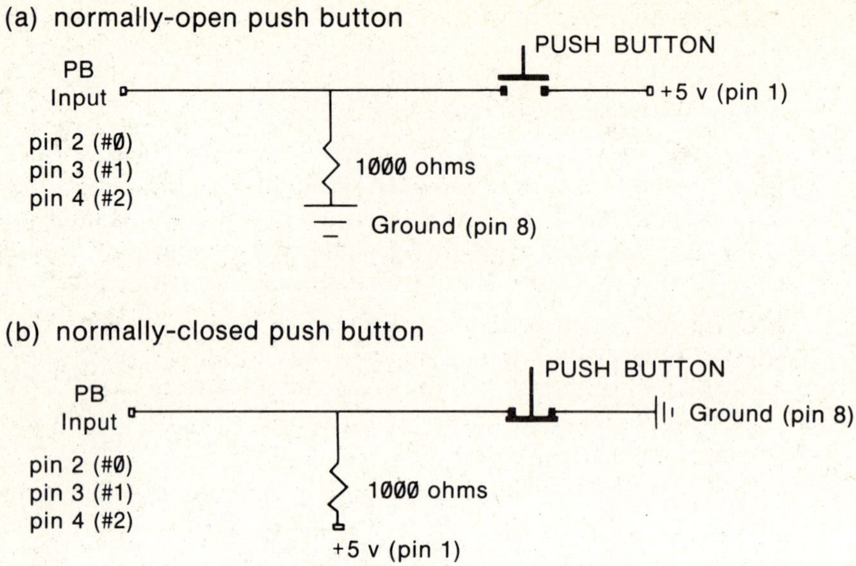

Figure 1Ø-4. Interfacing push buttons to the game I/O connector.

//e reserves for that button. As explained earlier, if this bit is on (1), then the button is being pressed; if it is off (Ø), the button is not being pressed. This means that if you PEEK this memory location from Applesoft, then the number you read is greater than or equal to 128 if the button is pressed or less than 128 if it is not.

Two keys on the //e's keyboard are actually directly connected to the game I/O connector's push-button input lines. These are the OPEN-APPLE and CLOSED-APPLE keys that flank the space bar. These two keys are connected to PBØ and PB1, respectively.

The presence of these two keys enables you to easily experiment with the concept of game-paddle switches without having to do any circuit design at all. Let's write a simple little program to test the status of PBØ, the OPEN-APPLE key.

The I/O memory location reserved for PBØ is 49249. To read this location from an Applesoft program, you would use the PEEK(49249) command. Enter the following simple Applesoft program and run it:

```
100 IF PEEK(49249)>127 THEN PRINT "DOWN WE GO!"
200 IF PEEK(49249)<128 THEN PRINT "BACK AGAIN!"
300 GOTO 100
```

While the program is running, periodically press and release the OPEN-APPLE key. You will find that when it is pressed, the message

```
DOWN WE GO!
```

will appear, and that when it is released, you will see the message

```
BACK AGAIN!
```

By changing the address that is PEEKed, you can easily test the status of any of the other push buttons, including the one you wired up yourself.

Remember that the switches connected to the push-button inputs on the game I/O connector need not be push buttons. Any type of switch can be connected, including toggle switches, reed switches, blow switches, pressure switches, and magnetic switches.

ANNUNCIATOR OUTPUTS

There are four one-bit outputs on the game I/O connector that are called "annunciators" and are referred to as ANØ, AN1, AN2, and AN3. The original purpose of providing these outputs on the //e's predecessor, the Apple II, was apparently to allow the Apple to drive a series of control lights. We will show you how to do that shortly.

The annunciator output signals are standard 74LS series transistor-transistor-logic (TTL) outputs, so they can also be used to control other TTL devices (logic gates, integrated circuits, and so on), or to drive relays, speakers, and many other devices. See the references at the end of the chapter for further information on TTL logic and digital electronics.

Each annunciator output is controlled by a pair of I/O memory locations, as indicated in Table 1Ø-3. These I/O memory locations are called "soft switches" because switching the states of the annunciators can be achieved only by accessing memory locations in software. If you read or write the first location in the pair, the

Table 1Ø-3. Annunciator I/O memory locations.

Address *Hex*	*(Dec)*	*Symbolic Name*	*Description*
$CØ58	(4924Ø)	CLRANØ	Turn off annunciator Ø.
$CØ59	(49241)	SETANØ	Turn on annunciator Ø.
$CØ5A	(49242)	CLRAN1	Turn off annunciator 1.
$CØ5B	(49243)	SETAN1	Turn on annunciator 1.
$CØ5C	(49244)	CLRAN2	Turn off annunciator 2.
$CØ5D	(49245)	SETAN2	Turn on annunciator 2.
$CØ5E	(49246)	CLRAN3	Turn off annunciator 3.
$CØ5F	(49247)	SETAN3	Turn on annunciator 3.

annunciator will be turned off; if you read or write the second location, it will be turned on. When an annunciator is in the "off" state, the voltage on its pin goes low (near Ø volts) and when it is in the "on" state, the voltage goes high (near 5 volts).

It is simple to control the states of the annunciators from an Applesoft program. In general terms, to put annunciator #N (N=Ø,1,2,3) into the off position, you would use the command

```
POKE 49240+2*N,0
```

and to put annunciator #N into the on position, you would use the command

```
POKE 49241+2*N,0
```

To make things even simpler, you could include a flag variable in your program, say "F", where F=1 if you want the on position and F=0 if you want the off position, so that the command

```
POKE 49240+F+2*N,0
```

will be the only one you need to use to control the states of the annunciators.

Experimenting with the Annunciators

The best way to learn more about the annunciators is to wire up a simple circuit and experiment with them it. One such circuit is set out in Figure 1Ø-5. This circuit allows you to control one light-emitting diode (LED) through each of the annunciators. Figure 1Ø-5 contains both the schematic diagram and the pictorial diagram for this circuit. You will have to obtain four LEDs, four 33Ø-ohm resistors, and a 4Ø49B Hex Inverter integrated circuit from an electronic parts store before you can build this circuit. Once you obtain them, use the pictorial diagram to assemble the circuit. Note that LEDs, being diodes, can pass current only in one direction, so you should be careful to orient them properly (anode to +5v). The resistors are used to limit the current flowing through the LEDs to a safe level. The hex inverter integrated circuit is used to "buffer," or strengthen, the annunciator output levels so that they will be capable of lighting the LEDs. As its name suggests, the inverter also reverses the signal coming from the annunciator. That is why the anodes of the LEDs are connected to +5v: when the annunciator is low (off), the output from the inverter will be high (+5v), no current will flow through the LED, and so it will be off as expected.

Now that you've assembled this circuit, what can you do with it? Well, since you can turn any LED on or off by reading one of

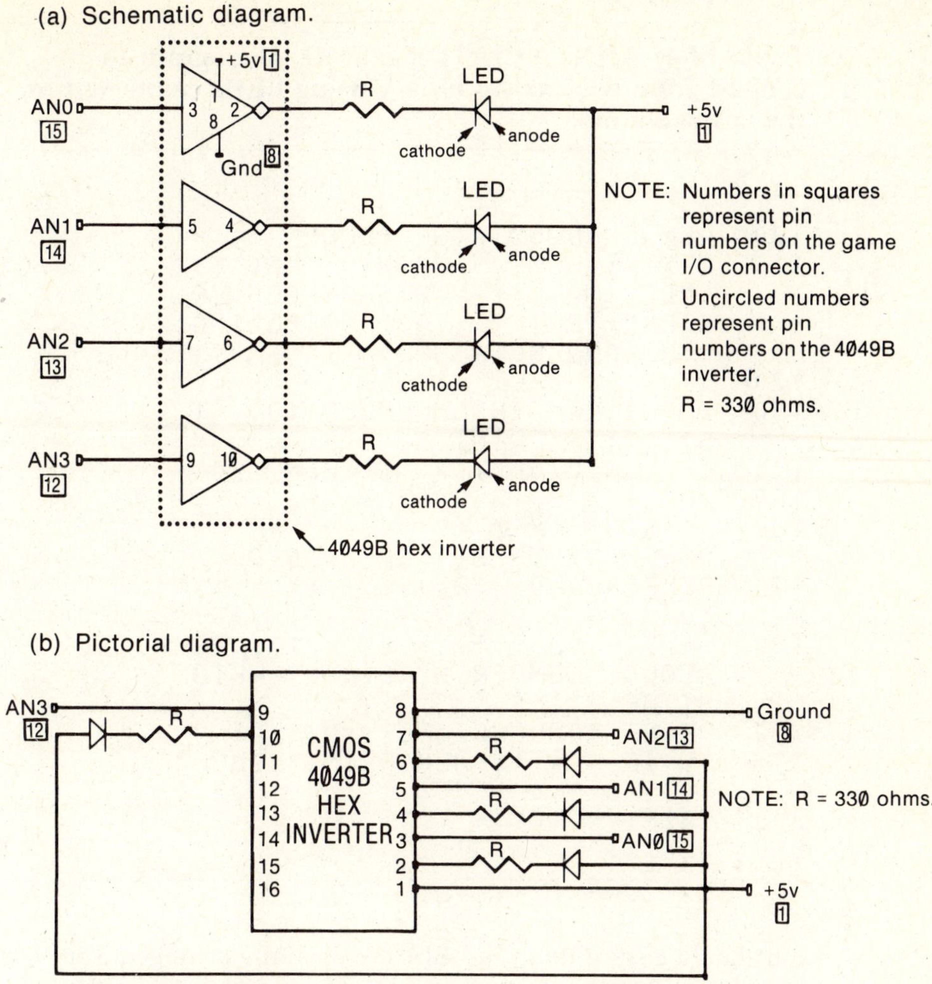

Figure 10-5. Game I/O connector LED experiments.

its associated annunciator I/O memory locations, you could easily write a program that would cause the circuit to act as a blinking four-bulb emergency flasher. In addition, the LEDs could be used as indicator lights for displaying the status of up to four on/off switches.

The sample program in Table 10-4 illustrates one interesting application: converting a decimal number to its binary equivalent. When the program is run, you will be asked to enter a decimal number between 0 and 15 and then its binary equivalent (that will be in the range 0000 . . . 1111) will be displayed using the four LEDs on the protoboard. A lighted LED corresponds to a '1' and an LED that is off corresponds to a '0'. Before running the program,

Table 10-4. ANNUNCIATOR DEMO. A program to convert from decimal to binary using LEDs connected to the annunciators.

```
]LIST

100  REM "ANNUNCIATOR DEMO"
110  TEXT : HOME : PRINT  TAB( 5)
     ;"DECIMAL ---> BINARY CONVER
     SION": PRINT  TAB( 9);"USING
      THE ANNUNCIATORS"
120  VTAB 5: CALL  - 958
130  INPUT "ENTER A NUMBER (0...1
     5): ";Y: PRINT
140  IF Y < 0 or Y > 15 THEN 120
150  FOR I = 3 TO 0 STEP  - 1
160 X =  INT (Y / (2 ^ I)): REM
     CHECK "I"TH BIT OF NUMBER
170  POKE 49240 + 2 * I + (X = 1)
     ,0
180 Y = Y - (2 ^ I) * (X = 1): REM
     REDUCE NUMBER BY BINARY WEIG
     HT OF BIT
190  PRINT "ANNUNCIATOR #";I;": "
     ;: IF X = 1 THEN PRINT "ON"
     : GOTO 210
200  PRINT "OFF"
210  NEXT I
```

you should ensure that the LEDs are spatially arranged from left to right in descending numerical order (that is, AN3-AN2-AN1-AN0).

You should realize by now that even though this project is an extremely simple one, the annunciators can be used to control much more complex circuits. For example, they can be used to control the number displayed on a seven-segment LED or to activate any one of a number of other simple logic circuits.

Special Use for AN3

There is one annunciator output that is used in a special way by the //e: AN3. As was discussed in Chapter 7, this annunciator allows you to select or deselect double-width high-resolution and low-resolution graphics.

STROBE OUTPUT

This is a single-bit output that can be used to send a momentary pulse (a "strobe") to an external circuit. Such a pulse may be required to change the state of an on/off device or to latch data into the circuit so that it will not change until after it has been read or sent.

As indicated in Table 10-5, the strobe signal is controlled by GCSTROBE ($C040). The signal is normally kept at a high-voltage level (+5v) but when this location is accessed by a read operation (such as an Applesoft PEEK), it drops to a low-voltage level (near 0v) for about half a microsecond before returning to a high level.

Table 10-5. Game connector strobe I/O memory location.

Address Hex	*(Dec)*	*Symbolic Name*	*Description*
$C040	(49216)	GCSTROBE	Generate a game I/O connector strobe signal.

SUMMARY OF GAME I/O CONNECTOR LOCATIONS

Table 10-6 contains a list of all of the I/O locations on the //e that relate to the game I/O connector.

Table 10-6. Summary of all game I/O connector I/O locations.

Address Hex	*(Dec)*	*Symbolic Name*	*Description*
$C040	(49216)	GCSTROBE	Generate a game I/O connector strobe signal.
$C058	(49240)	CLRAN0	Turn off annunciator 0.
$C059	(49241)	SETAN0	Turn on annunciator 0.
$C05A	(49242)	CLRAN1	Turn off annunciator 1.
$C05B	(49243)	SETAN1	Turn on annunciator 1.
$C05C	(49244)	CLRAN2	Turn off annunciator 2.

(continued)

Table 10-6. Summary of all game I/O connector I/O locations (continued).

Address Hex	(Dec)	Symbolic Name	Description
$C05D	(49245)	SETAN2	Turn on annunciator 2.
$C05E	(49246)	CLRAN3	Turn off annunciator 3.
$C05F	(49247)	SETAN3	Turn on annunciator 3.
$C061	(49249)	PB0	Status of push button 0 (bit 7).
$C062	(49250)	PB1	Status of push button 1 (bit 7).
$C063	(49251)	PB2	Status of push button 2 (bit 7).
$C064	(49252)	GC0	Status of game controller 0 (bit 7).
$C065	(49253)	GC1	Status of game controller 1 (bit 7).
$C066	(49254)	GC2	Status of game controller 2 (bit 7).
$C067	(49255)	GC3	Status of game controller 3 (bit 7).
$C070	(49264)	GCRESET	Reset the game controllers.

FURTHER READING FOR CHAPTER 10

On reading the game paddles . . .

B. Sander-Cederlof, "Reading Two Paddles at the Same Time," *Apple Assembly Line*, March 1982, p. 1. A program to simultaneously read two game paddle inputs.

On generating music through the annunciators . . .

M.A. Cross, "Apple Audio Processing," *Byte*, April 1980, p. 212. How to generate multiphonic sound through the annunciators.

On interfacing a numeric keypad . . .

M. Harvey, "Numeric Key Pad Lab!," *Nibble*, Vol. 1, No. 5 (1980), pp. 28-29. How to hook up a numeric keypad to the game I/O connector.

On interfacing a lie detector . . .

D.B. Curtis, "To Tell the Truth," *Kilobaud Microcomputing*, August 1981, pp. 87-89. How to hook up a lie-detecting device to the game paddle inputs.

On interfacing a joystick . . .

"Dual Joysticks for Under $15.ØØ," *Nibble*, Vol. 1, No. 2 (1980), p. 13. How to hook up a joystick to the game paddle inputs.

On interfacing a thermistor . . .

C.J. Kershner, "A Digital Thermometer for the Apple II," *Micro*, March 198Ø, p. 21. How to hook up a thermistor to the game paddle inputs.

On interfacing a light pen . . .

D.J. Lilja, "Build a Simple Light Pen for the Apple II," *Byte*, June 1983, pp. 395-4Ø6. How to hook up a light pen to the push button inputs.

On TTL logic and digital electronics . . .

D. Lancaster, *TTL Cookbook*, Howard W. Sams and Co., Inc., 1976.

11

Peripheral-Card Expansion Slots

One of the main reasons that the //e and its predecessors, the Apple II and the Apple II Plus, have proved to be so popular is that it is relatively simple to interface to them a multitude of external devices such as printers, disk drives, modems, music synthesizers, and so on. Devices such as these can be controlled by the //e through special peripheral cards that can be inserted into any of the seven 5Ø-pin expansion connectors (or slots) found at the back of the //e's motherboard. I/O circuitry on these peripheral cards can be controlled by accessing addresses within the //e's I/O memory space from $CØ9Ø to $CØFF.

The seven slots on the //e are numbered from 1 to 7, with the leftmost slot (as viewed from the keyboard end) representing slot 1. The //e also contains an eighth slot, called the auxiliary connector, into which Apple's 8Ø-column text card can be installed. It is located at the left side of the //e's motherboard in front of the other slots. The auxiliary connector is markedly different from the other slots and different interfacing methods must be followed to use it.

In this chapter, we will take a look at some of the rules that must be followed when designing and using peripheral cards. We will also see how the //e allocates memory space and I/O memory locations to peripheral cards.

PERIPHERAL-CARD I/O MEMORY LOCATIONS

Apple has developed certain hardware conventions that should be adhered to whenever peripheral cards are being designed. Fortunately, the vast majority of manufacturers have followed these conventions, thus making it possible to plug several peripheral cards into the //e at the same time and use them without fear of interference or irreconcilable conflicts.

The first of these conventions relates to the I/O memory locations within the //e's I/O memory space that are to be used by the I/O circuitry on the peripheral card in a given slot. As we saw in Chapter 2, this I/O space extends from $C000 to $C0FF. The convention is that whenever a peripheral card is plugged into one of the seven standard slots, it must only make use of the sixteen I/O memory locations from $C080+$10*s to $C08F+$10*s, where "s" is the slot number. The I/O memory locations assigned to each of the seven expansion slots on the //e are shown in Table 11-1.

It is the responsibility of the designer of the peripheral card to ensure that the I/O circuitry on the card remains inactive until an I/O memory location assigned to the slot into which that card has been inserted has been accessed. This can be done fairly easily because the //e generates a low-voltage signal on pin 41 of the slot connector, called the DEVICE SELECT signal, whenever this condition is met (the voltage at this pin is normally high). In the usual case, the I/O circuitry on the peripheral card will be connected to the DEVICE SELECT pin in such a way that it will be operative only when DEVICE SELECT is low. When the circuitry becomes operative, the low four address lines from the 6502 microprocessor can be examined (or "decoded") to determine which of the 16 I/O memory locations has been selected, and then the specific action that has been associated with that particular location can be performed.

Some peripheral cards that are available for the //e do not adhere to the I/O memory locations convention. These are the multifunction cards, which typically combine two or three discrete I/O circuits on one physical card. A card such as this allows each of its

Table 11-1. Peripheral-card I/O memory locations.

Slot Number	*I/O Memory Locations*
Slot 1	$C090–$C09F
Slot 2	$C0A0–$C0AF
Slot 3	$C0B0–$C0BF
Slot 4	$C0C0–$C0CF
Slot 5	$C0D0–$C0DF
Slot 6	$C0E0–$C0EF
Slot 7	$C0F0–$C0FF

distinct circuits to be controlled as if it was contained on a card plugged into another physical slot.

The phenomenon of allowing one physical card to behave as if it occupied several slots is called "phantom slotting." Phantom slotting is made possible by circuitry on the peripheral card that is capable of reacting to an I/O memory location reserved for a slot other than the one into which the card has been installed. Special address decoder circuits similar to those which the //e uses to determine when to generate an active DEVICE SELECT signal are used for this purpose.

If peripheral cards are used that are using phantom slotting techniques, it is important to ensure that no card is inserted into the physical slot that is being phantomed. If a card is inserted there by mistake, then two separate I/O operations could be activated at the same time and this is probably not what was intended.

PERIPHERAL-CARD ROM

Each peripheral card that plugs into the //e is permitted to contain memory. The second hardware convention developed by Apple relates to the address space that may be used by any ROM or RAM memory included on the peripheral card (it's usually ROM). According to this convention, each peripheral card is assigned 256 bytes of memory within the space from $C1ØØ to $C7FF; this memory space is called peripheral-card ROM. The memory space assigned to each slot is shown in Table 11-2.

A 256-byte page of memory has been allocated to each slot to permit *intelligent* peripheral cards to be attached to the //e. The page is normally used by a ROM that contains device drivers writ-

Table 11-2. Peripheral-card ROM spaces reserved for expansion slots.

Slot Number	*Memory Space*
Slot 1	$C1ØØ–$C1FF
Slot 2	$C2ØØ–$C2FF
Slot 3	$C3ØØ–$C3FF
Slot 4	$C4ØØ–$C4FF
Slot 5	$C5ØØ–$C5FF
Slot 6	$C6ØØ–$C6FF
Slot 7	$C7ØØ–$C7FF

ten in 65Ø2 assembly language that allow for simplified control of the peripheral by providing a set of subroutines that can be used to perform the basic I/O and status-reading operations normally associated with it. If these drivers could not be stored on the peripheral card in this way, they would have to be loaded into RAM memory whenever the //e was turned on and this would be highly inconvenient.

There are two Applesoft (and DOS) commands that can be used to redirect character input and output to the peripheral-card ROM area: IN#s and PR#s. Both of these commands cause Applesoft to jump to a subroutine that starts at location $CsØØ on the peripheral card, where "s" is the slot number. This subroutine is responsible for initializing the device and then, if necessary, for altering the //e's input and output links in order to redirect all further character input and output requests to subroutines contained in the peripheral-card ROM area. See Chapters 6 and 7 for further information on the //e's input and output links.

A character input subroutine contained in ROM on the peripheral card must return the inputted character in the 65Ø2 accumulator with the high-order bit set to one and with the X and Y registers unchanged (this is the protocol used by the standard keyboard input subroutine). A character output subroutine can expect to find the character to be outputted in the accumulator (with its high-order bit set to one) when it takes control and it must return with the A, X, and Y registers unchanged.

The //e generates a special signal that simplifies the interfacing of the 256-byte memory page on a peripheral card. This is called the I/O SELECT signal and it appears at pin 1 of the slot connector. I/O SELECT is normally high, but becomes low at a given slot whenever any address within the 256-byte memory page allocated to that slot is accessed. The low signal it produces can be used to enable the memory chips being used so that the starting address of the ROM will automatically take on the proper value in whatever slot the card is installed ($C1ØØ for slot 1, $C2ØØ for slot 2, and so on).

As we saw in Chapter 8, the same address space encompassed by peripheral-card ROM ($C1ØØ . . . $C7FF) is used by built-in internal ROM that holds the extensions to the standard system monitor, self-test subroutines, and the 8Ø-column firmware. Before programs in peripheral-card ROM can be used, the INTCXROM switch must be turned off by writing to INTCXROMOFF ($CØØ6) and, if any ROM in slot 3 is to be used, the SLOTC3ROM switch must be turned on by writing to SLOTC3ROMON ($CØØB). In the normal course of events, INTCXROM will always be off, so you shouldn't have to worry about adjusting it before peripheral cards can be used. If an 8Ø-Column Text Card has been installed in the auxiliary slot, however, then SLOTC3ROM will initially be off and must be turned on before accessing the ROM on a card in slot 3. Note, however, that if SLOTC3ROM is on, the //e's special 8Ø-column firmware that supports the text card cannot be used because the physical memory in which it is contained will be temporarily inactive.

PERIPHERAL-CARD EXPANSION ROM

The //e also permits each peripheral card to contain a 2,Ø48-byte area of memory that is mapped to locations $C8ØØ . . . $CFFF. This area is called peripheral-card expansion ROM and is used whenever additional space is needed to hold programs that control the peripheral device.

Before making use of any subroutines within the expansion ROM space for any particular card, the expansion ROMs in all peripheral cards must first be disabled. If this were not done, then several different physical locations might be active that correspond to the same logical address and this is not tolerated by the 65Ø2 microprocessor. This is where Apple's third convention comes into play. This convention states that the circuitry on each peripheral card must turn off its expansion ROM whenever location $CFFF is accessed. Fortunately, most peripheral cards adhere to this convention. Thus, to turn off all the peripheral-card expansion ROMs, an instruction such as

```
STA $CFFF
```

or

```
LDA $CFFF
```

must be executed. (This instruction is usually contained in the standard peripheral-card ROM—it obviously cannot be contained in the peripheral-card expansion ROM.) After this has been done, the circuitry on the peripheral card must be such that the card's expansion ROM will be enabled as soon as an address in the card's 256-byte peripheral card ROM is accessed. After the card's expansion ROM space has been enabled like this, it will remain enabled until all expansion ROMs are turned off again with a subsequent access of $CFFF.

PERIPHERAL-CARD SCRATCHPAD RAM

It is often necessary for the program running in the ROMs contained on a peripheral card to make use of RAM memory locations so that it can store information that may change from time to time. These locations are referred to as "scratchpad" RAM. For example, it may be necessary to store the current status of a device, a constant such as "slot number" or "16 times slot number" or a default command value. Any RAM memory location could be used for such purposes, but unless that location is specifically reserved for use by a peripheral device, it could be overwritten by any program that uses the same location.

Apple's fourth convention relates to the RAM memory locations reserved for use as scratchpad RAM. If a peripheral card is installed in slot "s", then it may make use of the following RAM locations: \$478+s, \$4F8+s, \$578+s, \$5F8+s, \$678+s, \$6F8+s, \$778+s, \$7F8+s. The specific addresses that are available for use at each slot are set out in Table 11-3.

The base addresses set out in Table 11-3 are used by DOS 3.3 and for the storage of information that indicates the status of the system. For example, \$5F8 holds the value \$Cs, where "s" is the slot number from which DOS 3.3 was booted, and \$7F8 holds the value \$Cs, where "s" is the slot number of the peripheral device whose ROM was last accessed.

You will recall from Chapter 7 that the scratchpad locations are all contained within the area of memory dedicated for use by the text screen and the low-resolution graphics screen (\$400 . . . \$7FF). Remember, however, that not all of the bytes from \$400 to \$7FF

Table 11-3. Peripheral-card scratchpad RAM locations.

Base	*Slot Number*						
Address	*1*	*2*	*3*	*4*	*5*	*6*	*7*
\$478	\$479	\$47A	\$47B	\$47C	\$47D	\$47E	\$47F
\$4F8	\$4F9	\$4FA	\$4FB	\$4FC	\$4FD	\$4FE	\$4FF
\$578	\$579	\$57A	\$57B	\$57C	\$57D	\$57E	\$57F
\$5F8	\$5F9	\$5FA	\$5FB	\$5FC	\$5FD	\$5FE	\$5FF
\$678	\$679	\$67A	\$67B	\$67C	\$67D	\$67E	\$67F
\$6F8	\$6F9	\$6FA	\$6FB	\$6FC	\$6FD	\$6FE	\$6FF
\$778	\$779	\$77A	\$77B	\$77C	\$77D	\$77E	\$77F
\$7F8	\$7F9	\$7FA	\$7FB	\$7FC	\$7FD	\$7FE	\$7FF

are used by the screen display circuitry; in fact, there are a total of 64 unused locations which are called "screenholes." It is these screenholes that are used for peripheral-card scratchpad storage.

THE AUXILIARY CONNECTOR AND SLOT 3

The auxiliary connector on the //e is designed to hold the //e's 8Ø-column text card or extended 8Ø-column text card. For historical reasons, when either of these two cards is plugged in, the //e reacts in such a way that it thinks that a card has been plugged into slot 3. This means that the 8Ø-column display is enabled by entering an Applesoft PR#3 command, that the ROM supporting the 8Ø-column display occupies locations $C3ØØ to $C3FF (and $C8ØØ to $CFFF), and that the scratchpad RAM areas used by this ROM are those normally reserved for a card in slot 3. In "emulating" slot 3, Apple is simply adhering to another convention that stems from Apple II and Apple II Plus days: that an 8Ø-column card is to be installed in slot 3.

As you might guess, if an 8Ø-column text card is installed in the auxiliary connector, there are considerable problems in using any peripheral card that is installed in slot 3 at the same time. In a nutshell, the problem arises because the //e initially prevents any ROMs on a peripheral card in slot 3 from being used by turning off the SLOTC3ROM soft switch (see Chapter 8) in order to select internal ROM memory from $C3ØØ . . . $C3FF. Even with SLOTC3ROM off, however, it is still possible to use a peripheral card in slot 3 by using a driver program that resides in main RAM memory and that uses only the I/O memory addresses used by the device in slot 3 and not the ROM subroutines on the peripheral card. Unfortunately, it may not be possible to do this if commercial software is being used since it becomes difficult, if not impossible, to interface RAM drivers of this sort.

As we saw earlier in this chapter, and in Chapter 8, the ROM on a peripheral card in slot 3 can be activated even if an 8Ø-column text card is present in the auxiliary slot by turning on SLOTC3ROM by writing to SLOTC3ROMON ($CØØB). When this is done, a PR#3 or IN#3 command will not transfer control to $C3ØØ in the internal 8Ø-column firmware ROM but rather it will transfer control to the same address in the slot 3 ROM. This means that the device interfaced to slot 3 can be used in the normal manner (but the 8Ø-column text card subroutines will be temporarily disabled).

PROGRAMMING FOR PERIPHERAL CARDS

Programs that are to be stored in the ROM area of a peripheral card have to be carefully written. There are two fundamental restrictions on such programs: first, they must be *relocatable* and, second, they must adhere to certain software protocols established by Apple.

Relocatability

A program is said to be relocatable if it can be run in any part of memory without having to be changed. This is an important attribute for a peripheral-card program because it means that the peripheral card can be placed in any of the //e's seven standard interface slots and still operate properly. (Remember that if the card has been properly designed, the beginning address of the ROM will automatically change if the card is placed in another slot—it will be $C1ØØ for slot 1, $C2ØØ for slot 2, and so on.)

There are two main reasons why a program may not be relocatable. One reason is that the program may read data from or store data to absolute memory locations that are within the program boundaries itself. If this is done, then when the program is moved, the old locations will still be accessed and this is likely not what was intended.

The second reason that the program may not be relocatable is that it contains JSR or JMP instructions that transfer control to instructions within the program itself. Since both of these instructions use the absolute addressing mode, when the program is moved by changing slots, the absolute addresses specified will stay the same and the program will no longer operate properly. Any change in program flow should be done by using branch-on-condition instructions (such as BNE, BPL, BCC, and BCS), which use relative, rather than absolute, addressing. For example, instead of jumping to a location called TARGET using the instruction

```
JMP TARGET
```

you could use relocatable code such as this:

```
SEC
BCS TARGET
```

Because slot independence of the peripheral card is such an important feature, peripheral-card ROM driver subroutines must never use absolute addressing to access I/O memory locations or the scratchpad RAM locations. Instead, indexed addressing must be used where the base addresses are fixed at locations that will be the same for each slot.

For example, to read the third of the sixteen I/O memory locations for a given slot, an instruction like this:

```
LDA $C082,X
```

should be used, where X holds 16 times the slot number (alternately, the Y register could be used as the index). This makes the instruction slot independent.

Scratchpad RAM locations should be accessed using a similar method; the only difference is that the index register will contain the slot number itself. For example, to access the second scratchpad RAM location for a given slot, the following instruction should be used:

```
LDA $4F8,X
```

where X contains the slot number.

The above two examples bring up an important question: how does the program in the peripheral-card ROM know which slot the peripheral card has been placed in? This information cannot be stored in the peripheral-card ROM because this would prevent the card from being operable in any slot. The slot number can be determined by using a rather tricky software technique that takes advantage of the fact that whenever the 65Ø2 executes a JSR (jump-to-subroutine) instruction, it saves the current value of the program counter on the stack (the "return address"). If the subroutine is called from a program contained within the peripheral-card ROM space, the high-order byte of the return address will be of the form $Cs, where "s" is the slot number. Thus, "s" can be deduced by finding this byte in the stack area and examining it.

Here is how this technique works in practice. First, the peripheral-card ROM subroutine must perform a JSR to a location that contains an RTS (return-from-subroutine) instruction. A convenient location to use for this purpose is $FF58 because Apple has guaranteed that this location will always contain an RTS instruction. After the JSR and RTS instructions have been executed, the 65Ø2 stack pointer will be pointing to a byte of the form "$Cs", where "s" is the slot number, and the stack will look something like this:

aa
Cs ← stack pointer
bb
cc
dd
.
. (to bottom of stack)

where aa, bb, cc, and dd represent hexadecimal numbers. "$Csaa" is the address minus 1 of the next in-line instruction to be executed after the subroutine to which JSR passes control finishes. The byte being pointed to by the stack pointer can be obtained by executing the following instructions:

```
TSX              ;Put stack pointer into X index
LDA $100,X       ;Get "$Cs" byte off stack
AND #$0F         ;Convert "$Cs" to "$0s"
TAX              ;Put slot number in X
```

After these instructions have been executed, the slot number will be in the X register and can be used to properly access I/O memory locations (if it is first multiplied by 16) and scratchpad RAM locations.

Software Protocols

Apple has also established several software protocols that the programs contained in the ROMs of any peripheral cards should adhere to. Many of these protocols are important only if the peripheral card is going to be used in connection with the Apple Pascal language rather than Applesoft. Even though we are not looking at Apple Pascal in this book, these Pascal-related protocols will be summarized for the sake of completeness.

If you want to study implementations of the following protocols, refer to Apple's source listing for the //e's internal 8Ø-column firmware (in "*Reference Manual Addendum: Monitor ROM Listings*") or for the Apple super serial card (contained in the reference manual for that peripheral).

Applesoft Protocol

The Applesoft software protocol requires that the initialization, input, and output subroutines for a peripheral card begin at those fixed locations shown in Table 11-4.

Table 11-4. Applesoft software protocol.

Subroutine	*Starting Address*
Initialization	$CsØØ
Character Input	$CsØ5
Character Output	$CsØ7

s = slot number.

Note that this protocol is not adhered to by some of Apple's older peripheral cards, namely, the parallel printer interface card and the communications card. These cards represent special cases and must be treated as exceptions by any program that needs to know the absolute locations of the initialization, input, and output subroutines.

Pascal 1.Ø Protocol

Pascal 1.Ø expects initialization, input, and output subroutines on a peripheral card to begin at different locations than those expected by Applesoft. These locations are shown in Table 11-5.

Besides supporting these subroutines, the peripheral card must have the values $38 and $18 stored at locations $CsØ5 and $CsØ7, respectively. If these values are not present, the peripheral card will be ignored by Pascal 1.Ø.

Pascal 1.1 Protocol

Pascal 1.1 is a significant upgrade to its predecessor, Pascal 1.Ø. It supports a much more flexible software protocol for peripheral devices that enables it to easily determine not only that a usable device has been installed, but also what kind of device it is.

Table 11-5. Pascal 1.Ø software protocol.

Subroutine	*Starting Address*
Initialization	$C8ØØ
Character input	$C84D
Character output	$C9AA

Interface cards that support Pascal 1.1 must contain a table at $CsØD to $Cs13 in the peripheral-card ROM that contains the offsets from $CsØØ of various subroutines that Pascal 1.1 may need to use. The primary subroutines are those for initialization, input, output, and I/O status. However, two other subroutines, one for control of the device and the other for interrupt handling, can also be included. A description of the meaning of each entry in this offset table is shown in Table 11-6. Note that the last two offsets contained in the table are not actually used because Pascal 1.1 does not use Device Control and Interrupt Handler subroutines.

Before any of the subroutines referred to in Table 11-6 are called, the 65Ø2 X register must contain $Cs (where "s" is the slot number) and the Y register must contain $sØ. In addition, if the Character Output subroutine is being called, the byte to be outputted must be contained in the accumulator. If the I/O status subroutine is being called, the accumulator must contain the request code: Ø means "Are you ready for output?" and 1 means "Is any input ready?"

After the subroutine has performed its duties, the X register will contain an error code; this code will be Ø if no error actually occurred. If the Character Input subroutine was called, the character read will be returned in the accumulator. If the I/O Status subroutine was called, the status of the carry flag must be checked to determine the status. Only if the carry flag is set is the device ready to perform I/O.

Table 11-6. Pascal 1.1 software protocol.

Address of Offset	*Subroutine Description*
$CsØD	Initialization
$CsØE	Character input
$CsØF	Character output
$Cs1Ø	I/O status
$Cs11	Continuation byte: $ØØ if the following two offsets are used
$Cs12	Device control
$Cs13	Interrupt handler

Table 11-7. Peripheral-card ROM identification bytes.

Address	*Value*
$CsØ5	$38 (SEC opcode)
$CsØ7	$18 (CLC opcode)
$CsØB	$Ø1 (generic signature byte)
$CsØC	$ci (device signature from Table 11-8)

ROM Identification Bytes

Four other bytes in the peripheral-card ROM are used by Pascal 1.1 to allow I/O devices to be identified. The addresses for these bytes, and the values stored there, are set out in Table 11-7.

The device signature byte at $CsØC is not currently used by Pascal 1.1 but may be examined by a program that is operating to determine the type of peripheral card installed in the slot. The first hexadecimal digit of the signature ("c") represents the general device class, as shown in Table 11-8, and the second digit ("i") represents a unique identifier that has been assigned to the device by Apple. The identifier makes it possible to determine the precise model of the interface card being used.

Table 11-8. Pascal 1.1 device class digits.

Device Class Digit	*Description of Class*
$Ø	<Reserved>
$1	Printer
$2	Joystick or other X-Y input device
$3	Serial or parallel I/O device
$4	Modem
$5	Sound or speech device
$6	Clock
$7	Mass storage device (disk drive)
$8	8Ø-column card
$9	Network or bus interface
$A	Special purpose (none of the above)
$B–$F	<Reserved>

FURTHER READING FOR CHAPTER 11

On hardware interfacing techniques . . .

J.S. Titus, D.G. Larsen, and C.A. Titus, *Apple Interfacing*, Howard W. Sams & Company, Inc., 1981. The hardware aspects of interfacing devices to the Apple's slots.

J.W. Coffron, *The Apple Connection*, Sybex, 1982.

J.E. Uffenbeck, *Hardware Interfacing with the Apple II Plus*, Prentice-Hall, Inc., 1983. A good introduction to hardware interfacing with lots of examples.

On software protocols . . .

B. Haynes, *Attach-BIOS for Apple II Pascal 1.1*, International Apple Core, 1980. This booklet explains the Pascal 1.1 firmware protocols.

Apple //e Design Guidelines, Apple Computer, Inc., 1982. This book reviews all of Apple's software protocols and "preferred" programming practices.

Appendix I

American National Standard Code for Information Interchange (ASCII) Character Codes

ASCII Code Hex	Dec	Symbol		Keys to Press
$ØØ	ØØØ	NUL	(Null)	CONTROL @
$Ø1	ØØ1	SOH	(Start of header)	CONTROL A
$Ø2	ØØ2	STX	(Start of text)	CONTROL B
$Ø3	ØØ3	ETX	(End of text)	CONTROL C
$Ø4	ØØ4	EOT	(End of transmission)	CONTROL D
$Ø5	ØØ5	ENQ	(Enquiry)	CONTROL E
$Ø6	ØØ6	ACK	(Acknowledge)	CONTROL F
$Ø7	ØØ7	BEL	(Bell)	CONTROL G
$Ø8	ØØ8	BS	(Backspace)	LEFT-ARROW or CONTROL H
$Ø9	ØØ9	HT	(Horizontal tabulation)	TAB or CONTROL I
$ØA	Ø1Ø	LF	(Line feed)	DOWN-ARROW or CONTROL J
$ØB	Ø11	VT	(Vertical tabulation)	UP-ARROW or CONTROL K
$ØC	Ø12	FF	(Form feed)	CONTROL L
$ØD	Ø13	CR	(Carriage return)	RETURN or CONTROL M
$ØE	Ø14	SO	(Shift out)	CONTROL N
$ØF	Ø15	SI	(Shift in)	CONTROL O
$1Ø	Ø16	DLE	(Data link escape)	CONTROL P
$11	Ø17	DC1	(Device control 1)	CONTROL Q
$12	Ø18	DC2	(Device control 2)	CONTROL R
$13	Ø19	DC3	(Device control 3)	CONTROL S
$14	Ø20	DC4	(Device control 4)	CONTROL T
$15	Ø21	NAK	(Negative acknowledge)	RIGHT-ARROW or CONTROL U
$16	Ø22	SYN	(Synchronous idle)	CONTROL V
$17	Ø23	ETB	(End of transmission block)	CONTROL W
$18	Ø24	CAN	(Cancel)	CONTROL X
$19	Ø25	EM	(End of medium)	CONTROL Y
$1A	Ø26	SUB	(Substitute)	CONTROL Z
$1B	Ø27	ESC	(Escape)	ESC or CONTROL [
$1C	Ø28	FS	(Field separator)	CONTROL \
$1D	Ø29	GS	(Group separator)	CONTROL]
$1E	Ø3Ø	RS	(Record separator)	CONTROL ^
$1F	Ø31	US	(Unit separator)	CONTROL _

$2Ø	Ø32	(Space)	SPACE BAR
$21	Ø33	!	SHIFT 1
$22	Ø34	"	SHIFT '
$23	Ø35	#	SHIFT 3
$24	Ø36	$	SHIFT 4
$25	Ø37	%	SHIFT 5
$26	Ø38	&	SHIFT 7
$27	Ø39	'	'
$28	Ø4Ø	(	SHIFT 9
$29	Ø41	)	SHIFT Ø
$2A	Ø42	*	SHIFT 8
$2B	Ø43	+	SHIFT =
$2C	Ø44	,	,
$2D	Ø45	-	-
$2E	Ø46	.	.
$2F	Ø47	/	/
$3Ø	Ø48	Ø	Ø
$31	Ø49	1	1
$32	Ø5Ø	2	2
$33	Ø51	3	3
$34	Ø52	4	4
$35	Ø53	5	5
$36	Ø54	6	6
$37	Ø55	7	7
$38	Ø56	8	8
$39	Ø57	9	9
$3A	Ø58	:	SHIFT ;
$3B	Ø59	;	;
$3C	Ø6Ø	<	SHIFT ,
$3D	Ø61	=	=
$3E	Ø62	>	SHIFT .
$3F	Ø63	?	SHIFT /

(continued)

ASCII Code Hex	Dec	Symbol	Keys to Press
$4Ø	Ø64	@	SHIFT 2
$41	Ø65	A	SHIFT A
$42	Ø66	B	SHIFT B
$43	Ø67	C	SHIFT C
$44	Ø68	D	SHIFT D
$45	Ø69	E	SHIFT E
$46	Ø7Ø	F	SHIFT F
$47	Ø71	G	SHIFT G
$48	Ø72	H	SHIFT H
$49	Ø73	I	SHIFT I
$4A	Ø74	J	SHIFT J
$4B	Ø75	K	SHIFT K
$4C	Ø76	L	SHIFT L
$4D	Ø77	M	SHIFT M
$4E	Ø78	N	SHIFT N
$4F	Ø79	O	SHIFT O
$5Ø	Ø8Ø	P	SHIFT P
$51	Ø81	Q	SHIFT Q
$52	Ø82	R	SHIFT R
$53	Ø83	S	SHIFT S
$54	Ø84	T	SHIFT T
$55	Ø85	U	SHIFT U
$56	Ø86	V	SHIFT V
$57	Ø87	W	SHIFT W
$58	Ø88	X	SHIFT X
$59	Ø89	Y	SHIFT Y
$5A	Ø9Ø	Z	SHIFT Z
$5B	Ø91	[	[
$5C	Ø92	\	\
$5D	Ø93	]	]
$5E	Ø94	ˆ	SHIFT 6

$5F	Ø95	_		SHIFT -
$6Ø	Ø96	`		`
$61	Ø97	a		A
$62	Ø98	b		B
$63	Ø99	c		C
$64	1ØØ	d		D
$65	1Ø1	e		E
$66	1Ø2	f		F
$67	1Ø3	g		G
$68	1Ø4	h		H
$69	1Ø5	i		I
$6A	1Ø6	j		J
$6B	1Ø7	k		K
$6C	1Ø8	l		L
$6D	1Ø9	m		M
$6E	11Ø	n		N
$6F	111	o		O
$7Ø	112	p		P
$71	113	q		Q
$72	114	r		R
$73	115	s		S
$74	116	t		T
$75	117	u		U
$76	118	v		V
$77	119	w		W
$78	12Ø	x		X
$79	121	y		Y
$7A	122	z		Z
$7B	123	{		SHIFT [
$7C	124	|		SHIFT \
$7D	125	}		SHIFT]
$7E	126	~		SHIFT `
$7F	127	▌	(Rubout)	DELETE

Appendix II

6502 Instruction Set and Cycle Times

Instruction Mnemonic	*Assembler Operand Format*	*Opcode Byte*	*Number of Bytes*	*Number of Clock Cycles*
ADC	#num	69	2	2
	zpage	65	2	3
	zpage,X	75	2	4
	(zpage,X)	61	2	6
	(zpage),Y	71	2	5*
	abs	6D	3	4
	abs,X	7D	3	4*
	abs,Y	79	3	4*
AND	#num	29	2	2
	zpage	25	2	3
	zpage,X	35	2	4
	(zpage,X)	21	2	6
	(zpage),Y	31	2	5*
	abs	2D	3	4
	abs,X	3D	3	4*
	abs,Y	39	3	4*
ASL	[accumulator]	ØA	1	2
	zpage	Ø6	2	5
	zpage, X	16	2	6
	abs	ØE	3	6
	abs,X	1E	3	7
BCC	disp	9Ø	2	2**
BCS	disp	BØ	2	2**
BEQ	disp	FØ	2	2**
BIT	zpage	24	2	3
	abs	2C	3	4
BMI	disp	3Ø	2	2**
BNE	disp	DØ	2	2**

(continued)

Instruction Mnemonic	*Assembler Operand Format*	*Opcode Byte*	*Number of Bytes*	*Number of Clock Cycles*
BPL	disp	1Ø	2	2**
BRK	[implied]	ØØ	1	7
BVC	disp	5Ø	2	2**
BVS	disp	7Ø	2	2**
CLC	[implied]	18	1	2
CLD	[implied]	D8	1	2
CLI	[implied]	58	1	2
CLV	[implied]	B8	1	2
CMP	#num	C9	2	2
	zpage	C5	2	3
	zpage,X	D5	2	4
	(zpage,X)	C1	2	6
	(zpage),Y	D1	2	5*
	abs	CD	3	4
	abs,X	DD	3	4*
	abs,Y	D9	3	4*
CPX	#num	EØ	2	2
	zpage	E4	2	3
	abs	EC	3	4
CPY	#num	CØ	2	2
	zpage	C4	2	3
	abs	CC	3	4
DEC	zpage	C6	2	5
	zpage,X	D6	2	6
	abs	CE	3	6
	abs,X	DE	3	7
DEX	[implied]	CA	1	2
DEY	[implied]	88	1	2
EOR	#num	49	2	2
	zpage	45	2	3
	zpage,X	55	2	4
	(zpage,X)	41	2	6
	(zpage),Y	51	2	5*
	abs	4D	3	4
	abs,X	5D	3	4*
	abs,Y	59	3	4*
INC	zpage	E6	2	5
	zpage,X	F6	2	6
	abs	EE	3	6
	abs,X	FE	3	7

Instruction Mnemonic	*Assembler Operand Format*	*Opcode Byte*	*Number of Bytes*	*Number of Clock Cycles*
INX	[implied]	E8	1	2
INY	[implied]	C8	1	2
JMP	abs	4C	3	3
	(abs)	6C	3	5
JSR	abs	2Ø	3	6
LDA	#num	A9	2	2
	zpage	A5	2	3
	zpage,X	B5	2	4
	(zpage,X)	A1	2	6
	(zpage),Y	B1	2	5*
	abs	AD	3	4
	abs,X	BD	3	4*
	abs,Y	B9	3	4*
LDX	#num	A2	2	2
	zpage	A6	2	3
	zpage,Y	B6	2	4
	abs	AE	3	4
	abs,Y	BE	3	4*
LDY	#num	AØ	2	2
	zpage	A4	2	3
	zpage,X	B4	2	4
	abs	AC	3	4
	abs,X	BC	3	4*
LSR	[accumulator]	4A	1	2
	zpage	46	2	5
	zpage,X	56	2	6
	abs	4E	3	6
	abs,X	5E	3	7
NOP	[implied]	EA	1	2
ORA	#num	Ø9	2	2
	zpage	Ø5	2	3
	zpage,X	15	2	4
	(zpage,X)	Ø1	2	6
	(zpage),Y	11	2	5*
	abs	ØD	3	4
	abs,X	1D	3	4*
	abs,Y	19	3	4*
PHA	[implied]	48	1	3
PHP	[implied]	Ø8	1	3
PLA	[implied]	68	1	4

(continued)

Instruction Mnemonic	*Assembler Operand Format*	*Opcode Byte*	*Number of Bytes*	*Number of Clock Cycles*
PLP	[implied]	28	1	4
ROL	[accumulator]	2A	1	2
	zpage	26	2	5
	zpage,X	36	2	6
	abs	2E	3	6
	abs,X	3E	3	7
ROR	[accumulator]	6A	1	2
	zpage	66	2	5
	zpage,X	76	2	6
	abs	6E	3	6
	abs,X	7E	3	7
RTI	[implied]	4Ø	1	6
RTS	[implied]	6Ø	1	6
SBC	#num	E9	2	2
	zpage	E5	2	3
	zpage,X	F5	2	4
	(zpage,X)	E1	2	6
	(zpage),Y	F1	2	5*
	abs	ED	3	4
	abs,X	FD	3	4*
	abs,Y	F9	3	4*
SEC	[implied]	38	1	2
SED	[implied]	F8	1	2
SEI	[implied]	78	1	2
STA	zpage	85	2	3
	zpage,X	95	2	4
	(zpage,X)	81	2	6
	(zpage),Y	91	2	5*
	abs	8D	3	4
	abs,X	9D	3	4*
	abs,Y	99	3	4*
STX	zpage	86	2	3
	zpage,Y	96	2	4
	abs	8E	3	4
STY	zpage	84	2	3
	zpage,X	94	2	4
	abs	8C	3	4
TAX	[implied]	AA	1	2
TAY	[implied]	A8	1	2
TSX	[implied]	BA	1	2

Instruction Mnemonic	Assembler Operand Format	Opcode Byte	Number of Bytes	Number of Clock Cycles
TXA	[implied]	8A	1	2
TXS	[implied]	9A	1	2
TYA	[implied]	98	1	2

* Add one clock cycle if a page boundary is crossed.

** Add one clock cycle if a branch occurs to a location in the same page; add two clock cycles if a branch occurs to a location in a different page.

See Table 2-3 in Chapter 2 for a description of the assembler operand formats.

Appendix III

Apple //e Soft Switch, Status, and Other I/O Locations

NOTE: The "Usage" column in the following tables indicates how a particular location is to be accessed:

"W" means "write to the location."
"R" means "read from the location."
"RW" means "read from or write to the location."
"R7" means "read and check bit 7 to determine the status."
"RR" means "read from the location twice in a row."

The term "aux." refers to auxiliary memory on an 8Ø-column text card; "main" refers to built-in internal memory. "BSR" refers to the //e's 16K bank-switched RAM space from $DØØØ–$FFFF.

Memory Management Soft Switches

Address Hex	*(Dec)*	*Usage*	*Symbolic Name*	*Action Taken*	*Note*
$CØØØ	(49152)	W	8ØSTOREOFF	Allow PAGE2 to switch between video page1 and page2	1
$CØØ1	(49153)	W	8ØSTOREON	Allow PAGE2 to switch between main and aux. video memory	1
$CØØ2	(49154)	W	RAMRDOFF	Read-enable main memory from $2ØØ–$BFFF	4

(continued)

Memory Management Soft Switches (continued)

Address Hex	(Dec)	Usage	Symbolic Name	Action Taken	Note
$C003	(49155)	W	RAMRDON	Read-enable aux. memory from $200–$BFFF	4
$C004	(49156)	W	RAMWRTOFF	Write-enable main memory from $200–$BFFF	4
$C005	(49157)	W	RAMWRTON	Write-enable aux. memory from $200–$BFFF	4
$C006	(49158)	W	INTCXROMOFF	Enable slot ROM from $C100–$CFFF	5
$C007	(49159)	W	INTCXROMON	Enable main ROM from $C100–$CFFF	5
$C008	(49160)	W	ALZTPOFF	Enable main memory from $0000–$01FF and make main BSR available	5
$C009	(49161)	W	ALTZPON	Enable aux. memory from $0000–$01FF and make aux. BSR available	
$C00A	(49162)	W	SLOTC3ROMOFF	Enable main ROM from $C300–$C3FF	5
$C00B	(49163)	W	SLOTC3ROMON	Enable slot ROM from $C300–$C3FF	5

Video Soft Switches

Address Hex	(Dec)	Usage	Symbolic Name	Action Taken	Note
$C00C	(49164)	W	80COLOFF	Turn off 80-column display	
$C00D	(49165)	W	80COLON	Turn on 80-column display	
$C00E	(49166)	W	ALTCHARSETOFF	Turn off alternate characters	
$C00F	(49167)	W	ALTCHARSETON	Turn on alternate characters	
$C050	(49232)	RW	TEXTOFF	Select graphics mode	
$C051	(49233)	RW	TEXTON	Select text mode	
$C052	(49234)	RW	MIXEDOFF	Use full screen for graphics	2

Video Soft Switches (continued)

Address Hex	(Dec)	Usage	Symbolic Name	Action Taken	Note
$CØ53	(49235)	RW	MIXEDON	Use graphics with four lines of text	2
$CØ54	(49236)	RW	PAGE2OFF	Select page1 display (or main video memory)	1
$CØ55	(49237)	RW	PAGE2ON	Select page2 display (or aux. video memory)	1
$CØ56	(49238)	RW	HIRESOFF	Select low-resolution graphics	1,2
$CØ57	(49239)	RW	HIRESON	Select high-resolution graphics	1,2

Soft Switch Status Flags

Address Hex	(Dec)	Usage	Symbolic Name	Status Description	Note
$CØ1Ø	(49168)	R7	AKD	1 = a key is being pressed Ø = all keys are released	3
$CØ11	(49169)	R7	BSRBANK2	1 = bank2 of BSR is available Ø = bank1 of BSR is available	
$CØ12	(4917Ø)	R7	BSRREADRAM	1 = BSR is active for read operations Ø = $DØØØ–$FFFF ROM is active for read operations	
$CØ13	(49171)	R7	RAMRD	Ø = main $2ØØ–$BFFF is active for read operations 1 = auxiliary $2ØØ–$BFFF is active for read operations	4
$CØ14	(49172)	R7	RAMWRT	Ø = main $2ØØ–$BFFF is active for write operations 1 = auxiliary $2ØØ–$BFFF is active for write operations	4

(continued)

Soft Switch Status Flags (continued)

Address Hex	(Dec)	Usage	Symbolic Name	Status Description	Note
$CØ15	(49173)	R7	INTCXROM	1 = main $C1ØØ–$CFFF ROM is active Ø = slot $C1ØØ–$CFFF ROM is active	5
$CØ16	(49174)	R7	ALTZP	1 = aux. zero page + stack is active; aux. BSR is available Ø = main zero page + stack is active; main BSR is available	
$CØ17	(49175)	R7	SLOTC3ROM	1 = slot $C3 ROM is active Ø = main $C3 ROM is active	5
$CØ18	(49176)	R7	8ØSTORE	1 = PAGE2 switches main/aux. Ø = PAGE2 switches video pages	1
$CØ19	(49177)	R7	VERTBLANK	1 = vertical retrace is on Ø = vertical retrace is off	
$CØ1A	(49178)	R7	TEXT	1 = a text mode is active Ø = a graphics mode active	
$CØ1B	(49179)	R7	MIXED	1 = mixed graphics and text Ø = full-screen graphics	2
$CØ1C	(49180)	R7	PAGE2	1 = video page2 selected OR aux. video page selected	1
$CØ1D	(49181)	R7	HIRES	1 = high-resolution graphics Ø = low-resolution graphics	1,2
$CØ1E	(49182)	R7	ALTCHARSET	1 = alternate character is on Ø = primary character is on	

Soft Switch Status Flags (continued)

Address Hex	(Dec)	Usage	Symbolic Name	Status Description	Note
$CØ1F	(49183)	R7	8ØCOL	1 = 8Ø-column display is on Ø = 4Ø-column display is on	

Notes:

1. If 8ØSTORE is ON, then PAGE2OFF activates main video RAM ($4ØØ–$7FF) and PAGE2ON activates auxiliary video RAM. If HIRES is also ON, then PAGE2OFF also activates main high-resolution video RAM ($2ØØØ–$3FFF) and PAGE2ON also activates auxiliary high-resolution video RAM.

   If 8ØSTORE is OFF, then PAGE2OFF turns on text page1 mode and PAGE2 turns on text page2 mode. If HIRES is also ON, then PAGE2OFF also selects high-resolution page1 mode and PAGE2ON selects high-resolution page2 mode.
2. The HIRES and MIXED switches are meaningful only if the TEXT switch is OFF (i.e., a graphics mode is active).
3. Reading this switch will cause the keyboard strobe (bit 7 of $CØØØ) to be cleared.
4. The RAMRD and RAMWRT switches do not affect the video RAM area from $4ØØ-$7FF if the 8ØSTORE switch on ON or the high-resolution graphics area from $2ØØØ-$3FFF if the HIRES switch is ON as well. In these situations, these RAM areas are controlled by the PAGE2.
5. The SLOTC3ROM switches affect $C3ØØ. . .$C3FF only if INTCXROM is OFF.

Annunciator Soft Switches (READ or WRITE)

Address Hex	(Dec)	Usage	Symbolic Name	Action Taken
$CØ58	(4924Ø)	RW	CLRANØ	Turn off annunciator Ø
$CØ59	(49241)	RW	SETANØ	Turn on annunciator Ø
$CØ5A	(49242)	RW	CLRAN1	Turn off annunciator 1
$CØ5B	(49243)	RW	SETAN1	Turn on annunciator 1
$CØ5C	(49244)	RW	CLRAN2	Turn off annunciator 2
$CØ5D	(49245)	RW	SETAN2	Turn on annunciator 2
$CØ5E	(49246)	RW	CLRAN3	Turn off annunciator 3
$CØ5F	(49247)	RW	SETAN3	Turn on annunciator 3

Input/Output Locations for Built-In Devices

Address Hex	(Dec)	Usage	Symbolic Name	Action Taken (or Status)
$CØØØ	(49152)	R	KBD	Keyboard data (bits Ø . . . 6)
		R7	KBD	1 = keyboard stroke is on Ø = keyboard stroke is off
$CØ1Ø	(49168)	RW	KBDSTRB	Clear keyboard strobe
		R7	AKD	1 = a key is being pressed Ø = all keys are released
$CØ2Ø	(49184)	R	CASSOUT	Toggle the state of the cassette output port
$CØ3Ø	(492ØØ)	R	SPEAKER	Toggle the state of the speaker
$CØ4Ø	(49216)	R	GCSTROBE	Generate a game I/O connector strobe signal
$CØ6Ø	(49248)	R7	CASSIN	1 = cassette input on
$CØ61	(49249)	R7	PBØ	1 = push button Ø is on
$CØ62	(4925Ø)	R7	PB1	1 = push button 1 is on
$CØ63	(49251)	R7	PB2	1 = push button 2 is on
$CØ64	(49252)	R7	GCØ	Ø = game controller Ø timed out
$CØ65	(49253)	R7	GC1	Ø = game controller 1 timed out
$CØ66	(49254)	R7	GC2	Ø = game controller 2 timed out
$CØ67	(49255)	R7	GC3	Ø = game controller 3 timed out
$CØ7Ø	(49264)	R	GCRESET	Reset the game controllers

Bank-Switched RAM Soft Switches

Address Hex	(Dec)	Usage	Symbolic Name	Action Taken
$CØ8Ø	(4928Ø)	R	READBSR2	Select Bank2, read BSR, write-protect BSR
$CØ81	(49281)	RR	WRITEBSR2	Select Bank2, read ROM, write-enable BSR
$CØ82	(49282)	R	OFFBSR2	Select Bank2, read ROM, write-protect BSR
$CØ83	(49283)	RR	RDWRBSR2	Select Bank2, read BSR, write-enable BSR
$CØ88	(49288)	R	READBSR1	Select Bank1, read BSR, write-protect BSR
$CØ89	(49289)	RR	WRITEBSR1	Select Bank1, read ROM, write-enable BSR
$CØ8A	(4929Ø)	R	OFFBSR1	Select Bank1, read ROM, write-protect BSR
$CØ8B	(49291)	RR	RDWRBSR1	Select Bank1, read BSR, write-enable BSR

Note: Addresses $CØ84 . . . $CØ87 and $CØ8C . . . $CØ8F duplicate the functions of addresses $CØ8Ø . . . $CØ83 and $CØ88 . . . $CØ8B, respectively.

Peripheral-Card I/O Memory Locations

I/O Memory Locations	*Description*
$CØ9Ø–$CØ9F	Reserved for use by slot 1
$CØAØ–$CØAF	Reserved for use by slot 2
$CØBØ–$CØBF	Reserved for use by slot 3
$CØCØ–$CØCF	Reserved for use by slot 4
$CØDØ–$CØDF	Reserved for use by slot 5
$CØEØ–$CØEF	Reserved for use by slot 6
$CØFØ–$CØFF	Reserved for use by slot 7

Appendix IV

Apple //e Page 3 Vectors

Address	Contents (DOS 3.3)	Contents (ProDOS)	Description
\$3DØ–\$3D2	JMP \$9DBF	JMP \$BEØØ	A JMP instruction to the DOS 3.3 or ProDOS warm-start entry point. A call to this vector will reconnect DOS without destroying the Applesoft program in memory. Use the "3DØG" command to move from the system monitor to Applesoft.
\$3D3–\$3D5	JMP \$9D84	JMP \$BEØØ	DOS 3.3: a JMP instruction to the DOS 3.3 cold-start entry point. A call to this vector will initialize DOS 3.3 to the state it was in when it was first loaded and will clear the Applesoft program in memory. ProDOS: a JMP instruction to the ProDOS warm-start entry point.
\$3D6–\$3D8	JMP \$AAFD		A JMP instruction to the DOS 3.3 file manager.
\$3D9–\$3DB	JMP \$B7B5		A JMP instruction to the DOS 3.3 RWTS subroutine.
\$3DC–\$3E2	LDA \$9DØF LDY \$9DØE RTS		A subroutine that loads the A register with the high-order address and the Y register with the low-order address of the DOS 3.3 file manager parameter list.

Address	Contents (DOS 3.3)	(ProDOS)	Description
$3E3–$3E9	LDA $AAC2 LDY $AAC1 RTS		A subroutine that loads the A register with the high-order address and the Y register with the low-order address of the DOS 3.3 RWTS parameter list (called IOB).
$3EA–$3EC	JMP $A851		A JMP instruction to the DOS 3.3 subroutine that causes it to accept new I/O links and reconnect itself. This subroutine must be called to properly install new I/O subroutines without affecting DOS 3.3 (See Chapters 6 and 7).
$3ED–$3EE			The address of the subroutine to be called by XFER ($C314) is stored here.
$3EF	$4C		A JMP opcode. (DOS 3.3 sets this byte but does not use it.)
$3F0–$3F1	$FA59	$FA59	The address of the subroutine to which control is to be passed when a BRK instruction is executed (low-order byte first).
$3F2–$3F3	$9DBF	$BE00	The address of the subroutine to which control is to be passed when a RESET interrupt is generated (low-order byte first).
$3F4	$38	$1B	POWERED-UP BYTE. The reset vector at $3F2 is used only if the number stored here is equal to the logical exclusive-OR of the number stored at $3F3 and the constant $A5.
$3F5–$3F7	JMP $FF58	JMP $BE03	A JMP instruction to the subroutine to which control is to be passed when the Applesoft "&" command is executed.

Address	Contents (DOS 3.3)	(ProDOS)	Description
$3F8–$3FA	JMP $FF65	JMP $BEØØ	A JMP instruction to the subroutine to which control is to be passed when the system monitor's USER command (⟨CTRL-Y⟩) is entered.
$3FB–$3FD	JMP $FF65	JMP $FF59	A JMP instruction to the subroutine to which control is to be passed when an NMI interrupt is generated.
$3FE–$3FF	$FF65	$BFEB	The address of the subroutine to which control is to be passed when an IRQ interrupt is generated (low-order byte first).

NOTES: All addresses are stored with the low-order byte first.

For descriptions of the specific vectors that DOS 3.3 and ProDOS set up from $3FØ–$3FF, refer to Tables 5-2 and 5-12 in Chapter 5.

Appendix V

Additional Programs on the Optional Diskette

There are four "bonus" programs on this book's optional program diskette that are not described within the main body of the text. These programs are all DOS 3.3 utility programs and will not operate in a ProDOS environment. Let's look at them now.

RAMDISK

You will recall from Chapter 5 that ProDOS defines a disk volume called /RAM that walks and talks just like a real disk drive but that is really just a block of auxiliary RAM memory residing on the extended 8Ø-column text card. DOS 3.3 does not automatically define a RAMdisk such as this when it is started up, but you can run the RAMDISK program to install it into DOS 3.3.

To run RAMDISK, enter Applesoft direct mode and then enter the command

```
BRUN RAMDISK
```

After the program starts to run, you will be asked to enter a slot number and a drive number for the RAM disk. The slot number must be between 1 and 7, inclusive, and the drive number must be 1 or 2. Be careful, however, not to specify a drive/slot combination that relates to an actual disk drive; if you do, then you won't be able to use that drive while the RAMdisk is active.

Once the slot and drive information has been entered, the RAM disk will be automatically "initialized" and will be ready for use. You will find that, from a software point of view, it behaves exactly like a real disk drive, except that it has a storage capacity of only 4ØK.

DISK MAP

DISK MAP is a useful DOS 3.3 utility program that draws a map of the sector usage on a diskette on the low-resolution graphics screen. To run the program, enter Applesoft direct mode and then enter the command

```
BRUN DISK MAP
```

After you do this, you will be asked to insert any diskette and to press any key to begin. DISK MAP maps each sector on the disk to a unique position in a 16×35 rectangular grid map. The vertical axis of the map represents the sector number from Ø (top) to 15 (bottom); the horizontal axis represents the track number from Ø (left) to 34 (right).

Differently colored low-resolution blocks are used to indicate the usage of any particular sector. If the block is blue, then the sector is in use and readable; if it is white, then the sector is in use but not readable (that is, the sector is damaged). If the block is grey, then the sector is not being used.

DISK MAP also displays the amount of free space on the diskette and the volume number of the diskette.

COMMAND CHANGER

DOS 3.3 supports a total of 28 different commands that can be used from Applesoft. The names of these commands are found within the copy of DOS 3.3 that is stored on every initialized diskette.

You can use the COMMAND CHANGER program to change the command names to (almost) any other name that you prefer. There are only two caveats to keep in mind when entering new names:

- the total number of characters in all 28 names must not exceed 132.
- one command name cannot be the same as the first part of another command name. For example, if you rename DELETE as KILL, then you can't have another command name that has K-I-L-L as the first four characters.

To run the COMMAND CHANGER program, first enter Applesoft direct mode and then enter the command

```
RUN COMMAND CHANGER
```

After you do this, the first command name (INIT) will be displayed in inverse video and you will be asked to enter a new name for it. If you prefer to keep the same name, just press <RETURN>. After INIT has been dealt with, the other 27 DOS 3.3 commands will be displayed, one-by-one, and you will be asked to redefine them as well.

After all the commands have been displayed, the new commands will be saved to diskette. The next time that the diskette is booted, the new command names will be active.

DISK VOLUME CHANGER

Whenever you use the DOS 3.3 CATALOG command, the 12-character phrase "DISK VOLUME " appears at the top of the list of files that are displayed, followed by the disk volume number.

With the DISK VOLUME CHANGER program, you can modify the copy of DOS 3.3 that is stored on a diskette so that any other 12-character phrase will be displayed instead.

You can run DISK VOLUME CHANGER by entering Applesoft direct mode and then entering the command

```
RUN DISK VOLUME CHANGER
```

After you do this, you will be asked to enter the new 12-character phrase. After you enter it, it will be saved to disk on top of the old phrase. This means that the next time the diskette is booted, you will see your own phrase instead of "DISK VOLUME " whenever the diskette is cataloged.

Appendix VI

Recent Enhancements to the Apple //e

In March, 1985, Apple Computer, Inc. announced an interesting enhancement to the Apple //e: four new chips to replace the 65Ø2 microprocessor, the character generator ROM, and the two Applesoft and system monitor ROMs used in the original version of the //e. The main reasons for the enhancement were to make the //e more closely compatible with the Apple //c and to facilitate the development of mouse-based software by including 32 graphic icons (called "MouseText") in the character generator ROM and rewriting the system monitor output subroutine to work with them. Other reasons were to allow lower-case command entry from Applesoft and the system monitor, to improve the way in which the //e responds to interrupts from peripherals, and to fix a few minor, but annoying, bugs that had been discovered in the code stored in the original //e ROMs.

Despite the ROM changes, most programs written for the original //e will run properly on the enhanced //e. Just to be safe, Apple informed most major software developers of the proposed ROM change well in advance of the public announcement so that incompatibility problems could be cleared up before the new ROMs were in the hands of general users.

All Apple //e units manufactured after March, 1985 were shipped with the four new chips already installed. Owners of the original //e can have the chips installed by an authorized Apple dealer for about $7Ø.

When an enhanced Apple //e is booted, the message "Apple //e" is displayed at the top of the screen (the original Apple //e displays "Apple]["). You can also examine two identification bytes in the system monitor to determine what version of the Apple II you are using. The value stored at location $FBB3 is used to distinguish an Apple //e or //c from other members of the Apple II family. If it's $Ø6, then you're either working with the //e (original or enhanced version) or the //c. The value stored at $FBCØ indicates the precise version: $EA for an Apple //e with original ROMs, $EØ for a //e with the enhanced ROMs, or $ØØ for an Apple //c.

In this appendix, we will take a close look at the //e enhancements and see how they improve the performance of the Apple //e.

THE NEW MICROPROCESSOR: "65CØ2"

The new microprocessor for the Apple //e is the same as the one used in the Apple //c, the 65CØ2. As its name suggests, the 65CØ2 is a close relative of the 65Ø2 that it replaces. In fact, every program that runs with the 65Ø2 will also run with the 65CØ2 (with rare exceptions). The converse is not true, however, since the 65CØ2 supports some ten instructions that are unknown to the 65Ø2. Here are brief descriptions of these new instructions:

```
BRA -- Branch relative always
DEA -- Decrement accumulator
INA -- Increment accumulator
PHX -- Push the X register on the stack
PHY -- Push the Y register on the stack
PLX -- Pop the X register from the stack
PLY -- Pop the Y register from the stack
STZ -- Store zero in memory
TRB -- Test and reset memory bits with accumulator
TSB -- Test and set memory bits with accumulator
```

The 65CØ2 also supports two useful new addressing modes that can be used by some of its instructions: absolute indexed indirect and zero-page indirect.

ABSOLUTE INDEXED INDIRECT. This addressing mode can be used with the JMP instruction only. Its assembler form is

```
JMP ($1234,X)
```

The effective address is calculated by first adding the contents of the X-register to the address specified in the operand to get an intermediate location. The address stored at this intermediate location, and the next location, is the effective address, the address to which the JMP instruction will pass control.

ZERO-PAGE INDIRECT. The operand for this addressing mode is a single byte that represents a location in zero page. The effective address is simply the address stored at this and the very next location. This means that the zero-page indirect mode is the same as the 65Ø2's zero-page indexed indirect mode, but without the X indexing. An instruction of the form

```
STA ($E0)
```

is used with an assembler to indicate that the zero-page indirect mode is to be used.

There are several minor differences between the 65Ø2 and 65CØ2 that may affect the performance of some programs. For example, the cycle times for some instructions are different, the BIT instruction behaves differently when the immediate addressing mode is used, and an indirect JMP command on a page boundary is handled differently. (Because of a 65Ø2 design error, a JMP ($xxFF) instruction transfers control to the address stored at $xxØØ and $xxFF, not $(xx+1)ØØ and $xxFF, as might be expected. This instruction behaves properly on the 65CØ2.)

Read the data sheet for the NCR Corporation version of the 65CØ2 for detailed descriptions of its instruction set and addressing modes.

By the way, the "C" in 65CØ2 stands for CMOS, an acronym for Complementary Metal Oxide Semiconductor. This is the name for the process used to manufacture the transistors that form the 65CØ2 integrated circuit. A CMOS integrated circuit consumes far less power than a functionally identical circuit built using conventional technology. It will run cooler and can be operated by a smaller power supply.

THE NEW CHARACTER GENERATOR ROM : "MouseText"

The new character generator ROM contains the definitions of thirty-two graphic icons that can be displayed on the screen if the //e's alternative character set has been turned on. (It is automatically turned on when you enter a PR#3 command to enter the 8Ø-column display mode.) This set of icons is called MouseText and is shown in Figure VI-1. As you can see, MouseText is made up of many useful symbols, such as representations of the two "Apple" keys, different kinds of arrows, shading blocks, and so on. Some of the icons can even be displayed next to one another to create other useful images, such as a running man or a file folder. As the name MouseText suggests, the icons are meant to be used primarily in programs that use the Apple Mouse input device to point to and select commands and functions.

Mouse Text ICON	ASCII character	Video RAM value
	@	$40
	A	$41
	B	$42
	C	$43
	D	$44
	E	$45
	F	$46
	G	$47
	H	$48
	I	$49
	J	$4A
	K	$4B
	L	$4C
	M	$4D
	N	$4E
	O	$4F
	P	$50
	Q	$51
	R	$52
	S	$53
	T	$54
	U	$55
	V	$56
	W	$57
	X	$58
	Y	$59
	Z	$5A
	[	$5B
	/	$5C
	]	$5D
	^	$5E
	_	$5F

Figure VI-1. The MouseText character set.

A MouseText icon is displayed on the video screen whenever a number between $4Ø and $5F is stored in the //e's video RAM memory. With the original //e ROMs installed, these numbers correspond to inverse upper-case characters and six special symbols.

New subroutines in the //e's 8Ø-column firmware make it quite simple to display MouseText using standard Applesoft PRINT statements. To do this, you must follow these steps (after the 8Ø-column firmware has been activated):

- Turn on inverse video.
- Enable the firmware's handling of MouseText.
- Print the standard ASCII characters that correspond to the special MouseText characters that are to be displayed (see Figure VI-1).
- Turn on normal video.
- Disable the firmware's handling of MouseText.

Here is a short program that prints out the entire MouseText character set:

```
100 PRINT CHR$(4);"PR#3": REM SELECT 80-COLUMN FIRMWARE
200 PRINT CHR$(27);
300 PRINT CHR$(15);"@ABCDEFGHIJKLMNOPQRSTUVWXYZ[\]^_
";CHR$(14);
400 PRINT CHR$(24)
```

Here is what the four control characters in lines 2ØØ through 4ØØ are used for:

*CHR$(27)	:	Tells the firmware to display MouseText characters.
*CHR$(15)	:	Turns on inverse video.
*CHR$(14)	:	Turns on normal video.
*CHR$(24)	:	Turns off the MouseText feature.

When the display of MouseText has been enabled and reverse video is on, the 8Ø-column firmware converts printed characters having ASCII codes from $CØ ('@') through $DF ('_') to the MouseText characters having codes from $4Ø through $5F. Thus, in the above program you will not see a reverse video display of standard ASCII characters, but rather the complete MouseText character set.

THE NEW SYSTEM MONITOR

All system monitor commands can now be entered in upper- or lower-case characters. Other improvements are the inclusion of a search command and a simple assembler, and the ability to specify ASCII codes by character rather than by hexadecimal code.

Entry of ASCII Characters

ASCII characters can now be used with the system monitor STORE command (":"), or any other monitor command, in a much more convenient way. Rather than entering the hexadecimal ASCII code for a character, you can precede the character itself with a tick mark ("'"). (That's the character marked on the key to the immediate left of RETURN.) For example, use 'G instead of C7 when you want to enter the ASCII code for G.

Here's what to enter to place the word "Inside" into memory beginning at $300 (don't type the asterisk—it's just the monitor's prompt symbol):

```
*300:'I 'n 's 'i 'd 'e
```

Notice that each ASCII character is separated from the next by a blank space.

The Search Command

The new system monitor ROM includes a search command that allows you to find one- or two-byte patterns stored in a specified area of memory. To find a two-byte pattern, say "ED FD", in the standard system monitor area beginning at $F800 and ending at $FFFF, you would use the command

```
*FDED<F800.FFFFS
```

When a matching pattern is found, its address is displayed on the screen followed by a hyphen.

Notice that the byte pattern specified in the command line is the *reverse* of the actual pattern to be found. Also, there is no blank space between the two search bytes.

To find the occurrence of a single byte, say the ASCII code for "L", anywhere in the block from $2000 to $2FFF, use the command

```
*'L<2000.2FFFS
```

You can, of course, specify the ASCII code for "L" instead of using the tick notation.

The Mini Assembler

Another useful addition to the system monitor is a "mini assembler" that can be used to quickly enter 6502 programs in assembly language (mnemonic) form rather than machine language (hexadecimal bytes) form. Unfortunately, the mini assembler does not recognize the ten new instruction mnemonics that are unique to the 65C02.

To enter the mini assembler from the system monitor, enter the "!" command. After you do this, the mini assembler's "!" prompt symbol will appear and you can start entering a program.

To enter a program line, first type in the address of the 6502 instruction, a colon, and then the instruction mnemonic and its operand. If you do this properly, the starting address of the instruction, the hexadecimal bytes for the instruction, and the instruction mnemonic and operand will be displayed. If you make a mistake, you will hear a beep, the line will be reprinted, and a "^" will appear beneath the character that caused the error.

After the first line has been successfully entered, you can enter subsequent lines just by typing a space and then the next instruction; the code generated will be placed in succeeding memory locations.

The mini assembler assumes that all numbers and addresses that you enter are in hexadecimal form, even if a leading "$" sign is not used. The instruction mnemonics and operand formats that it recognizes are the standard ones used by most assemblers. However, symbolic labels for memory locations or data cannot be used as with standard assemblers.

To leave the mini assembler and return to the system monitor, press [RETURN] at the beginning of any line.

Changes in Escape Sequences

Two new keyboard escape sequences have been added to the //e's standard input subroutine: ESC [control-D] and ESC [control-E].

ESC [control-D] is used to disable the printing of any control characters that are sent to the standard output subroutine, other than the codes for carriage return ($8D), line feed ($8A), backspace ($88), and bell ($87). The //e reacts in special ways to several other control characters that are sent to its output subroutine when the 80-column firmware is being used. For example, if a [control-U] character is printed in 80-column mode, the 40-column display will be turned on. This is a handy way of exiting 80-column mode, but what if you happen to be communicating with a remote computer through a modem and it sends you a [control-U] character for some reason? Before you know it, you will pop out of 8Ø-column mode and you will be left scratching your head wondering what happened. To avoid this type of trouble it is best to enter the ESC [control-D] sequence before running such a program. You can re-enable the handling of the control codes later by entering the ESC [control-E] sequence.

The upper-case restrict escape sequences, ESC R and ESC T, are not supported by the enhanced ROMs. In the original ROMs, these sequences are used to activate and deactivate an input mode where all lower-case text that is not entered within quotation marks is converted to upper-case. This mode is no longer required since Applesoft and system monitor commands can now be entered in both upper- and lower-case characters.

Improvements in Interrupt Handling

Interrupts are handled badly on the Apple II, Apple II Plus, and the original Apple //e because both DOS 3.3 and the system monitor use location $45 for data storage and this location is overwritten when an interrupt occurs. With the enhanced //e ROMs in place, however, the integrity of $45 is preserved and interrupts are handled properly.

The interrupt request (IRQ) interrupt vector on the enhanced //e (at $FFFE/$FFFF) now points to $C3FA, the address of the monitor's interrupt handling subroutine. This subroutine ultimately passes control to NEWIRQ at $C4ØØ.

NEWIRQ is responsible for saving the state of the system when the interrupt occurs and then setting it to the following standard state:

- Main memory is active for reading and writing
- The ROM space from $DØØØ to $FFFF is active
- The main stack and zero page are active
- The main text page is active
- If the alternative stack is active, the current stack pointer is stored at $1Ø1 (in the alternative stack) and the main stack pointer is set equal to the value stored at $100 (in the alternative stack). For this scheme to work properly, any program that turns on the alternative stack must also store the value of the main stack pointer at $1ØØ. Here's the code that will do the trick:

```
PHP         ;Save status
SEI         ;Disable interrupts for this
```

```
STA $C009 ;Turn on alternative stack
TSX       ;Transfer SP to X
STX $100  ;Save main SP
PLP       ;Restore interrupt status
```

After this has been done, the alternative stack pointer can be set up.

Once this standard state has been set up, the interrupt handler calls the user's own interrupt handler (its address is stored at $3FE/ $3FF). After it finishes (with an RTI instruction), the original state of the system is restored, and control returns to the interrupted program.

Slot 3 Peripheral Cards

When the original Apple //e is turned on, or RESET is pressed, the internal slot 3 firmware is always enabled if an 8Ø-column text card is installed, or disabled if it is not.

The situation is different with the enhanced Apple //e. If there is a peripheral card installed in slot 3 that has the following two identification bytes:

```
$C305 = $38
$C307 = $18
```

then the peripheral card slot 3 firmware is turned on, even if an 8Ø-column text card is also installed. This means that the slot 3 peripheral will be used when a PR#3 command is entered, and not the 8Ø-column text card.

The firmware in a slot 3 peripheral card must contain a special sequence of four instructions beginning at $C3F4 to support the //e's new internal interrupt handling subroutine:

```
$C3F4:  STA $C081   ;Read ROM, write RAM
        JMP $FC7A   ;
        BIT $C015   ;Get INTCXROM status
        STA $C007   ;Select internal ROM
```

If these instructions are not present, you will not be able to use interrupts on the new //e.

OTHER CHANGES

- Applesoft commands can now be entered in upper- or lower-case characters.

- It is possible to boot directly from a ProFile hard disk when the //e is turned on or RESET is pressed.
- The bug-induced ESC [control-L] sequence that transfers control to $4CCE has been removed.
- The code for the Applesoft HTAB, TAB, SPC, and PRINT commands has been rewritten to ensure that these commands work properly in 8Ø-column mode.
- Even or odd window widths are now supported.
- The Applesoft GET command and the monitor RDKEY ($FDØC) subroutine will now return the ESC or right-arrow keycode.

For more information on the Apple //e enhancements, see *About Your Enhanced Apple //e: Programmer's Guide,* a publication of Apple Computer, Inc. This book also contains a source listing of the new system monitor ROM.

Index